BROKEN TABLETS

JONATHAN P. RIBNER

BROKEN TABLETS

The Cult of the Law in French Art
from David to Delacroix

UNIVERSITY OF CALIFORNIA PRESS

Berkeley   Los Angeles   Oxford

The publisher gratefully acknowledges the contribution
provided by the Art Book Endowment Fund of the
Associates of the University of California Press,
which is supported by a major gift of the Ahmanson
Foundation.

University of California Press
Berkeley and Los Angeles, California
University of California Press, Ltd.
Oxford, England
© 1993 by
The Regents of the University of California
Library of Congress Cataloging-in-Publication Data
Ribner, Jonathan P.
Broken tablets : the cult of the law in French art from
David to Delacroix / Jonathan P. Ribner.
p.   cm.
Includes bibliographical references and index.
ISBN 0-520-07749-0
1. Arts, French. 2. Arts, Modern—19th century—
France. 3. Law in art. 4. Arts—Political aspects—
France. I. Title.
NX549.A1R5   1993
700'.1'03—dc20   92-23046
CIP
Printed in the United States of America
9 8 7 6 5 4 3 2 1
The paper used in this publication meets the mini-
mum requirements of American National Standard
for Information Sciences—Permanence of Paper for
Printed Library Materials, ANSI Z39.48-1984. ∞

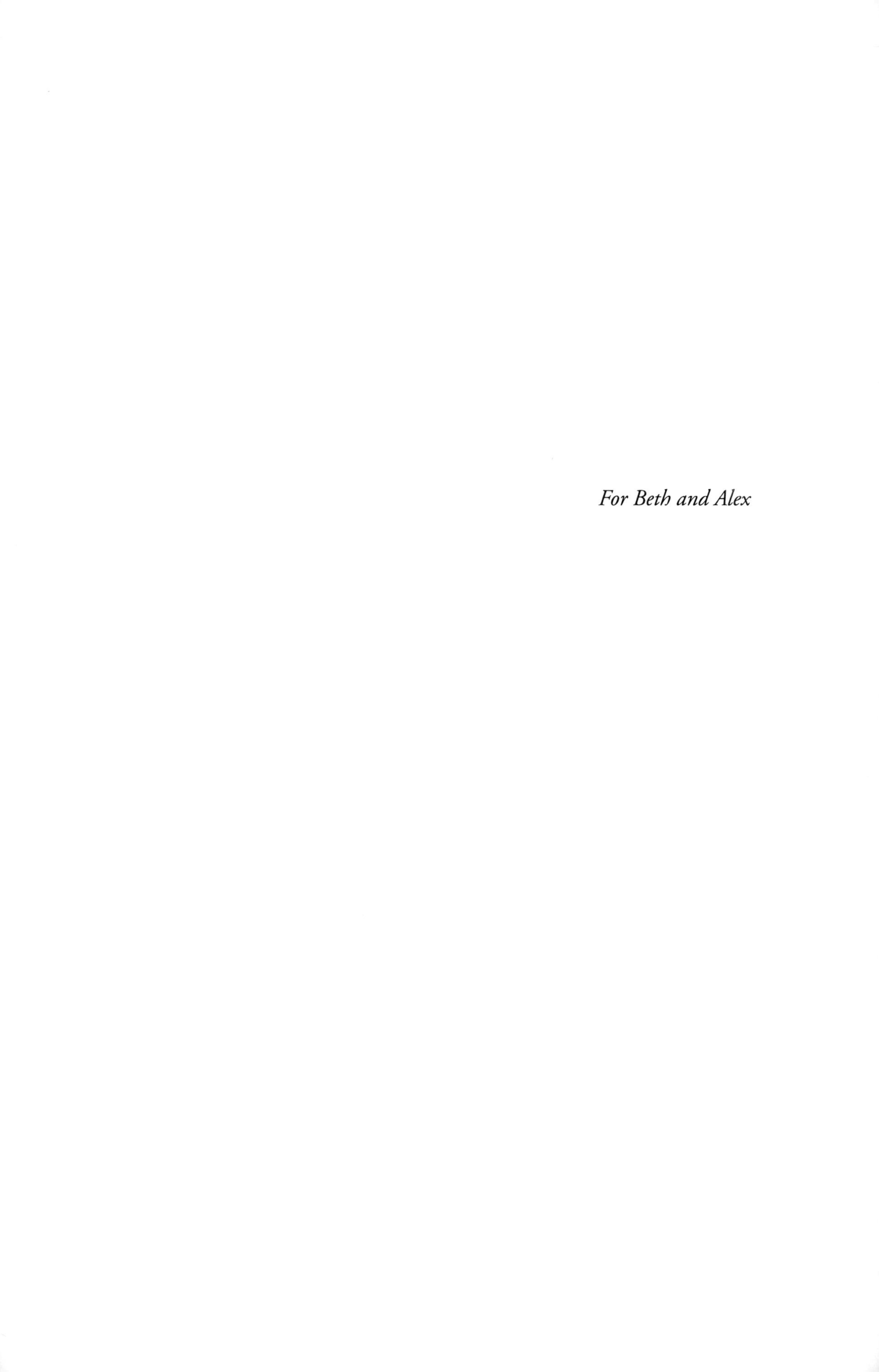

For Beth and Alex

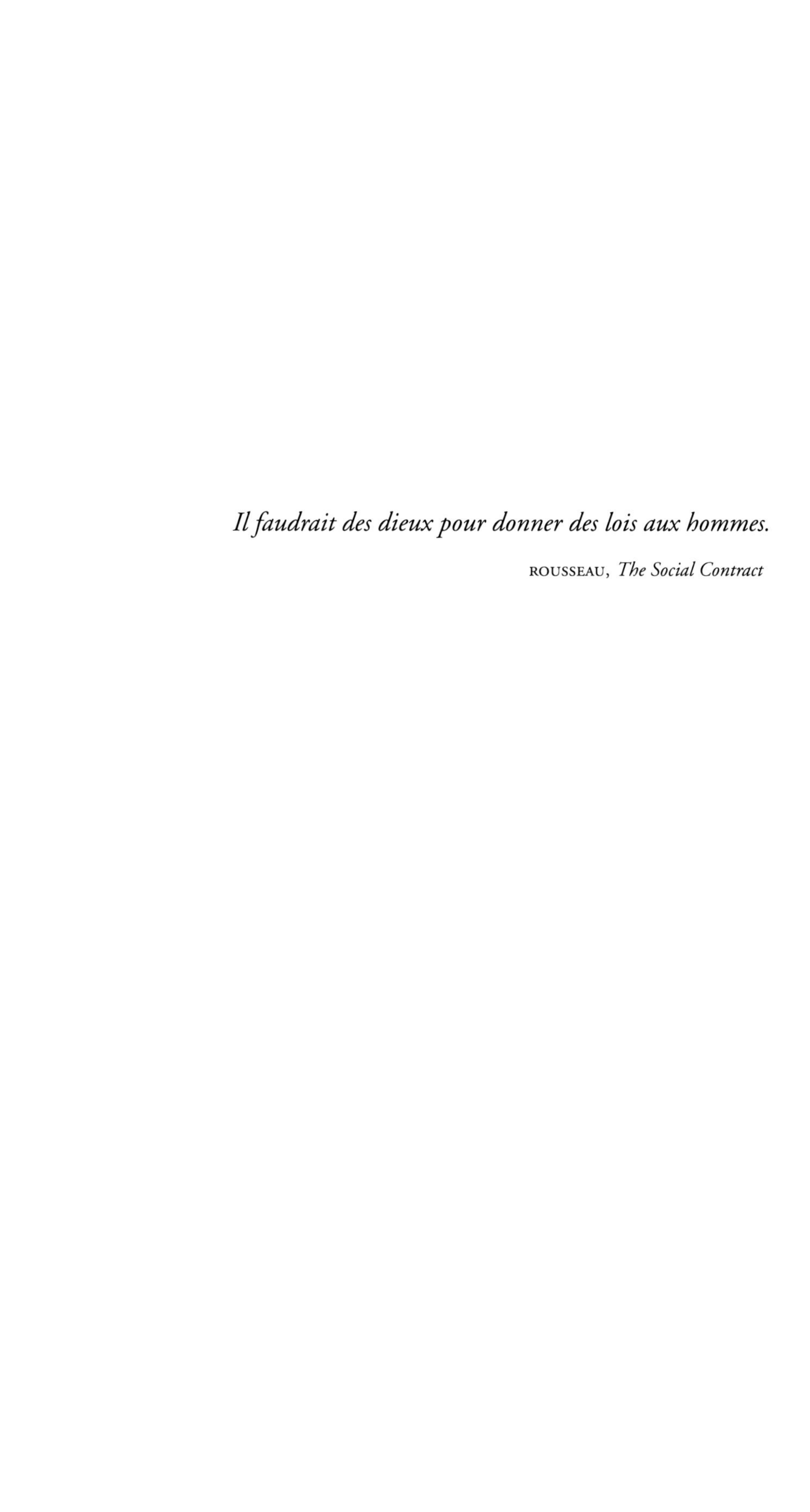

Il faudrait des dieux pour donner des lois aux hommes.

ROUSSEAU, *The Social Contract*

Contents

Acknowledgments

A Fellowship for Recent Recipients of the Ph.D. from the American Council of Learned Societies and a Junior Fellowship in the Boston University Society of Fellows in the Humanities allowed me to devote the 1987–88 academic year to this book. Boston University provided further support with a Faculty Research Seed Grant and a Special Summer Term Research Support Grant. A generous grant to Boston University from the Florence Gould Foundation covered the cost of color illustrations and photographic reproduction rights.

For assistance and hospitality, I am grateful to numerous museum, library, and government professionals. I extend special thanks to Pascal Aumasson, Musée d'Histoire, Saint-Brieuc; Rhoda Bilansky and Ruth Thomas, Mugar Memorial Library, Boston University; Noëlle de Chambrun, Consulate of France, Boston; Philippe Couton, Réunion des Musées Nationaux; Jean-Marie Darnis and Yvonne Goldenberg, Musée de la Monnaie; Theodore Feder, Art Resource; Blanche Grinbaum and C. Carrer, Musée Thomas Henry, Cherbourg; Geneviève Gareau, Caisse Nationale des Monuments Historiques et des Sites; Philippe Grunchec, Ecole Nationale Supérieure des Beaux-Arts; Sinclair Hitchings and Karen Shafts, Print Department, Boston Public Library; Françoise Monet and Jeanine Dodu, Assemblée Nationale library; Jean-Daniel Pariset, Archives Nationales and the Musée de l'Histoire de France; and Sylvie de Turckheim-Pey, Departement des Monnaies, Médailles et Antiques, Bibliothèque Nationale. I remain grateful to Roseline Bacou, Jacques Foucart, Louis-Antoine Prat, Pierre

Rosenberg, and Maurice Sérullaz of the Musée du Louvre for their kindness while I was working on the dissertation from which this book developed.

Many kind individuals provided welcome support and expertise during this endeavor. In particular, I would like to thank Aaron Fogel, Fern Luskin, Naomi Miller, Christopher Ricks, Kim Sichel, Ken Simpson, Scott Sprenger, and Stefan Tessler for their unstinting encouragement; Jeffrey Mehlman and Reva Wolf for helpful bibliographic suggestions; David Wisner for bringing his work on the cult of the legislator to my attention; and Gregory Leftwich and Susan von Daum Tholl for translations from Latin (translations from French, unless otherwise indicated, are my own).

A number of scholars generously read and critiqued the manuscript, in whole or in part, at various stages of completion. I wish to thank Nina Athanassoglou-Kallmyer for encouraging me to include the Palais-Bourbon library material in this book; Patricia Hills for her editorial prowess; Fred Licht for his vast erudition; Linda Nochlin for introducing me to new pathways of thinking; and Henri Zerner for his keen eye and perceptive comments.

The greatest challenge posed by this project was the pursuit of research outside the field of art history. I am deeply grateful to Frank Paul Bowman of the Department of Romance Languages, University of Pennsylvania, for his reading of the manuscript. Professor Bowman's work in the literature and intellectual history of nineteenth-century France is a model of interdisciplinary achievement. I am honored by his support.

Christopher Riopelle, associate curator, European Painting and Sculpture before 1800, Philadelphia Museum of Art, has been a loyal friend and a scholarly resource of astonishing breadth. The manuscript benefited greatly from his learning and insight.

Two mentors who shaped my thinking and inspired my love of art history deserve special recognition. My heartfelt thanks extend to John Hunisak, whose spellbinding lectures at Middlebury College convinced me to become an art historian. The manuscript was strengthened by his thoughtful commentary. Robert Rosenblum, my dissertation advisor, continues to be a source of inspiration. His supportive reading of the manuscript has meant much to me.

I am saddened that the late Gert Schiff will not read these lines. His generosity, and his encouragement of my work at the dissertation level, are fondly remembered.

Many thanks are due to Deborah Kirshman, fine arts editor at the University of California Press, for her highly professional handling of this project. For countless points of clarification, I am indebted to the outstanding editorial talent of Stephanie Fay.

While working on this book, the memory of my parents, Irving Ribner and Roslyn G. Ribner Reichler, was never distant. They taught me to value art, history, and literature. Recollections of my father—reading, typing, and smoking his pipe, surrounded by volumes of Shakespeare and Marlowe—are inseparable from my commitment to scholarship.

Having lost my parents, I am fortunate to have enjoyed the unwavering support of my mother-in-law, Mary Nicklas; my late father-in-law, Bill Nicklas; my step-father, Merton Reichler; and my brother, Clifford. For their solidarity in this project, I am also grateful to Julia Allan, Terry Ashley, Monroe and Prudence Green, Irwin Greenblatt, Nancy Nicklas, and Sara and Debby Reichler.

My wife, Beth Nicklas, and our son, Alex, gave the most to this book.

More than two decades before the drafting of France's first constitution, Jean-Jacques Rousseau wrote of the difficulty of creating durable laws. The founders of nations, he argued, imputed durability to their laws by claiming a divine source for them. But only an individual of extraordinary genius—a Moses, for example—can produce laws that lend credence to this mythic pedigree: "The great soul of the legislator is the true miracle that substantiates his mission."[1] Rousseau's thoughts resonate like prophecy in light of the rapid collapse of France's early constitutions and the regimes that produced them. His lofty association of law with religion, moreover, foreshadows the veneration of the law during the Revolution. When the nation was invested with legislative power, the law—that ancient social concept and fundamental instrument of power—was perceived in a thrillingly unfamiliar light. It became the focus of a veritable cult, given characteristic expression in 1791 by Gilbert Romme (1750–1795), the patriotic founder of the Tennis Court Society (originally called the Society of Friends of the Law), who declared, "Law is the religion of the state, which must also have its ministers, its apostles, its altars, and its schools."[2] Two centuries later, such passionate devotion to the law seems as remote as the joy that accompanied the destruction of the Bastille. But from 1789 to 1848—a period that saw the introduction of constitutional, parliamentary government and the adoption of the Code Napoléon—law and lawgiving were imbued with evocative power, expressed in art and poetry as well as in political discourse.

This book examines the representation of law and the legislator during the troubled beginnings of constitutional government in France. I argue that each of France's early constitutional regimes had recourse to imagery suggesting the divine origin or sacred character of its laws; this imagery changed to reflect the way these regimes sought to establish their legitimacy; and the legitimating discourse itself was subject to subversion and co-option by opponents of these regimes. I hope to shed light on a quest for authority and legitimacy that reached from the public realm of constitutional law, national politics, and propaganda to the private world of the self-aggrandizing artist and poet.

Between 1789 and 1848 in France the cult of the law flowered and then withered. Two famous images of the French legislature bracket the period. In the Salon of 1791 Jacques-Louis David exhibited a drawing, *The Tennis Court Oath*, charged with heady optimism (Plate 1); in this work he anticipated a painting that was intended to fittingly commemorate the pledge of the self-proclaimed National Assembly—France's first national legislature—to remain united until it had firmly established a constitution.[3] In David's reconstruction of this event of June 20, 1789, a seething multitude is ordered by a centripetal force that at once mirrors the new spirit of national solidarity and recalls the Assembly's insistence on the unity and permanence of the nation's legislative power. The participants are portrayed with all the flattering resources of the French academic tradition that David had done so much to reinvigorate during the previous decade. Heroically framed legislators take their oath with gestures and expressions as incisive as David's contour; it is as if they had been physically remade in accord with their mission of national regeneration. Mirabeau's face, so famously pockmarked, shines without a blemish. The physical bearing of the diminutive Robespierre is as impressive as his patriotic fervor. David's rigorously abstract composition is animated by the feelings attributed to Gilbert Romme and his Tennis Court Society when, on the first anniversary of the Tennis Court Oath, they reenacted the constitutional pledge: "A religious convulsion took hold of their souls; they let out shouts of joy toward heaven, in gratitude for liberty."[4] David's drawing, in a similar spirit of piety, represents the Assembly, headed by three clerics—Abbé Grégoire, Dom Gerle, and the Protestant minister Rabaut Saint-Etienne—taking its vow amid providentially engineered wind and lightning.

Forty-three troubled years separate David's drawing from Daumier's *Legislative Belly* (Fig. 1),[5] whose title plays on the French term for legislature, *corps législatif.*

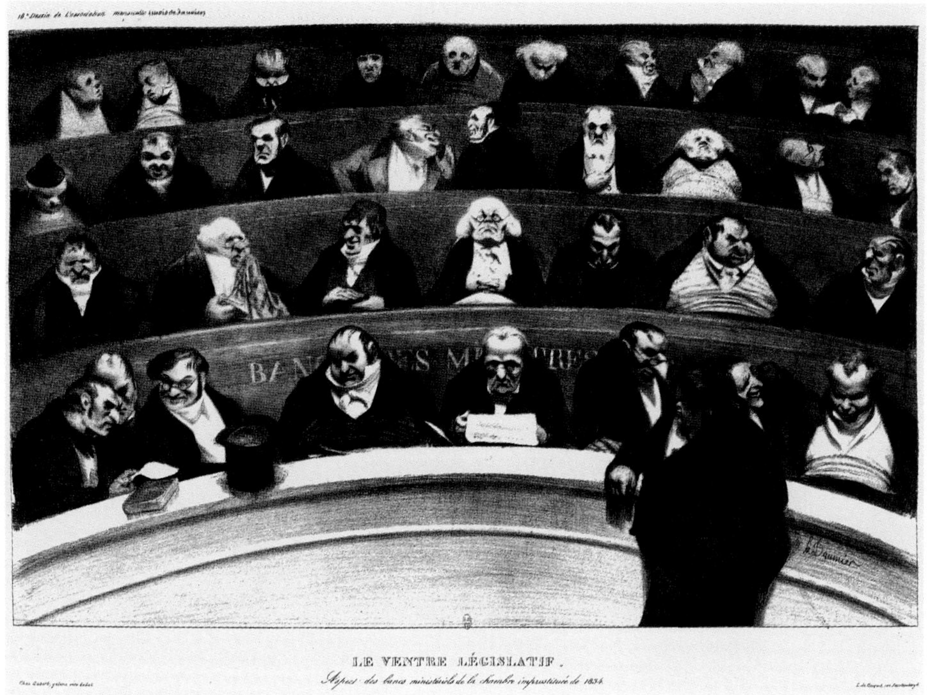

FIG. I.   H. Daumier, *The Legislative Belly*, 1834. Bibliothèque Nationale, Paris.

Daumier portrayed the ministers and deputies who were the bulwark of the July Monarchy—a regime created in the name of constitutional integrity—as round-shouldered bureaucrats sitting smugly like so many chairs in the Louis-Philippe style. Whereas David generated a sense of exhilaration through upraised arms, steeply converging walls, and umbrella-bending wind, Daumier emphasized the ponderous bulk of the chamber through the protruding bellies that rhyme so ungracefully with the curves of the newly renovated assembly hall. *The Legislative Belly* suggests why one of the outstanding legislators of the July Monarchy, the poet Lamartine, complained to his colleagues of the Palais-Bourbon that "France is a nation which is bored."[6]

The making and abandonment of nine constitutions in France between the Revolution of 1789 and that of 1848 explains how constitutional government could inspire such extremes of enthusiasm and disgust.[7] The legislative proliferation and waste are all the more striking in contrast with the American

Constitution, which, though amended and subject to radical differences in interpretation, has remained intact. The turbulence of French constitutional history can be associated with both ongoing political instability and the continued production of a potent political symbolism that legitimated the present and negated the immediate past. This impulse to wipe the slate clean and start anew was part of the revolutionary heritage. The symbolic aspect of French constitutional law, moreover, accounts for its interest as the subject of art.

The divinely inspired legislator played a large role in late eighteenth- and nineteenth-century French culture. That the Spartan Lycurgus enjoyed the blessings of Apollo and that Numa, the legendary second king of Rome, gained legislative wisdom from conversing with the nymph Egeria was known from Plutarch's *Parallel Lives*—a work firmly integrated into the French tradition by Jacques Amyot's classic translation (1559). Any French reader would have known Fénélon's *Aventures de Télémaque* (1699), which recounts with great sentimental force how Ulysses' son painfully learned virtue and legislative wisdom from Minerva. And of course there was Moses.

Imagery of Moses and the Ten Commandments is my concern in this study. The association of these motifs with the law and with authority was as sacred and fundamental as the Catholic catechism from which French children memorized the Ten Commandments. An attraction to the authority of Moses, furthermore, was deeply embedded in French Romanticism. Since the display of distinguished French religious art of the late eighteenth and nineteenth centuries in The Age of Revolution exhibition (Detroit Institute of Arts, 1975), the post-revolutionary revival of scriptural subject matter has received considerable attention.[8] The new range of significance carried by Old Testament imagery in this period, however, has gone relatively unnoticed.[9] Although many of the images in this book refer to Moses and the divine law of the Ten Commandments, the imagery itself is transvalued under the pressure of new secular concerns.

The theme of divine legislation crossed political boundaries. Moses and the Ten Commandments and the legendary lawgivers Numa and Lycurgus were invoked by revolutionary republicans, Napoleonic authoritarians, Restoration ultra-royalists, and Orleanist constitutional monarchists. Much of the political sentiment with which I am concerned is resolutely authoritarian; some of it is anti-democratic and reactionary. In considering such unsympathetic currents of opinion, my book has been preceded by The Dreyfus Affair exhibition at the

Jewish Museum, New York, and by the work of Zeev Sternhell and Michel Winock.[10] Each of these precedents, concerned with anti-Semitism, nationalism, and anti-parliamentarianism in France during the late nineteenth and twentieth centuries, offers instructive examples of how the most unpleasant ideologies can be approached without sentiment or oversimplification.

My own approach is both thematic and interdisciplinary. Although the visual evidence provided by painting, sculpture, prints, and medals has determined the shape and focus of my book, the imagery employed by contemporary politicians and poets is also integral to the argument, thus allowing access to some unfamiliar affinities between the art objects and their context. I consider some works—the bronze doors of the Madeleine, Préault's *Tuerie,* and Delacroix's paintings in the Palais-Bourbon library, for example—that are both thematically important and valuable as works of art; major literary works like Alfred de Vigny's "Moïse" and Lamartine's *Jocelyn* are similarly crucial to my discussion. My interest in other works—schematically propagandistic prints and medals produced under the Revolution and Empire, for example—is primarily iconographic. These works nevertheless bring both theme and historical context into better focus. Given the abstract nature of law, much of the imagery in question is allegorical. Accordingly, this study examines allegory itself during the period when the Davidian tradition matured and was transformed.

Although this is a thematic study, it is organized with respect for the political chronology of France between the revolutions of 1789 and 1848. In the final pages I consider the continued erosion of the French cult of the law during the second half of the nineteenth century. It seems appropriate to end a story of conflict between lofty ideals and brute reality on an elegiac note.

CHAPTER ONE

The Revolutionary Cult of Law

David's drawing *The Tennis Court Oath* gives little evidence of the controversy that attended the birth of France's first constitution (Plate 1). A swarm of outstretched arms converges on the president of the National Assembly as he leads his colleagues in their pledge of unity. Only one figure, cringing in the lower right corner like an allegory of damnation, refuses to participate. He is Martin Dauch, representative to the Estates-General from the bailiwick of Castelnaudary, who refused to take an oath he felt would compromise his allegiance to the king. His resistance sets in relief the enthusiasm of the patriots, who seem spiritually and physically invigorated as they surrender their will to the national cause. Embodied in David's rigorously choreographed demonstration of unanimity is a cherished revolutionary belief, proclaimed in the Declaration of the Rights of Man and Citizen: "Law is the expression of the general will. All citizens have the right to contribute personally, or by their representatives, to its formation."[1]

The revolutionary equation of lawmaking with national sovereignty, persuasively visualized by David, challenged one of the most venerable French monarchic traditions. Prior to the Revolution, the French king was invested with a legislative supremacy articulated by the seventeenth-century theorist of absolutism, Charles Loyseau: "Il n'y a que le Roy seule, qui puisse faire des loys" (Only the King can make laws.)[2] In practice, the absolute monarch's legislative power was limited. It could transgress neither the dictates of religion nor the "fundamental laws of the kingdom," a body of custom and written law that, among other things, prescribed the royal succession, forbade abdication of the throne, and

6

attributed the power to vote on taxes to the Estates-General.[3] Monarchic legislative power was also limited to the administration of justice and the maintenance of custom.[4] And so arbitrarily was the law executed that "for men of the Old Regime," Alexis de Tocqueville complained, "the place that the idea of law should occupy in the human mind was vacant."[5]

A new perspective on the law opened during the second half of the eighteenth century when the legislator's role in improving human society emerged as a prominent topic in literature.[6] The dialogue *On Legislation* (1776) by the *philosophe* Abbé Gabriel Bonnot de Mably (1709–1785) is an example. "Nothing is impossible for a capable legislator," Mably's principal interlocutor maintains; "he holds, so to speak, our hearts and our minds in his hands; he can make new men."[7] Here is a foreshadowing of the optimism with which David's *Tennis Court Oath* is charged. For those touched by this Enlightenment current, the roles of lawgiver and moral preceptor were indistinguishable. Accordingly, the *Encyclopédie* emphasized the role of the lawgiver in directing the education of children so as to inspire "humanity, benevolence, public virtues, private virtues, love of honesty, [and] passions useful to the state."[8] The cult of the lawgiver was given especially solemn expression by the author of *The Social Contract*.[9] Rousseau's fascination with the figure of the lawgiver was informed by a belief that good laws could inculcate virtue.

The legislator's prestige was never more inflated than during the French Revolution, when Rousseau's lofty speculations seemed on the verge of realization. For Emmanuel-Joseph Sieyès (1748–1836), the leading theorist of the National Assembly, the legislator's function was to "enlighten men about their happiness" and to "correct the evils caused by nature and by men."[10] "The legislator commands the future," proclaimed Saint-Just, that stern advocate of the Reign of Terror. "It is his role to desire good and to perpetuate it; it is his role to make men what he wishes them to be."[11] In the words of "Ça Ira," the song that filled the air at the great Paris Festival of the Federation, July 14, 1790: "Du législateur tout s'accomplira" (The legislator will accomplish everything).

Such unbounded confidence in the benevolence of the law speaks of the revolutionary legislators' unfamiliarity with their role. To them a constitution was an electrifyingly novel thing. Before the late eighteenth century the French rarely used the word *constitution* in the modern sense of a body of law instituting and regulating the political order of a society.[12] Most of the deputies to the National

Assembly initially understood their charge to be the restoration of monarchic tradition to the financially and politically bankrupt nation. Thus in anticipation of the salutary effect of their constitution, the participants in the Tennis Court Oath pledged to "maintain the true principles of monarchy."[13] Amid controversy, an audaciously comprehensive notion of the nation's constituent (i.e., constitution-making) power eventually prevailed.[14] Respect for monarchic tradition gave way to a decision to create a new government that would rule and regenerate France.

Leading this radical movement was Deputy Sieyès, who declared in his famous pamphlet *Qu'est-ce que le Tiers état?* that the will of the nation "is always legal; it is the law itself." Elsewhere he maintained that the nation, in exercising the constituent power ("the greatest, the most important of its powers"), must be unconstrained.[15] In accord with this bold idea of the nation's constituent power, David conceived *The Tennis Court Oath* as a massive demonstration of coordinated muscular force and included the irreverent detail of lightning striking the royal chapel of Versailles.

Severed from the person of the king, revolutionary law was at once depersonalized and venerated as the expression of the general will. This veneration was expressed in representations of the constitution and the Declaration of the Rights of Man and Citizen in the roundheaded form traditionally associated with the Ten Commandments.[16] At the same time, the depersonalization of the law can be associated with a taste for certain objects, such as the insignia of the Legislative Assembly (Plate 2).

Having provided France with the means to its regeneration, the Constituent Assembly was succeeded, in 1791, by the Legislative Assembly, mandated to make laws in accordance with the constitution. The Legislative Assembly decreed on July 12, 1792, that its insignia would take the form of tablets of the law inscribed RIGHTS OF MAN and CONSTITUTION, to be worn on a tricolored ribbon, draped across the chest, by deputies engaged in official business.[17] The roundheaded white enamel tablets set in gilded copper demonstrated the Legislative Assembly's pompous taste. "The Triumph of the Law," a song commemorating Jacques-Guillaume Simoneau, the mayor of Etampes killed in a food riot on March 3, 1792, and honored three months later by a Festival of the Law, was in a similar spirit: "Hail . . . to the law! Honor to the citizen who remains loyal to it! Triumph to the magistrate who knows how to die for it! . . . May one cherish it, may one fear it! New French people, march, march under its sign!"[18]

It is tempting to view the tablets worn by the Legislative Assembly as a transposition of the Christian doctrine of grace triumphant over law. For the era of constitutional law had superseded the rule of the monarchy by divine grace. Reference to the tablets of Moses was all the more appropriate in that revolutionary law was intended to share the brevity and immutability of the Ten Commandments. The president of the Convention's Committee of Legislation, Jean-Jacques-Régis Cambacérès, declared regarding his project for a Civil Code (1793) that "few laws suffice for honest men; there are never enough for the wicked." Once these laws were written, "one must dread touching this sacred deposit."[19] As Michelet pointed out, the simple rhyme of the song "Ça Ira" mimicked the simple form in which the Ten Commandments were taught to French children.[20] Behind the lofty rhetoric of the Declaration of the Rights of Man and Citizen the constitutional historian Maurice-Charles-Emmanuel Deslandres discerned the self-image of the Constituents as "nouveaux Moïses."[21]

The revolutionaries' veneration of tablets addressed the emotional void opened when the law was dissociated from the person of the monarch and attached to the written text. When Gilbert Romme and his Tennis Court Society celebrated the first anniversary of the Tennis Court Oath, a bronze tablet, inscribed with the oath and borne like a "sacred ark" by four Bastille combatants, was carried onto the holy ground of the Versailles tennis court and affixed to the wall.[22] The patriotic newspaper *Révolutions de Paris* reported that the procession at the festival held in the spring of 1792 to honor the mutinous Swiss guards of Châteauvieux "opened with the Declaration of the Rights of Man, written on two stone tablets as the Decalogue [i.e., Ten Commandments] of the Hebrews is represented to us, though it is no match for our Declaration." "Four citizens," according to the paper, "proudly carried this venerable burden on their shoulders."[23] On July 14, 1792—two days after the Mosaic insignia was decreed for the Legislative Assembly—a bronze tablet inscribed with the Declaration of the Rights of Man and Citizen was placed in a chest with a copper-bound volume of the constitution and other revolutionary memorabilia and deposited in the foundation of a monument to Liberty being built at the former site of the Bastille.[24]

The sanctity of the law was repeatedly belied by the relentless political instability and violence of the 1790s. The king played an integral role in the governmental mechanism defined by the Constitution of 1791. But that document, unable to survive the increasingly radical course of the Revolution, became obsolete less than a year after its acceptance. In September 1792 the Legislative Assembly was dissolved, the monarchy abolished, and France declared a republic. The National Convention was assembled to write a new constitution, which, unlike that of 1791, would be submitted to a nationwide vote of confidence. Even the Declaration of the Rights of Man and Citizen was not spared: the new Constitution of Year I (June 24, 1793) was headed by a longer, more truculent version of it than that adopted by the Constituents in 1789. In a print by Louis Laurent after Jean-Jacques-François Lebarbier, the thirty-five articles of the new declaration are inscribed on the familiar roundheaded tablets (Fig. 2).[25]

To lend prestige to the new constitution, the government held the Festival of Unity and Indivisibility on August 10, 1793, the anniversary of the monarchy's collapse. Organized by Jacques-Louis David and conducted by Hérault de Séchelles, the president of the National Convention, the festival expressed a bold vision of regenerated France radically different from that which had inspired the Constituent Assembly. The spectacle was at once steeped in a serene primitivist vision of rebirth and aflame with regicidal anger, thus anticipating the coupling of lofty civic zeal with unthinkable crime during the Reign of Terror. Far from unified as it confronted the armed might of the monarchic powers of Europe, France was torn by civil war. But as Mona Ozouf has pointed out, the Festival of Unity and Indivisibility made no reference to the conflicts that imperiled the nation.[26]

The festivities commenced at the former site of the Bastille before a fountain of regeneration, represented by a colossal Egyptoid figure of Nature from whose breasts flowed water. This drink was shared by members of the nation's Primary Assemblies—the regional assemblies that, according to the new constitution, would vote on laws as well as choose the citizens who would elect the national legislature. These delegates carried bouquets of wheat and fruit to symbolize the "sublime alliance . . . between agriculture and legislation" of the ancient republican peoples who had regarded Ceres as "the legislator of societies."[27] They proceeded to the Boulevard Poissonnière, where an arch of triumph had been erected honoring the women who had marched on Versailles demanding bread in October 1789. The crowd assembled at the Place de la Révolution (now the Place de la Concorde) before moving on to the Place des Invalides, where a colossal allegorical sculpture, *The French People Crushing the Hydra of Federalism,* was displayed.[28]

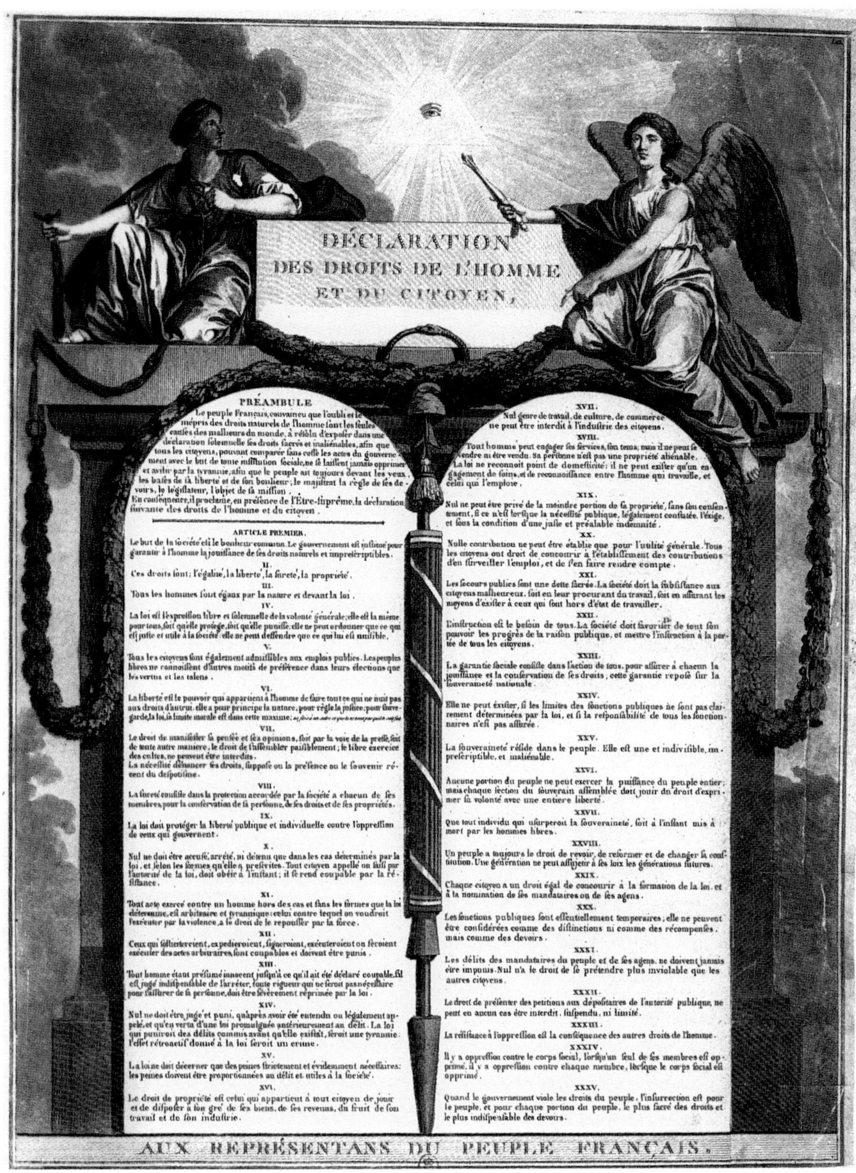

FIG. 2. L. Laurent after J.-J.-F. Lebarbier, *Declaration of the Rights of Man and Citizen,* c. 1793. Bibliothèque Nationale, Paris.

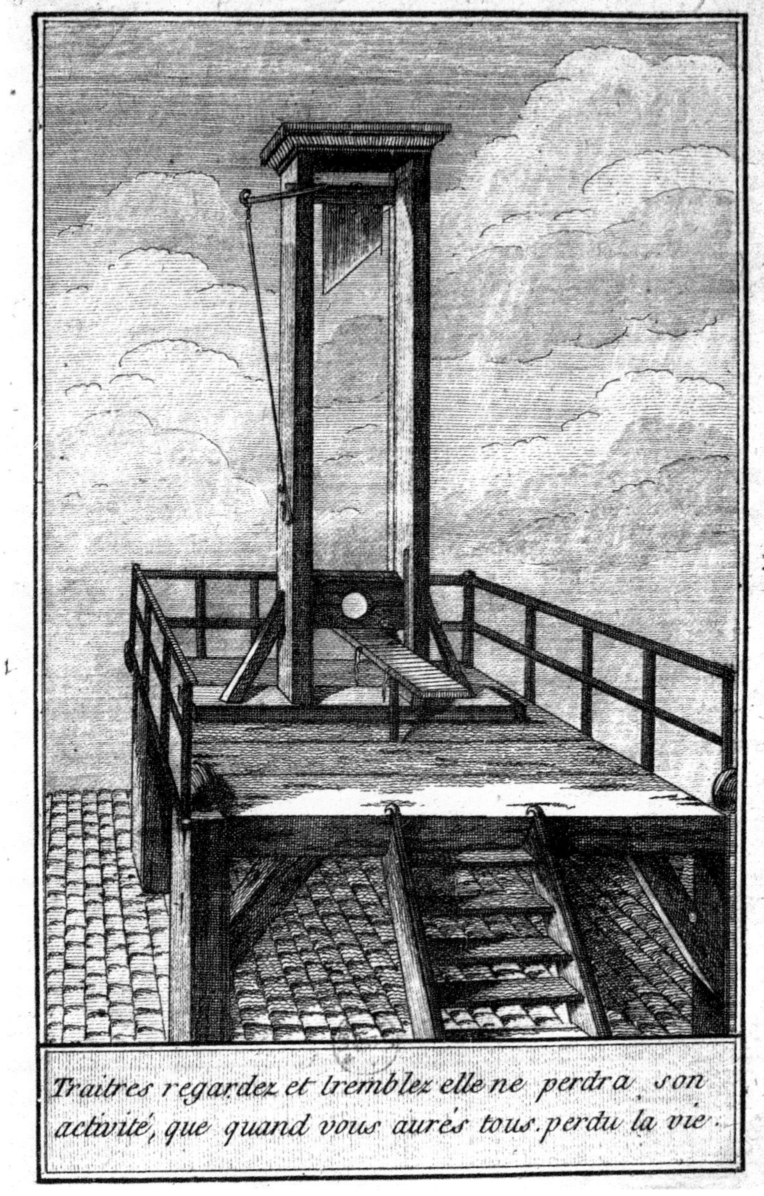

FIG. 3. J.-B.-M. Louvion, *The Dagger of Patriots is the Axe of the Law*, c. 1793. Bibliothèque Nationale, Paris.

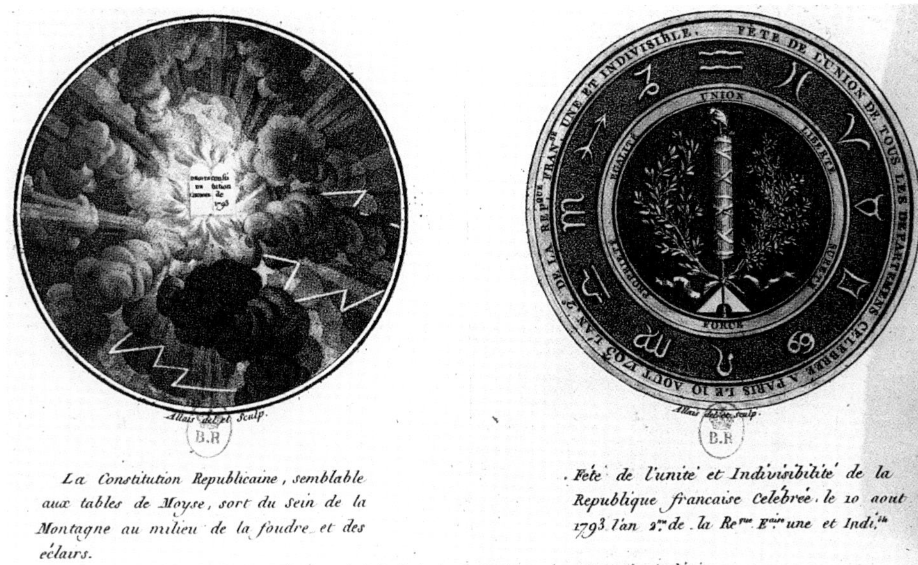

FIG. 4.   L.-J. Allais, print commemorating the Festival of Unity and Indivisibility, 1793. Bibliothèque Nationale, Paris.

At the site where Louis XVI had been executed, the president of the Convention proclaimed: "Here the axe of the law struck the tyrant."[29] Such a reference to the guillotine expresses the fearsome aspect of the law under the Terror (Fig. 3);[30] here the Enlightenment concept of law as creative and regenerative yields to the Old Regime and biblical notion of law as retributive and lethal. The phrase "axe of the law," moreover, could have been uttered only when the law had been resolutely depersonalized, severed from the person of the king, as it had been, gruesomely, with the decapitation of Louis XVI, January 21, 1793.

The festivities concluded at the Champ-de-Mars where, only three years earlier, the Festival of the Federation had celebrated the fidelity of the king and the nation to the previous constitution. Documentation of France's acceptance of the new constitution was placed on the Altar of the Fatherland and the constitution was enclosed in a cedar ark, as if it bore the very words of Jehovah. The event was commemorated in a print by Louis-Jean Allais that compares the Constitution of 1793 with the tablets Moses received on Mount Sinai (Fig. 4). The caption below

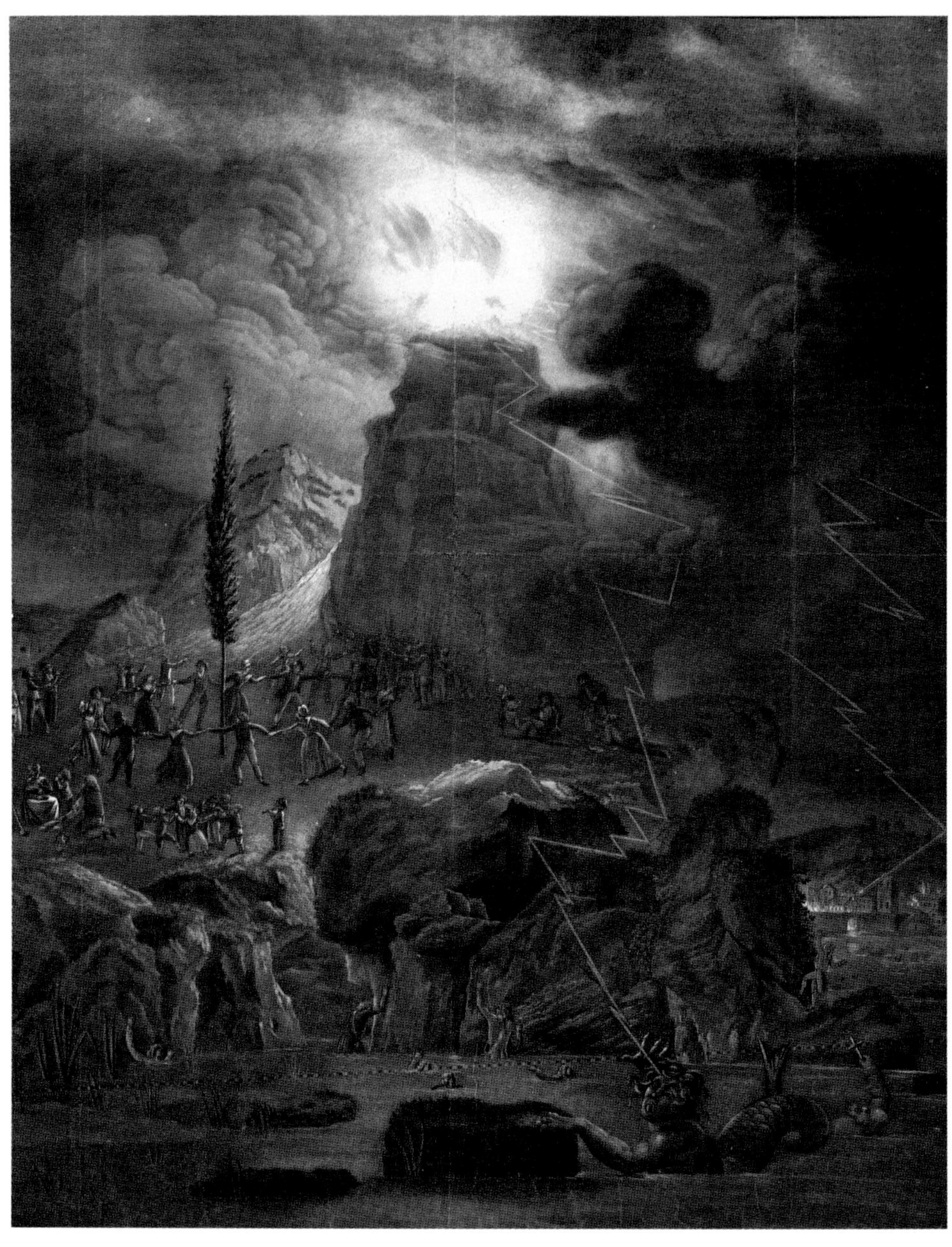

FIG. 5.   P.-M. Alix after Boissier,
The Triumph of the Mountain, c. 1794.
Bibliothèque Nationale, Paris.

reads: "The republican constitution, like the tablets of Moses, comes from the heart of the mountain in the midst of thunder and lightning."[31]

Such biblical rhetoric struck a common chord with the Constitution of 1793, whose final article states that the text of the constitution and the Declaration of the Rights of Man and Citizen are "engraved on tablets in the midst of the assembly and in public places." Similarly, the new Declaration of the Rights of Man and Citizen includes the fearsome commandment, reminiscent of Old Testament prescriptions for summary justice, that "any individual who would usurp sovereignty shall instantly be put to death by free men" (art. 27). And the Mount Sinai allusion flattered the radical section of the Convention popularly known as the Mountain because its members sat on the highest benches of the assembly hall.[32] A color print by Pierre-Michel Alix (Fig. 5) treats the same theme: in it a pair of fiery tablets (not visible in the photograph) send down bolts of lightning against the enemies of the Revolution while a patriotic multitude make merry around a liberty tree.[33] The author of a contemporary broadside entitled *The Mountain of Liberty; Mountain of Sinai, Source of French Regeneration, Protected by the Supreme Being* professed to "believe in the holy constitution, accepted by the French people August 10, 1793."[34]

Such was the value the revolutionaries placed on tangible representations of the law that objects bearing the imprint of outdated laws, viewed as abominations, were subject to official vandalism. On April 25, 1793, the Convention ordered the exhumation and mutilation of the tablet with the 1789 Declaration of the Rights of Man and Citizen and the volume of the Constitution of 1791 deposited in the foundation of a projected monument on the former site of the Bastille. These objects were now deemed "contrary to the general system of liberty [and] equality of the one and indivisible Republic." On May 3 the decree that this act be performed in two days was presented in the name of the Committee of Public Instruction by Gilbert Romme, whose Tennis Court Society had so passionately honored the authors of these tainted laws. The exhumed objects, Romme specified, "will be broken at the site and the fragments deposited in the national archives as a historical monument."[35] The violated book and broken tablet, now in the National Archives, resonate with morbid pathos (Plate 3 and Fig. 6). Like David's *Tennis Court Oath*—the monument to national unity that could not be completed in the face of political discord—these forlorn objects negate the revolutionary myth of the permanence and sanctity of the law.

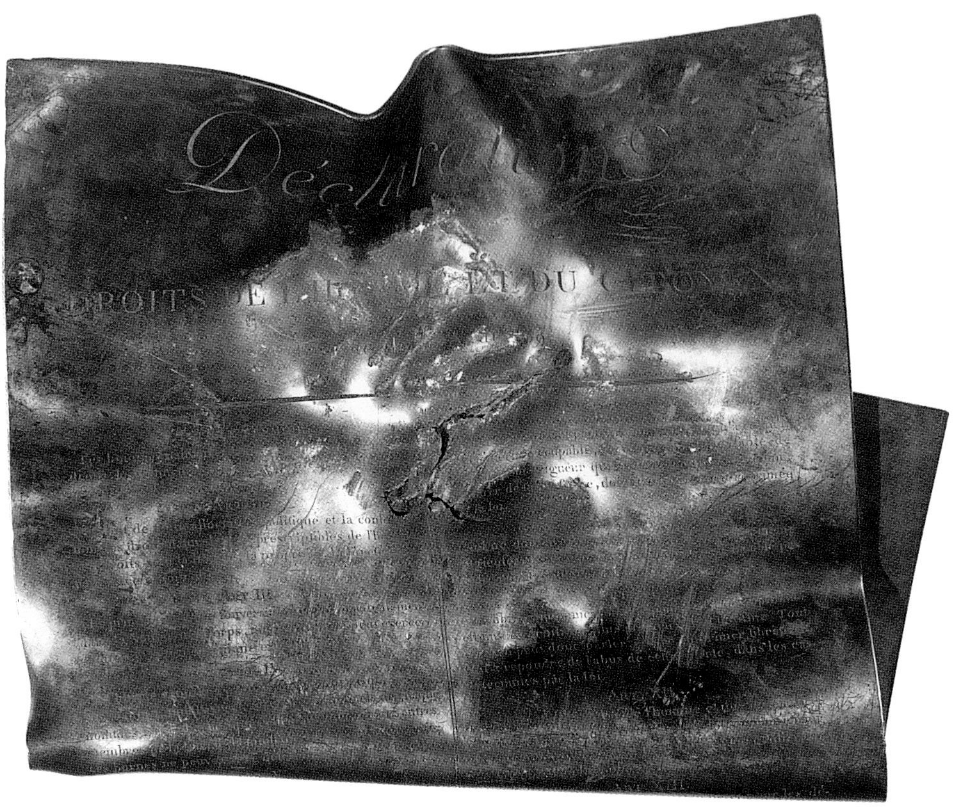

FIG. 6.   Bronze tablet inscribed with the 1789 Declaration of the Rights of Man and Citizen, vandalized in 1793. Archives Nationales, Paris.

The Constitution of 1793 was never put into effect following its poetic consecration at the Festival of Unity and Indivisibility. In the final act of a popular theater spectacle written by two members of the Convention and based on the festival of August 10 a citizen sang: "Oh holy constitution! Your salutary influence will soon dissipate the illusions of the peoples of the earth!"[36] But the perils of war and subversion seemed to necessitate the postponement of this salutary influence. The survival of the Republic of Virtue demanded a stronger executive power than that defined by the new constitution. While France suffered the despotism of the

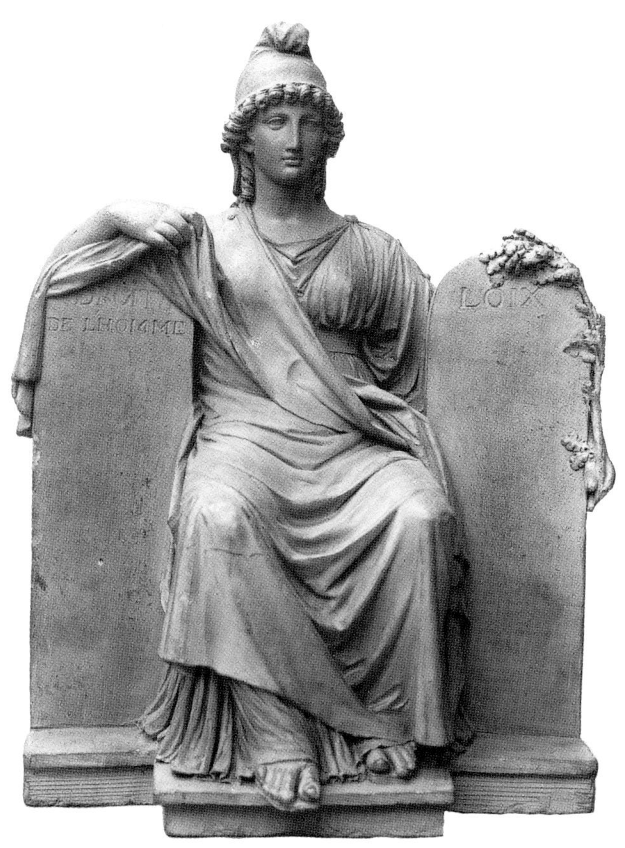

FIG. 7.   J. Chinard, *La République,*
1794. Louvre, Paris.

Committee of Public Safety, the Constitution of 1793 was kept in reserve. It remained in the Convention's assembly hall, safely enclosed in its cedar ark.

No hint of this state of affairs is given by Joseph Chinard's austere terra-cotta known as *La République* (Fig. 7), produced a little more than two months before the execution of Robespierre and the end of the most radical phase of the Revolution. Apparently a model for a monument that, like so many revolutionary projects, was never realized, Chinard's coldly placid figure in a Phrygian cap holds roundheaded tablets, inscribed RIGHTS OF MAN and LAWS, and an oak branch, emblematic of strength.[37]

The dictatorship of the legislature, initiated by the Constituents and brought to a terrible climax during the Terror, ended with the reaction of Thermidor. Robespierre was guillotined, and France was given yet another constitution. The Constitution of Year III (August 22, 1795)—it lasted almost five years, longer than any other revolutionary constitution—opened with a Declaration of the Rights and Duties of Man and Citizen, among which was the pronouncement that "no one is a good man if he does not frankly and religiously observe the laws" (art. 5). This homage to the revolutionary cult of law, however, was not backed by confidence in the nation's legislators. A five-member Directory held executive authority, and the legislature was cautiously divided into two separate assemblies. A Council of Five Hundred proposed laws to the 250 members of the Council of Ancients. Identification medals by Nicolas-Marie Gatteaux (1751–1832), distributed to members of the two legislative chambers, display the familiar revolutionary iconography of the law: Mosaic tablets, inscribed with the title of the new constitution, are superimposed on the level of equality and encircled by a serpent biting its tail, emblematic of "the long destinies of the republic and the stability of its legislation" (Fig. 8).[38] This conventional panoply ignored the turmoil of Directory France, beset by financial collapse, brigandage, and rebellion.

Hatred of the legislature had shadowed the development of representative government in France since the days of the Constituent Assembly. But popular French anti-parliamentarianism reached a new intensity during the summer and fall of 1795, when the Convention was purged of its radical element and the directorial Constitution of Year III was instituted.[39] How could there be respect for the law under the Directory when the government relied on measures so exceptional that this phase of the Revolution has been characterized as a permanent coup d'état?[40]

From the outset, the revolutionary legislative record was the subject of a formidable literature of denunciation.[41] It is ironic, in this regard, that detractors of the Constituent Assembly found ammunition in the very passages from *The Social Contract* that most exalted the legislator. For these critics Rousseau's lofty notion of the lawgiver set into relief the weakness of the Assembly.[42]

The most resounding attack came from across the English Channel. Edmund Burke, in *Reflections on the Revolution in France,* reprinted eleven times within a year of its appearance in 1790, established a position that became a mainstay of the French Right. Burke denied that a constitution could be "made," insisting

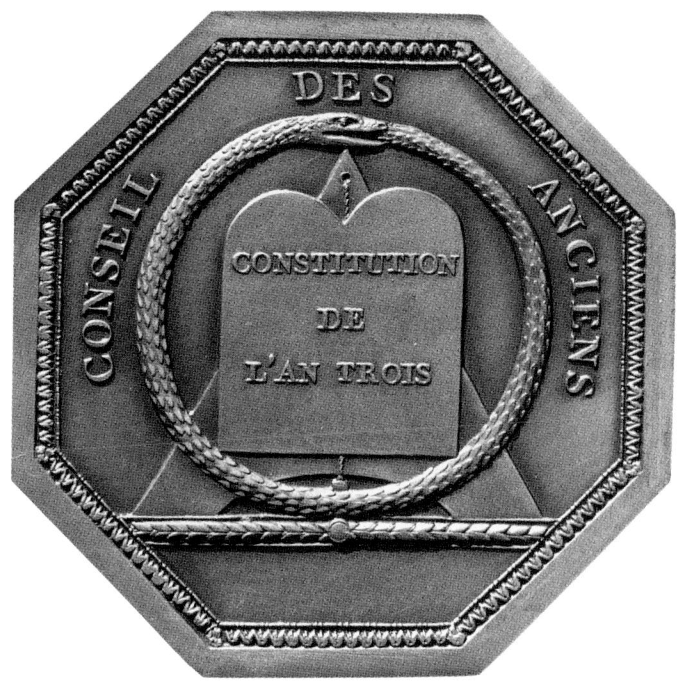

FIG. 8.   N.-M. Gatteaux, membership
medal for the Council of Ancients
(obverse), 1797. Musée de la Monnaie,
Paris.

that it had to evolve slowly and organically out of social institutions and history, as it had in England, where liberty "has its gallery of portraits, its monumental inscriptions, its records, evidences, and titles." Ignoring this principle, the legislators of France, behaving "like the comedians of a fair before a riotous audience," have given their nation a "monster of a constitution."[43]

Burke's *Reflections* were applauded by the counter-revolutionary French journal *Acts of the Apostles*.[44] With an anti-parliamentarian bile that prefigures *La Caricature* in the 1830s, this satirical royalist paper (November 1789–October 1791) denounced the "debased tigers" of the Constituent Assembly who had forced

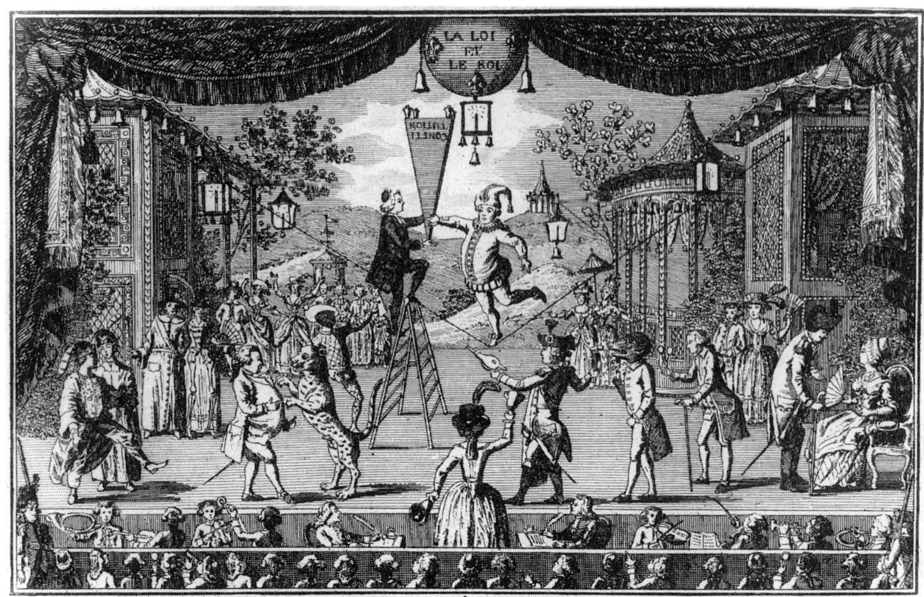

FIG. 9.   *Opening of the Club of the Revolution*, from *Actes des apôtres*, 1790. Widener Library, Harvard University.

Louis XVI to submit to their "ghastly laws."[45] In *Opening of the Club of the Revolution* (Fig. 9), published with an explanatory text as the frontispiece to the second volume, the nation's legislators display none of the dignity David would give them in *The Tennis Court Oath* (see Plate 1). This caricature engages the revolutionaries in a grotesque stage farce, complete with orchestra and fanciful Asiatic scenery. Atop a ladder, Sieyès hands an unwieldy constitution (the inverted pyramid) to Guy-Jean Target, who, because he often served as orator for the Constitution Committee, was malevolently viewed as father to the constitution by the counter-revolutionary press.[46] "Persuaded that a competent juggler could hold it in equilibrium," Sieyès has entrusted the constitution "to the dexterity of the academician Target." Deputy Antoine Barnave is said to be costumed as the Rights of Man: "a shark snout, & decrees in the form of principles in every buttonhole, give him a very expressive air." The bizarre display at the center of the

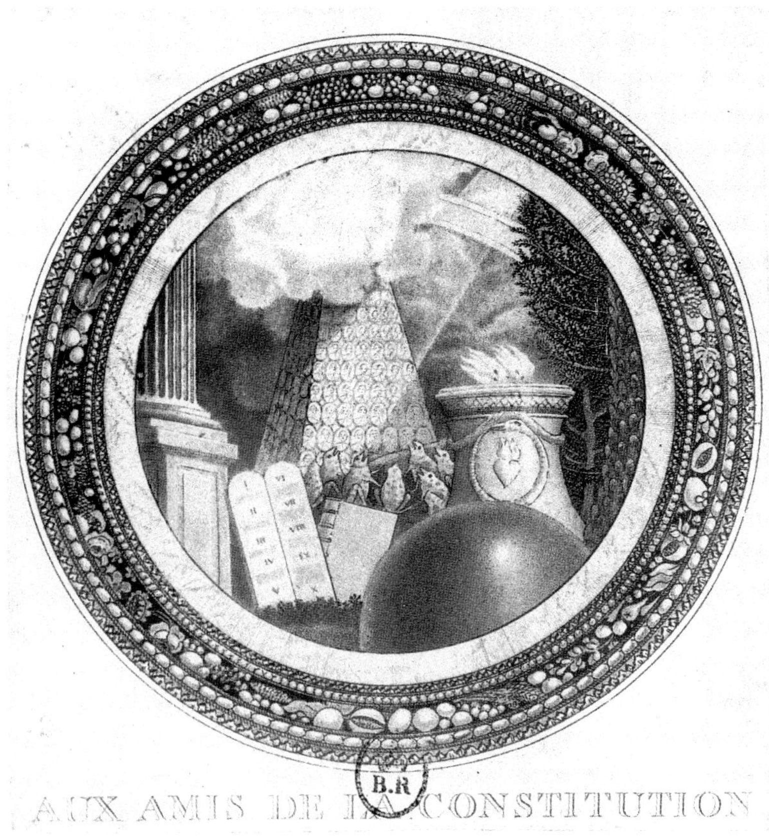

FIG. 10.   *To the Friends of the Constitution,* c. 1791. Bibliothèque Nationale,
Paris.

proscenium (a balloon filled with flammable air, a lighted lantern, and "the agreeable sound of little bells") symbolizes the "patriotic fire that exalts our divine legislators, the enlightenment and talents that they have shown, and the noise that
their eternal operations make in the universe."[47]

Counter-revolutionary caricaturists treated the revolutionary motif of the
roundheaded tablets of the law with similar derision. Consider, for example, a
curious allegorical tondo dedicated to the radical Jacobin Club, originally called
the Society of the Friends of the Constitution (Fig. 10).[48] At the foot of a pyramid

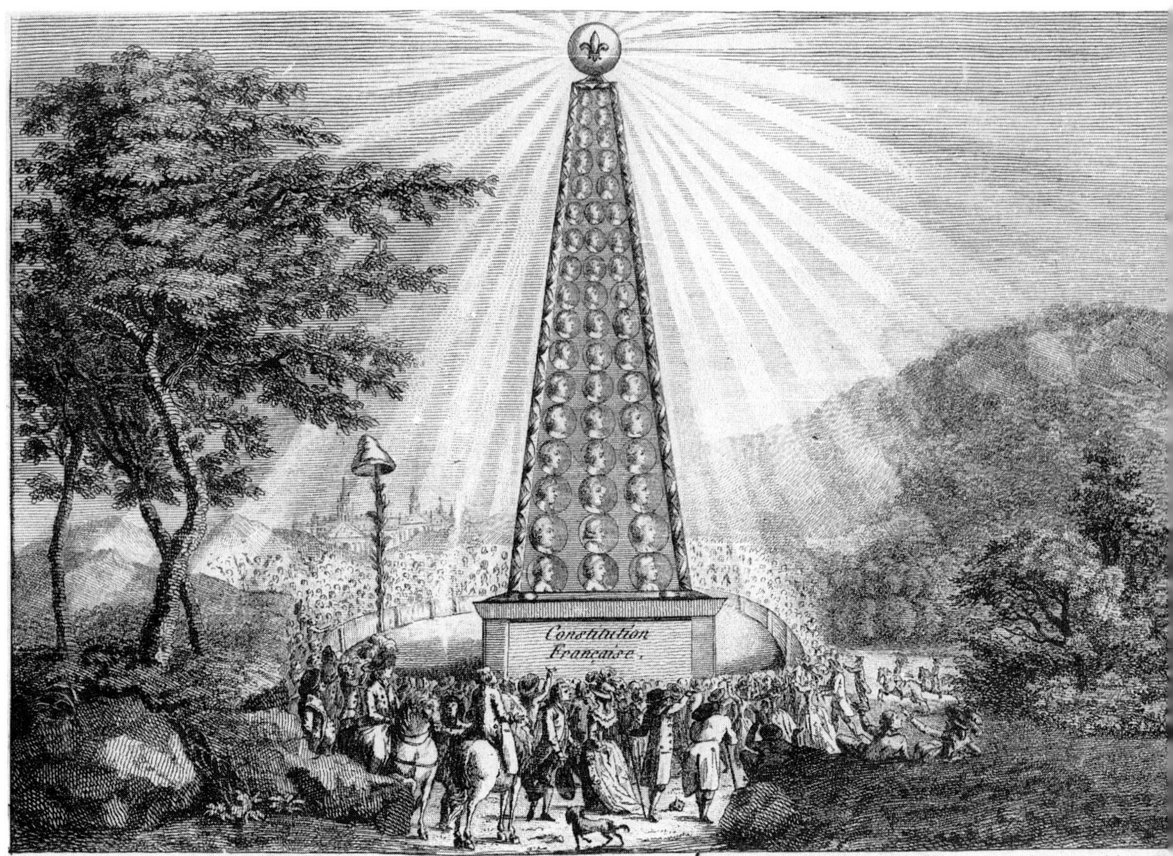

FIG. II.   *Homage to the National Assembly,* c. 1791. Bibliothèque Nationale, Paris.

encrusted with portraits—its prototype can be found in a revolutionary print *Homage to the National Assembly* (Fig. II)—a chorus of frogs croak in praise of the revolutionary legislators. Its summit obscured by clouds, this monument to folly stands amid an oppressive clutter of emblems. Flames rise from an altar whose serpent of eternity bears a suspiciously goose-like head. The tablets of the Ten Commandments and a bound volume that probably represents the Constitution of 1791 are pressed close to the adoring amphibians.

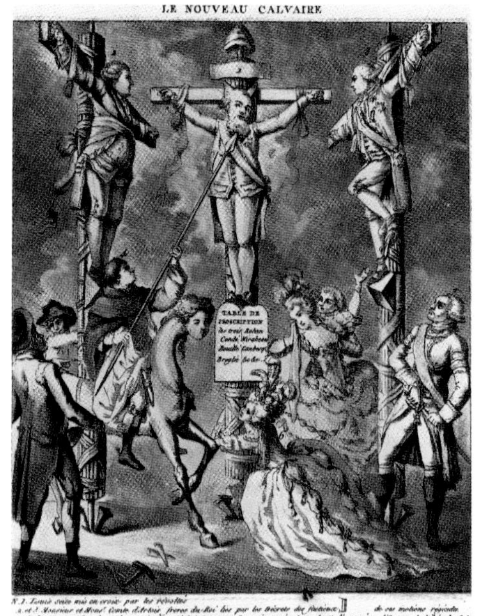

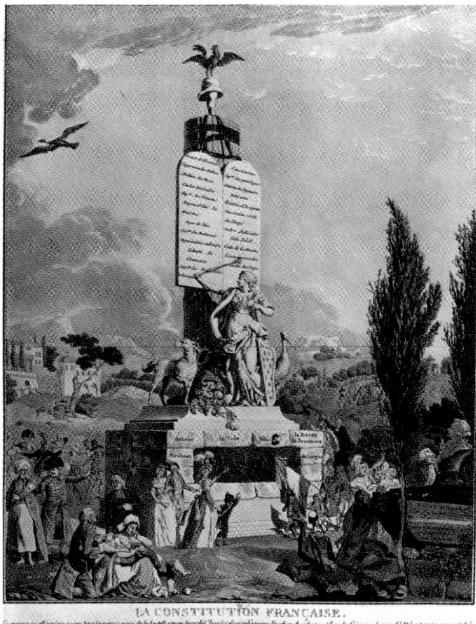

FIG. 12.   Attributed to M. Webert, *The New Calvary*, 1792. Bibliothèque Nationale, Paris.

FIG. 13.   *The French Constitution*, 1791. Bibliothèque Nationale, Paris.

A more ominous transformation of the tablets of the law occurs in *The New Calvary* (Fig. 12), a print sold and perhaps created by Michel Webert (b. 1769), an engraver and dealer in pornographic and royalist prints condemned to the guillotine in 1794.[49] This print contrasts with a revolutionary image of 1791, *The French Constitution* (Fig. 13). There, a stately personification of the nation uses the scepter of legislative power to engrave a roster of revolutionary reforms on colossal roundheaded tablets of the law suspended from a fasces. *The New Calvary* transforms these revolutionary emblems into instruments of torture. Flanked by his brothers, the future Louis XVIII and Charles X, Louis XVI is crucified above

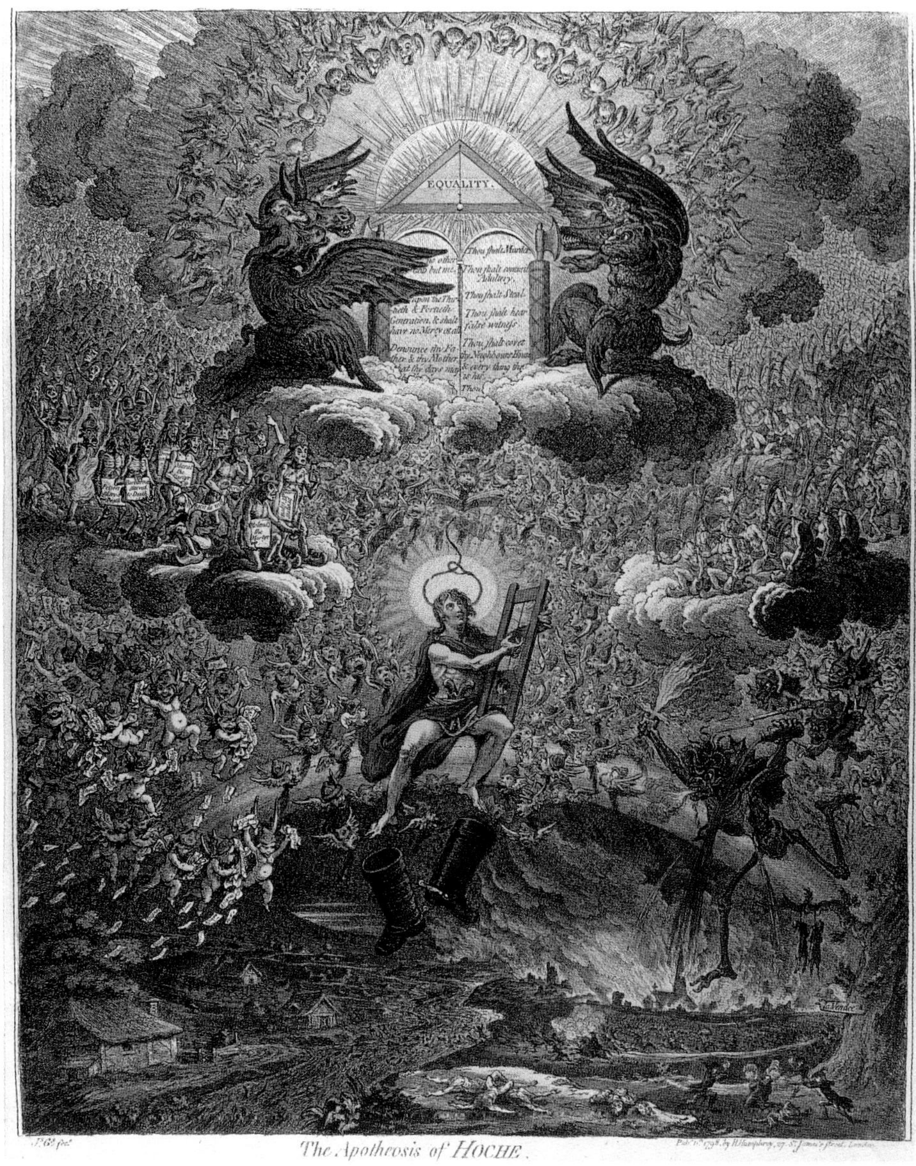

FIG. 14.   J. Gillray, *The Apotheosis of Hoche,* 1798. Yale Center for British Art, Paul Mellon Collection, New Haven, Conn.

roundheaded tablets that bear the names of those banished and anathematized by the Revolution. As the queen pleads for vengeance and the prince of Condé draws his sword, the king is offered a bitter sponge.[50]

The roundheaded tablets of revolutionary law served as a butt for the black humor of the British caricaturist James Gillray (1757–1815) in *The Apotheosis of Hoche,* an apocalyptic travesty of Hoche's funeral, September 19, 1797 (Fig. 14).[51] The republican anglophobe general, who on July 21, 1795, annihilated a counter-revolutionary assault force that attempted to land at the western coastal town of Quiberon, is cast in the dual role of Orpheus and Antichrist. In a grotesque mimicry of the civilizing legislator-poet Orpheus, Hoche plays a guillotine-lyre above a devastated landscape amid a satanic host of *sans-culotte* cherubim. Between two apocalyptic beasts are roundheaded tablets inscribed with a satanic inversion of the Ten Commandments.

Burke's attack on the Revolution was seconded in loftier terms by Joseph de Maistre in *Considérations sur la France* (1796), a book then little known in France but esteemed by the exiled aristocracy.[52] Maistre's fervent devotion to absolute monarchy and revealed religion was informed by a cruel wit worthy of Voltaire. "The more one examines the most apparently active figures of the Revolution," he asserted, "the more one finds in them something passive and mechanical." Maistre viewed the Revolution as a providential purification and punishment that would culminate in the triumph of the French monarchy: "Never has Divinity shown itself more clearly in any human event." And if Providence "employs the most vile instruments, that is because it is punishing in order to regenerate."[53] Such regeneration was hardly of the kind anticipated by those who took the Tennis Court Oath.

Maistre, who later wrote an essay condemning the very idea of written law, had unbounded contempt for revolutionary legislation.[54] The Revolution had created many laws, he argued, because it lacked a legislator. Although he considered Rousseau "perhaps the most mistaken man in the world," Maistre agreed with the author of *The Social Contract* that durable institutions must have a divine basis.[55] Like other counter-revolutionary polemicists, he invoked the *ancienne constitution* of France—the unwritten laws and customs by which monarchic France had been ruled for centuries—at the expense of the revolutionary legislators:

France, it is by the noise of infernal songs, the blasphemies of atheism, the cries
of death and long groans of innocence with its throat cut, by the light of con-
flagrations, on the debris of the throne and altars, watered by the blood of the
best of kings and an innumerable crowd of other victims . . . that your seducers
and your tyrants have founded what they call *your liberty.*

Against these horrors Maistre held up divine Providence, which would lead
France back to its *ancienne constitution.*[56]

Maistre's caustic brilliance had a ponderous counterpart in the theoretical writing of Viscount Louis-Gabriel-Ambroise de Bonald (1754–1840).[57] In *Théorie du
pouvoir politique et religieux dans la société civile, demontrée par le raisonnement &
par l'histoire* (1796), written in exile in Heidelberg, he anathematized the political
heresies of modern France. In accord with pre-revolutionary usage, Bonald
defined *constitution* as the traditional, patriarchal, and Catholic order of monarchic society. He regarded the very idea of a man-made constitution as absurd. He
presented this position in uncompromising terms at the opening of *Théorie du
pouvoir:*

I believe it possible to demonstrate that man can no more give a constitution
to religious or political society than he can give weight to the body or extension
to matter and that, far from being able *to constitute* society, man, by his inter-
vention . . . can only delay the efforts that society makes to arrive at its natural
constitution.[58]

Bonald held up Catholicism and monarchy as the foundations of an immutable social order revealed by God ("the supreme Legislator") through the
miracle of language. One of the few copies of *Théorie du pouvoir* to escape
confiscation by the Directory fell into the hands of General Napoleon Bonaparte.
Napoleon was supposedly so impressed by the treatise that he wrote to Bonald,
offering to have the government pay for a new edition.[59]

Revolutionary law received its ultimate insult on 19 brumaire, Year VIII
(November 10, 1799), the day after the abrupt transfer of the two legislative coun-
cils from Paris to Saint-Cloud. In response to General Bonaparte's defiance of the
Constitution of Year III, a dissident faction among the Five Hundred shouted
"Hors la loi!" To be deemed "outside the law" was a crime punishable by immediate execution. Lucien Bonaparte, president of the Council of Five Hundred,
saved both the coup d'état and his impetuous brother by having his recalcitrant

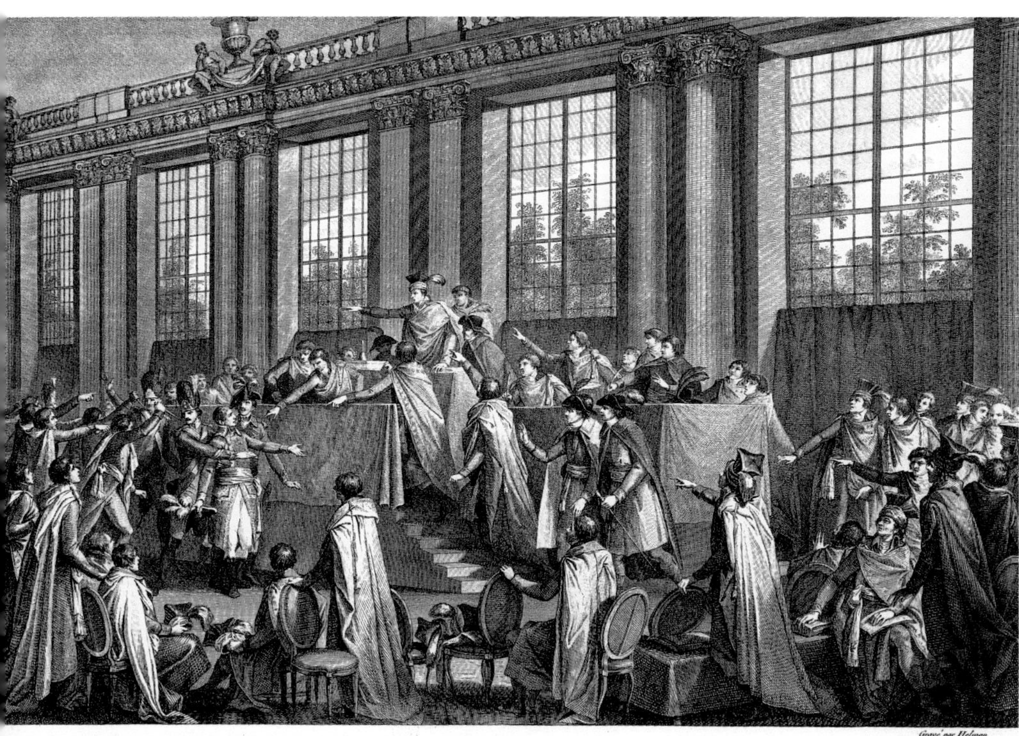

FIG. 15.   I.-S. Helman after
C. Monnet, *Day of Saint-Cloud,
18 Brumaire, Year VIII,* c. 1801.
Bibliothèque Nationale, Paris.

colleagues removed from the premises at gunpoint. Madame de Staël received with sorrow the news that "General Bonaparte had triumphed, the soldiers having dispersed the national representation; and I . . . felt in that instant a difficulty in breathing that has since become, I believe, the malady of all those who have lived under the authority of Bonaparte."[60]

The official interpretation of Bonaparte's confrontation with the legislature is represented in a print by Isidore-Stanislas Helman that shows the general beset—like Julius Caesar or the betrayed Christ—by a mob brandishing daggers (Fig. 15).[61] Less respectfully, the last moments of the Constitution of Year III

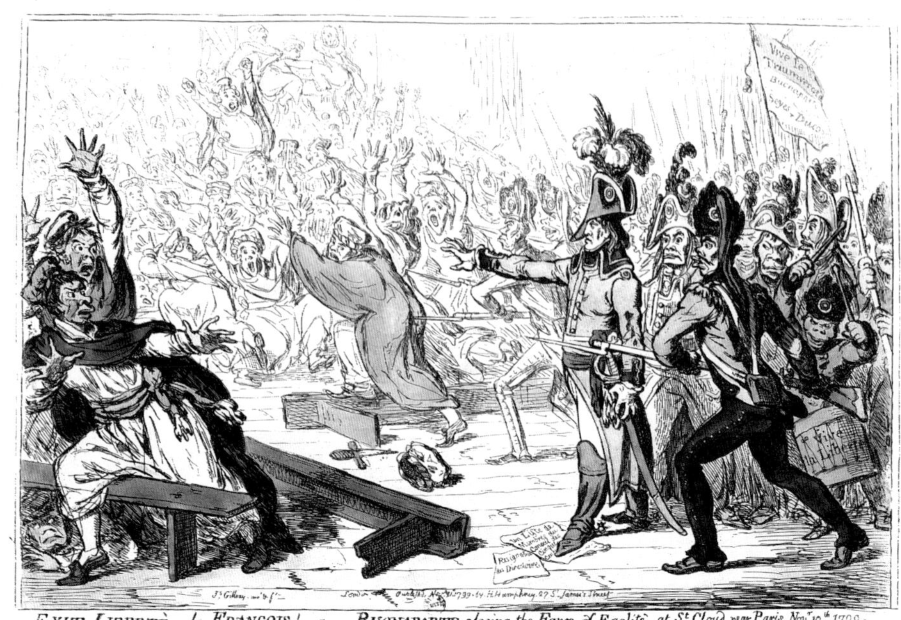

FIG. 16.   J. Gillray, *Exit Libertè a la Francois!* 1799. Bibliothèque Nationale, Paris.

were commemorated by Gillray in a print published November 21, 1799, *Exit Libertè a la Francois! or Buonaparte Closing the Farce of Egalitè* (Fig. 16).[62] This act of anti-parliamentary violence—whose brutishness Gillray conveys— closed definitively the period of buoyant optimism represented by the Declaration of the Rights of Man and Citizen, by David's drawing *The Tennis Court Oath,* and by the revolutionary festivals.

CHAPTER TWO

Legislative Imagery under Napoleon

France emerged from a decade of revolutionary strife hungering for order. Emmanuel-Joseph Sieyès's support of Napoleon's coup d'état is a telling indication of this political climate. The theorist who in a more innocent phase of the Revolution had been a leading advocate of the nation's constituent power and of the Declaration of the Rights of Man and Citizen was willing to take drastic measures to end the lawlessness of directorial France. In the aftermath of the coup Sieyès compiled notes for a constitution, in which he wrote that "authority must come from above and confidence from below" and that a constitution should be "short and obscure."[1]

Following the forcible dispersion of the Council of Five Hundred, Sieyès collaborated with Napoleon—who now bore the title of first consul—in drafting a new constitution. To his dismay and that of his collaborators, Napoleon, whom they had envisioned as a mere instrument to effect constitutional change, was unwilling to share the power seized by force. With this uncompromising attitude and the backing of his loyal army Napoleon could not be resisted. He altered Sieyès's complex project, molding the Constitution of Year VIII (December 13, 1799) to concentrate power in his own hands.

The dictator was at once a child of the Revolution and a grandson of the Old Regime. Though he continued the Revolution's war against the European monarchies and realized the dream of a rationally ordered and centralized France regulated by a single code of civil law, Napoleon returned the nation to Catholicism and had himself crowned as emperor. In Napoleonic France, moreover, the revolutionary cult of the law was transformed. The ambivalence toward the revolutionary heritage that would characterize Napoleonic France was expressed succinctly when, following the coup d'état of 18–19 Brumaire, the three consuls of the provisional government, Napoleon, Sieyès, and Pierre-Roger Ducos, presented the new authoritarian Constitution of Year VIII to the nation for approval. "Citizens," the consuls declared, "the Revolution is fixed in the principles by which it began: it is finished."[2]

The revolutionary legislators were too busy making and destroying constitutions to fulfill the intention, stated in the Constitution of 1791, that the nation be provided with a "code of civil laws, common to all the kingdom." Under Napoleon, the focus of legislative activity shifted from the public to the private domain, that is, from constitutional to civil law.[3] And a vast campaign of legal codification was undertaken: the famous Code Napoléon (Civil Code) of 1804 was followed by codes of civil procedure (1806), commerce (1807), and criminal procedure (1808) and by a penal code (1810). Although some great jurists of the Old Regime had attempted to unify the nation's welter of customary law (followed in the northern half of France), written Roman law (followed in the Midi), and royal ordinances,[4] the task required the centralized administrative vigor of Napoleonic France.

In 1812 Jacques-Louis David depicted Napoleon as a tireless legislator in a portrait commissioned by Alexander Douglas, a Scottish nobleman, art collector, and admirer of Bonaparte (Plate 4). It is almost 4:15 A.M., and the candle burns low. Napoleon, the artist explained, had spent the night absorbed in his work on the code; having ceased his labor, he stands alert, ready to buckle on his sword and review his troops.[5] Such fortitude and industry, made all the more impressive by David's insistence on the corporeality of the man, are echoed by the fiercely erect feline leg of the work table and by the Napoleonic bees decorating the massive regal chair. On the chair and table a sword and the rolled code symbolize Napoleon's accomplishments as warrior and lawmaker, which Louis de Fontanes, the president of the imperial Legislative Body, was fond of invoking.[6] Appropriately, a volume of Plutarch lies near his feet to recall for David's contemporaries the legendary legislative prowess of a Lycurgus or a Numa.

Napoleon presided over more than half of the 102 sessions in which the work of the Civil Code commission was discussed before the Council of State. Notwithstanding his lack of legal sophistication, he contributed to the code's emphasis on paternal authority and the protection of property. Although he sup-

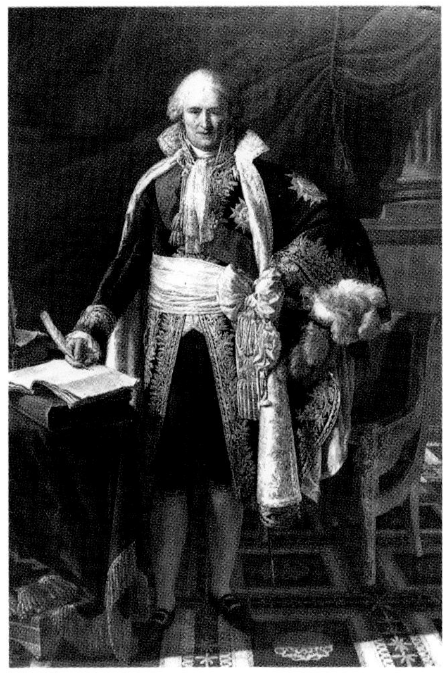

posedly complimented David for truthfully revealing how "at night I work for my subjects' happiness,"[7] he was hardly the author of the durable and internationally influential body of law that bears his name. Such is the persuasive power of David's stately arrangement of scrupulously rendered symbolic details that the genesis of the Code Napoléon is veiled behind the charismatic person of the great leader.

The Code Napoléon was drafted by a commission of jurists appointed in 1800 and headed by Jean-Etienne-Marie Portalis (1746–1807).[8] A lawyer in the *parlement* of Aix under the Old Regime, Portalis had served as president of the Council of Ancients and was exiled as a result of the anti-royalist coup of 18 Fructidor (September 4, 1797). Appointed minister of religion in 1804, he had been deeply involved in directing French religious affairs since the signing of the Concordat with the Vatican in 1801. It was appropriate that this pious jurist was both minister of religion and chief drafter of the Civil Code, for Napoleonic France inherited from the revolutionary legislators a quasi-religious attitude toward the law. Although Napoleon's legal expert was nearly as blind as Justice (he squints weakly in his official regalia in Claude Gautherot's portrait, Fig. 17), he had a prodigious memory.[9]

Portalis and his associates wanted a code that, like Roman law, would be a universally valid expression of "written reason." Surely the code commission was flattered when the tribune Louis-François-Alexandre Goupil de Préfelne told the Legislative Body that the code "will merit the title *written reason of our century.*"[10] But the middle-aged jurists of the commission were pragmatists who, moreover, perceived reason in the traditions they knew. Accordingly, they avoided innovation and attempted to strike a compromise between Roman law, custom, royal ordinances, and revolutionary legislation.[11]

Although Napoleon regarded the code as one of his principal achievements, he was disturbed by its dryness, which confirmed his belief that the "vice of our modern legislators is an inability to speak to the imagination."[12] Convinced that the stability of his regime depended on its power to "dazzle and astonish,"[13] Napoleon wanted his code to inspire awe. Official demonstrations of amazement and gratitude were in order.

With the promulgation of the Code Napoléon (under the title Civil Code of the French People) on March 21, 1804, France resounded with hyperbolic praise of the first consul's legislative prowess. In gratitude for the Civil Code, the Legislative Body decreed that a bust of Bonaparte be placed in the midst of their assembly hall in the Palais-Bourbon. The project was amplified to a life-sized sculpture, *The First Consul Offering the Civil Code to the French People,* with the inscription: TO BONAPARTE FROM THE LEGISLATIVE BODY. On the advice of Vivant Denon, Napoleon's chief artistic director, the commission was given to Antoine-Denis Chaudet (1763–1810).[14] The original design that called for civilian dress was modified so that Napoleon would be draped like a caesar. As an engraving of Chaudet's lost statue indicates, this work gave the "restorer of laws" an appropriately august bearing (Fig. 18).[15]

No less grandiose in evoking the legislative stature of the emperor was a relief ensemble by Jean-Guillaume Moitte (1746–1810) on the west wall of the Cour Carré of the Louvre, *History Inscribing upon Her Tablet the Names of Napoleon the Great and the Legislators Moses, Numa, and Lycurgus* (Fig. 19).[16] The elegantly mannered poses and richly linear drapery of Moitte's group were intended to be in stylistic accord with the existing sixteenth-century reliefs by Jean Goujon.[17] History, flanked by busts of Herodotus and Thucydides, inscribes the name of France's great legislator in the presence of four representatives of the sacred mysteries of law. Numa—the legendary second king of Rome, whose laws were

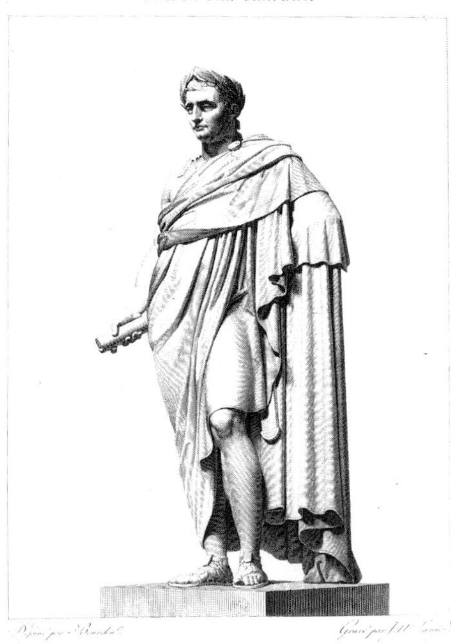

FIG. 18.   J.-N. Laugier after Bourdon, engraving of A.-D. Chaudet, *The First Consul Offering the Civil Code to the French People* (1805), c. 1820. Bibliothèque Nationale, Paris.

FIG. 19.   J.-G. Moitte, *History Inscribing upon Her Tablet the Names of Napoleon the Great and the Legislators Moses, Numa, and Lycurgus*, c. 1805–7. Cour Carré, Louvre, Paris.

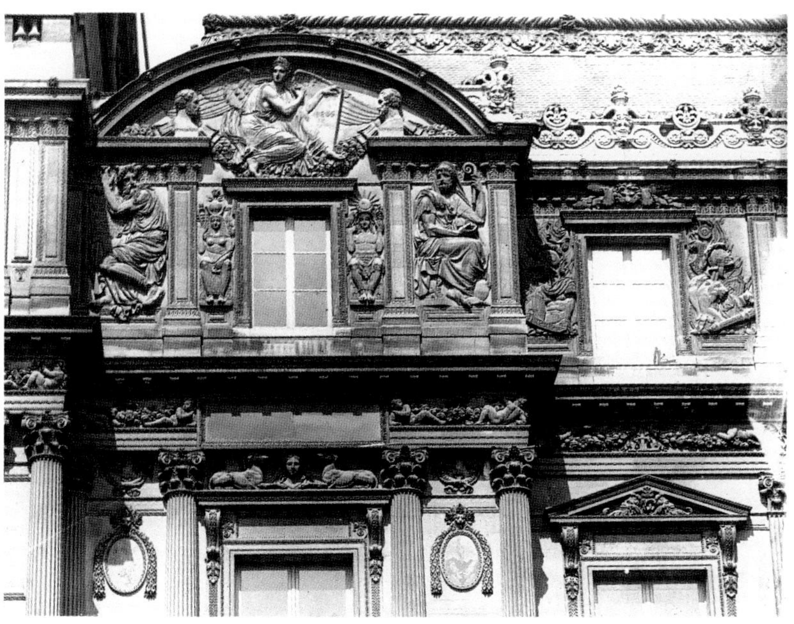

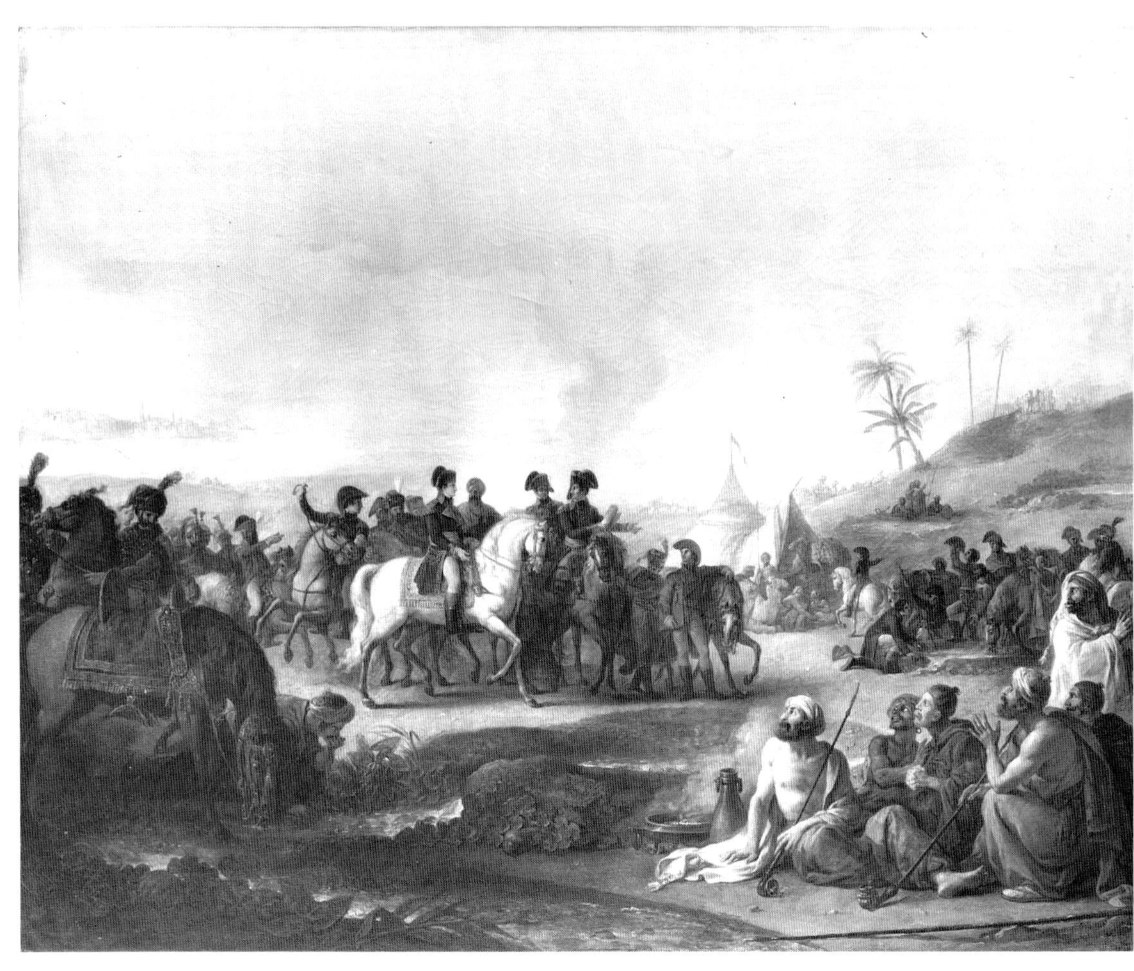

FIG. 20.　J.-S. Barthélemy, *The Passage of the Isthmus of Suez and His Majesty Visiting the Wells of Moses,* Salon of 1808. Musée National du Château de Versailles.

inspired by the nymph Egeria—holds attributes of priesthood and prophecy, the wand of augury and a vestal flame;[18] Moses points to the celestial source of his inspiration.[19] The pose of this Moses derives from conventional representations of Saint John the Baptist, suggesting, further, that the Hebrew legislator is a prophet of Napoleonic legal genius. The Egyptian god Isis and the mythic demigod Manco-Capac, who brought civilization to the Incas, are peculiar iconographic elements, not included in a preserved bronze-cast sketch. These figures were apparently added as arcane references to the divine nature of legislative genius.[20] Such imagery fit the Napoleonic practice of referring to lawyers by the Roman title "priests of the laws."[21]

A painting commissioned by Vivant Denon in 1806 from Moitte's friend the Old Regime history painter Jean-Simon Barthélemy (1743–1811) also implied that Napoleon was following in the tracks of Moses.[22] The flattering biblical resonance of *The Passage of the Isthmus of Suez and His Majesty Visiting the Wells of Moses* (Fig. 20) was subtly accented in the official guide to the Salon of 1808, which noted that before visiting the fountains of Moses, Napoleon had crossed the Red Sea at a ford accessible only at low tide.[23] Although Salon critics were not enthusiastic about the work, the emperor personally offered his compliments to the painter, who spoiled the occasion with his speechlessness.[24]

The aggrandizement of Napoleon's personal stature as lawgiver in Chaudet's statue and Moitte's relief group represented a departure from the revolutionary tradition of honoring the law. Even though the legislature exercised a dictatorship until the fall of Robespierre, the revolutionary notion that law was the expression of the general will theoretically divested legislators of individual political authority; they were but vehicles through which the general will of the nation was realized.[25] Although Napoleon maintained this revolutionary doctrine his regime associated the general will not with the legislature but with the charismatic dictator.

Between the Tennis Court Oath and the Directory, revolutionary politics had been dominated by the legislature. But Napoleon—who seized power through an act of anti-parliamentary violence—almost obliterated the power and autonomy of the legislature and reinstated pre-revolutionary executive power with a vengeance. In 1804 he bluntly characterized his position: "I am the constituent power."[26] "Legislation incarnate" was an epithet supposedly applied to him by Second Consul Cambacérès.[27] Such uncompromising personalization of the law recalls the Old Regime concept of the monarch as supreme legislator. "This was the first time since the Revolution," Madame de Staël noted, "that you heard a proper name in everyone's mouth." Previously, "one said the Constituent Assembly had done such and such, the people, the Convention; now one only spoke of the man fated to take the place of all others and render the human species anonymous by monopolizing celebrity."[28]

The Napoleonic practice of inscribing Bonaparte's name in the constitution reflected this personalization of the law. Whereas the revolutionary constitutions had upheld Rousseau's insistence that law remain unsullied by particulars, the Constitution of Year VIII cited the three consuls by name, and the imperial Constitution of Year XII (May 18, 1804) specified the positions of Napoleon's heirs in the line of succession to the throne.

On September 3, 1807, the new Civil Code was renamed Code Napoléon.[29] This change of title, which consolidated the fiction of Napoleon's authorship, occurred within days of the huge state funeral (August 29) of Portalis, the venerable jurist who had headed the Civil Code commission. The tribune Georges-Antoine Chabot (known as Chabot de l'Allier) announced the new title to the Legislative Body, justifying the official use of what had long been used "spontaneously" by pointing out how the emperor, with his "triumphant hands," had established France's civil laws:

> He was constantly seen participating in the discussion [of the code] . . . directing it with profound ideas and with forceful reasoning. He consistently displayed knowledge that astonished the most consummate jurists and established all [of the code's] fundamental principles through the comprehensive workings of a creative genius to which nothing seems foreign.

In a contention alien to the depersonalized notion of the law embraced by the legislators of the Revolution, l'Allier insisted that Napoleon's greatness would guarantee the durability of the code: "A great name, that is the best safeguard of the laws, and the surest means to convey their authority."[30]

In 1802, when the nation was voting to make Napoleon consul for life, an enthusiastic admirer denounced, in verse, the "timid laws" that would limit the duration of Bonaparte's rule.[31] "A constitution must not interfere with the process of government or be written in a way that would force the government to violate it," the first consul said before the Council of State in Year X (1801–1802). "Every day brings the necessity to violate constitutional laws; it is the only way, otherwise progress would be impossible."[32] Napoleon's willingness to sacrifice constitutional integrity to political expediency was consistent with his contempt for representative institutions.

Even under the Directory, Napoleon had nursed ominous plans for the nation's legislators. In 1797 he told his future foreign minister Talleyrand that the ideal legislature would be "without rank in the Republic, impassive, without eyes and without ears," that it would "no longer swamp us with a thousand circumstantial laws that annul themselves by their absurdity and constitute us a nation with three hundred volumes-in-folio of laws."[33]

Napoleon first unleashed his hostility toward the revolutionary legislative tradition in his authoritarian Constitution of Year VIII, which divided the process of legislation—introduction, deliberation, and voting—among three bodies: the Council of State, the Tribunate, and the Legislative Body. The Senate chose members for each of the three and served as a tribunal for constitutional questions. Legislation was initiated by the "government"—that is, the first consul with the advice of his administrative court, the Council of State. The Tribunate—purged in 1802 after resisting the first project of the Civil Code commission—discussed the proposed laws but could not vote on them. The Legislative Body voted on measures presented to it by the Tribunate but was barred from deliberation, under pain of discipline. The mute and generally docile Legislative Body, composed largely of obscure but now affluent former revolutionaries, was thus a mere shadow of the great revolutionary legislative assemblies.

The dictatorship initiated by the Constitution of Year VIII was strengthened by amendments that make up two additional constitutions. According to the Constitution of Year X (measures enacted August 2 and 4, 1802) Napoleon, named consul for life, was empowered to legislate and to interpret and define the constitution through edicts issued through the Senate (senatus consulta).[34] Rich rewards of land and residences guaranteed the Senate's allegiance. The Legislative Body would henceforth be convoked and dissolved at the will of the government. With the Constitution of Year XII (May 8, 1804) Napoleon was elevated to the imperial throne.

The difficult task of bringing luster to the captive legislature was handled with aplomb by Louis de Fontanes,[35] who during his remarkable career rode the changing

winds of French politics with an agility that earned him a large entry in the satirical *Dictionnaire des girouettes* (Dictionary of weathercocks; 1815).[36] A moderate
during the early years of the Revolution, Fontanes, like Portalis, was forced to
emigrate by the anti-royalist coup of 18 Fructidor (September 4, 1797). Following
a year of exile in England, Fontanes returned to France, where in 1804 he became
president of the Legislative Body. While he quietly insisted on the autonomy and
dignity of this assembly, his official speeches were such masterpieces of obse-
quiousness that a satirical pamphlet published under the Restoration ridiculed
him by simply quoting from his Napoleonic addresses.[37] "The man before whom
the universe is silent is also the man in whom the universe has confidence,"
Fontanes declared of Napoleon on March 5, 1806. If the universe was not silent
before the emperor, the Legislative Body generally was. "He is both the terror and
the hope of peoples. . . . As soon as the wise saw him . . . they recognized in him
all the signs of domination."[38] This was appropriate praise of a ruler who had
reduced the legislature to an assembly of mutes.

Even as the Legislative Body was wholly subordinate to him, Napoleon was
concerned to clothe this living symbol of his supremacy as lawgiver in appropriate dignity.[39] To this end some modifications of the building in which the Legislative Body assembled were carried out under official command. Bernard Poyet
(1742–1824) designed a majestic flight of steps and an imperial portico for the
Seine facade of the Palais-Bourbon (Fig. 21), which served as Napoleon's "Temple
of Laws."[40] The emperor, however, was displeased with the result.[41] Jean-Baptiste
Regnault's fiercely revolutionary painting *Liberty or Death* (Salon of 1795), which
had been on view since 1799 in the assembly hall of the Council of Five Hundred
in the Palais-Bourbon, was removed. It was replaced by *The Signature of the
Preliminaries of Leoben,* by Guillaume Guillon (called Lethière), representing an
early manifestation of Napoleon's dictatorial resolve.[42] In addition to Chaudet's
First Consul Presenting the Civil Code to the French People, portraits of Napoleon
and Josephine in imperial costume were purchased from Ingres and Lethière.[43]

Although the cold glamour of Ingres's *Napoleon on His Imperial Throne* has
proved irresistible to late twentieth-century eyes familiar with Pop Art and Photo-
Realism, the artist was deeply pained to learn that this strangely hieratic and air-
less portrait (Fig. 22) had failed at the Salon of 1806, where the likeness was
faulted as well as the resemblance to the fifteenth-century art of Jan van Eyck.
Modern commentators, noting among the sources for the portrait the *God the*

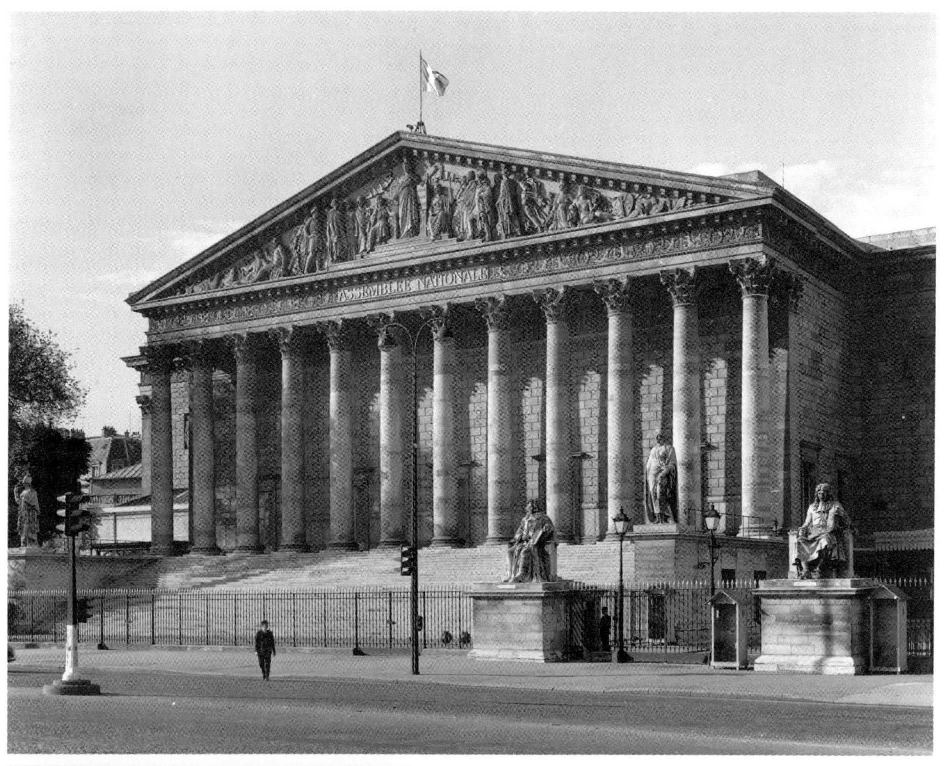

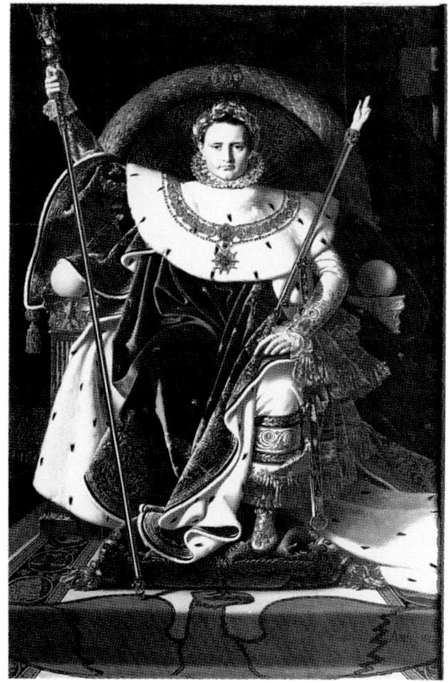

FIG. 21.   B. Poyet, Seine facade of
Palais-Bourbon, 1806– 8. Paris.

FIG. 22.   J.-A.-D. Ingres, *Napoleon
on His Imperial Throne*, 1806. Musée de
l'Armée, Paris.

Father panel from Jan van Eyck's Ghent altarpiece, plundered for display in Paris, have delighted in Ingres's forceful archaism, in which compositional rigidity is startlingly combined with minute detail. The stylistic archaism reinforces references to Charlemagne—the sword and hand of justice supposedly borne by the medieval emperor and restored, or perhaps manufactured anew, for Napoleon's coronation.[44] Such references, common in Napoleonic propaganda before the 1806 Salon, could have been additional irritants to contemporary critics.[45]

Although Ingres's imperial portrait, purchased by the Legislative Body prior to the 1806 Salon, was apparently not an official commission, it was an appropriate one. It offers an unblushing expression of the emperor's domination over the Legislative Body.[46] At the time of its purchase, it was intended for the chambers of President Fontanes, but it was relegated (along with Lethière's portrait of the empress) to the office of the quaestors, who, as treasurers of the Legislative Body, had purchased the works.

That Ingres's portrait was sent to this undistinguished location is not surprising given the critics' response to it. Before the Salon, however, this portrait would have seemed a fitting ornament for the chambers of Fontanes. Ingres's presentation of the emperor as a new Charlemagne, timelessly enthroned with the props Fontanes had recommended for the imperial coronation,[47] struck a common chord with the pious nostalgia for the Middle Ages professed by the president of the Legislative Body. Shortly after the imperial coronation, Fontanes joyfully observed:

> Ten centuries have passed since the epoch when France saw a similar spectacle.
> A monarchy of fourteen hundred years that seemed buried beneath so many
> ruins has suddenly reappeared with its ancient splendors, and almost all the
> diadems that the family of the Martels [i.e., the family of Charlemagne] had
> lost are again reunited on the same head.

This singular event, explained Fontanes, had been made possible by the restoration of Catholicism in France: only religion "explains and consecrates the greatest mystery, that of power and obedience."[48]

The construction by Chaudet, Moitte, and Ingres of a Napoleon whose legislative authority was both timeless and superhuman was consonant with the emperor's decision to convoke the Grand Sanhedrin—the ancient Jewish governing body that had not met since the destruction of the Second Temple by Titus in A.D. 70. This meeting, February 9–March 13, 1807, was a legal pageant intended to guarantee that the religious and cultural traditions of Napoleon's Jewish subjects would not interfere with their civic duty.[49] Moreover, it publicized Napoleon's Mosaic role of legislating to the Jews.[50]

The compatibility between Jewish custom and French law had been discussed by the Assembly of Jewish Notables, convoked by Napoleon on March 7, 1806. This assembly argued that only the Grand Sanhedrin could rule on matters of Jewish polity. His imagination stirred, the emperor wrote to Minister of the Interior Jean-Baptiste de Nompère de Champagny on August 23, 1806, ordering the convocation of the Grand Sanhedrin. Its deliberations, the emperor wrote, would have "the force of ecclesiastical and religious law" and would "stand as a second legislation of the Jews." The authority of the Sanhedrin's acts would ensure their placement "next to the Talmud as articles of faith and principles of religious legislation."[51] To solemnize the meeting, it was held in the former Chapel of Saint Jean, adjoining the Hôtel de Ville (site of the Assembly of Jewish Notables), which was fitted with a temporary decor. David Sintzheim, chief rabbi of Strasbourg, presided over the proceedings. A portrait by Michel-François Demane-Demartrais shows the bicorned hat that Sintzheim was required to wear in his official capacity (Fig. 23). This fanciful headdress, reminiscent of the ancient Levitical miter and the horns of Moses, was not part of contemporary rabbinical regalia. It was apparently designed to reinforce the spirit of pseudo-religious solemnity in which the Sanhedrin's deliberations were clothed.[52]

A commemorative medal by Duprès (pseudonym for Nicolas-Guy-Antoine Brenet, 1770–1846), after a design by Vivant Denon (Fig. 24), baldly represented Napoleon superseding Moses.[53] Here, the emperor presents the roundheaded tablets of the law to Moses, who kneels in supplication. The law, Sintzheim declared in his closing discourse,

> returned to its original purity, is going to regain its ancient splendor; and the
> miraculous bush of our divine legislator is going to burn with a new flame
> without ever being consumed. . . . And you, Napoleon, . . . you the idol of
> France and Italy, you the terror of the haughty, the consoler of the human race
> . . . the elect of the Lord, Israel raises a temple to you in its heart.[54]

Such unblushing flattery was *de rigueur* at the proceedings.

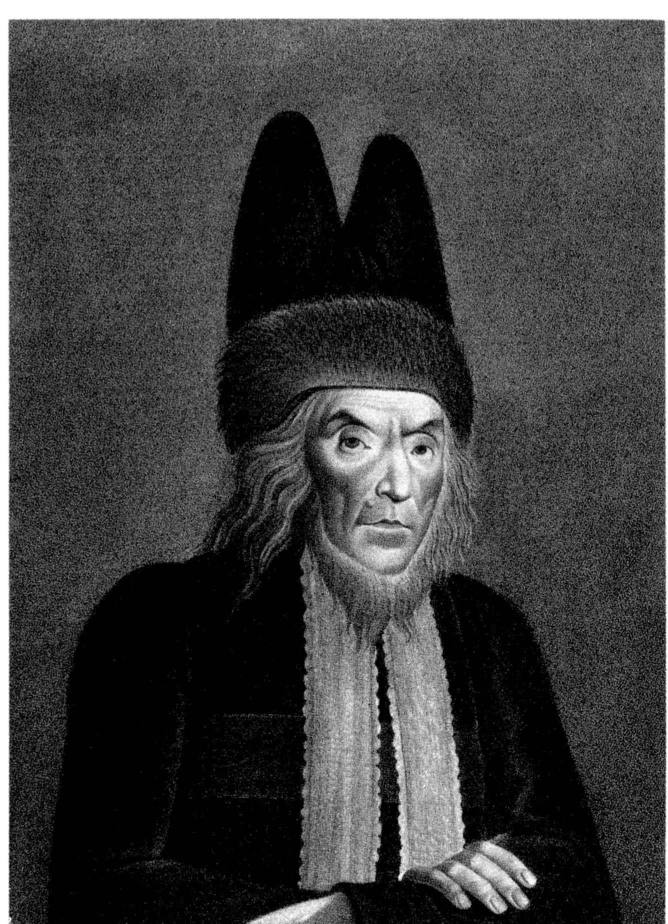

The official line that the meeting of the Grand Sanhedrin was an act of imperial clemency was as fictive as the notion that the Code Napoléon was born of
Bonaparte's legislative genius. The Grand Sanhedrin was an instrument of coer-
cion rather than liberation, and the proceedings were followed by the promulgation of the "décret infame," March 17, 1808, which introduced a series of brutal
anti-usury reforms at the expense of the Jews of eastern France.[55]

Another Napoleonic project, the *Imperial Catechism* published in 1806,[56] osten-
sibly introduced uniformity into Catholic worship; actually, it taught obedience
to the state in the guise of religious instruction. The work was largely copied from
the *Catechism of the Diocese of Meaux* (1687), by the great seventeenth-century

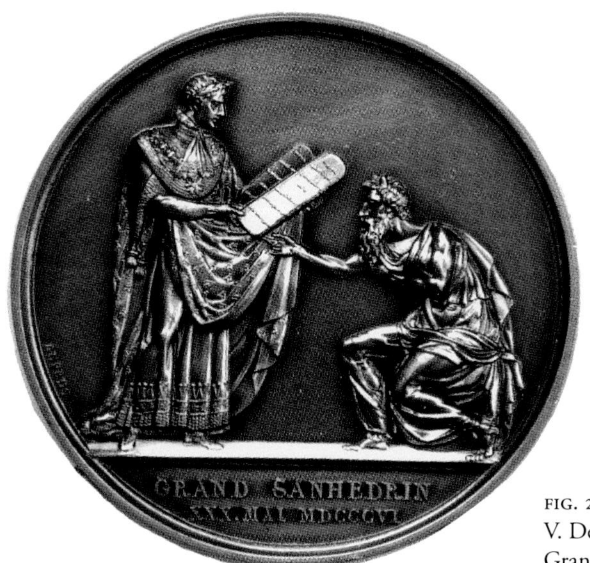

FIG. 24.   N.-G.-A. Brenet after
V. Denon, medal commemorating the
Grand Sanhedrin, c. 1807. Musée de la
Monnaie, Paris.

defender of Catholic orthodoxy and divine right absolutism, Jacques-Bénigne
Bossuet. Napoleon, however, insisted on drafting one section of the text, whose
importance was indicated by an asterisk. The lesson on the Fourth Commandment, "Honor thy father and mother," thus explained that love, respect, and obedience were due Napoleon "because God, who creates empires and distributes
them according to his will, in lavishing gifts on our emperor . . . has established
him as our sovereign, has rendered him minister of his might and his image
on Earth. To honor and serve our emperor is thus to honor and serve God
Himself."[57]

Such politicizing of the catechism went far beyond Bossuet's interpretation of
this commandment as prohibiting disobedience toward pastors, kings, and magistrates.[58] Many political catechisms, teaching republican dogma in a liturgical for-
mat, were published during the Revolution.[59] In such publications could be found,
for example, "The Ten Commandments of the French Republic," which directed
the young to pursue all tyrants (even if they were "further than Hindustan"), to be
willing to shed their blood in the defense of law and virtue, and to honor August
10—the date of the monarchy's downfall.[60] Bonaparte's reintegration of this genre

of secular indoctrination into a Catholic context was typical of his synthesis of Old Regime and revolutionary tradition.

Beyond the element of personal aggrandizement (for which Napoleon had an insatiable appetite), references to divine legislation in imperial propaganda suggest that the emperor subscribed to the notion—articulated in Rousseau's chapter on the legislator in *The Social Contract*—that laws, to be durable, needed a divine pedigree. This attachment to the divine basis of law also reflects Napoleon's conviction that religion was integral to the social order, a conviction affirmed in the Concordat, the treaty with Pope Pius VII signed in 1801 and proclaimed the following year, which recognized Catholicism as the religion of the majority of the French people in return for the Vatican's official recognition of the French republic.

With Catholicism officially reinstated, free rein could be given to the piety that during the Revolution had inflamed the rebels of the Vendée region in the west of France and had consoled the aristocracy in exile. The resurgent vigor of post-revolutionary Catholicism was encouraged by the irresistible lyricism of Chateaubriand's *Génie du christianisme* (The genius of Christianity; subtitled, The beauties of the Christian religion), released four days before the Concordat was proclaimed in what was later characterized by Sainte-Beuve as a "coup de théâtre et d'autel."[61] This book was the fruit of Chateaubriand's exile in England, shared with Fontanes, who would serve as the president of Napoleon's Legislative Body.

Between the winter of 1797 and the summer of 1798, Chateaubriand tearfully rediscovered Christianity under the influence of his mother's death and the opinions of Fontanes. This change of heart was aesthetic as well as religious: Chateaubriand realized the unparalleled fecundity of Christianity, which had inspired magnificent literature, virtuous institutions, and the tender—and distinctly modern—emotion of melancholy. With such timely thoughts, the *Génie du christianisme* was marvelously attuned to the sense of loss and the need for submission to authority that were felt so acutely in post-revolutionary France. In the Bible, Chateaubriand found poetry unsurpassed in primitive vigor and moral purity—decisively superior to Homer.

Although the narratives of the Old Testament were a fundamental part of Christian tradition, Chateaubriand's focus on the literary merits of Hebrew Scripture had an exotic appeal in France at the turn of the nineteenth century, when most readers' knowledge of Moses and the Hebrews was limited to the abridged accounts of *histoire sainte* provided, with commentary, in the Catholic catechism and in popular religious digests.[62] And even though the Catholic hierarchy had traditionally viewed the laity's unguided reading of the Bible with suspicion, Bossuet, Abbé Claude Fleury, and the English bishop Robert Lowth had defended the literary excellence of Scripture in the seventeenth and eighteenth centuries. The Old Testament had inspired Racine's *Athalie* and *Esther,* and lesser figures, such as Jacques-Charles-Louis de Malfilâtre and Jean-Baptiste Rousseau, had translated and paraphrased the Psalms.[63] Chateaubriand's revival of this pious Old Regime tradition appealed to readers at once nostalgic for pre-revolutionary faith and fascinated by primitive literature.[64]

To reestablish Christian monarchic society on the ruins of the Old Regime and the Revolution, Chateaubriand located its foundation in the primeval authority of Moses, the prophets, and the patriarchs. This political orientation also informs his praise of Mosaic law. Chateaubriand offered poets the subject of Moses descending from Mount Sinai, his brow "adorned with two rays of fire, his face resplendent with the glories of the Lord." And Chateaubriand marveled at the miraculous durability of the commandments entrusted to Moses: "Laws of God, how little you resemble those of men!"[65] France's Catholic tradition offered an antidote to the legislative failures of the previous decade.[66] Fontanes, whose review praising the *Génie du christianisme* was published in the *Mercure de France* and reprinted in the official *Moniteur,* condemned the revolutionaries who "boasted of annihilating by their laws the religious beliefs that nature and habit have so profoundly engraved in the heart."[67]

Chateaubriand's counter-revolutionary perspective on Moses and the Ten Commandments was forcefully articulated in Louis de Bonald's *Législation primitive* (1802). On returning from exile, Bonald socialized with Chateaubriand, Fontanes, and Joubert in the reactionary Consulate salons of Napoleon's brother Lucien and sister Elisa Bacciocchi and of Chateaubriand's lover, Pauline de Beaumont. In the *Mercure de France* Chateaubriand was pleased to point out that the work of this "new legislator" confirmed "the literary and religious principles we have enunciated in the *Génie du christianisme.*"[68] Written during deliberations on the Code Napoléon, Bonald's dense treatise, like his earlier *Théorie du pouvoir,* denounced the heresies of the revolutionary legislative heritage.

Bonald argued that the proposed Civil Code, while necessary, must be understood as secondary to the natural, moral, and divine law that had served as the foundation of French legislation before the Revolution. Bonald identified this fundamental law with the Ten Commandments, which can be found "on the first page of every civil and criminal code of Christian peoples, just as it forms the first instruction of all men."[69] Following the example of Bossuet, whose name is reverently invoked in *Législation primitive,* Bonald traced all authority—political as well as religious—to Scripture. He maintained that the law revealed to Moses—"this primitive and general law, this natural, perfect, divine law"—was the only true constitution. Before it, the laws of the Revolution crumbled like those of ancient societies ignorant of the teachings of Moses and Christ and deceived by their leaders into believing that their false and absurd laws were inspired by the gods. But "a reasonable people wants to see, shining on the brow of the legislator who descends from the holy mountain with the tablets of the law, the mysterious authority that guarantees his communion with divinity."[70]

Although Bonald posed as a new Bossuet, denouncing the heresies of modern France, his preoccupation with fundamental principles of law reveals his debt to revolutionary thought.[71] He criticized the Declaration of the Rights of Man and Citizen as an incomplete imitation of the Ten Commandments. The legislators of the Revolution had foolishly erred, he argued, in not using the Ten Commandments themselves as their principle of law.

Napoleon shared Bonald's conviction that society takes precedence over the individual and that France needed, above all, obedience and uniformity. But for Napoleon religion was only a means to secure his authority. Bonald, Chateaubriand, and Fontanes would have to wait until the Bourbon Restoration for the fulfillment of the counter-revolutionary aspirations nursed under the Consulate and Empire.

Less than a decade after the divinity of Napoleonic authority was inscribed in the *Imperial Catechism,* the empire was crushed by its monarchic enemies. A French caricature from the spring of 1814 shows Napoleon marching into exile with a bundle of imperial ordinances hanging from a broken scepter and a copy of the great code under his arm (Fig. 25).[72]

When Napoleon returned from exile one year later for the final brief adventure that ended at Waterloo, he was bereft of the authority represented by Chaudet and Ingres in the effigies purchased by the Legislative Body. The restored emperor convinced his liberal opponent Benjamin Constant to draft an amendment to the imperial constitutions to introduce a measure of liberty he was no longer in a

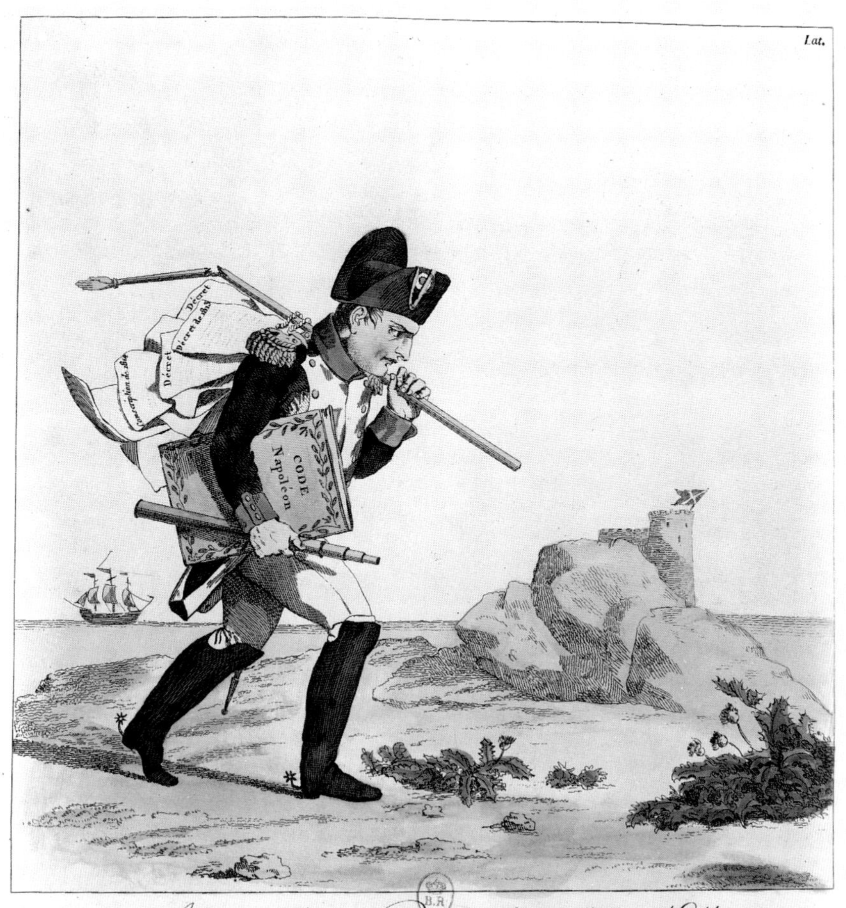

FIG. 25. *Arrival of Napoleon on the Island of Elba,* 1814. Bibliothèque Nationale, Paris.

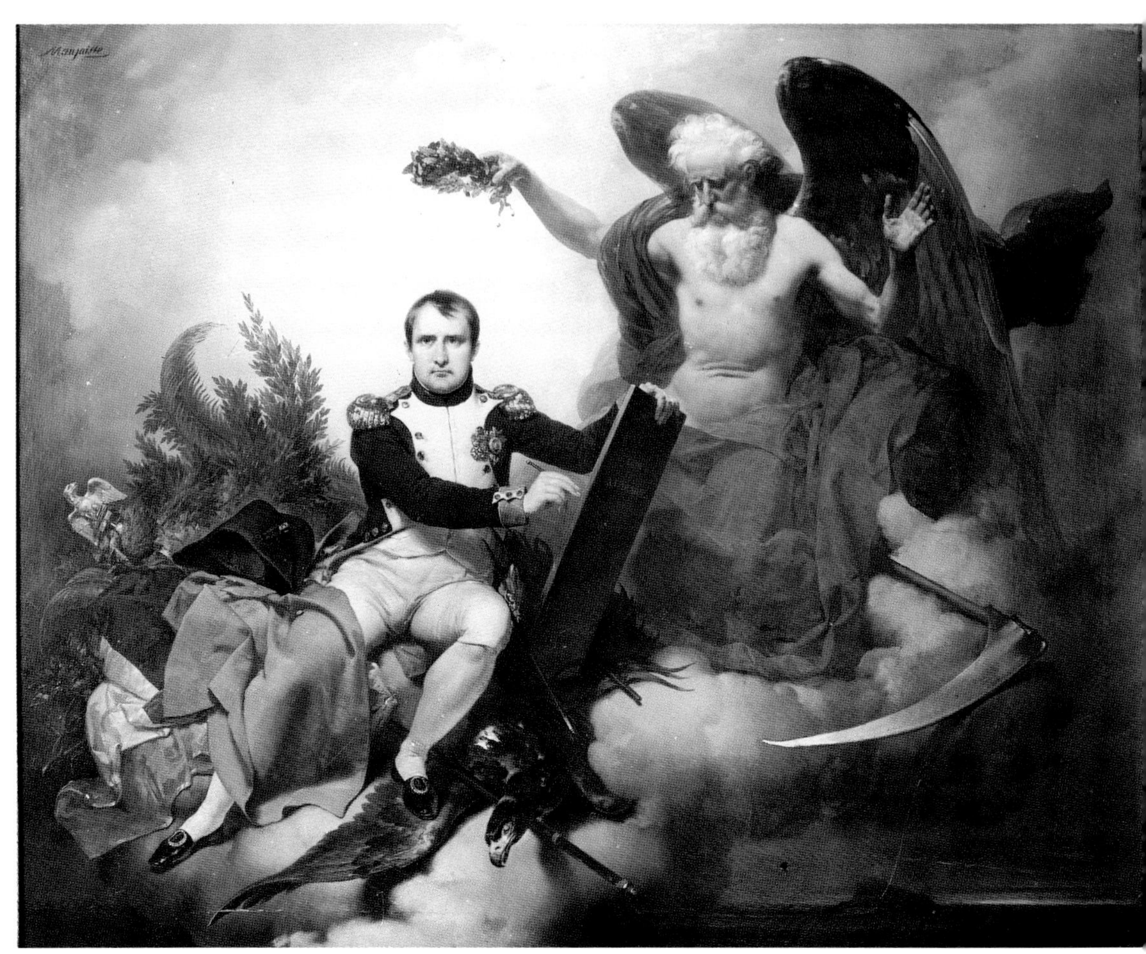

FIG. 26.   J.-B. Mauzaisse, *Allegory of Napoleon Writing the Code*, Salon of 1833. Musée National du Château de Malmaison.

position to deny. The Additional Act of April 22, 1815, called the Benjamine after its author, modified the balance of governmental power at the expense of the executive. As in the constitutional charter recently granted by the restored Louis XVIII, legislative power was to be shared with a bicameral legislature of peers and deputies. The preamble states that Napoleon had postponed establishing liberal institutions solely to maximize the extent and stability of a great European federation: "Our goal is henceforth only the growth of French prosperity and the solidification of public liberty."[73]

Although this hasty constitutional reform was no more durable than the regime of One Hundred Days, the myth of Napoleon's legislative genius survived. In a painting exhibited in the Salon of 1833 by Jean-Baptiste Mauzaisse (1784–1844), Napoleon sits on a cloud far above the somber island of Saint Helena, to which he was exiled after Waterloo (Fig. 26). A conflation of Zeus and Saint John the Evangelist in his crisply detailed uniform, he inscribes his code on a tablet while a reverent figure of Time crowns him.[74] Such hyperbole is characteristic of the cult of Napoleon that flourished during the July Monarchy, when the nation waxed nostalgic over the lost glories of the empire and the cult of the law entered its twilight.

CHAPTER THREE

Legislative Imagery under the Bourbon Restoration

When Louis XVIII returned to France in 1814, the tricolored flag carried by the armies of the Republic and the Empire was replaced by Bourbon white and the *fleur-de-lis*. Although the return to the old monarchic colors symbolized the identification with the Old Regime in France between 1814 and 1830, the Bourbon Restoration could hardly erase the previous quarter-century of French history. Imperial artists and politicians shifted their allegiance to the Bourbon monarchy, but the new regime maintained such Napoleonic institutions as the Council of State and the Legion of Honor. The Code Napoléon proved similarly durable, though it was shorn of its divorce provision and renamed Civil Code of the French People.[1] In granting a constitutional charter to the nation, Louis XVIII tacitly accepted the irreversibility of the Revolution. And by imitating the Napoleonic cult of the legislator the Restoration attempted to reinstate the Old Regime association of the law with monarchic will.

The preamble to the Bourbon Charter of 1814 exemplifies the Restoration's explicit denial and implicit co-option of the modern French political tradition. Here the revolutionary discourse of reason, universality, natural rights, and the general will is silenced. In place of a Declaration of the Rights of Man and Citizen there is a reference to divine Providence, which, "recalling us [i.e., Louis XVIII] to our states after a long absence, has imposed on us great obligations." The 1814 charter, whose principles have been sought "in the French character and in the venerable monuments of past centuries," is dissociated from French history since 1789. For "we have effaced from our memory, as we would wish that one could efface from history, all the misfortunes that have afflicted the fatherland during our absence." Instead, French monarchic judicial and administrative reforms are cited as precedents for modifying the exercise of the authority that "in France resides entirely in the person of the king."

The original draft of the preamble was provided by none other than Louis de Fontanes, who repudiated the revolutionary heritage with the same rhetorical flair he had shown so often in flattering Napoleon. His text deserves to be read in the original French:

> Un pouvoir supérieur à celui des peuples et des monarques fit la société et jeta sur la face du monde des gouvernements divers: il faut plutôt en diriger la marche qu'en expliquer les principes. Plus leurs bases sont anciennes et plus elles sont vénérables; qui veut trop les chercher s'égare; qui les touche de trop près devient imprudent et peut tout ébranler. Le sage les respect et baisse la vue devant cette auguste obscurité qui doit couvrir le mystère social comme les mystères religieux.

> A power greater than peoples and monarchs made society and molded the different governments of the earth. It is our duty to manage them rather than to explain their principles. The older their foundations, the more we reverence them. Whoever tries too hard to understand them errs; whoever tampers with them imprudently can bring all to ruin. Whoever is wise respects them and bows before that majestic obscurity that must cloak both society and religion in mystery.[2]

Fontanes's rhetoric epitomizes that of critics of the Revolution under the Consulate and Empire who denigrated the eighteenth-century tradition of critical inquiry—Pierre-Simon Ballanche, for example, the Lyonnais mystic whose *Du sentiment considéré dans ses rapports avec la littérature et les arts* (1801) offered many of the same arguments as the later, but more famous, *Génie du christianisme* of Chateaubriand. Ballanche held that "the same divine power that reserves the right to establish and consolidate social institutions wanted to place their sacred constitution behind a veil that the hand of innovators cannot raise with impunity."[3]

The preamble to the 1814 charter—both in Fontanes's original draft and in Count Jean-Claude Beugnot's less pungent final version—testifies to the passage into mainstream French politics of the counter-revolutionary apology for throne

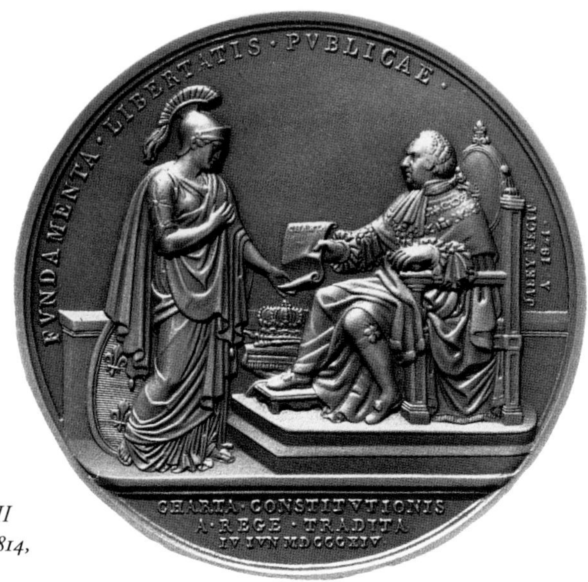

FIG. 27.   J.-L.-N. Jaley, *Louis XVIII*
Granting the Constitutional Charter, 1814,
1821. Musée de la Monnaie, Paris.

and altar articulated under the Consulate and Empire by Fontanes, Chateau-briand, and Bonald.[4] Fontanes's participation in drafting the preamble suggests his importance in providing ideological continuity between Napoleonic and Restoration France.

In accord with the Old Regime notion of the monarch as supreme legislator, the Charter of 1814 was granted (*octroyé*) by Louis XVIII to his subjects. A com-memorative medal by Jean-Louis-Nicolas Jaley (1802–1866) represented the offi-cial interpretation of this reform as an act of royal volition (Fig. 27).[5] It is instruc-tive to compare this medal with a print commemorating Louis XVI's acceptance of the Constitution of 1791 (Fig. 28), a more innocent moment in French consti-tutional history. The print shows Louis XVI, hand on heart, vowing to maintain the constitution, held by a regal personification of France; in Jaley's medal France touches her breast in deference as she receives the charter from Louis XVIII. Whereas Louis XVI stands respectfully, virtuously, Louis XVIII sits enthroned, his severe countenance and exposed calf smacking of pre-revolutionary monarchic prerogative. Brenet's medal commemorating the Grand Sanhedrin (see Fig. 24) shows the legislator and recipient on similarly unequal footing.

The political history of the Bourbon Restoration was shaped by an uneasy compromise between the acceptance of constitutional reform and the assertion

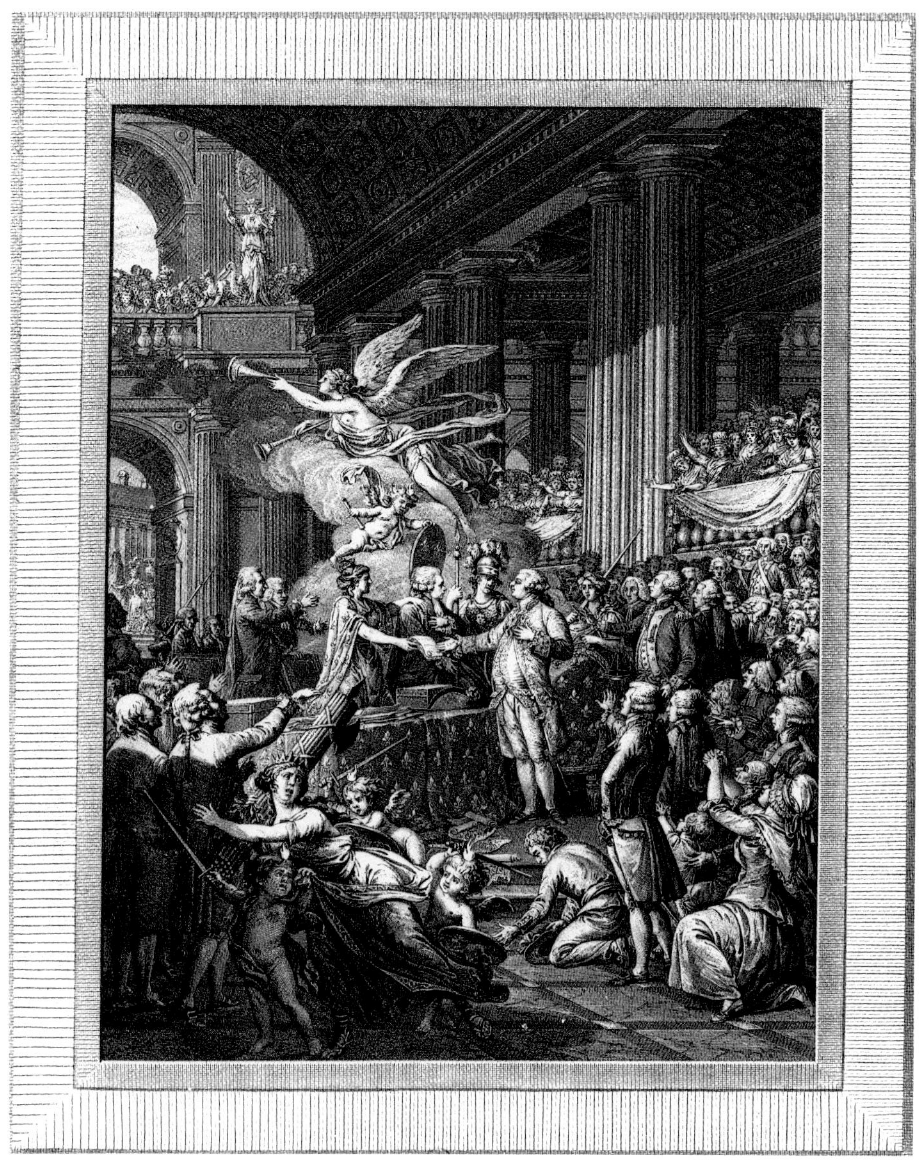

FIG. 28.   F.-A. David after
N. Lejeune, *Louis XVI Solemnly
Accepts the Constitution at the National
Assembly, September 14, 1791*, 1791.
Bibliothèque Nationale, Paris.

of monarchic prerogative. Committed to the exercise of royal authority in accord with the constitutional charter, the regime stubbornly aspired to pre-revolutionary absolutism, an aspiration especially apparent after the coronation in 1824 of Louis's ultra-royalist brother, Charles X. To dignify this uncomfortable position, an iconography of divine legislation was employed in a cycle of paintings commissioned by the government to decorate four rooms in the Louvre that were remodeled in 1825 as new chambers for the Council of State.

The Council of State played an integral part in the conflict between constitutional legality and royal prerogative that colored politics under the Restoration. Deriving from the corps of professional administrators who counseled Old Regime monarchs and bearing the name of one of the principal cogs in Bonaparte's political machine, the Council of State was linked to both monarchic absolutism and Napoleonic authoritarianism.[6] Under the Restoration, it functioned outside the scope of constitutional control, offering advice to the cabinet of royal ministers and arbitrating administrative conflicts. The liberal opposition particularly disliked it, objecting to its extra-legal character.

When the Council of State was reorganized by an ordinance of August 26, 1824, it moved to the royal palace of the Louvre.[7] Because it was supposed to be presided over by the monarch, explained Minister of Justice and Keeper of the Seals Count Charles-Ignace de Peyronnet, "it is contrary to all decorum [*contraire à toutes les convenances*] that this body assemble anywhere but in the palace of the king."[8] The ordinance, issued by a conservative ministry under Count Jean-Baptiste-Séraphin-Joseph de Villèle, was meant to reconcile royal authority with constitutional responsibility. The oath of new members of the Council of State was revised to include loyalty to the charter as well as the king, and the government was no longer to have the power, called *destitution,* to remove unwanted council members. A final exercise of this power, however, gave an ultra-royalist cast to the new Council of State.[9] According to François Guizot—who before becoming Louis-Philippe's prime minister was a member of the liberal opposition under the Restoration—such ambivalence was typical of Villèle, who always strove to attribute to the king both liberal opinions and those that recalled Old Regime absolutism.[10]

Under the direction of Viscount Louis-François-Sosthène de La Rochefoucauld, of the Department of Fine Arts, and Count Louis-Nicolas-Philippe-Auguste de Forbin, general director of the royal museums, the government commissioned twenty-seven artists in 1826 to provide paintings for the new chambers.[11] The painters—most now known only to specialists—included a number of Prix de Rome laureates as well as Eugène Delacroix, Ary Scheffer, and Paul Delaroche. In the opinion of the conservative critic Etienne-Jean Delécluze, the artists chosen were the "elite of the present school."[12] Two of the decorated ceilings remain visible, and a number of canvases are preserved in French provincial museums. In addition, many of the works were reproduced in the *Musée de peinture et de sculpture*. Together with the description of the ensemble in the Salon *livret* of 1827, these remains give an idea of the decorative program.[13]

Although visitors to the Salon of 1827 could view the new Council of State rooms, the decorations were intended for an elite audience. On the ceiling of the principal assembly hall is M.-J. Blondel's *France, in the Midst of the Legislator Kings and French Jurisconsults, Receives the Constitutional Charter from Louis XVIII* (Fig. 29).[14] The late Louis XVIII, avuncular but august, sits, with Wisdom, Prudence, Justice, and Law, high above the Seine on "the throne of his ancestors, to represent legitimacy" (pour caractériser la Légitimité).[15] At his feet a regal personification of France humbly receives the charter. The event transpires with a graciousness absent from Jaley's commemorative medal, which apparently served as Blondel's model (see Fig. 27). The monarchs and legists of the Old Regime looking on approve. Montesquieu and Henri IV (holding the Edict of Nantes) relax in the unlikely company of a delighted Louis XIV. To suggest the confidence inspired by the law, a putto sleeps on an open book inscribed CODE. A hostile critic remarked in the *Journal du Commerce* that "young France has armed itself against the arbitrariness of the ordinances and decisions of the Council of State, not by sleeping on the codes, but by studying them with perseverance."[16]

In associating the charter with divine will and traditional Bourbon largess, Blondel's ceiling painting echoes the sentiments of the charter's preamble. This didactic program continues in the coving, where monarchic precedents for the charter are illustrated in illusionistic bronze reliefs. Placed between *Louis the Fat [Louis VI] Chartering the First Town* and *Saint Louis [Louis IX] Granting the Pragmatic Sanction* is *The Spirit of Law Showing the Charter to Hope and Faith* (Fig. 30). Here Christian virtues enact an unfamiliar constitutional pantomime. The Mosaic posturing of the putto Spirit of the Laws—like the obtrusively tangible anchor of Hope—points to that uncomfortable mixture of the literal and the ideal characteristic of late Davidian history painting. The unintentional

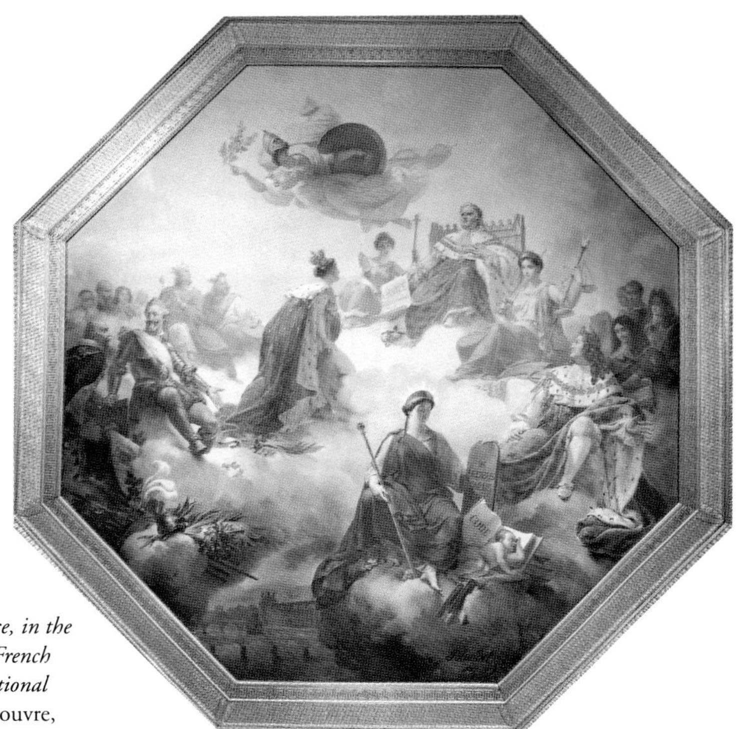

FIG. 29.   M.-J. Blondel, *France, in the Midst of the Legislator Kings and French Jurisconsults, Receives the Constitutional Charter from Louis XVIII,* 1827. Louvre, Paris.

FIG. 30.   M.-J. Blondel, *The Spirit of Law Showing the Charter to Hope and Faith,* 1827. Louvre, Paris.

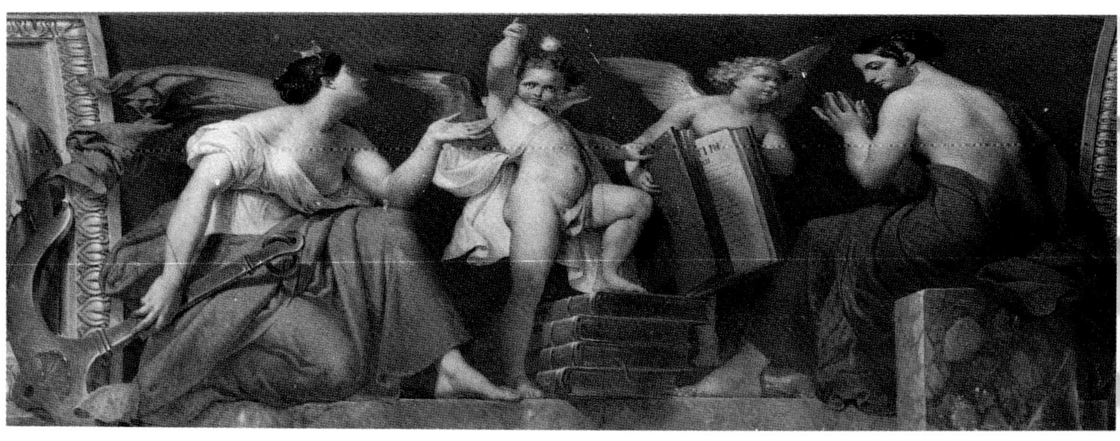

comedy of this allegorical scene, moreover, hints at the shortcomings of the Bourbon Restoration's variant of the cult of law. "The Spirit [of the Laws] lacks inspiration," the critic from the *Journal du Commerce* noted, "and Faith seems to grimace as it beholds the book of our destiny."[17]

The royal throne in the room with Blondel's ceiling paintings symbolically referred to the king's presiding, by proxy, over the Council of State.[18] Never actually occupied, the throne serves as a reminder that Napoleon's energetic employment of the Council of State had no sequel under the Restoration; and it symbolizes the inability of the Bourbon regime to keep alive the Old Regime notion of the monarch as supreme legislator, triumphantly reinstated by Napoleon.

On the ceiling of the fourth room Jean-Baptiste Mauzaisse rephrased in Bourbon terms the Napoleonic theme of divine legislative inspiration. In his *Divine Wisdom Giving the Laws to the Kings and Legislators* (Plate 5),[19] Moses, leading an encyclopedic host of legislators—including an Indian chief, George Washington, William Penn, Muhammad, and Confucius as well as Numa, Solon, and Lycurgus—receives the law from Divine Wisdom, whose entourage includes Prudence, Equity, and Clemency.[20] Envy and Calumny are banished by the sword as Louis XVIII and other French monarchs watch from the clouds.[21] The critic Auguste Jal, evidently hostile toward the regime, explained that Mauzaisse had gallantly separated the legislators from the French kings, not wanting "to mingle the very Christian kings with just any sort of people" (Le peintre n'a pas voulu confondre les rois très-chrétiens avec toute sorte de gens).[22]

In its invocation of legendary, prototypical legislators, Mauzaisse's ceiling painting can be considered a Bourbon sequel to Moitte's relief group in the Cour Carré (see Fig. 19).[23] As in Blondel's ceiling painting, Mauzaisse reverts to the baroque allegorical tradition that seamlessly and felicitously links human events and acts of divine will. The persuasive power of the allegory, however, is blunted by a discursive specificity of historical and contemporary reference that lends an air of masquerade to Mauzaisse's legislators.

Legendary legislators as prototypes of the French monarch were repeatedly invoked in the Council of State rooms. Beneath Blondel's octagonal ceiling painting in the assembly hall hung his portraits of the divinely inspired legislators Lycurgus, Solon, Numa, and Moses—the last seated in stiff majesty like a *salvador mundi* (Fig. 31).[24] *The Law Descends to the Earth, Establishes Her Domain, and Distributes Her Benefits*, by Michel-Martin Drolling (1786–1851) is bordered

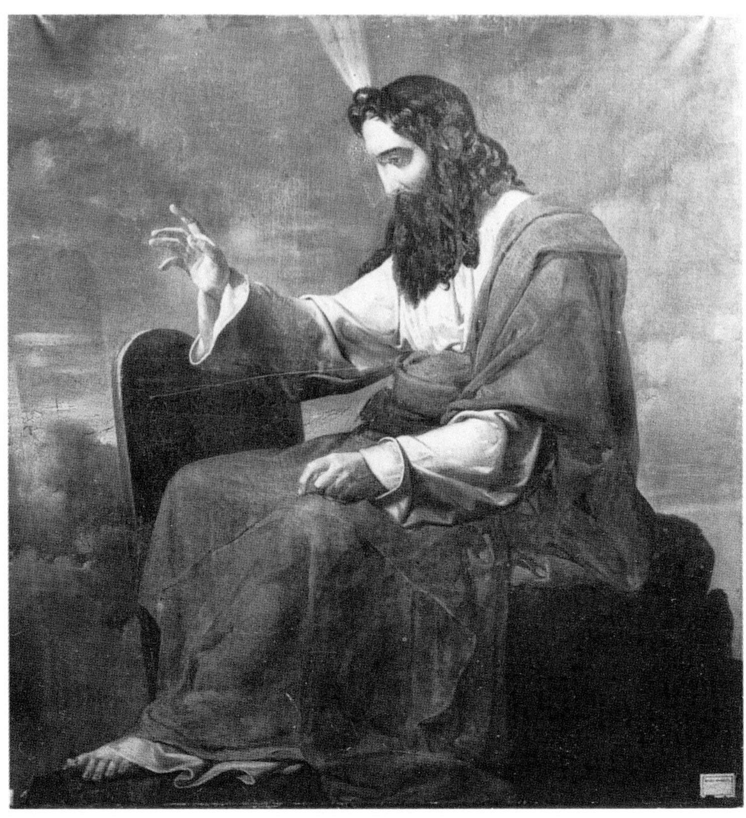

FIG. 31.   M.-J. Blondel, *Moses,*
1826–28. Louvre, Paris (on deposit in
the Musée d'Histoire, Saint-Brieuc).

with roundels inscribed with the names Moses, Numa, Charlemagne, and Justinian (Fig. 32).[25] Below this chilly reprise of Guido Reni's *Aurora* hung *Moses, Legislator* (Michel Marigny; destroyed in the Palais d'Orsay fire, 1871), *Numa Giving Laws to the Romans* (Léon Cogniet; Montbéliard), *Charlemagne Presenting the Capitularies to the Assembly of Francs* (Ary Scheffer; Versailles), and *Emperor Justinian Drafting His Laws* (Delacroix).

Delacroix's large canvas (3.71 x 2.76 meters; lost in the Palais d'Orsay fire, 1871) is known from an old photograph and from a superb sketch of 1826–27 in the Musée des Arts Décoratifs (Plate 6).[26] The enthroned Justinian, inspired by an angel and dictating to a scribe, is based on traditional representations of the

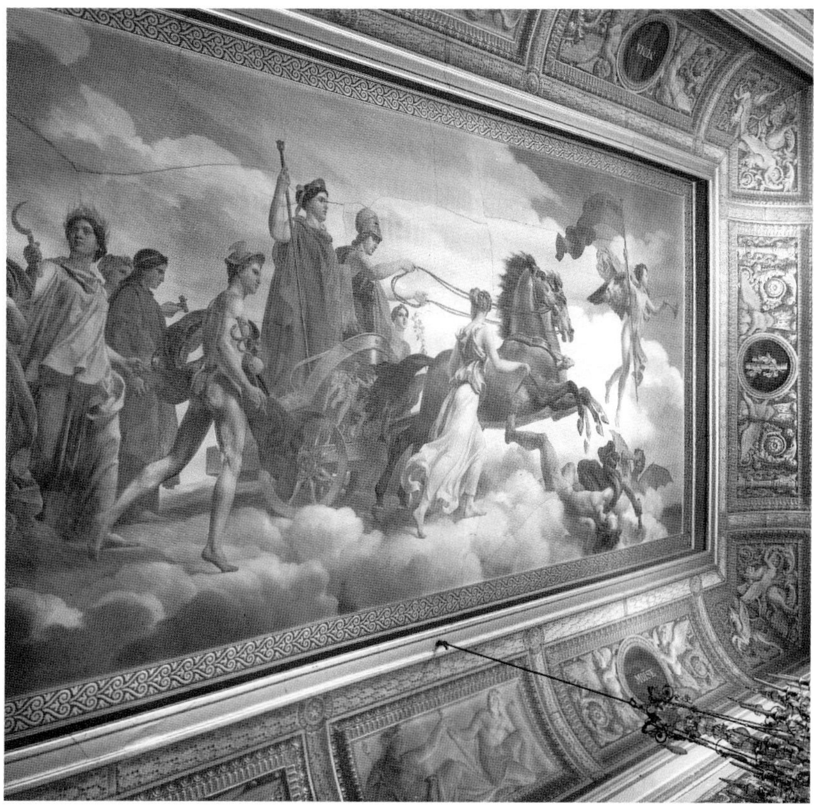

FIG. 32.   M.-M. Drolling, *The Law
Descends to the Earth,* 1827. Louvre, Paris
(no longer visible).

Evangelists. The emphatic gestures, bold chiaroscuro, and warm tonality of the
sketch suggest that Delacroix brought to this motif an operatic amplitude and a
material opulence that recall the contemporary *Death of Sardanapalus.* Justinian's
extravagantly stylized pose suggests at once the flux of inspiration and the aloof
authority of the lawgiver. Contemporary accounts of the lost painting speak of
jewel-encrusted draperies that must have made the *Justinian* seem all the more
remote and exotic. Delacroix's representation of the attributes of divine inspiration seems deliberate, for Justinian himself was principally a compiler and codifier
of earlier Roman law. But the emphasis on the divine origins of law was also in
keeping with the decorative cycle for which the work was painted.

The ancient lawgivers honored in the Council of State rooms were complemented by *Saint Louis Rendering Justice under the Oak of Vincennes* (Fig. 33) by Georges Rouget (1784–1869).[27] Illustrating the traditional doctrine maintained by the Charter of 1814 (art. 57) that "all justice emanates from the king," the painting shows Louis IX calmly executing justice amid a reverential audience. Similarly, two paintings in the first room, *The Clemency of Augustus toward Cinna and His Accomplices* (Pierre Bouillon; destroyed in Saint-Malo during World War II) and *The Act of Clemency of Marcus Aurelius toward the Rebels of His Asian Provinces* (Alexandre-Charles Guillemot; destroyed in Saint-Malo during World War II) provided antique exemplars of the royal power to grant clemency preserved by the charter (art. 67)—a prerogative all the more precious in the wake of a quarter-century of civil and political strife. Illustrations of heroic Old Regime magistrates refer obliquely to the violence of recent French history. Among these was the most admired work of the cycle, Paul Delaroche's pathos-ridden *Death of President Duranti* (destroyed in the Palais d'Orsay fire, 1871).[28]

In invoking divinely inspired legislators and glorifying the Bourbon monarchy, the decorative program of the Council of State rooms embodied the aspiration of the regime to bolster the authority of the monarch.[29] Notwithstanding the splendor of Delacroix's *Justinian* and the poignant theatrics of Delaroche's *Death of President Duranti,* this pompous, redundant program has a hollow ring that suggests not only the weakness of Restoration history painting but also the disparity between the triumphant rhetoric of the preamble to the Charter of 1814 and the vulnerability of this post-Napoleonic constitutional monarchy.

Given the resurgence of piety under the Restoration, it is not surprising that Moses, who occupies a place of honor in Mauzaisse's ceiling painting for the Council of State, was an attractive legislative motif after 1814. This appeal was all the greater because of the flowering during the Restoration of the infatuation with the Bible introduced by the *Génie du christianisme.* Encouraged by the new edition of the Bible by Antoine-Eugène Genoude, the young poets Alphonse de Lamartine and Victor Hugo came of age intoxicated by Scripture.[30]

Because the Bible vogue was often allied to counter-revolutionary themes, the Republican songwriter Pierre-Jean de Béranger (1780–1857) denounced it, describing its practitioners as "bards inspired by the cashbox . . . [and] perfumers of the crown."[31] Such mockery would hardly have amused the young ultra-royalist Victor Hugo, who, according to his wife, wrote in a journal in 1816 that his

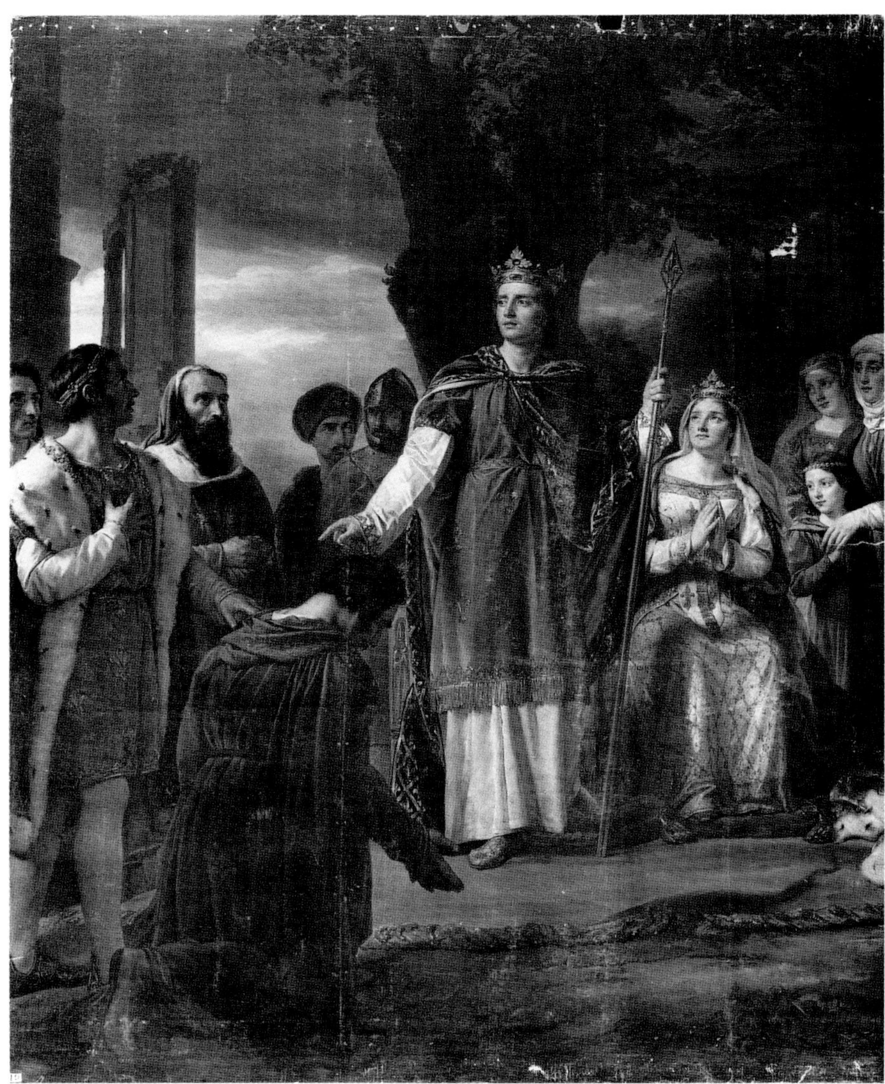

FIG. 33.   G. Rouget, *Saint Louis
Rendering Justice under the Oak of
Vincennes*, 1826. Musée National du
Château de Versailles.

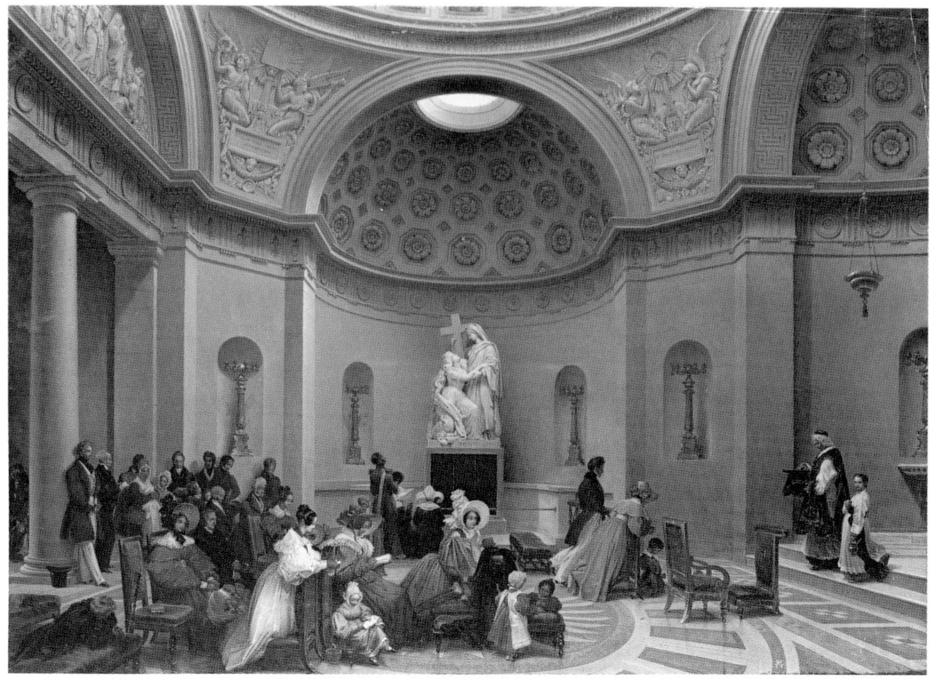

ambition was to be "Chateaubriand or nothing."[32] Bonald's *Législation primitive,*
with its elevation of Moses and the Ten Commandments at the expense of the revolutionary legislative tradition, foreshadowed the political significance of Mosaic
imagery in this reactionary climate.

The roundheaded tablets of the law were reconverted to Catholicism and
stripped of association with the rights of man in the hushed interior of the Expiatory Chapel (1816–24), which Chateaubriand thought "perhaps the most remarkable" building in Paris.[33] It had been constructed, with Chateaubriand's
blessings, by the former imperial architect Pierre-François-Léonard Fontaine
(1762–1853) on the site of the cemetery of the Madeleine, which, during the Revolution, had received the remains of Louis XVI, Marie-Antoinette, and other distinguished victims of the guillotine.[34]

Inside the chapel's severely classical central space, *The Apotheosis of Louis XVI* (1825) and *Marie-Antoinette Succored by Religion* (c. 1825) by the former imperial sculptors François-Joseph Bosio and Jean-Pierre Cortot lend grandeur to the fate of the royal couple. The base of *The Apotheosis of Louis XVI* is inscribed with Louis's profession of faith in the "commandments of God, . . . the sacraments, and the mysteries, such as the Catholic Church teaches them." The pendentives overhead bear emblematic relief sculptures by François-Antoine Gérard (1760–1843) that represent, according to the architect, "the four principal signs of our religion."[35] In one of these—visible in the meticulous rendering of the chapel in use by Lancélot-Théodore Turpin de Crissé (1781–1859)—Mosaic tablets in a glory are flanked by angels with attributes of martyrdom and immortality (Fig. 34). The Latin inscription beneath speaks of Christian duty: IF YOU WISH TO ENTER LIFE YOU MUST SERVE.[36] The revolutionary association of Mosaic tablets with the Declaration of the Rights of Man and Citizen lends poignance to this inscription, recalling Bonald's insistence on the sacrifice of individual rights to the duties owed to society and religion. "After long and bloody errors," Bonald concluded as he reflected on the Declaration of the Rights of Man and Citizen, "one realizes that it is necessary to speak to man a little less of his rights, a little more of his duties."[37]

Bonald was pleased when Lamartine dedicated to him "Le Génie" (1817), published in *Méditations poétiques* three years later.[38] In his poem Lamartine compared Bonald's revelation of the sacred and immutable foundations of society to Moses' reception of the law on Mount Sinai:

Ainsi, quand parmi les tempêtes,
Au sommet brûlant du Sina,
Jadis le plus grand des prophètes
Gravait les tables de Juda;
Pendant cet entretien sublime,
Un nuage couvrait le cime
Du mont inaccessible aux yeux,
Et, tremblant aux coups du tonnerre,
Juda, couché dans la poussière,
Vit ses lois descendre des cieux.

Ainsi des sophistes célèbres
Dissipant les fausses clartés
Tu tires du sein des ténèbres
D'éblouissantes vérités.
Ce voile qui des lois premières
Couvrait les augustes mystères,
Se déchire et tombe à ta voix;
Et tu suis ta route assurée,
Jusqu'à cette source sacrée
Où le monde a puisé ses lois.

Just as, long ago amid storms
On the burning peak of Sinai
The greatest of prophets
Engraved the tablets of Judah,
During the sublime encounter
A cloud covered the peak
Of the hidden mountain,
And, trembling at the thunderclaps,
Judah, prostrate in the dust,
Saw its laws come down from the skies.

So too, dispelling the false light
Of famous sophists,
You draw from the heart of darkness
Dazzling truths.
The veil that hides the august mysteries
Of the fundamental laws
Is torn and falls at your voice;
And you follow your certain path
To the sacred fountainhead
From which the world imbibed its laws.[39]

In using Mosaic imagery to aggrandize Bonald's battle against the hubristic falla-
cies of the Enlightenment and the Revolution, Lamartine was following Chateaubriand, who described Bonald's idol Bossuet, the seventeenth-century theologian
and historian, in similar terms. "Bossuet is more than a historian," Chateaubriand
wrote; "He is an . . . inspired priest, often with rays of fire on his brow, like the
legislator of the Hebrews."[40]

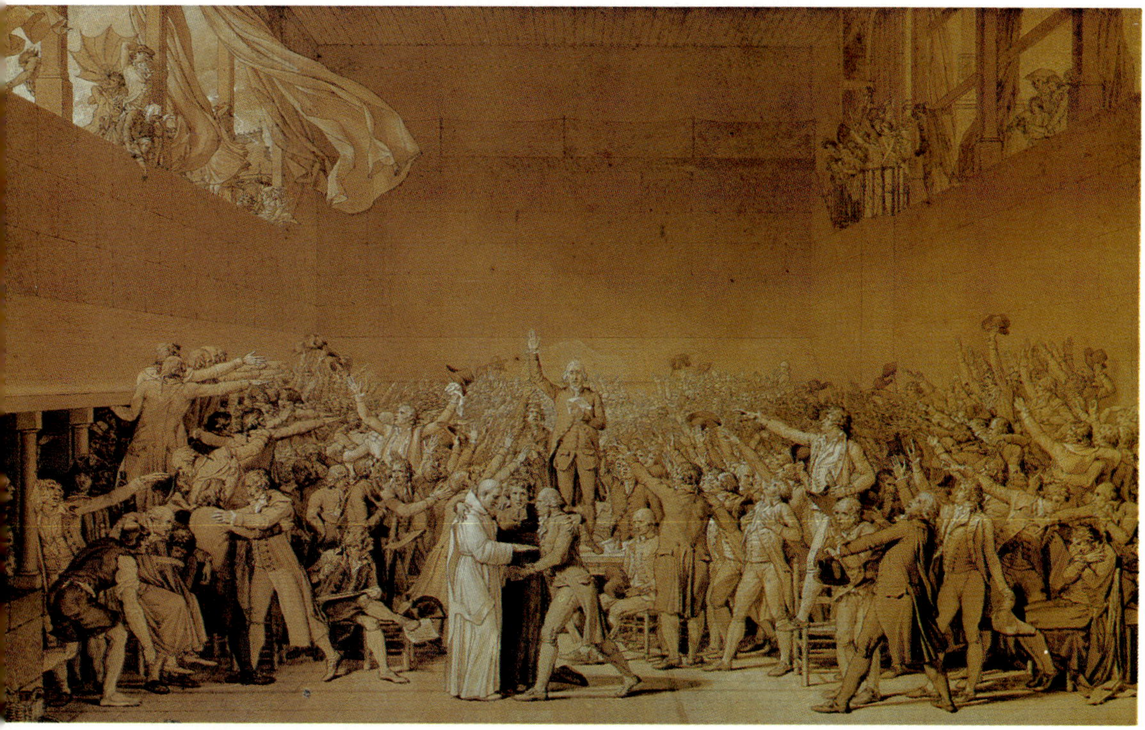

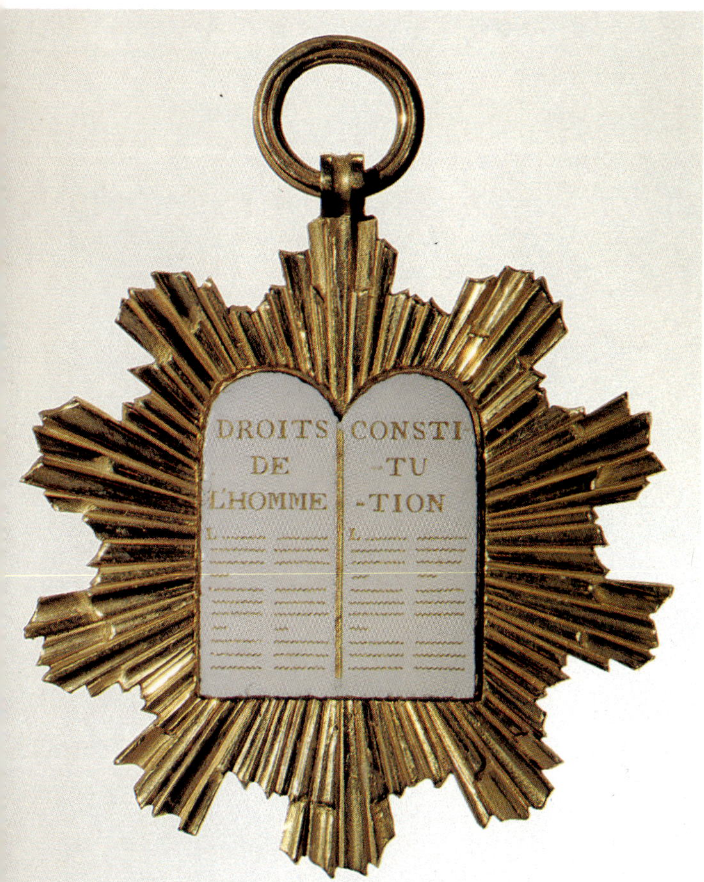

PLATE 1.   J.-L. David, *The Tennis Court Oath,* Salon of 1791. Louvre, Paris (on long-term loan to the Musée National du Château de Versailles).

PLATE 2.   Insignia of the National Legislative Assembly, 1792. Cabinet des Médailles, Bibliothèque Nationale, Paris.

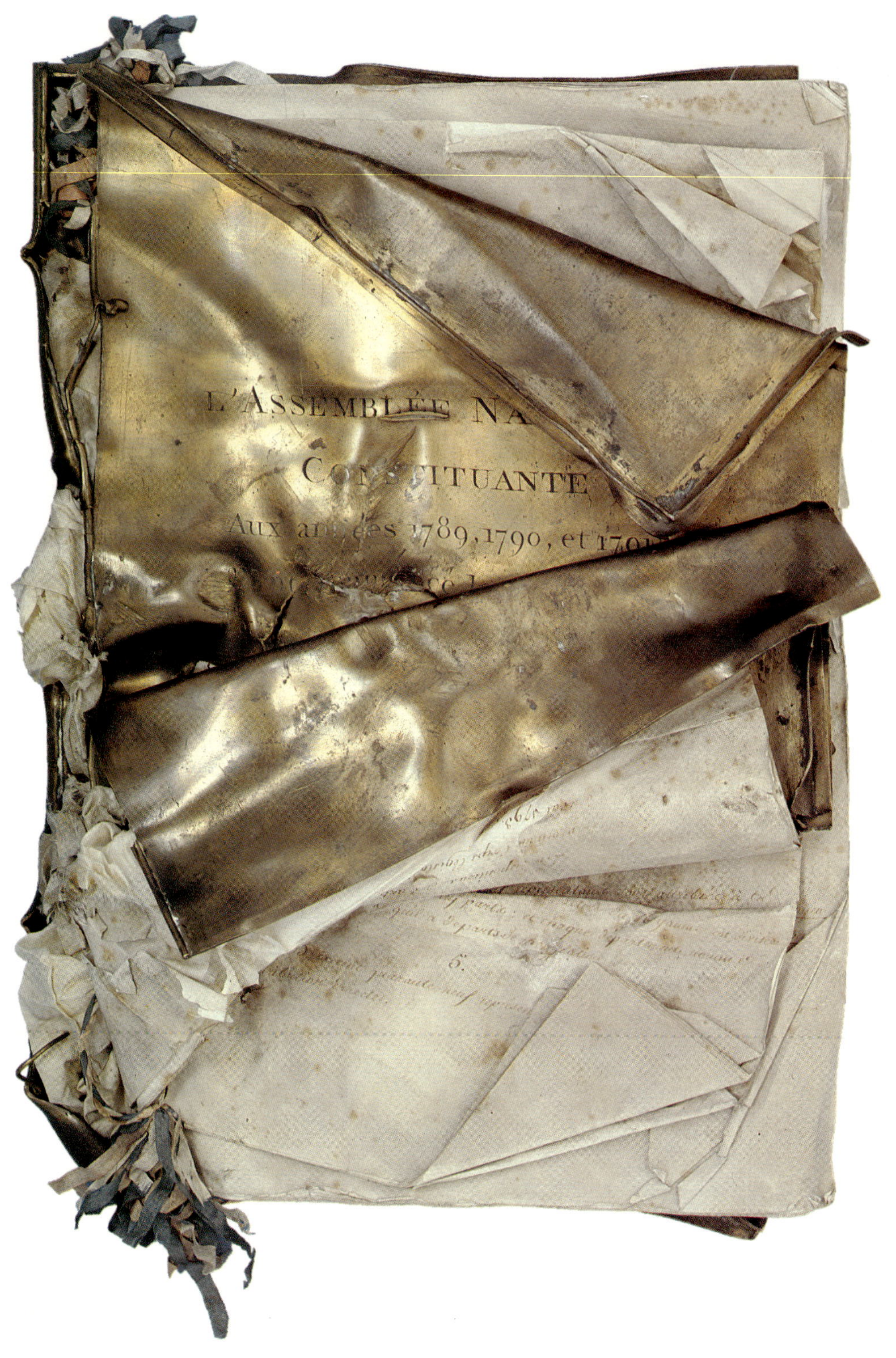

PLATE 3.   Copper-bound volume of the Constitution of 1791, vandalized in 1793. Archives Nationales, Paris.

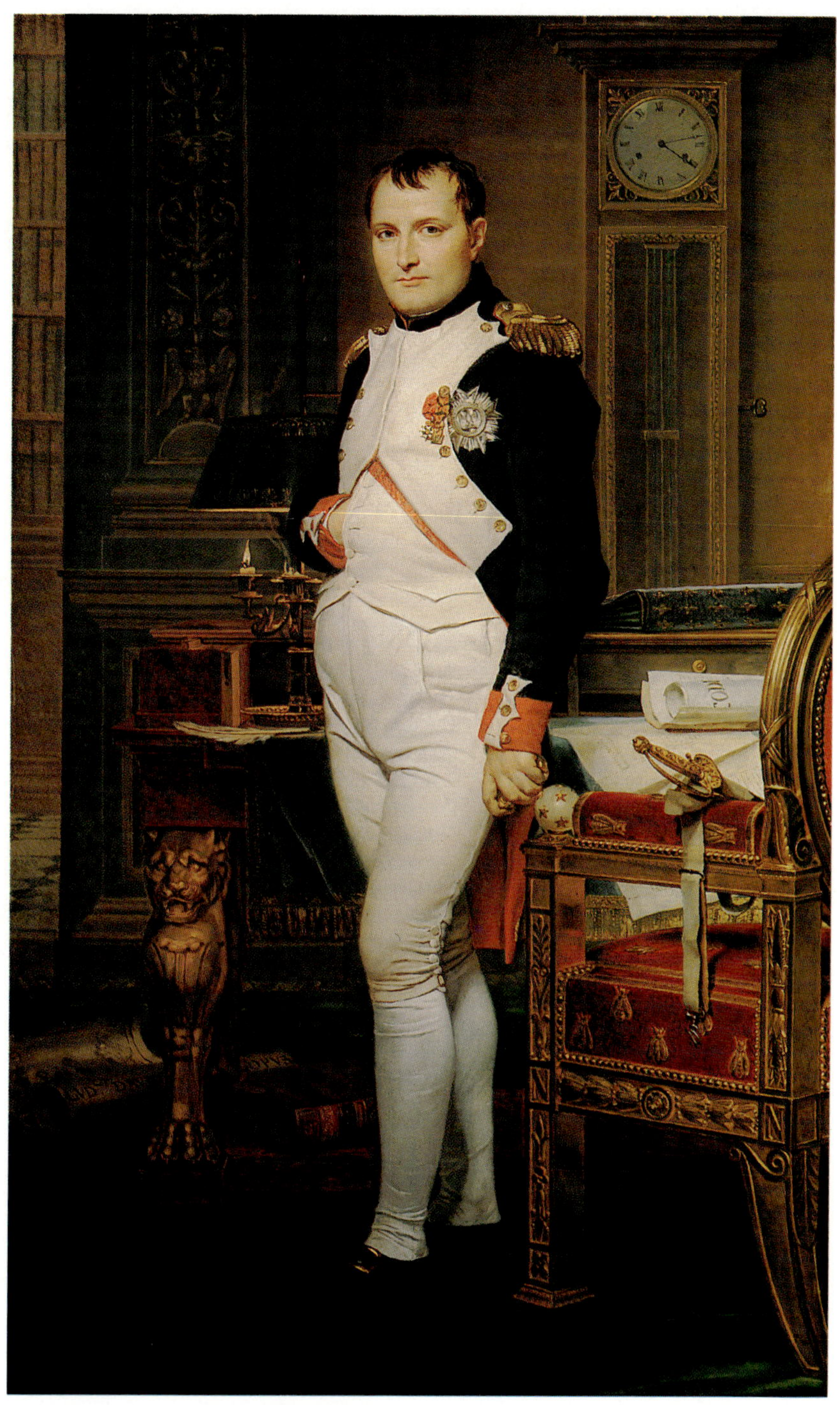

PLATE 4.   J.-L. David, *Napoleon in His Study*, 1812. National Gallery of Art, Samuel H. Kress Collection, Washington.

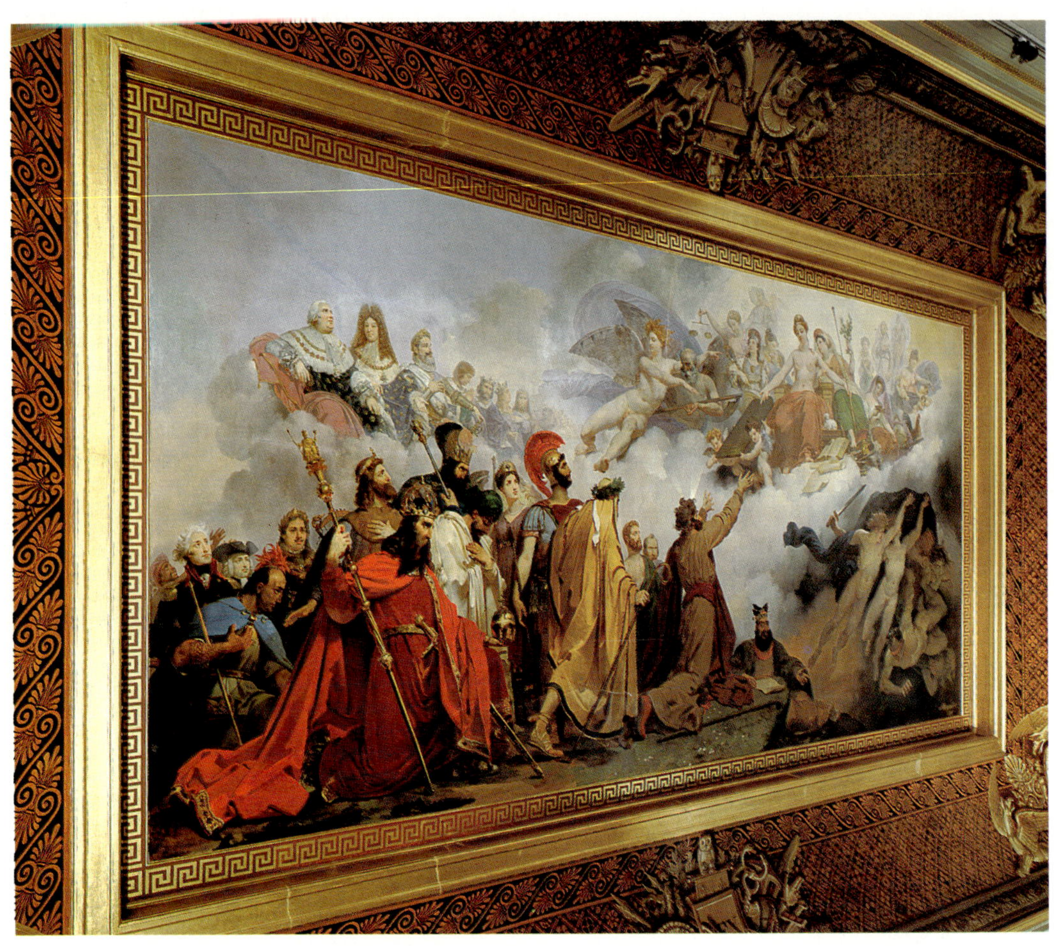

PLATE 5.   J.-B. Mauzaisse, *Divine Wisdom Giving the Laws to the Kings and Legislators*, 1827. Louvre, Paris.

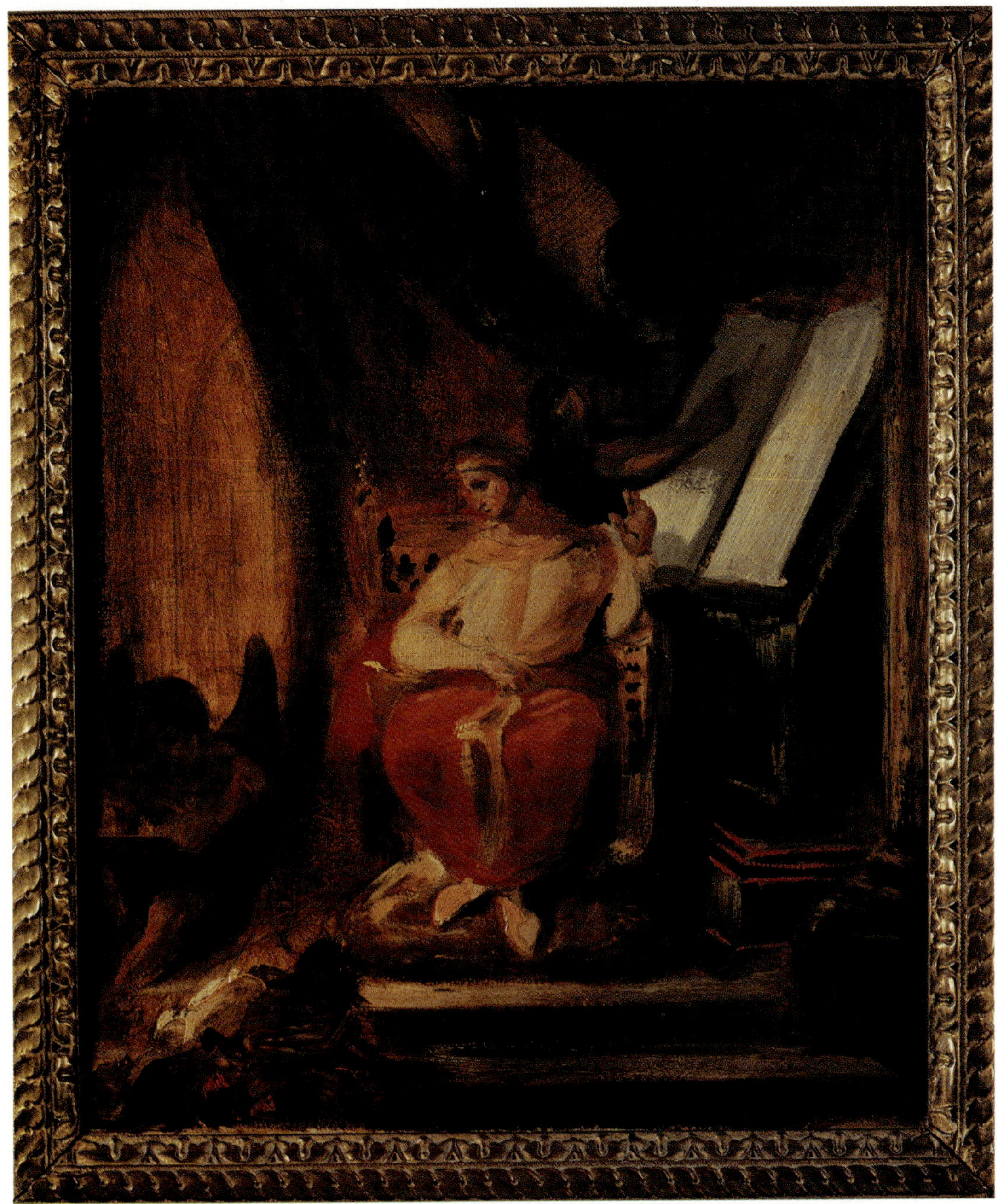

PLATE 6.   E. Delacroix, study for
The Emperor Justinian Drafting His Laws,
1826–27. Musée des Arts Décoratifs,
Paris.

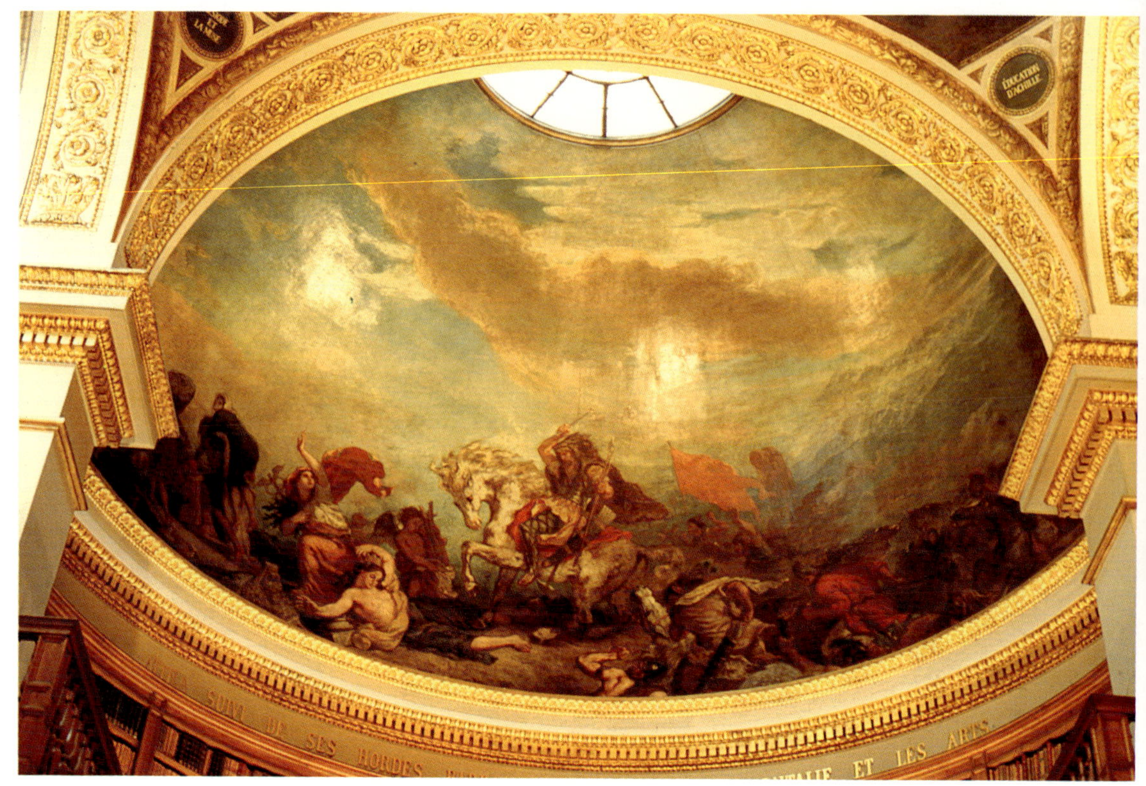

PLATE 7.   E. Delacroix, *Attila, Followed by His Barbarian Hordes, Tramples Italy and the Arts*. Palais-Bourbon, Paris.

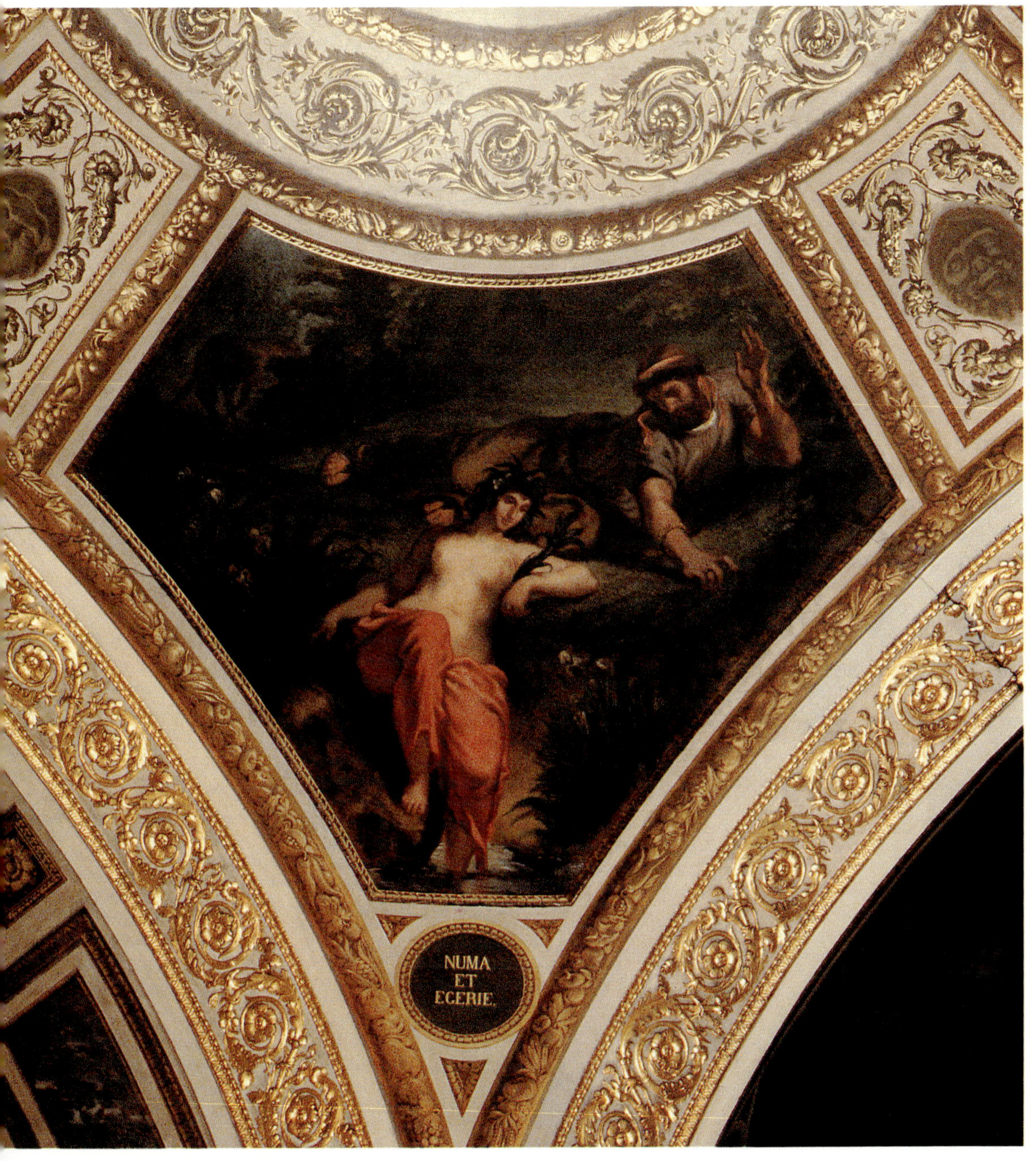

TE 8.   E. Delacroix, *Numa and
ria.* Palais-Bourbon, Paris.

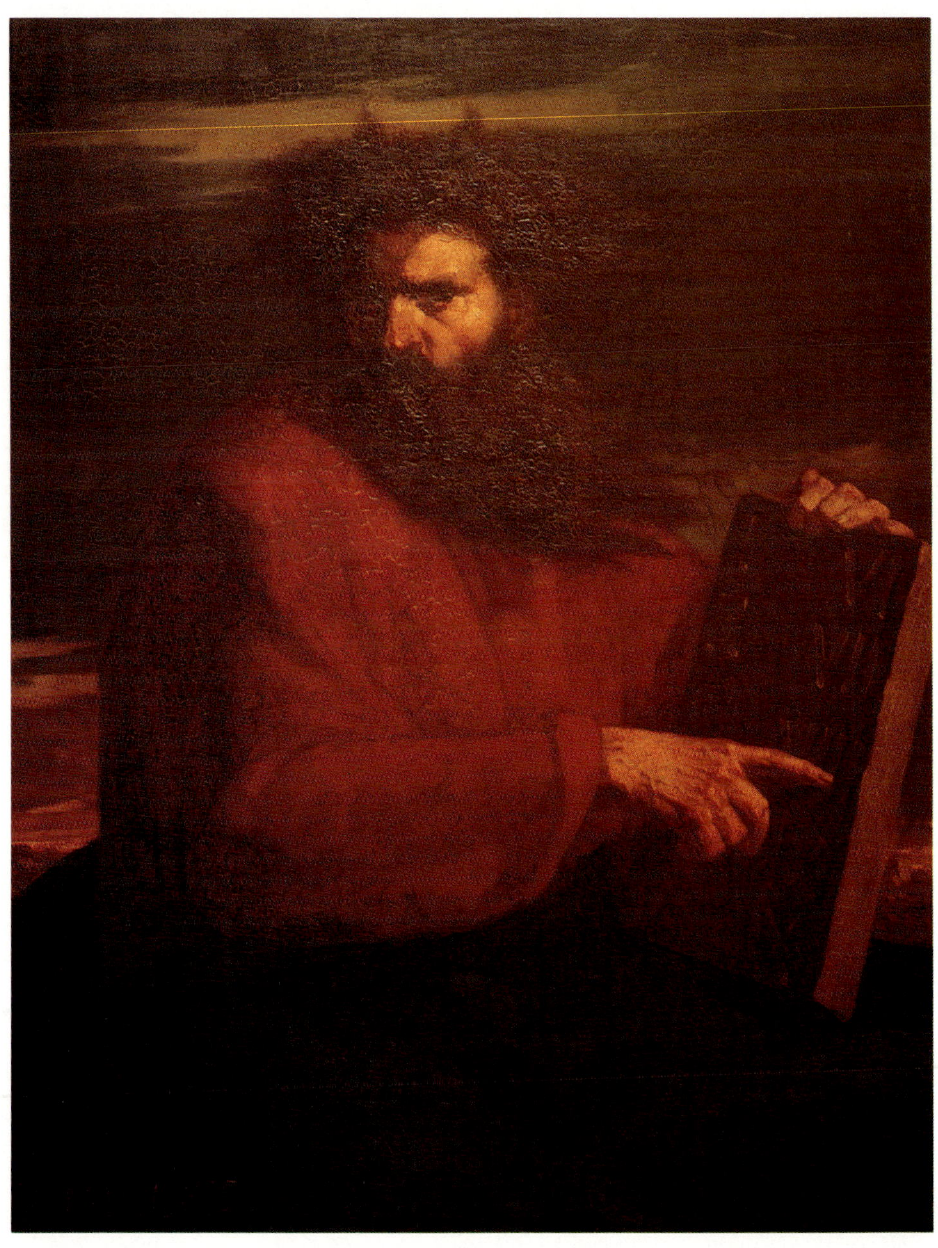

PLATE 9.   J.-F. Millet, *Self-Portrait as Moses,* 1841. Musée Thomas Henry, Cherbourg.

Lamartine (who, like Hugo, eventually cast off his youthful ultra-royalism) later distanced himself from his poem, asserting that when he wrote it he had not read Bonald but considered him "the honest and eloquent apostle of a sublime and hazy theocracy that would serve as the poetry of our political affairs if God deigned to name his earthly viceroys and ministers." The poet confessed that "my youthful imagination was fascinated by this totally oriental and biblical doctrine."[41]

Victor Hugo used similarly political references to Moses in one of his most reactionary odes, "Le Sacre de Charles X" (1825), written in honor of the splendid neo-medieval coronation of Louis XVIII's retrograde brother. The poem concludes with a prayer that God—whom the monarch has seen face-to-face, as if on Sinai—impart to the royal brow "two rays from your head." One month before "Le Sacre de Charles X" was written, Hugo and Lamartine had received the Legion of Honor for their defense of Catholicism and monarchy. This honor was conferred at the request of Sosthène de La Rochefoucauld,[42] who would shortly serve as one of the administrators in charge of the decoration of the Council of State suite.

In light of the association of Moses with royalism and counter-revolution in the Council of State rooms and in the poetry of Lamartine and Hugo, it is surprising that liberals also appealed to the authority of the biblical legislator during the Bourbon Restoration. For example, Stendhal, after seeing a performance of Rossini's opera *Mosè in Egitto* in Naples in 1818, recounted how it shattered his prejudice against Scripture, which he had associated with counter-revolution:

> Benedetti, in the role of Moses, appeared in a simple and sublime costume
> copied from the statue by Michelangelo in San Pietro in Vincoli, Rome; he had
> not addressed twenty words to the Eternal One before my received wisdom
> vanished; I no longer saw a charlatan changing his cane into a serpent . . . but a
> great minister of the Almighty making a vile tyrant tremble on his throne.[43]

Rossini's hero, clad in imitation of Michelangelo's revered figure (which will concern us later), revealed to Stendhal that Moses was an enemy of royal tyranny.

Joseph Salvador (1796–1873) publicly claimed Moses for the liberal cause in a controversial book of 1822. Unlike those who associated Moses with orthodoxy, obedience, and monarchy, Salvador, in *Loi de Moïse, ou Système religieux et politique des Hébreux,* identified him as the

author of the wisest and simplest system of public order that has ever been realized; the founder of the first known republic; the man who, having broken
the chains that oppressed his people, . . . made them swear to a constitution
founded on equality of rights and taught them that the law or reason must
hold sway.[44]

Salvador again argued that Moses was the founder of constitutional government in his *Histoire des institutions de Moïse et du peuple hébreu* (1828). The liberal
paper *Le Globe* responded enthusiastically:

There is a people more antique than Greek and Roman antiquity, whose rule
of law, equality, liberty, utility, nationality, and intellectual superiority were
highly acclaimed and recognized in the despotic Orient before the development of occidental civilization: the Hebrew people. The man who deserves to
be considered the true founder of free and legal government . . . is Moses.[45]

What brought notoriety to Salvador's *Histoire des institutions de Moïse* was his
claim that the condemnation of Christ had conformed to the law. Published only
four years after sacrilege had been officially defined as a capital crime (a measure
Bonald endorsed), the book produced an explosive reaction in the right-wing
press.[46] In his *Pastoral Instruction on the Progress of Impiety and on the Recent Direct
Outrages toward the Person of the Savior of Man*, February 2, 1829, the bishop of
Chartres attacked Salvador for attempting to replace the traditional conception of
Moses as the servant of God with the erroneous idea that "the famous legislator
was only inspired by his genius [and by] . . . the public good." Consequently, the
bishop argued, Salvador had transformed "this holy man" into "a republican more
extreme than the most violent demagogues of [17]93."[47]

Salvador's politically charged view of Moses had a comic counterpart in a pair
of anti-royalist Decalogue prints (c. 1827) that mimic the couplets in which the
Ten Commandments were taught in the catechism. A "Constitutional Decalogue,
Dedicated to the Friends of Public Liberty" prescribes fidelity to the constitutional charter (Fig. 35). A "Ministerial Decalogue," in contrast, prescribes fraud,
corruption, and hypocrisy under the sign of the backward-walking crayfish, stock
symbol of retrograde ultra-royalism (Fig. 36).[48] These prints—like Salvador's

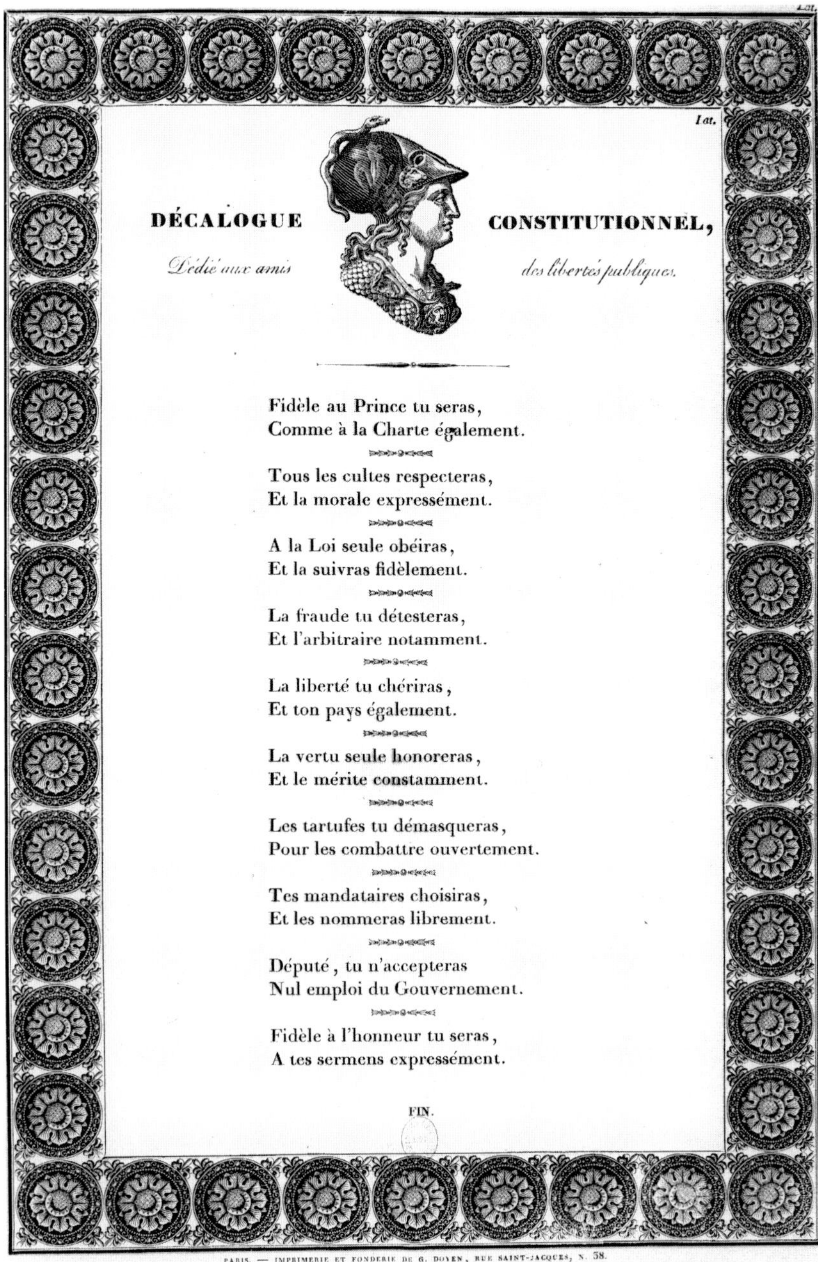

FIG. 35.   "Constitutional Decalogue,"
c. 1827. Bibliothèque Nationale, Paris.

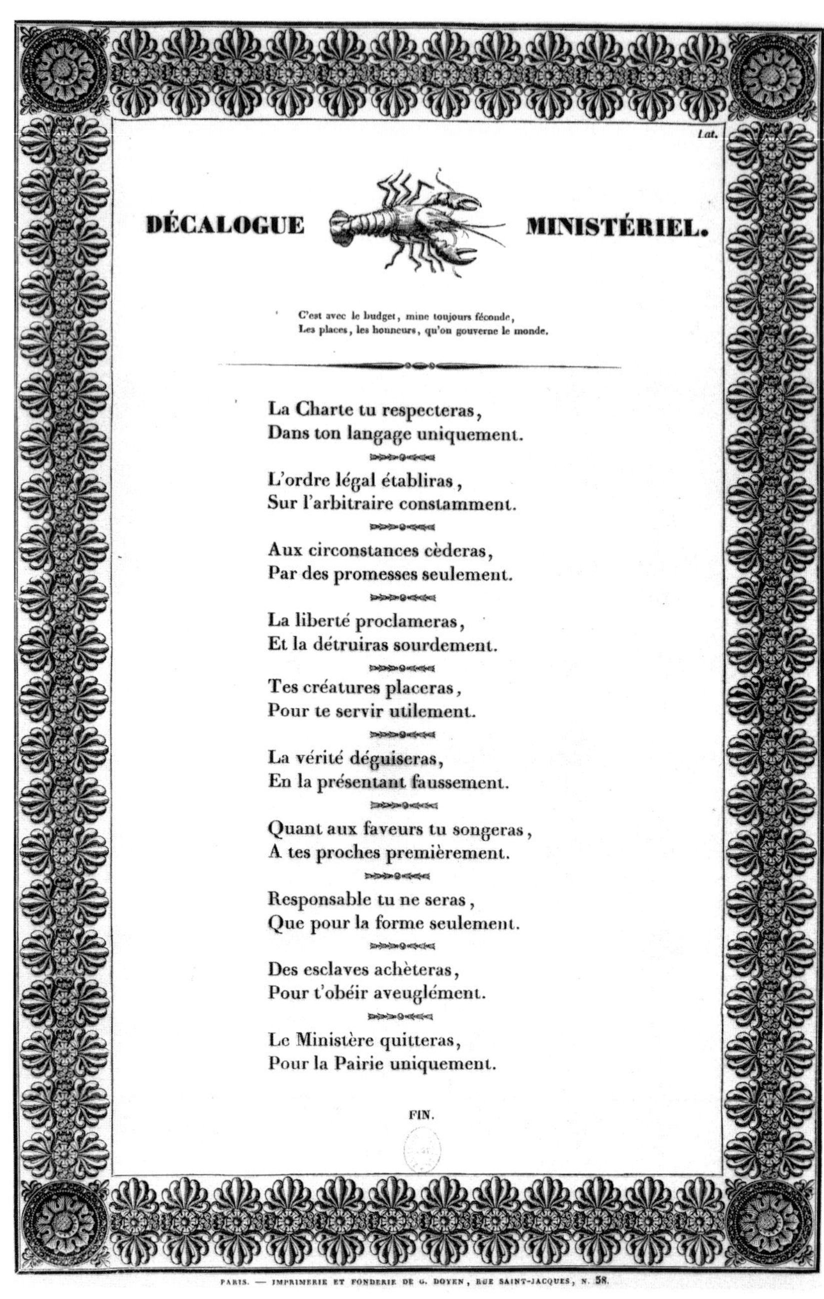

FIG. 36. "Ministerial Decalogue,"
c. 1827. Bibliothèque Nationale, Paris.

polemical studies of Mosaic legislation, the decorative program of the Council of State rooms, and Lamartine's ode to Bonald—speak of the broad appeal of Mosaic imagery in the ongoing crisis of authority that plagued, and eventually destroyed, the Bourbon Restoration.

CHAPTER FOUR

Law and Disorder under Louis-Philippe

In July 1830 the ministers of Charles X issued four ordinances intended to stifle freedom of the press and break legislative opposition to the crown. This unpopular action inflamed the liberal opposition that had gained an unlikely ally in Chateaubriand, who, soured by his loss of the Ministry of Foreign Affairs in 1824 and reborn as an outspoken opponent of press censorship, was scandalized by the ordinances, which presumed, in an Old Regime spirit (comme au temps du bon plaisir), that the king's authority superseded the law.[1]

Popular indignation over the four ordinances fueled a successful uprising that demonstrated the tenacious vitality of the principle inaugurated with the Constitution of 1791 that "in France no authority is superior to the law." With the cry "Long live the charter!" the elder branch of the Bourbon dynasty was driven from the French throne and the Charter of 1814 revised. No longer would the king have blanket authority, granted by article 14 of the Bourbon charter, to make "the regulations and ordinances necessary for the . . . security of the state."[2] And the monarch would never have the power "to either suspend the laws themselves or dispense with their execution" (Charter of 1830, art. 13).

Duke Louis-Philippe d'Orleans, lieutenant general of France and head of the younger branch of the French royal family, was elevated to the throne to protect the constitutional principles Charles X's ministers had disregarded. The new monarch's relationship to the Bourbon dynasty was complicated because his

This chapter is an expanded and revised version of the article "Henri de Triqueti, Auguste Préault, and the Glorification of Law under the July Monarchy," *Art Bulletin*, LXX, September 1988, pp. 486–501.

father, who had sported the name Philippe-Egalité during the Revolution, had voted for the death of Louis XVI. Louis-Philippe's distant blood kinship with his deposed predecessor did not guarantee his mandate to rule. Legal probity, symbolized by the inaugural oath of allegiance to the new constitutional Charter of 1830, invested the new king with authority; he acknowledged as much by insisting on legal rectitude in the daily business of government. François Guizot, one of Louis-Philippe's most loyal ministers, said that this Citizen King "made legal rule the basis of his domestic policy; he never asked his counselors to circumvent the law; he would have reminded them of [the law] himself if the occasion [for circumvention] had arisen, immediately observing, 'It's the law'—no matter how disagreeable or embarrassing it was to him."[3]

An unofficial bronze commemorative medal by Joseph-Arnold Pingret (1798–1862) expressed the idea that the revolution of 1830 had reestablished the law (Figs. 37, 38). The inscription NATIONAL LIBERTY RECONQUERED BY THE PEOPLE, JULY 27, 28, 29, 1830 encircles a laurel-crowned Liberty—a well-groomed Olympian cousin of Delacroix's famous heroine of the barricades—superimposed on the fasces of unity. The anti-clericalism of the inscription on the reverse reflects a decade and a half of oppressive Bourbon piety: TRIUMPH OF TRUTH OVER JESUITISM. An emblematic panoply honoring the reestablishment of the constitutional covenant includes the scales of justice, the mirror and serpent of prudence, and a Mosaic tablet inscribed REIGN OF THE LAWS.

Pingret's representation of the law as roundheaded tablets recalls any number of revolutionary images of the constitution and of the Declaration of the Rights of Man and Citizen; the revival of this revolutionary iconographic tradition under the July Monarchy was appropriate to the regime's professed veneration of the law. Nonetheless, the perception of the law was different from what it had been during the Revolution of 1789. Under Louis-Philippe, the law was not a miraculous source of national regeneration but a shield defending order and property. Thus Guizot said that Louis-Philippe considered the law "the best shield for the throne as well as for the citizenry."[4]

This conception of the law developed from the dangers faced by the regime. It became apparent at the outset of Louis-Philippe's reign that the regime represented the interests of the prosperous middle class and sympathized with neither the egalitarian sentiment nor the bellicose nationalism of those who had brought down the Bourbon Restoration. The July Monarchy was menaced in its early

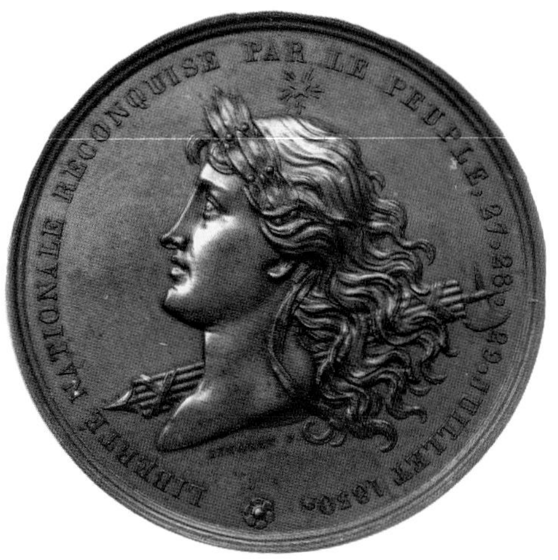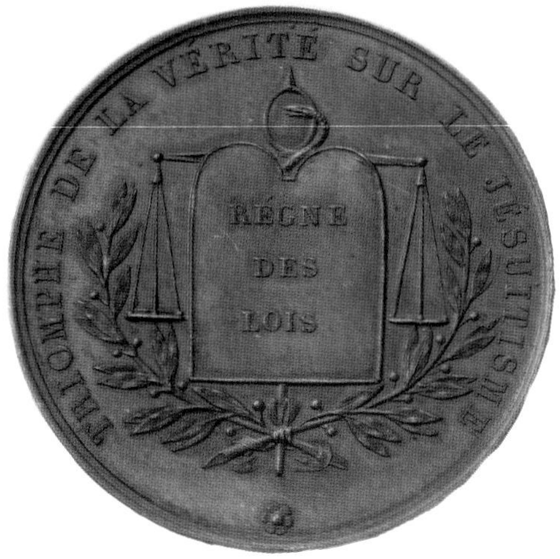

FIG. 37.   J.-A. Pingret, medal commemorating the July Revolution (obverse). Cabinet des Médailles, Bibliothèque Nationale, Paris.

FIG. 38.   J.-A. Pingret, medal commemorating the July Revolution (reverse). Cabinet des Médailles, Bibliothèque Nationale, Paris.

years from both the legitimist (pro-Bourbon) Right and the republican Left. An illiberal policy toward the regime's enemies was firmly established by Casimir Périer, president of the Council of Royal Ministers and minister of the interior from March 13, 1831, until his death on May 16, 1832. As the leader of Louis-Philippe's government, Périer professed a "cult of the law,"[5] whose severity is evident in an address to the Chamber of Deputies following the repression of an uprising in Lyon in 1831: "It is necessary to teach people who lay claim to the honor of being free that liberty is the despotism of the law." (From the audience, in response, came cries of "Bravo! Very Good!")[6]

Similar in its defensive spirit is a painting in grisaille by François-Edouard Picot (1786–1868), *July 1830: France Defends the Charter* (Fig. 39), commissioned for the ceiling of the Hall of 1830 in the Palace of Versailles.[7] Here the revolutionary roundheaded tablets of law are reborn as the Charter of 1830, and protected from blind royalist absolutism and masked republicanism. The Hall of 1830 was part of the historical museum Louis-Philippe created in the Palace of Versailles to glorify the history of France and to legitimize his own regime. The brash literal character

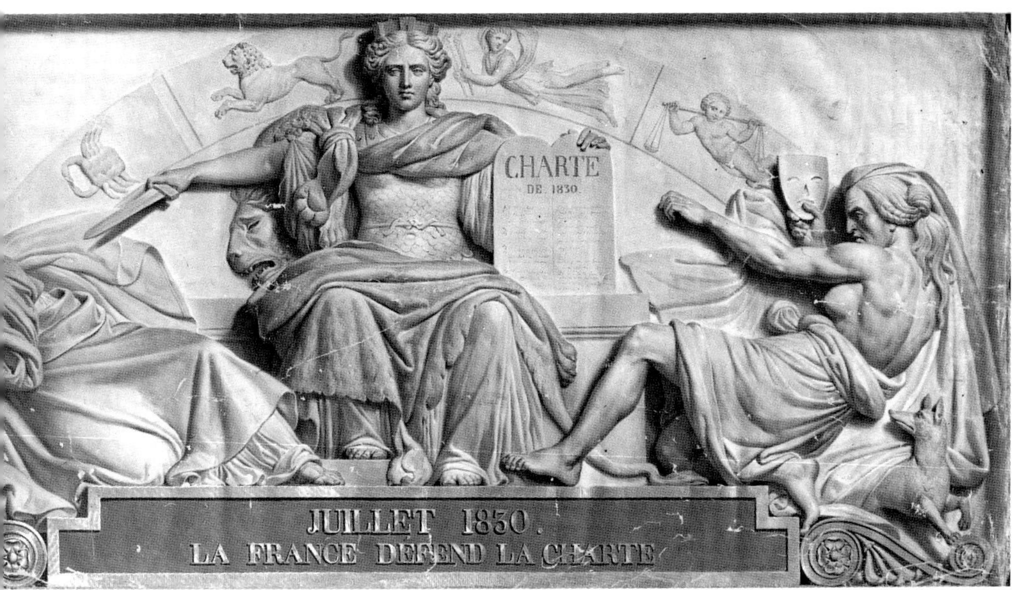

FIG. 39.   F.-E. Picot, *July 1830: France
Defends the Charter*, 1835. Paris, Louvre.

of Picot's allegory suited the propagandistic function of the room for which it was
commissioned.

The July Monarchy's cult of the law was expressed most elaborately in the decoration of the Palais-Bourbon. In 1828–33 Jean-Baptiste-Jules de Joly (1788–1865),
who succeeded Bernard Poyet as the architect responsible for the legislative palace,
directed the alteration and enlargement of the building.[8] Joly remodeled the
assembly hall, added a library, and designed a symmetrical suite of ceremonial
rooms appropriate to the nation's premier legislative body (Fig. 40).

At the opening of the annual legislative session, Louis-Philippe would go to the
Palais-Bourbon to deliver the "Speech from the Throne" to the legislature. He
would enter the palace not through the great Napoleonic portico on the Seine but
via the Court of Honor on the Rue de l'Université. A contemporary print shows
him mounting the palace steps at the head of a vast retinue (Fig. 41). As he
entered the palace via the new Salle Louis-Philippe (Fig. 42; G on plan), he would
see his own colossal effigy, swearing fidelity to the constitutional charter, in a richly
coffered barrel-vaulted gallery, where statues of four modern French legislators

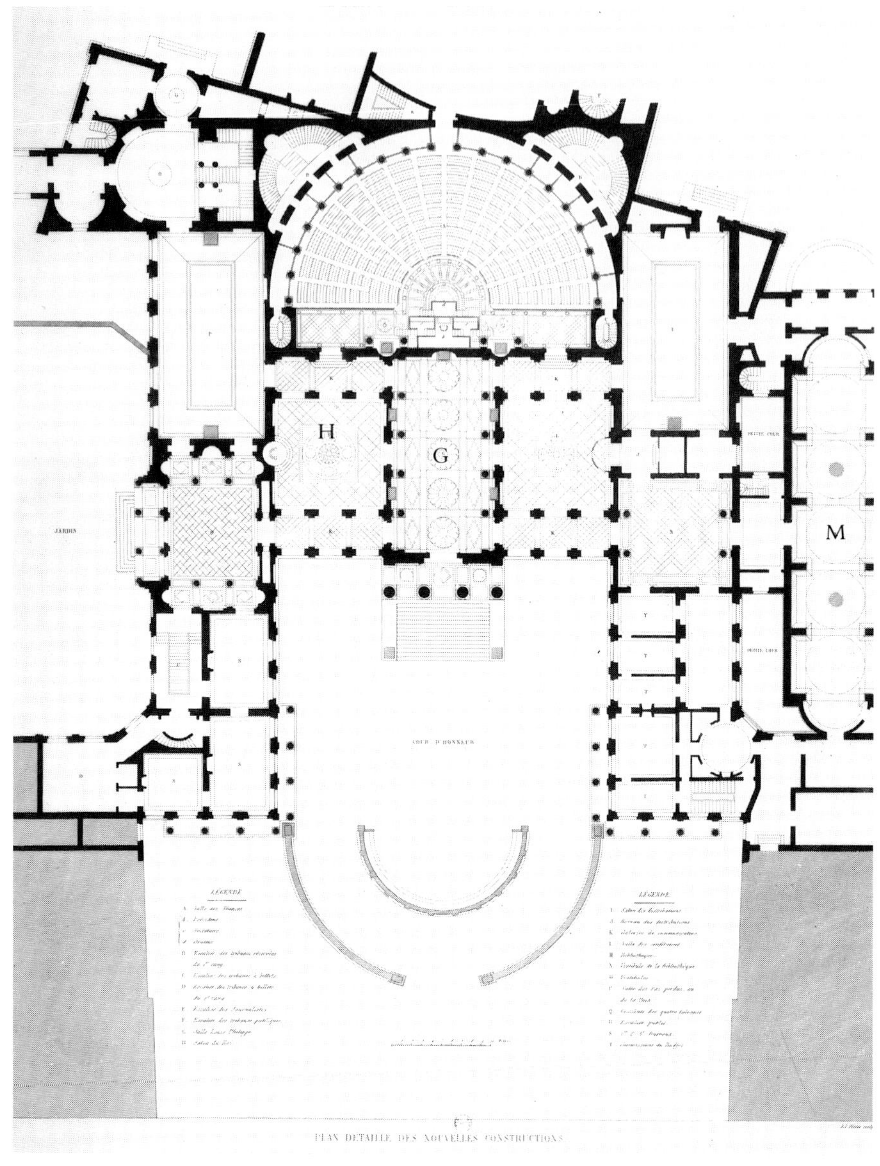

FIG. 40.   Plan of the Palais-Bourbon, from J. de Joly, *Plans, coupes, élévations et détails de la restauration de la Chambre des Députés*, Paris, 1840, plate 3.

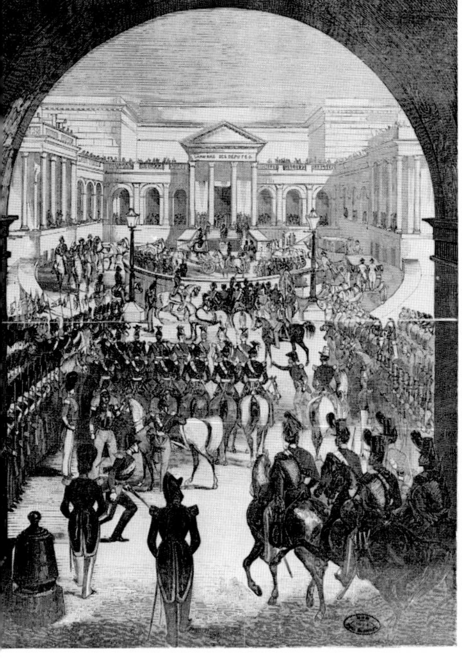
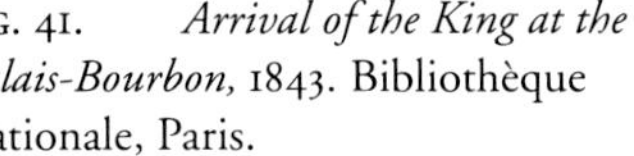
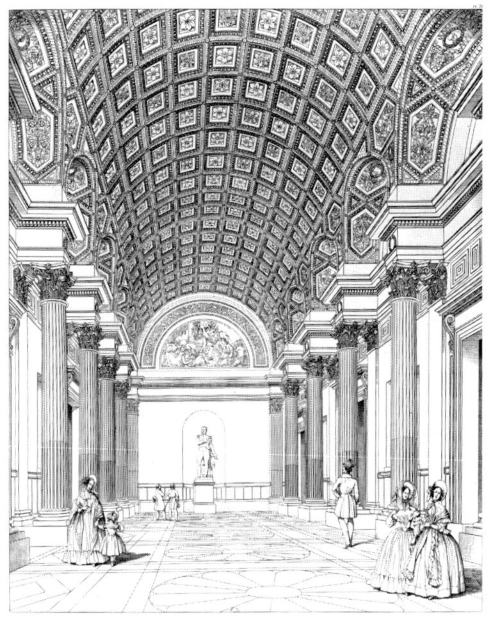

FIG. 41.   *Arrival of the King at the Palais-Bourbon,* 1843. Bibliothèque Nationale, Paris.

FIG. 42.   Salle Louis-Philippe, Palais-Bourbon, Paris, from J. de Joly, *Plans, coupes, élévations et détails de la restauration de la Chambre des Députés,* Paris, 1840, plate 29.

still stand in niches between freestanding Corinthian columns.[9] At either end of the Salle Louis-Philippe two large marble relief sculptures by Baron Henri-Joseph-François de Triqueti (1804–1874) celebrate the divine nature of law and its benefits to society (Figs. 43, 44).[10]

Protecting Law (*La Loi protectrice*) and *Avenging Law* (*La Loi vengeresse*) are semicircular compositions of life-size figures capped by Mosaic tablets inscribed LEX (Law). In *Protecting Law,* facing the entrance to the Salle Louis-Philippe, the tablets of the law are set in a panoply that features the caduceus of commerce and a hand of justice. To the left, a rustic family sleeps amid the tools and fruit of its labor under the protection of an armed woman. To the right, a book is inscribed by an infant-bearing mother to show the emanation of the law from the will of its beneficiaries (cf. Fig. 13, the revolutionary print *The French Constitution,* where

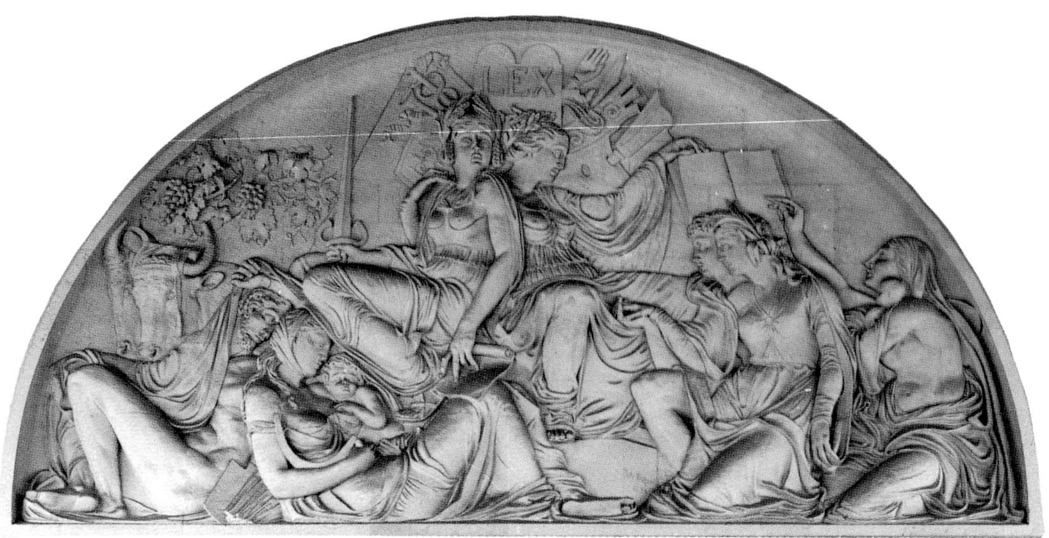

FIG. 43.   H. de Triqueti, *Protecting Law*, 1833–34. Salle Casimir-Périer (formerly called Salle Louis-Philippe), Palais-Bourbon, Paris.

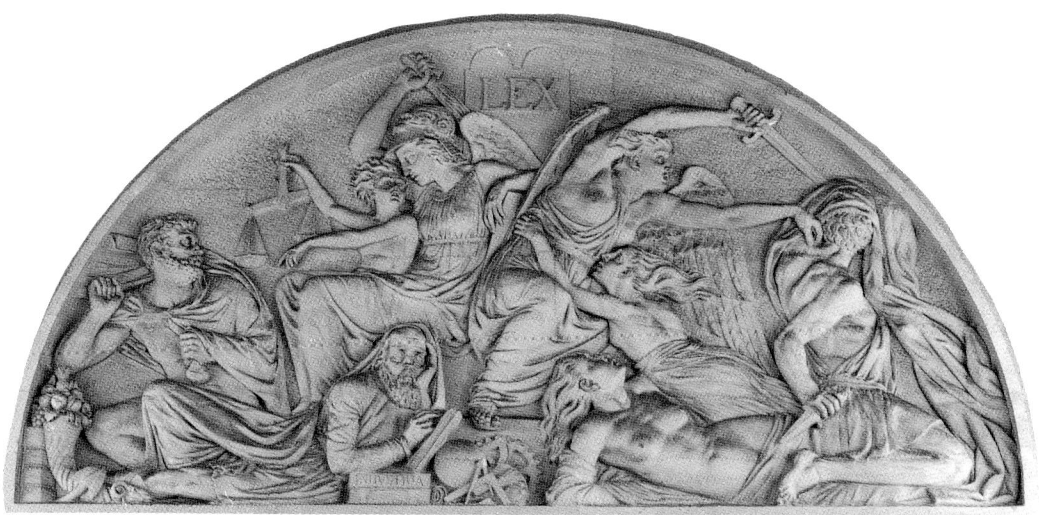

FIG. 44.   H. de Triqueti, *Avenging Law*, 1833–34. Salle Casimir-Périer, Palais-Bourbon, Paris.

the Nation inscribes the tablets of the law with the scepter of legislative power). A young couple clasping hands represents the covenant of marriage, revered as a fundamental cohesive element of society by the drafters of the Code Napoléon.[11] *Protecting Law* thus raises the law in triumph over fundamental human bonds: marriage, family, and labor.

Avenging Law, above the entrance, shows the nurturing of civilization under the fierce guardianship of the law. A philosopher resembling Socrates, protected by two winged figures, reclines beside attributes of industry, the arts, and science.[12] At either end of the lunette, perpetrators of murder and theft are apprehended. Whereas *Protecting Law* has a uniform relief and smooth ground, *Avenging Law* has a more irregular pattern and a rough ground that subtly dramatizes the theme of crime and punishment.

In the collection of the Ecole des Beaux-Arts is a pair of studies for *Protecting Law* and *Avenging Law,* each inscribed "présenté," that were apparently submitted to the ministry for approval (Figs. 45, 46). The firm and meticulous contour of the study for *Protecting Law* contrasts with the nervous vitality of that for *Avenging Law;* this contrast echoes the thematic counterpoint of the two lunettes more emphatically than do differences in ground texture and relief pattern in the finished marbles. Otherwise, the relief sculptures remained faithful to the drawings where, in the language of official allegory, homage is rendered to the entities the July Monarchy held scared: law, property, public order, agriculture, industry, and commerce. In these works, the revolutionary association of the law with regeneration and natural rights has been replaced by reference to material prosperity, punishment, and protection.

The pious glorification of the law in Triqueti's *Protecting Law* resembles that of "Les Laboureurs," a section of Lamartine's book-length poem *Jocelyn* (1836), written in the fall of 1835. Describing a scene of agricultural labor and rest, the poet sees a reflection of divine law in the earthly law of labor and the bond of familial love:

> Ô travail, sainte loi du monde,
> Ton mystère va s'accomplir;
> Pour rendre la glèbe féconde,
> De sueur il faut l'amollir!
> . . . .

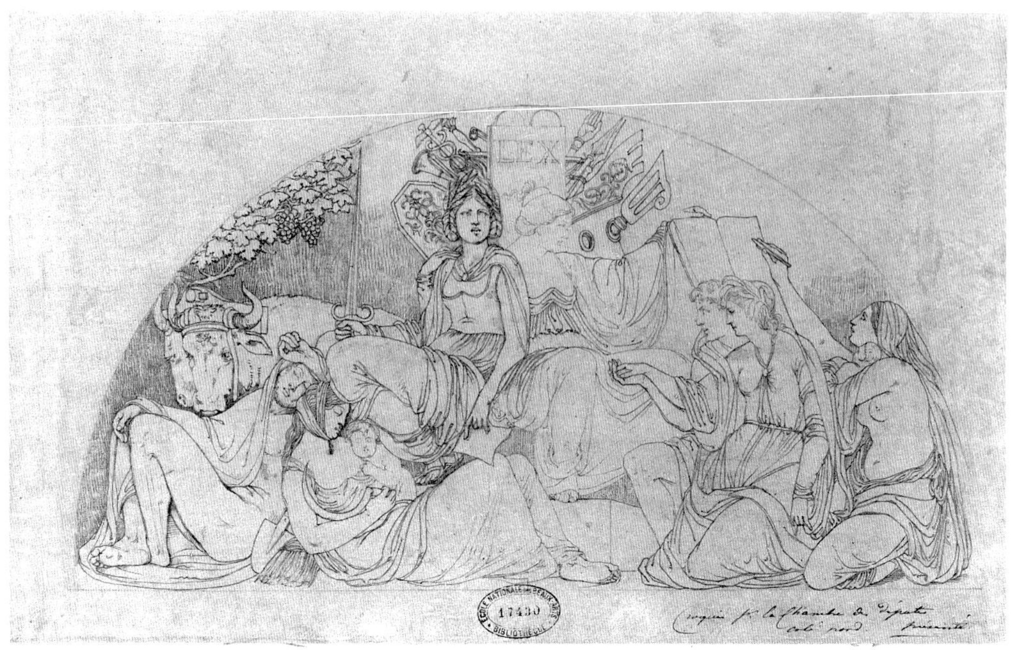

FIG. 45.　　H. de Triqueti, study for
Protecting Law, 1833. Ecole Nationale
Supérieure des Beaux-Arts, Paris.

FIG. 46 (*opposite*).　　H. de Triqueti, study
for *Avenging Law,* 1833. Ecole Nationale
Supérieure des Beaux-Arts, Paris.

Et pour consacrer l'héritage
Du champ labouré par leurs mains,
Les bornes firent le partage
De la terre entre les humains,
Et l'homme, à tous les droits propice,
Trouva dans son coeur la justice
Et grava son code en tout lieu,
Et pour consacrer ses lois même,
S'élevant à la loi suprême,
Chercha la juge et trouva Dieu!
. . . .
Oh! dormez sous le vert nuage
De feuilles qui couvrent ce nid,
Homme, femme, enfants leur image,
Que la loi d'amour réunit!
Ô famille, abrégé du monde,

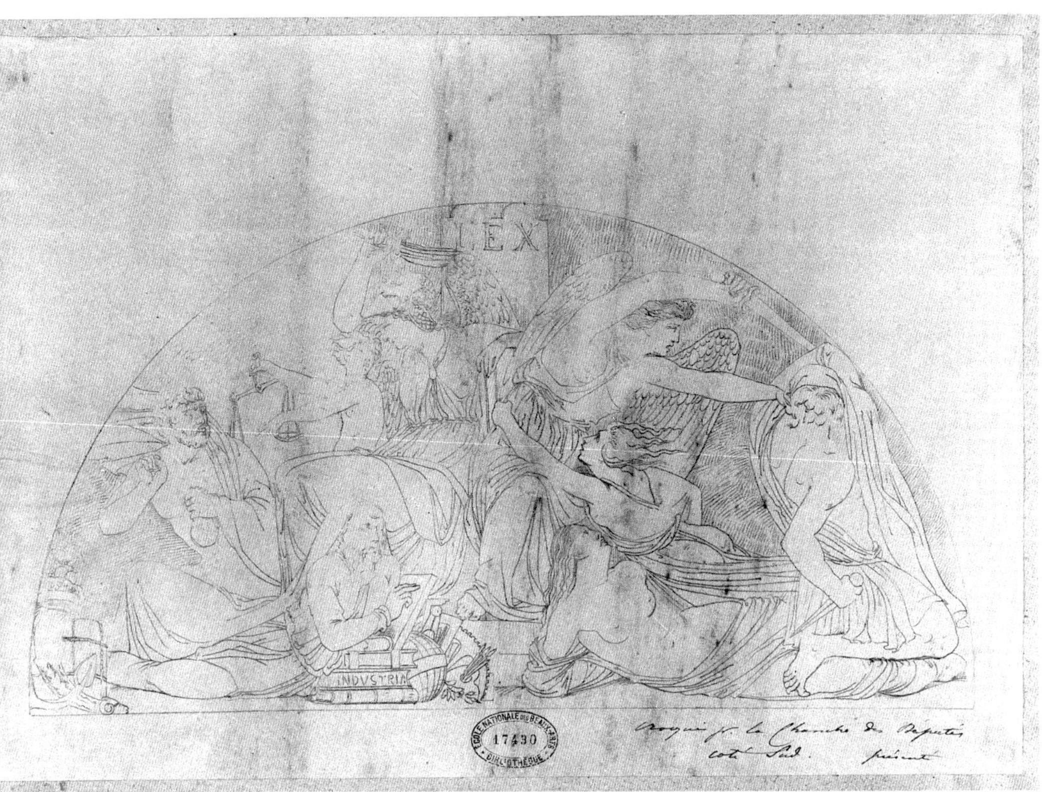

Instinct qui charme et qui féconde
Les fils de l'homme en ce bas lieu,
N'est-ce pas toi qui nous rappelle
Cette parenté fraternelle
Des enfants dont le père est Dieu?

Oh work, sacred law of the world,
Your rites shall be performed;
To make the soil fertile,
It must be watered with sweat!
. . . .
And to sanctify the heritage
Of the fields worked by their hands,
Boundaries divide the earth
Among humankind.
And man, respectful of all rights,

Found justice in his heart
And inscribed his code everywhere,
And to sanctify his laws,
Looked up to the supreme law,
Sought the judge, and found God!

. . . .

Oh! sleep under the cloud of
Green leaves that cover this nest,
Man, woman, and children in their parents' image,
United by the law of love!
Oh family, microcosm of the world,
Innate purpose that charms and makes fertile
The sons of man in this lowly place,
Is it not you that recalls to us
That fraternal kinship
Of the children of God?[13]

Although Lamartine said that "Les Laboureurs" was inspired by Léopold Robert's *Harvesters* (Salon of 1831),[14] I believe that his sympathy was also stirred by Triqueti's *Protecting Law.*

A member of the Chamber of Deputies since 1833, Lamartine had ample opportunity to view Triqueti's reliefs in the Salle Louis-Philippe. An outspoken advocate of charity, mercy, and moderation, Lamartine, who had once compared Bonald to Moses, now embraced the Orléans cult of law, order, and the protection of property.[15] In "Les Laboureurs" he associates the correspondence between divine and human law with agricultural boundaries (*bornes*).[16] "Property," he told his colleagues of the Palais-Bourbon, "is more than a legal right; it is a right of nature. It is society itself." And in the spirit of Casimir Périer's "despotism of the law" the legislator-poet declared in the same address—presented a month after the 1834 uprisings in Lyon and Paris—that "everything is legitimate against anarchy!"[17]

After entering the palace through the Salle Louis-Philippe, the king would receive deputations from the Chamber of Deputies and the Chamber of Peers in the new Salon du Roi—a square room with a throne set into a niche facing the entrance from the Salle Louis-Philippe (Fig. 47; H on plan). Delacroix's decoration of this room (1833–38) with allegories of justice, war, commerce, agriculture,

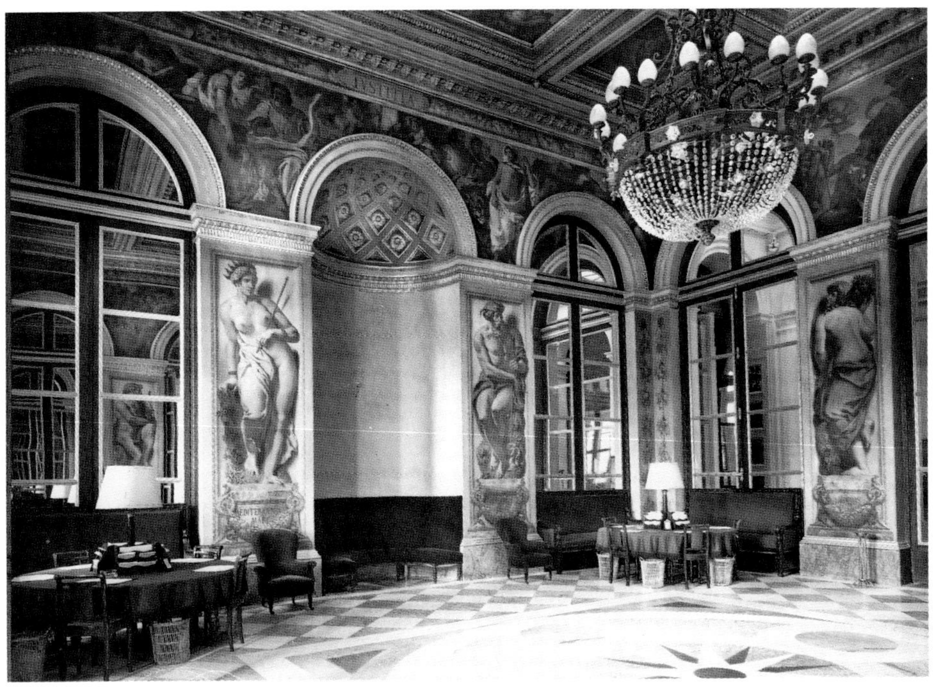

FIG. 47.   E. Delacroix, Salon du Roi,
1833–38. Palais-Bourbon, Paris.

and the principal waterways of France was appropriate to the monarch's function, as defined by article 13 of the charter:[18] "The king is the supreme chief of the state; he commands the forces of land and sea; declares war; makes treaties of peace, alliance, and commerce; . . . and makes the regulations and ordinances necessary for the execution of the laws."

Like Jacquot's colossal statue in the adjacent Salle Louis-Philippe (see Fig. 42), Delacroix's murals in the Salon du Roi represent a survival of the Napoleonic and Restoration association of law with the person of the ruler. The mural decoration above the throne niche—the first part visible, according to the artist, to someone entering the room—is devoted to the theme of justice.[19] This arrangement serves as a reminder that the Bourbon doctrine that "all justice emanates from the king" (Charter of 1814, art. 57) was preserved in the Charter of 1830 (art. 48).[20] The sympathetic critic Louis de Ronchaud noted that "M. Delacroix has indicated justice as the foremost of royal virtues."[21] Reference to the monarch is also made on the ceiling above the throne where, as the critic Gustave Planche noticed, a personification of Justice holds a scepter rather than the traditional scales.[22]

The Salon du Roi iconography reflected an element of Old Regime doctrine shared by the constitutional Bourbon and Orléans monarchies, and its regal flavor suited the monarch's preeminence in the legislative process. "Legislative power," according to article 14 of the charter, "is exercised collectively by the king, the Chamber of Peers, and the Chamber of Deputies." Each entity could initiate legislation, with tax legislation subject to prior vote by the deputies (art. 15); and, in marked contrast to Napoleonic parliamentary practice, each law was to be "freely discussed and voted for by the majority of each of the two chambers" (art. 16). But only the "inviolable and sacred" king—who held all executive power (art. 12)—could sanction and promulgate laws (art. 18). Concealed within the bourgeois hat and umbrella of the Citizen King, one of the regime's wittiest critics suggested, were the crown and scepter of absolute monarchy.[23]

In light of the continuity between the charters of 1814 and 1830 (the Orléans charter was, after all, based on that of the Bourbons), it is fitting that Delacroix's representation of Justice in the Salon du Roi quietly alludes to the association between law and divine inspiration that had been evident in the paintings for the Council of State (Delacroix had contributed the evangelical *Justinian* to that Bourbon decorative cycle). And it was appropriate for the critic Gustave Planche to compare the bulky legislator, seated in the frieze above the throne, to the Sistine prophets.[24] This thematic orientation also suggests why the artist might have modeled Prudence, to the left of this figure, on Raphael's sibyls in Santa Maria della Pace,[25] and why the bearded head closest to Force resembles that of Michelangelo's *Moses* (Fig. 48).[26]

Across the Seine from the Palais-Bourbon, the theme of divine legislation was treated in the colossal bronze doors that Triqueti, assisted by Etienne-Hippolyte Maindron (1801–1884), sculpted for the Church of the Madeleine (Fig. 49). Commissioned by the government in 1834 and emplaced in 1841, the doors illustrate the Ten Commandments through biblical narrative.[27]

Originally the subject of the doors was to have been the life of the patron saint of the church, Mary Magdalen; the modification of the program reflects the political agenda of Louis-Philippe's constitutional monarchy. In dedicating the church

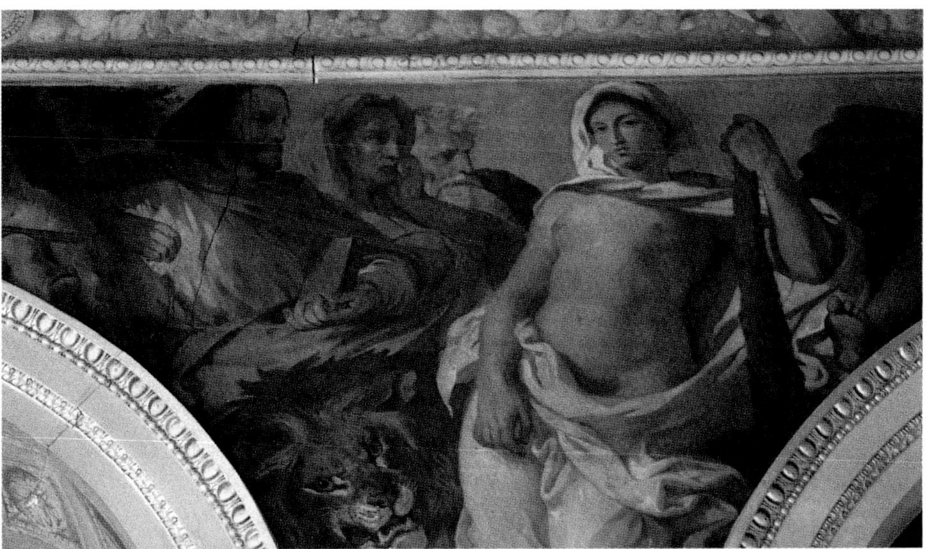

FIG. 48.   E. Delacroix, *Justice* frieze (detail), Salon du Roi, 1833–38. Palais-Bourbon, Paris.

to a penitent saint, the Bourbon Restoration referred to the nation's crimes during the Revolution, for in front of the church—in what is now the Place de la Concorde—Louis XVI had died on the guillotine.[28] The dedication suggests that the church was to have had a symbolic function similar to that of the Expiatory Chapel. Despite the commitment of the July Monarchy to ecclesiastical patronage, this expiatory reference to the Revolution had no place in its official art. On the contrary, the new regime aligned itself with popular sentiment as it focused on the nation's revolutionary and imperial past. Thus it publicized Louis-Philippe's military service during the Revolution and ceremonially returned the ashes of Napoleon to France in 1840.[29] Whereas Charles X had dedicated the square to Louis XVI and intended a statue of that king's apotheosis for its center, the July Monarchy—in a spirit of reconciliation—preferred a neutral obelisk and the name Place de la Concorde.[30] Inside the Madeleine, the Restoration plan for an altar sculpture of Mary Magdalen as a symbol of penitent France was not realized; instead, Carlo Marochetti sculpted *Mary Magdalen Exalted by Angels* (1834–41), and Jules-Claude Ziégler's painting *The History of Christianity* in the

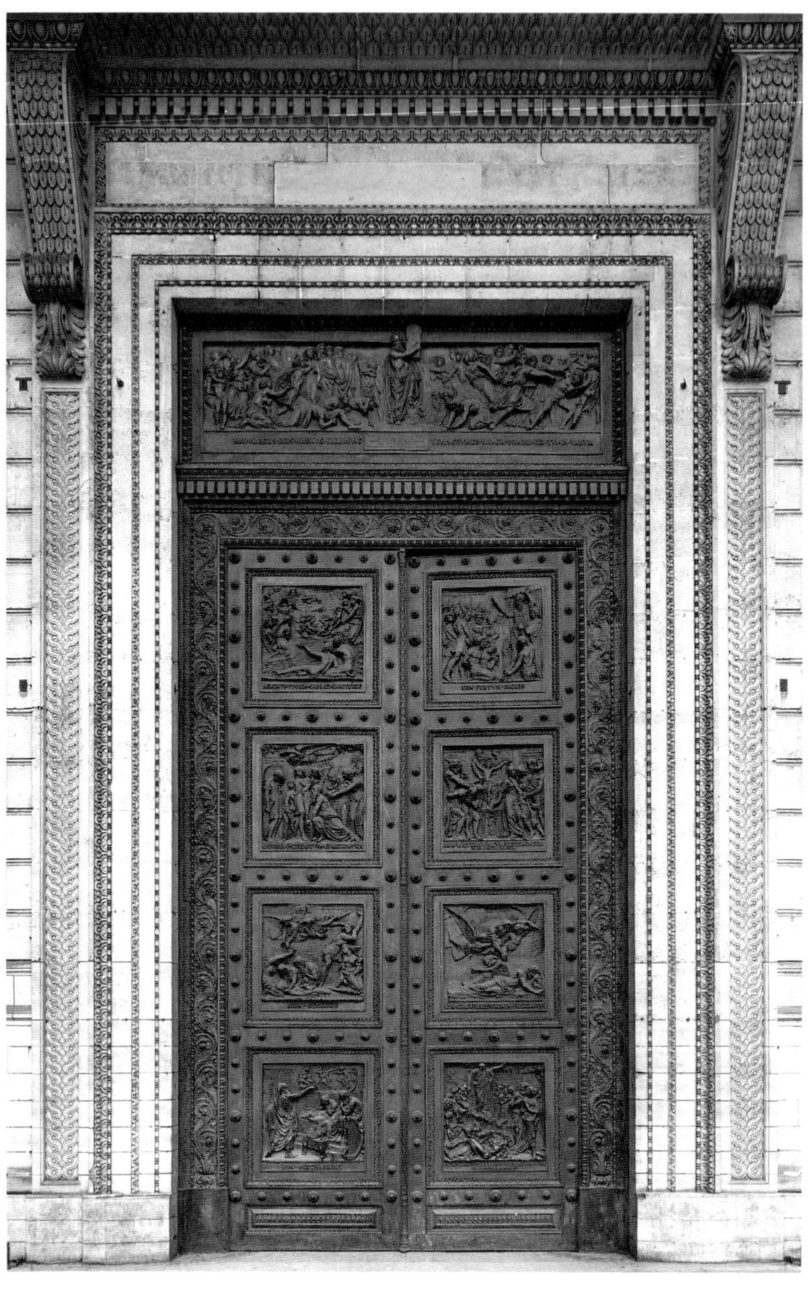

FIG. 49.   H. de Triqueti, *The Ten Commandments,* 1834–41. Paris, Madeleine.

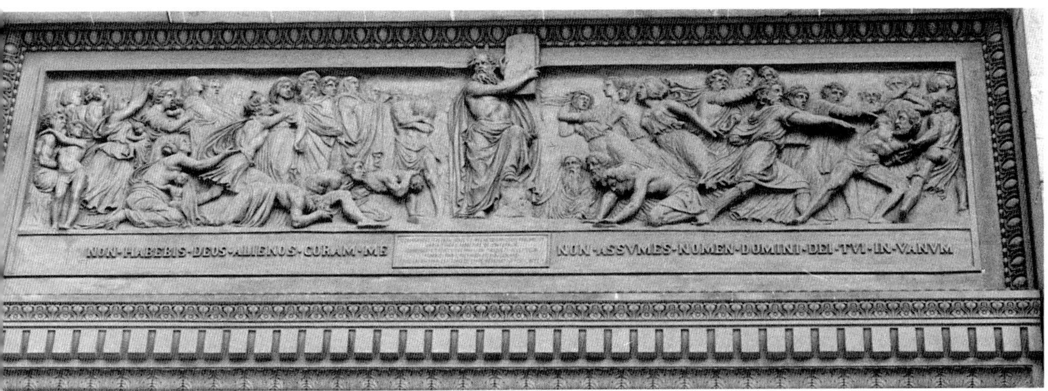

FIG. 50.   H. de Triqueti, *Proscription of Idolatry and Blasphemy*, 1834–41. Paris, Madeleine.

hemicycle (1837) represented the saint amid a historical, religious, and literary multitude that prominently includes Napoleon.[31]

Although there is little documentary evidence for the choice of subject for the Madeleine doors,[32] Adolphe Thiers, the minister in charge of the commission, shared a taste for Old Testament subjects with the Protestant Triqueti,[33] and the sculptor had employed the motif of the Mosaic tablets in his work in progress for the Salle Louis-Philippe, also commissioned by Thiers's ministry. This theme was especially suitable for a regime that looked to the law for its principal support.

The reliefs of the Madeleine doors are predominantly devoted to crime and punishment. The most solemn narratives employ a vehement emotional rhetoric absent from Triqueti's principal point of reference, the *Gates of Paradise* of Ghiberti—a work Thiers especially admired. Here are stern demonstrations of the "law of fear and terror," as Jewish legislation was characterized in a popular religious digest.[34] On the lintel (Fig. 50), the first two commandments (the proscription of idolatry and blasphemy) are represented by such emphatic demonstrations of anger and fear that a critic writing in *L'Artiste* mistakenly identified the subject as the *Last Judgment*.[35] At the center, a crowd of Hebrews prostrate themselves before Moses and the law with exaggerated awe. To the right, a bound criminal is hounded by accusers and dragged away for punishment.

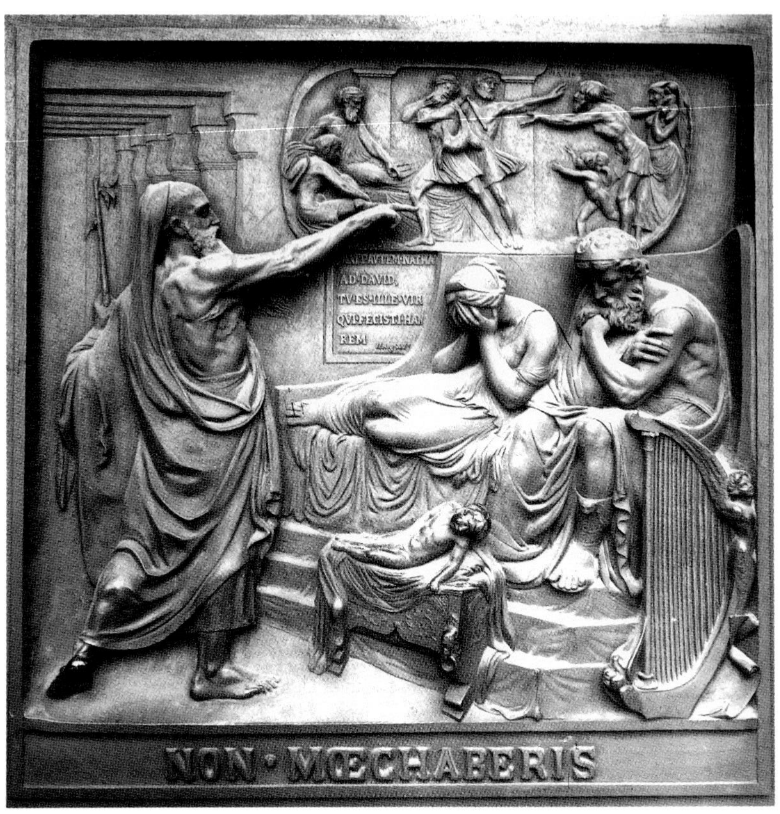

FIG. 51.   H. de Triqueti, *The Crime of Adultery (The Prophet Nathan Confronts King David)*, 1837. Paris, Madeleine.

A similar severity characterizes the bottom panel on the left door, representing the crime of adultery (Fig. 51). Here Triqueti condensed the aftermath of King David's seduction of Bathsheba, the wife of Uriah the Hittite (2 Samuel 12). David, seated beside Bathsheba, is overcome with remorse as the stern prophet Nathan confronts him. Nathan reveals David's crime through the parable of a rich man who steals a poor man's only lamb, narrated in a subsidiary zone. As a sign of divine wrath, David's illegitimate son lies lifeless before his guilty parents.

The prohibition against coveting a neighbor's property is represented by a solemn exemplar of retribution in the bottom panel of the right door (Fig. 52). King Ahab and Jezebel flee before the indignant Elijah, who predicts that dogs

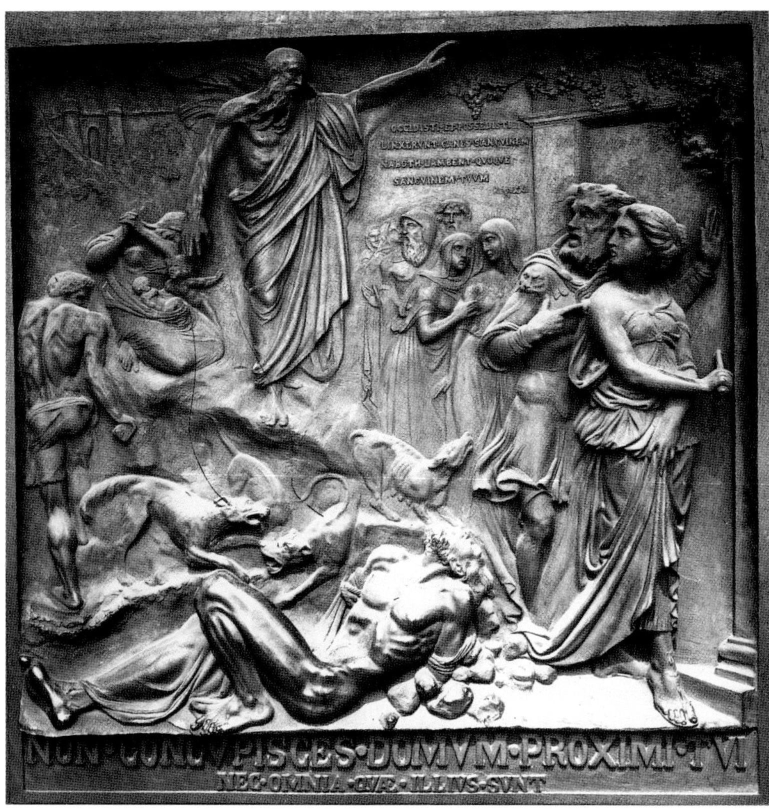

FIG. 52.   H. de Triqueti, *The Crime of Coveting a Neighbor's Property (Ahab and Jezebel Condemned by Elijah for the Murder of Naboth)*, 1837. Paris, Madeleine.

will lick the wicked king's blood and devour his guilty wife for coveting the vineyard of the murdered Naboth (1 Kings 21).[36]

The righteous anger with which Triqueti's bronze doors proclaimed the law of Moses reflected the young government's preoccupation with law and order as insurrection and subversion assailed it. Triqueti's patron Thiers was in the vanguard of the government's legal counter-offensive, and in the wake of a spectacular—and almost successful—attempt to assassinate Louis-Philippe in 1835, he championed the repressive September Laws that gagged the satirical press.[37] The righteous anger expressed in Triqueti's biblical narratives was matched by that of Duke Victor de Broglie, minister of foreign affairs, in a speech to the legislature favoring the passage of the September Laws. He extolled the regime's legal war against its enemies, in a speech that drew cries of "Bravo!" from the chamber:

> Rebellion . . . took to the streets; you have seen it knock on the doors of the king's palace . . . bare-armed, in rags, howling, uttering insults and threats, and thinking that it would prevail by fear. We have faced it; the law in hand . . . we have dissolved the anarchist organizations; we have arrested the leaders, scattered the soldiers . . . several times we have dragged it, in spite of its clamors, to the feet of justice, to receive its punishment.[38]

Commissioned by a government flattered by the association of its constitutional charter with the tablets of Moses, the Madeleine doors, with their stern imagery, constitute a resonant analogy to the regime's militant defense of the Charter of 1830.

The political significance of the Madeleine doors is amplified by their position in a large urban scheme commenced under Louis XV and completed during the July Monarchy (Fig. 53). A direct axis across the Place de la Concorde and the Seine links the Napoleonic porticoes of the Madeleine and the Palais-Bourbon (designated Corps législatif on the map, which dates from the Second Empire). This axis was bisected by another connecting the Tuileries palace (the residence of Louis-Philippe, destroyed during the Commune, at the west end of the Louvre) with the Arc de Triomphe de l'Etoile—the memorial to Napoleonic military glory completed under the July Monarchy. As an ensemble, the Palais-Bourbon, the Madeleine, the Tuileries, and the Arc de Triomphe formed a cross at whose center was the Place de la Concorde, site of the execution of Louis XVI.[39] The emotional charge of this central Parisian space was evocatively described by the ecclesiastical orator Lacordaire:

> When the foreigner descends the river that divides Paris, he encounters a square whose breadth and monuments invite his meditation. On one side there is the palace of the kings of France, and facing him, at the end of a long avenue, is a military arch of triumph. In a second perspective, which cuts the first in the form of a cross, two temples correspond to each other: one is that of laws, the other that of God. In the center rises an Egyptian obelisk, which disappears under an invisible monument present to all minds, the scaffold of Louis XVI. All of France is on this square: royalty, military glory, liberty, religion, revolution.[40]

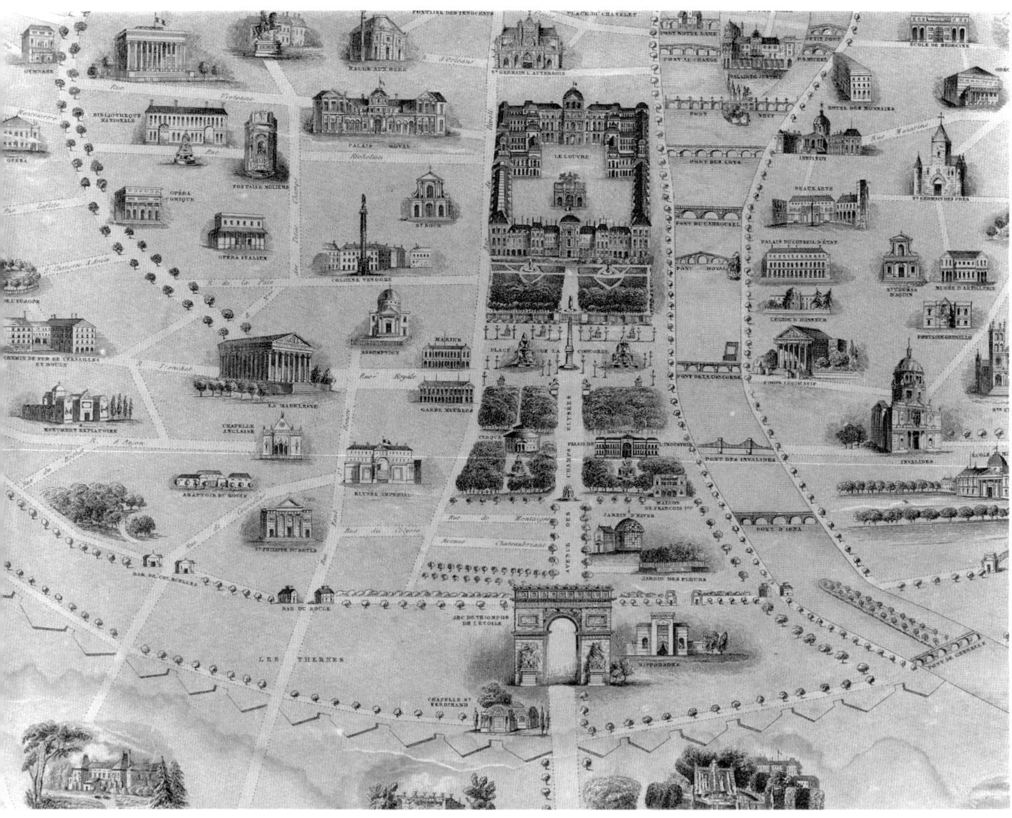

FIG. 53.   Place de la Concorde and environs, Paris (from the west; detail). From *Paris monumental et ses environs,* Paris, n.d. Boston Public Library.

The correspondence between the Madeleine and the Palais-Bourbon united the divine law of Moses with the legal foundation of the regime.[41]

Two cartoons published in *La Caricature* subverted the exalted official discourse of legitimacy and legality expressed in Triqueti's relief sculptures for the Palais-Bourbon and the Madeleine. In the April 2, 1835, issue Benjamin (Benjamin Roubaud, 1811–1847) satirized the government's devastating campaign of lawsuits against the opposition press in "The New Moses" (Fig. 54). Jean-Charles Persil, the minister of justice, is Moses striking the rock, labeled "liberty

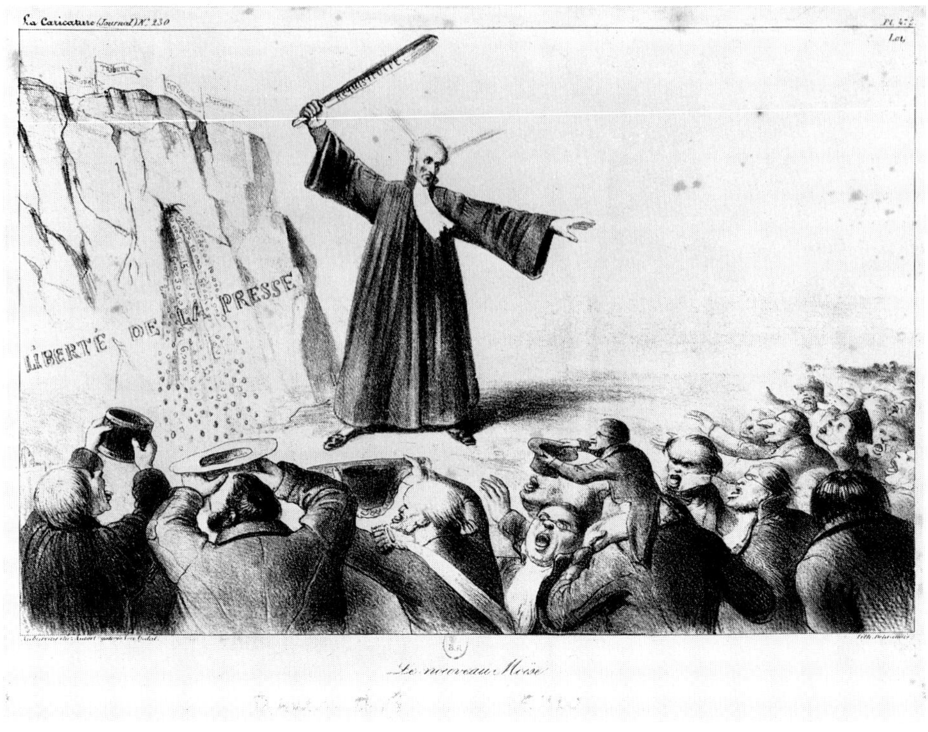

FIG. 54.   Benjamin, "The New Moses." *La Caricature*, April 2, 1835. Bibliothèque Nationale, Paris.

of the press," to produce water in the desert. The names of opposition papers appear on banners atop the rock. Persil's cudgel is labeled "requisitoire" (indictment); from the rock he has struck with it pours money, greedily gathered by members of the government as well as by Louis-Philippe, recognizable to readers of *La Caricature* by his misshapen head and mutton chops.[42]

Traviès (Charles-Joseph Traviès de Villers, 1804–1859) burlesqued biblical imagery in his "Adoration of the Golden Calf," published in the May 8, 1834, issue of *La Caricature* (Fig. 55).[43] Here Louis-Philippe's supporters are the idolatrous Hebrews who worshiped the golden calf while Moses received the divine law on Mount Sinai. These sycophants grovel before a pile of money bags labeled with examples of the regime's avarice (sinecures, secret funds, ministerial salaries) and topped by a giant radiant coin whose portrait in profile resembles that of

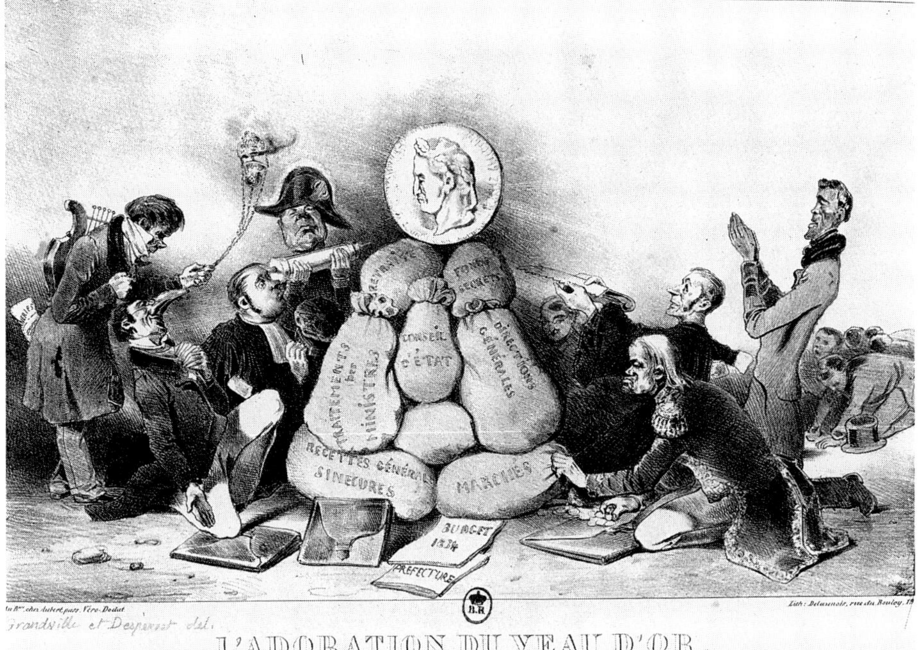

FIG. 55.   Traviès, "The Adoration of
the Golden Calf." *La Caricature,* May 8,
1834. Bibliothèque Nationale, Paris.

Louis-Philippe on the five-franc piece used during the July Monarchy.[44] Persil,
mocked as Père-Scie (Father Saw),[45] presents his toothy attribute like a saint in a
sacra conversazione. A final insult is the resemblance of the pyramid of money
sacks to the bloated and grimacing features of Louis-Philippe.

"The Adoration of the Golden Calf" and "The New Moses" belong to the
genre anathematized by Lamartine in an address to the chamber, August 21, 1835,
as "atrocious and seditious caricature, in which perversity of the heart toys with
crime and scoffs at the holy images of fatherland and religion."[46] The schematic
didacticism and encoded topical references of these caricatures make them negative counterparts to the flat-footed official allegory of Blondel and Mauzaisse in
the Council of State paintings and, under the July Monarchy, of such works as
Picot's *July 1830: France Defends the Charter.*

A more complex example of dissident art from the early July Monarchy is the large relief sculpture *Tuerie* by Auguste Préault (Fig. 56). Its thematic violence and stylistic daring shocked conventional taste at the Salon of 1834, one of whose visitors characterized the work as an "incredible farrago of every horror, wretchedness, misery, extravagance, monstrosity."[47] According to a famous anecdote, *Tuerie* was admitted to the Salon of 1834 solely at the insistence of the academician Jean-Pierre Cortot, who wanted it shown as a warning—like a criminal on a gibbet.[48]

No particular narrative is associated with the work, elusively described in the 1834 Salon *livret* as a "fragment épisodique d'un grand bas-relief."[49] *Tuerie*'s subject, as indicated by the laconic title, is slaughter itself, apparently gratuitous. Hugh Honour said of it, "There are visual reminiscences in it. . . . But there is no programme. . . . Its subject has never been satisfactorily explained, and it was perhaps conceived simply as a scene of violence."[50] David Mower has compared the work to a composite of passages from Auguste Barbier and Sir Walter Scott,[51] but this analogy locates the sculpture only in a general context: the Romantic taste for passion and violence. Jacques de Caso, by pointing out that other sculptors of the time deployed similar thematic violence and extravagant irregularity of relief, has made *Tuerie* seem less of an anomaly, but no less original.[52]

Although this evocative and idiosyncratic work resists identification with any single source, the visual evidence suggests that Henri de Triqueti's Law reliefs in the Salle Louis-Philippe contributed to its conception. Préault's transformation of this source was guided by a pessimistic impulse to repudiate Triqueti's glorification of the civilizing force of law.

There are sufficient figural similarities between *Tuerie* and *Avenging Law* (see Fig. 44) to suggest that Préault (1809–1879), who exhibited the plaster version of *Tuerie* in the Salon of 1834, was familiar with Triqueti's Law reliefs, commissioned the previous year. Principal among these is the resemblance of the hysterical mother at the center of *Tuerie* to the female victim at the right of *Avenging Law* who, with hair streaming behind, wildly seeks the protection of a winged avenger. In addition, the fury of Triqueti's sword-bearing avenger is echoed in a male profile in the upper right corner of *Tuerie;* the bearded thief on the left side of *Avenging Law* offers a conventional point of departure for the extravagantly grimacing African head that is desperately repulsed with both hands by a swooning long-haired woman in the upper left corner of *Tuerie;* and the baby in *Tuerie* seems an unfortunate cousin of the doughy-limbed child that lies at its mother's

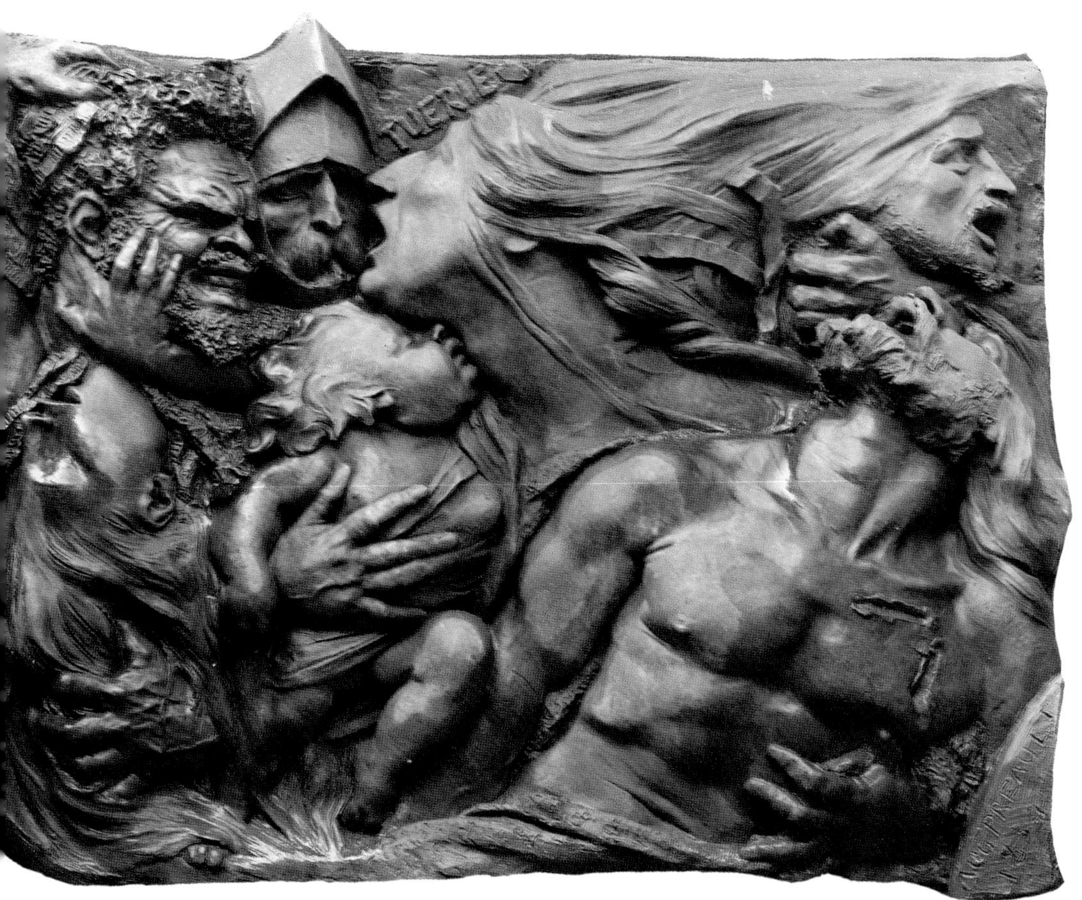

FIG. 56.   A.-A. Préault, *Tuerie* (Slaughter), 1834. Chartres, Musée des Beaux-Arts.

breast in *Protecting Law* (see Fig. 43). The startling scale of *Tuerie,* somewhat larger than life, recalls that of Triqueti's allegorical reliefs; the architect and critic Gabriel Laviron praised *Tuerie*'s suitability for an architectural setting—a quality that set it apart from the other sculpture at the Salon.[53] Particularly suggestive is Préault's placement of the word TUERIE in a position similar to that of the inscription LEX on the Mosaic tablets in Triqueti's reliefs. The inscriptions underscore the disparity between Triqueti's celebration of order, justice, and civilization under the aegis of law and Préault's evocation of blind, chaotic slaughter.

That Préault could have been spurred by a desire to negate Triqueti's Law
reliefs squares with the record of his notoriously caustic wit, characteristically
directed against authority and established taste.[54] Préault said he detested "conse-
crated platitudes."[55] The myth that law nurtured civilization smacked of hypocrisy
in light of the terrible events of the early July Monarchy. The escalating rhythm of
insurrection and repression of these years led, shortly after the opening of the
Salon of 1834, to the Rue Transnonain Massacre (April 14, 1834).[56] French sympathy had been deeply stirred by Russia's brutal subjugation of Poland in 1831. And
in the spring of 1832 more than eighteen thousand Parisians perished during a
cholera plague, in a climate of mass hysteria.[57] Considered in relation to Triqueti's
official allegories, the fragmented *Tuerie* resonates with the force characteristic of
the sculptor's conversation. According to Théophile Silvestre, "Préault never thoroughly develops an argument but runs and flies after violent or refined images
and comparisons. He also proceeds by ironic negations and imperious affirma-
tions, reinforced by sarcasm and nervous laughter in the modern manner."[58]

Unlike Triqueti's reassuring allegories, *Tuerie* has formal audacity as well as
aggressive content. Symmetry gives stability and regularity to both the spirited
Avenging Law and the serene *Protecting Law,* both of which uphold French sculptural tradition in their strict and elegant conformity to the wall plane. *Tuerie,* on
the contrary, has neither groundline nor symmetry; and the emphatically planar
composition emphasizes the suffocating compaction of the wracked bodies. This
sense of claustrophobia is intensified by the uncomfortable proximity of several
gaping mouths. The anatomical forms bulge so extravagantly that several passages—notably the dying man in the lower right—seem to have been conceived
in the round rather than in relief.

Tuerie and the Law reliefs are as different as the social and professional positions of the two sculptors. Triqueti was the son of Baron Michel de Triqueti, a
Piedmontese industrialist who had served as the ambassador of Sardinia to Russia
before the Revolution; Préault's father was a Parisian metalworker. Préault, noto-
rious as a pugnacious cultural dissident, was frequently rejected by the Salon
juries of the July Monarchy; the independently wealthy and amiable Triqueti enjoyed both respectability and royal favor.[59]

The subversiveness of *Tuerie* resembles that of a disturbing voice in contemporary French literature, Pétrus Borel (1809–1859). Préault's exact contemporary,
Borel was the most outrageous member of a rebellious literary and artistic circle,

the *Jeunes-France,* that included Théophile Gautier, Gérard de Nerval, and Préault's friend Célestin Nanteuil.[60] Préault aided Borel and his group in their famous attack on academic propriety at the premiere of Hugo's *Hernani,* February 25, 1830; and Préault has been identified as the "jeune sculpteur de beaucoup d'esprit et de talent"[61] who shouted at the elder members of the audience, "A la guillotine, les genoux!" (Guillotine the baldpates!).[62] The year before the exhibition of *Tuerie,* Borel wrote appreciatively of Préault's works in the Salon of 1833; impressed by the focus on suffering in *Two Poor Women* and *Beggary,* Borel praised the sculptor as one of the few who realized that the Romantic revolution in art was a moral issue, not one that called simply for a new literary subject matter.[63] Borel's *Champavert, contes immoraux,* published in 1833, resembles *Tuerie* in its violence.

This sadistic narrative, filled with suicide, murder, and rape, could be as brutally abrupt as *Tuerie.* The title story of the collection, "Champavert, le lycanthrope" (i.e., Champavert the wolfman), furiously maligns law and justice. Prior to committing suicide, Champavert goes with his lover to the grave of their illegitimate child, murdered in childbirth. He exhumes the skeleton, which he brandishes and flings away, indicting the laws that Triqueti was celebrating in the same year in the Palais-Bourbon:

> Law! virtue! honor! you are satisfied; here, take back your prey! . . . Barbaric
> world, you wanted it, here, look, it is your work, yours. Are you content with
> your victim? . . . Bastard! it's quite shameless of you to have wanted to be born
> without royal authorization, without a wedding announcement! Eh! law? eh!
> honor? . . . Barbaric law! ferocious prejudice! infamous honor! men! society!
> here! take your prey! . . . I surrender it to you!!![64]

An earlier passage from the same story offers yet another point of comparison to *Tuerie* in its frenetic enumeration of horrors. Champavert denounces as a lie the idealization of love:

> Let them come forth, the impostors, so that I can strangle them! the knaves
> who sing of love, who *garland* it and *pipe* it, who make it a chubby child,
> chubby with joys, let them come forth, the impostors, so that I can strangle
> them! To sing of love! . . . for me, love is hate, groans, cries, shame, mourning,
> iron, tears, blood, cadavers, bones, remorse; I have known no other! . . . Go
> ahead, rosy shepherds, sing of love, derision! bitter masquerade![65]

Gabriel Laviron, who admired *Tuerie* and whose portrait Préault exhibited in the Salon of 1833, wrote a sympathetic review of *Champavert, contes immoraux.* Praising the truth of the passions, murders, and "desolate philosophy" of the book, Laviron welcomed Borel's ruthless unmasking of public complacency and parodied the false smugness of offended readers in a list of recent horrors whose bitter irony foreshadows *Tuerie:*

> Why always horror, cadavers, bloody vicissitudes? decent folk will repeat; they have no place in our era, which is so calm, so uniform; because civilization, enlightenment. . . . From time to time there is some shooting under our windows . . . barricades, the dead that one walks on; another time, men that the crowd tears into pieces: last summer, cadavers that they piled into wagons like corded wood. . . . But since yesterday who gives any of that a thought, and what do you want from us with your gravedigger literature?[66]

Like Borel's contemporaneous writing, *Tuerie* embodies an implacable hostility to the middle-class ideals, values, and taste of the July Monarchy. The writer and sculptor are alike, moreover, in the distance of their revolutionary posturing from any concrete political engagement. Paul Bénichou has shown that political activism was foreign to Borel and his rebellious circle.[67] There is no documentation of Préault's political activity apart from the allegation after his death that he had "lifted two or three paving stones when barricades were raised against Charles X."[68]

Although *Tuerie* can be viewed as a negative counterpart to Triqueti's allegories in the Salle Louis-Philippe, its subversiveness remains implicit. Préault's sculpture lacks the black humor, the schematic didacticism, and the topical reference of contemporary images published in *La Caricature.* Unlike parody, with its constant and outspoken reference to the subverted prototype, *Tuerie* incorporates only traces of Triqueti's imagery, subsuming them in a melodrama whose anatomical truncations both amplify the emotional charge of the theme and reinforce the grandiose suggestion of a preserved fragment. Préault's avoidance of iconographic specificity—together with the broad modeling and the inclusion of the abstract title and medieval helmet—gives this massacre an evocative scope greater than that of Triqueti's official idealism, of *La Caricature'*s defamatory brutality, and of

Borel's gruesome exclamations. At the same time, comparison between *Tuerie* and Triqueti's Law reliefs suggests the inspirational force of rage in the dark period around 1834, when a scandalous discrepancy was perceived between official rhetoric and political reality.

The Swansong of Legislation: The Palais-Bourbon Library

The embellishment of the Palais-Bourbon that included Delacroix's paintings in the Salon du Roi and Triqueti's Law reliefs in the Salle Louis-Philippe culminated in the new library.[1] Like the paintings for the Bourbon Council of State suite in the Louvre and the artist's earlier decoration of the Salon du Roi, the Palais-Bourbon library cycle was intended for an elite and cultured audience. Delacroix created a lavish working environment for the legislators for whom the impressive collection of manuscripts, maps, medals, and some fifty-four thousand volumes was reserved.[2] From 1838 to 1847 the artist and his assistants worked on two large murals, painted on the curved hemicycles at either end of the room, and twenty pendentive scenes, in groups of four, in five domed cupolas (Fig. 57; M in Fig. 40). Set into gilded moldings, the twenty-two paintings crown the room, with its monumental Dutch oak bookcases and ranges of old leather bindings, with Delacroix's resonant reds and blue-greens.

The library paintings, one of the most ambitious decorative undertakings of the nineteenth century, offer a panorama of considerable iconographic complexity. A description of the work by the sympathetic critic Théophile Thoré, based on notes provided by the artist, indicates that the twenty pendentive paintings correspond roughly to the fields of study by which libraries were then classified.[3]

The principal entrance to the forty-two-meter room is at its center, beneath a cupola decorated with subjects pertaining to legislation and eloquence. The cupolas to the left are those of theology and poetry; those to the right are devoted to history and philosophy, followed by science.[4] With their subjects drawn from

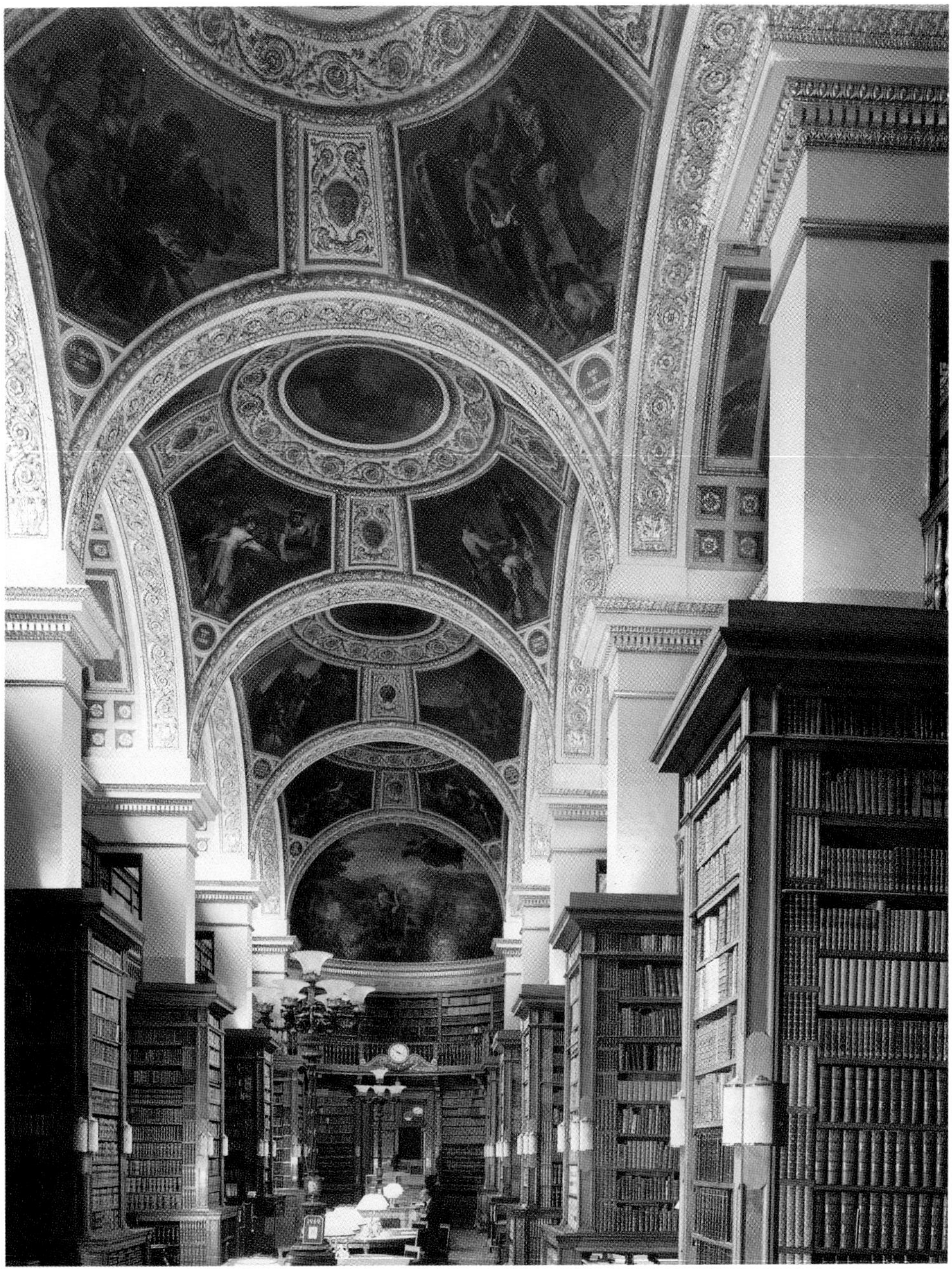

FIG. 57.   E. Delacroix, Palais-
Bourbon library paintings, 1838–47.
Palais-Bourbon, Paris.

Scripture and the classical tradition, the paintings reflect the civilization whose origin is represented in the right hemicycle by *Orpheus Comes to Civilize the Savage Greeks and to Teach Them the Arts of Peace* (Fig. 58). At the other end of the room, *Attila, Followed by His Barbarian Hordes, Tramples Italy and the Arts* dramatically closes the era initiated by Orpheus (Plate 7).

Even before the government decided to commission Delacroix to decorate the Palais-Bourbon library, on August 30, 1838, the artist had considered possible subjects, apparently with the aid of his learned friend Frédéric Villot. Enough documentation has survived to indicate that the program was determined only after the project was well under way.[5] Even before the ensemble was completely unveiled, the critic Louis de Ronchaud, who had written sympathetically of Delacroix's decoration of the Palais-Bourbon's Salon du Roi, admitted that he could not clearly comprehend "the mysterious correlation that must exist between these diverse subjects."[6] Similarly, Louis Clément de Ris, enthusiastic over parts of the cycle, nonetheless criticized the disunity of themes in the hemicycle and pendentive paintings.[7]

In 1968 George L. Hersey, attempting to dispel this confusion, proposed that the Palais-Bourbon library paintings have a comprehensive program based on the Neapolitan philosopher Giambattista Vico's *Scienza nuova seconda* (1744). To accommodate subjects that Delacroix could not have found there, however, Hersey was compelled to extrapolate from Vico's text. The elaborate and esoteric program presented by Hersey, moreover, has no counterpart in Delacroix's *oeuvre*.[8]

With the publication of Lee Johnson's catalogue and Anita Hopmans's analysis of the working method followed in the library commission, we can view this complex monument with greater clarity. Both commentators dispute Hersey's interpretation and accept, as basic to the work, the lack of strict organizational logic that troubled Ronchaud and Clément de Ris. For Johnson the program is a diverse collection of scenes of great men and events, appropriate to a library for politicians, that defies any consistent principle of organization. Hopmans is more emphatic in denying the programmatic consistency of the cycle. She convincingly demonstrates its improvisation. An initial plan to follow Jacques-Charles Brunet's system of library classification was only partially implemented.[9] Hopmans concludes that "the decorations in the Palais Bourbon became a mishmash of different plans and unplanned inspirations"; that no iconographic link exists between the hemicycles and the twenty pendentive paintings; and that only a taste for the

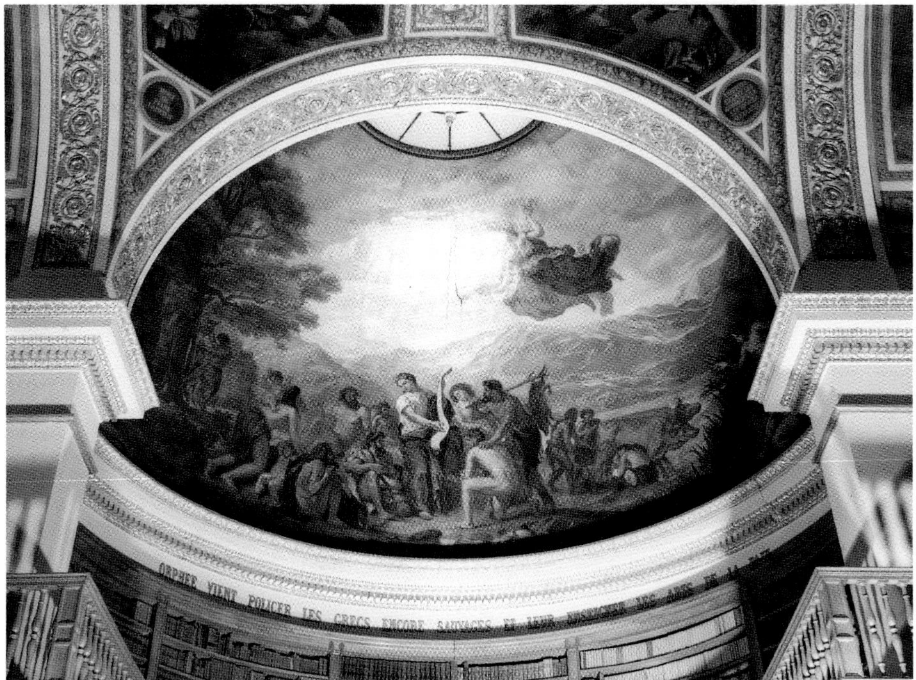

FIG. 58.   E. Delacroix, *Orpheus Comes to Civilize the Savage Greeks and to Teach Them the Arts of Peace*. Palais-Bourbon, Paris.

dramatic and the exemplary can account for the choice of subjects.[10] Although the cycle does lack a consistent program, it has elements of thematic coherence, not noted in the art-historical literature, that reflect the artist's concern to address the needs of the legislators who read and conversed beneath his paintings.

From the outset Delacroix planned to refer to great authors and bibliographic subjects—in accord with both the traditions of library decoration and the architect's general plans for the embellishment of the room.[11] The concern to link the paintings and the legislative institution itself apparently evolved in the course of the work. As late as November 1842, with the science and philosophy-history paintings almost ready to be installed, the remaining subjects of the decoration were not final. In the following year the artist was planning to place paintings pertaining to theology in the center cupola.[12] Delacroix's belated decision to devote

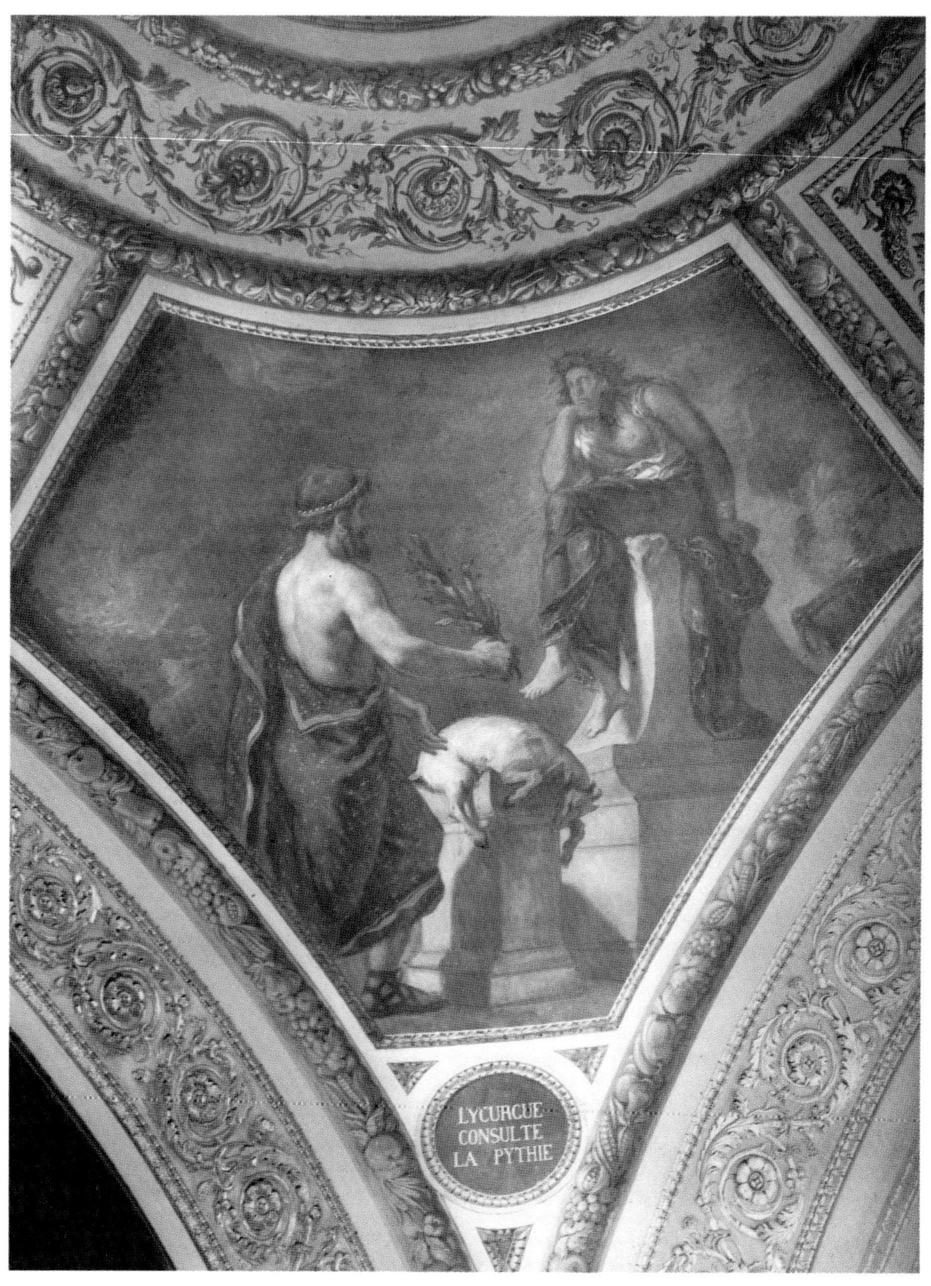

FIG. 59. E. Delacroix, *Lycurgus Consults the Pythian Sibyl.* Palais-Bourbon, Paris.

the central cupola to legislation and eloquence gave these themes a salience reinforced by the placing of the ideal point of view for the entire ensemble beneath this central cupola.[13]

Johnson aptly observes that this symmetrical configuration is reinforced by illusionistic cornices crowning the fictive oculus of each cupola. Whereas the cornice of the central dome is depicted with radial symmetry, the cornices of the four other cupolas are increasingly foreshortened in proportion to their distance from the central bay.[14] The placement of the cupola with Lycurgus, Numa, Demosthenes, and Cicero in this privileged position was analogous to the library's acquisition policy, which had changed in the early 1830s. Since the establishment of the collection during the Revolution, the librarians had sought rare and beautiful books and manuscripts in all fields. Under Louis-Philippe, this policy yielded to the pursuit of materials on legislation.[15]

The central cupola, the visual and the thematic fulcrum of the decorative cycle, includes representations of two familiar lawgivers. Lycurgus, bearing a laurel branch and gesturing toward a sacrificial goat, asks the Pythian Sibyl about the durability of Sparta's laws (Fig. 59). In the adjacent pendentive, Numa reclines gracefully in a clearing, conversing with his legislative muse, the nymph Egeria (Plate 8), who sits like a relaxed monarch, with leaves for a crown and a stem for a scepter. A deer grazes nearby. Lycurgus's consultation of the sibyl and Numa's woodland conversation suggest the authority and calm intimacy the great library offered readers.

We have seen how the divine inspiration of these legendary legislators was repeatedly invoked in the chambers of the Council of State to forge a noble pedigree for the Charter of 1814 and to glorify the Bourbon monarchy. A sheet of studies for the legislation paintings in the Palais-Bourbon library suggests derivation from the Council of State suite, for which Delacroix had painted *Justinian Drafting His Laws.*[16] This sheet, with the notations "Muhammad and his angel," "Numa and the nymph," "Charlemagne and a Christian angel," "Moses and God," and "the people receiving the law" (among others) also bears two sketches, which, like the Council of State *Justinian,* show an authoritative figure accompanied by an inspirational genius (cf. Fig. 60 and Plate 6).[17] That the artist had this Bourbon decorative cycle in mind when elaborating legislation subjects for the library is further suggested by notes on this sheet linking the "emancipation of the serfs" and "Fields of May" to "progress in civilization and the legislation

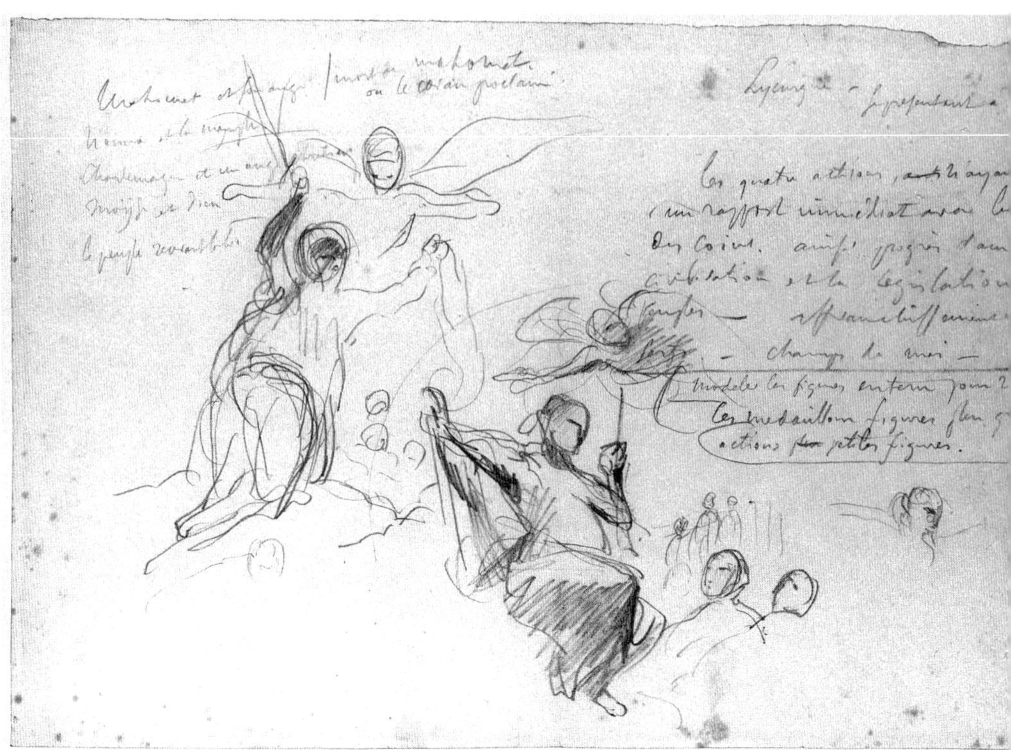

FIG. 60.   E. Delacroix, studies for legislation cupola of Palais-Bourbon library. Cabinet des Dessins, Louvre, Paris.

of peoples." The emancipation of the serfs and the Fields of May (general assemblies in which Charlemagne met with notables of the empire) were both examples of medieval monarchic reform dear to the Bourbon Restoration. Blondel's decoration of the main assembly room of the Council of State (1827) included a fictive bronze relief, *The Emancipation of the Serfs by Louis VI,* as a historical example of the enlightened royal legislative prerogative that had culminated in the constitutional Charter of 1814. And the preamble of that Bourbon Charter refers to the Fields of May as one of the Old Regime institutions that, having so often given proof of "zeal for the interests of the people, of fidelity to and respect for the authority of kings," was being replaced by the Chamber of Deputies.

Although in the Palais-Bourbon library Delacroix drew on the iconographic tradition, practiced under Napoleon and during the Restoration, that associates the legislator with divinity, the *Lycurgus* and *Numa* pendentives, like his *Justinian* for the Council of State, have an expressive vitality that sets them apart from earlier representations of ancient legislators, which were stock accessories to narrowly didactic programs. Delacroix's pendentives are narrative vignettes, the *Lycurgus* charged with dramatic expectation, the *Numa* infused with pastoral calm.

The theme of divine inspiration treated in the *Lycurgus* and *Numa* pendentives is echoed elsewhere in the library. In the poetry cupola, the sleeping Hesiod is inspired by a levitating muse in a serene floral setting like that in which Numa converses with the nymph Egeria (cf. Fig. 61 and Plate 8). Socrates, in the philosophy-history cupola, is accompanied, in the artist's words, by his "genius or familiar, who was perhaps only solitude itself or meditation, in which the true sages have always reinvigorated their souls and have drawn profound inspiration."[18] The philosopher, set apart by his red clothing from the somber, solitary grove, seems as dependent on the conventions of evangelical portraiture as the compositional sketches on the sheet of studies for the legislation and eloquence cupola (cf. Figs. 60 and 62).

Eloquence was a subject germane to the Chamber of Deputies. The French legislature had, since its revolutionary beginning, cultivated artful oration, a practice silenced by Napoleon but resumed under the Restoration and July Monarchy. The deliberations of the Chamber, spread daily before the newspaper-reading public, were conducted in the great tradition of parliamentary debate that the architect Joly invoked proudly in his publication of the Palais-Bourbon renovations.[19] Eloquence is represented in the central cupola by two famous orators of Greece and Rome who had long had a home in the Palais-Bourbon. The pose and physique of Demosthenes, who addresses the waves to accustom himself to the tumult of the Athenian assemblies, recall those of a bare-chested statue of him by Antoine-Léonard Dupasquier commissioned under the Directory for the assembly hall of the Council of Five Hundred and moved to the new library's entry hall in the course of Joly's remodeling of the legislative palace (cf. Figs. 63 and 64). Along with the representation of Demosthenes in the central cupola is one of Cicero, who vigorously points to the ill-gotten treasure of the wicked magistrate Verres (Fig. 65). François Masson's sculpture of the Roman orator was moved, with Dupasquier's *Demosthenes,* from the old Salle des Séances to the new library's entry hall.[20]

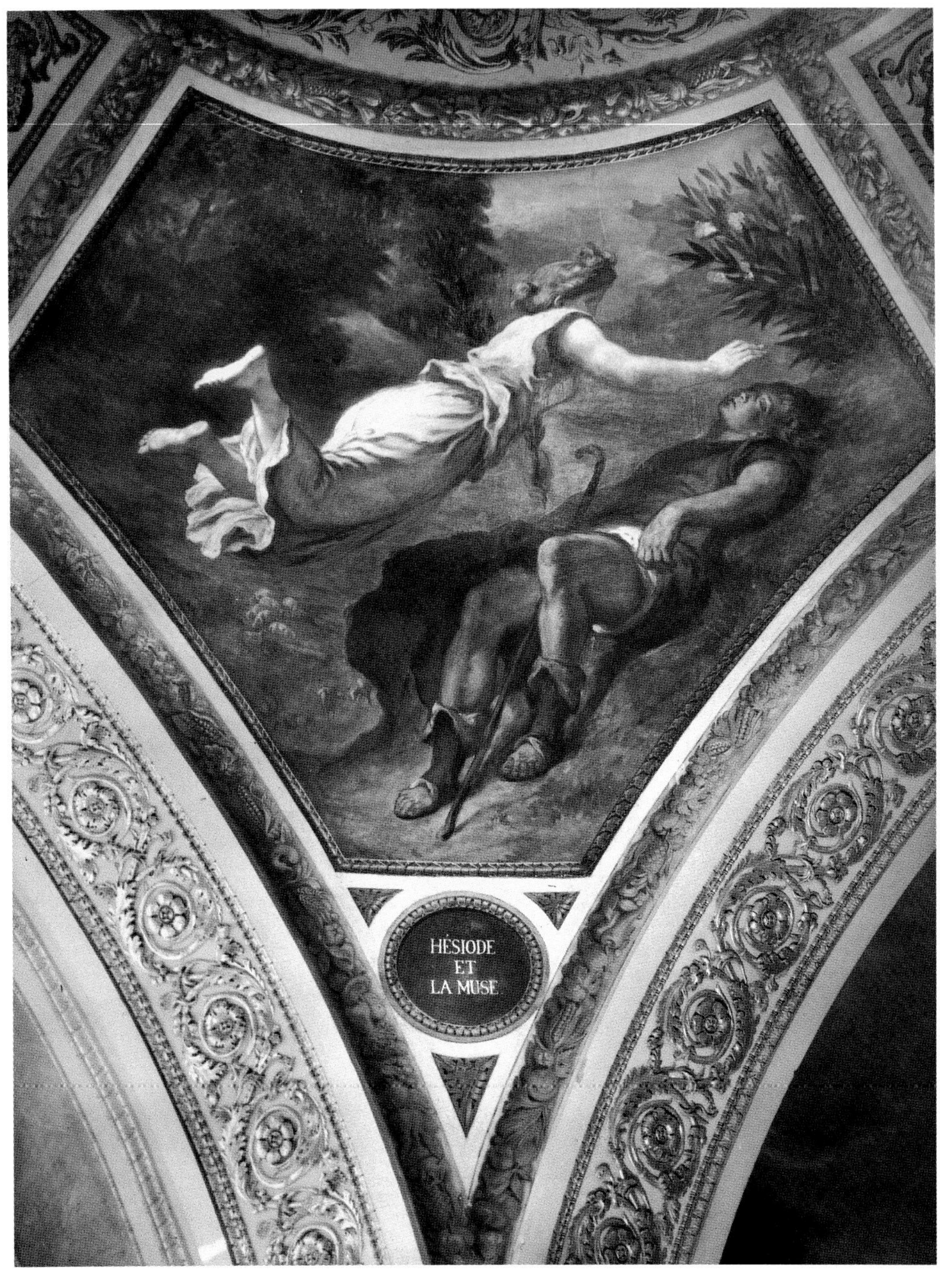

FIG. 61.   E. Delacroix, *Hesiod and the Muse.* Palais-Bourbon, Paris.

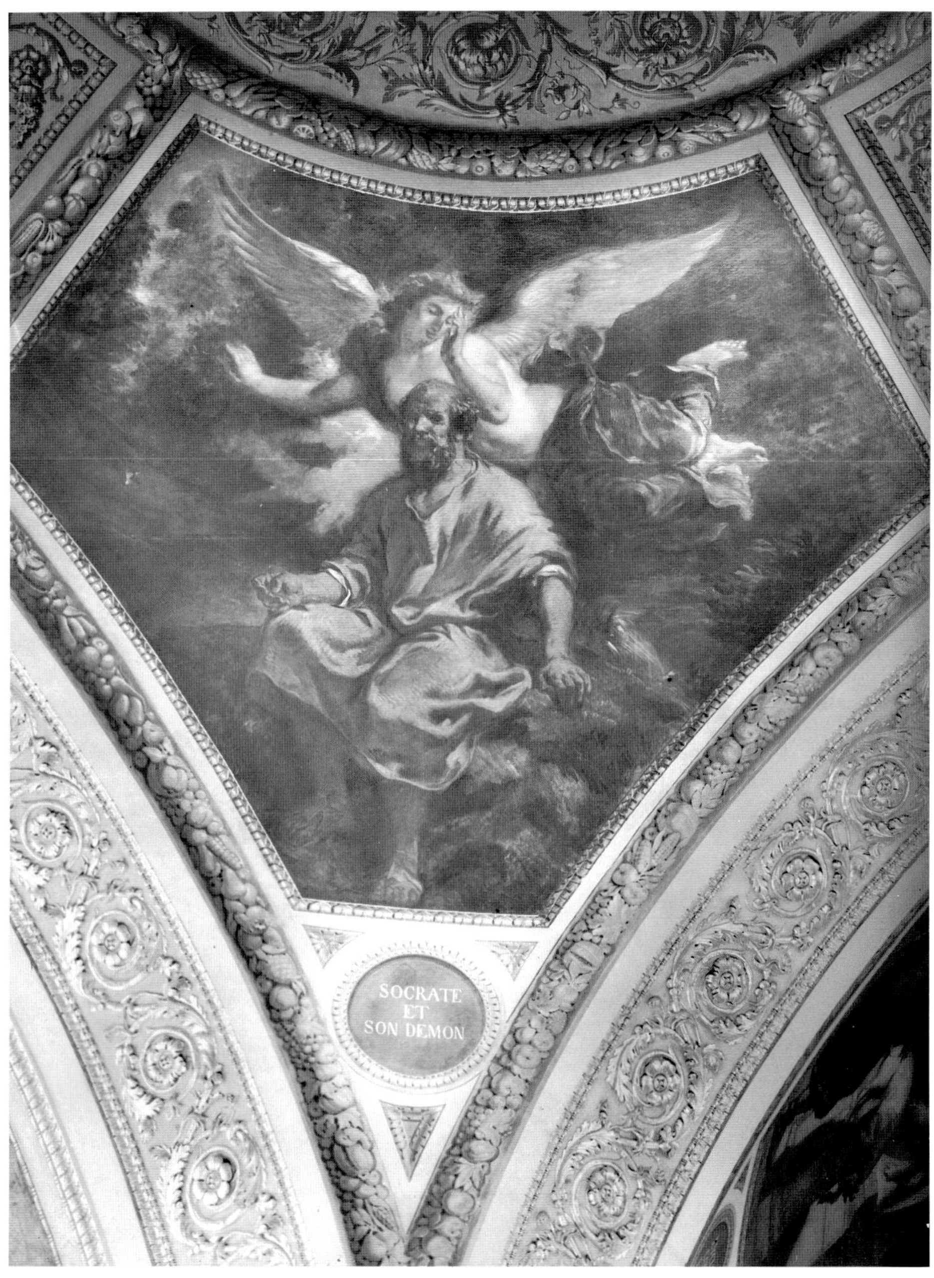

FIG. 62.   E. Delacroix, *Socrates and His Familiar.* Palais-Bourbon, Paris.

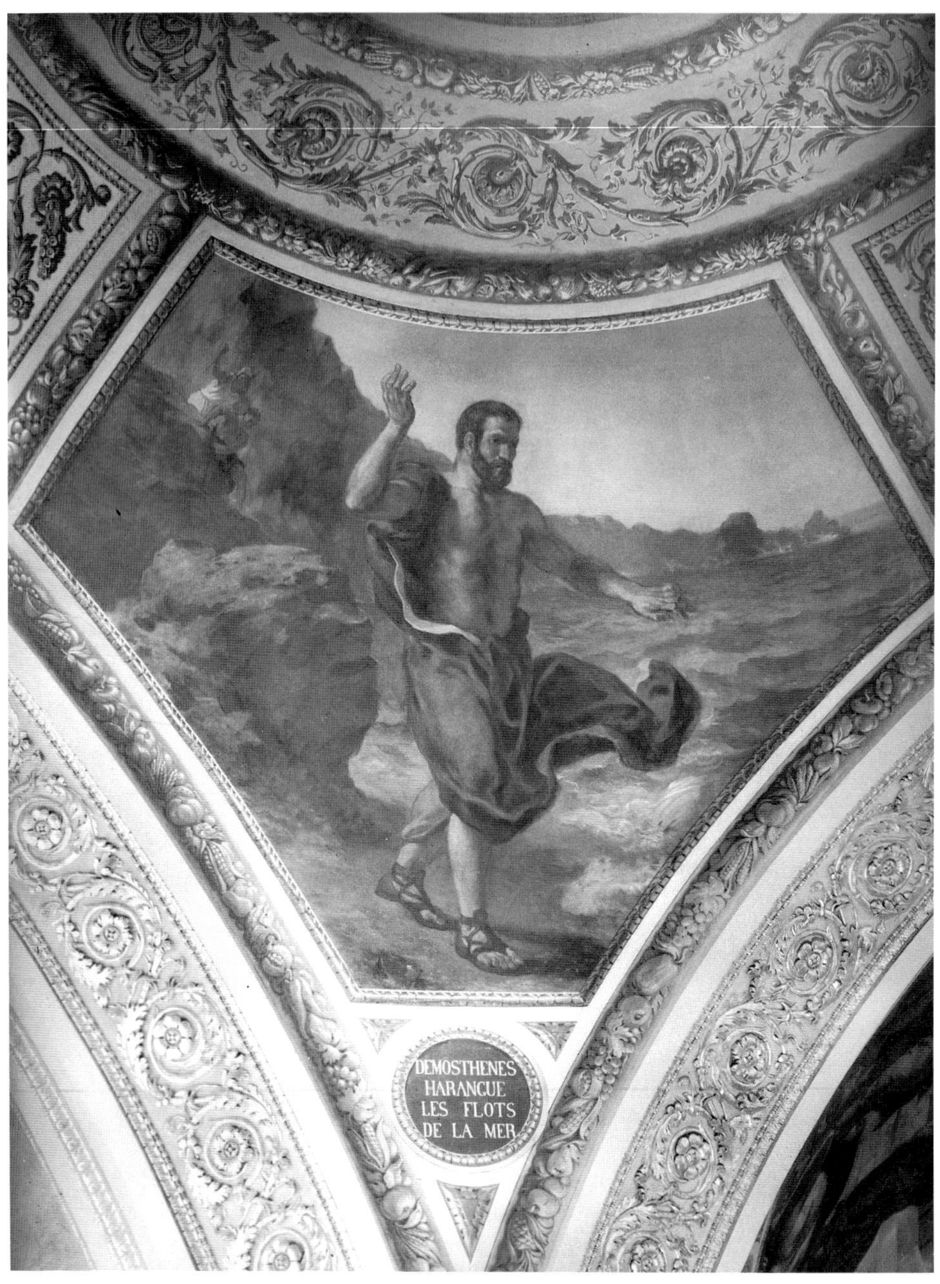

FIG. 63.   E. Delacroix, *Demosthenes Harangues the Waves of the Sea*. Palais-Bourbon, Paris.

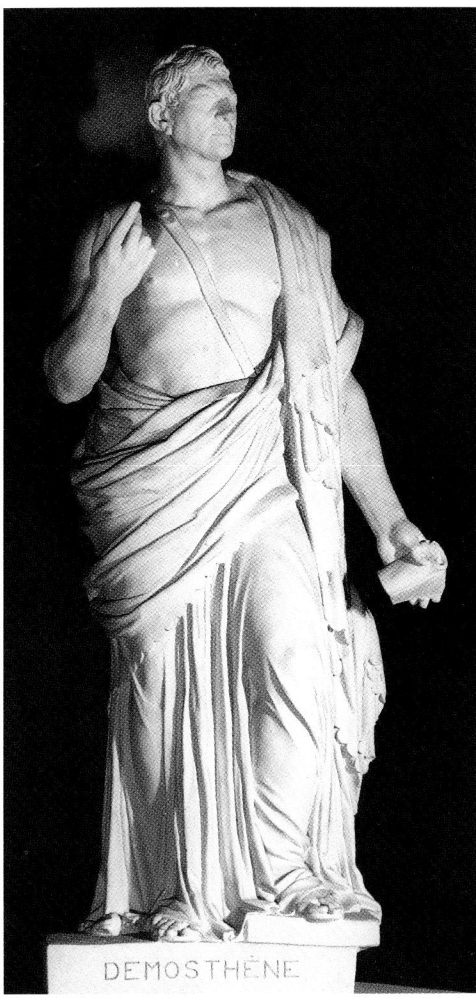

FIG. 64.   A.-L. Dupasquier,
Demosthenes, 1796–98. Palais-Bourbon,
Paris.

The two great hemicycles representing the birth and death of classical civilization and counterpointing the themes of peace and war also pay homage to the
unity of law and civilization. Under the auspices of Athena and Ceres, Orpheus
introduces an untamed company of old and young to the civilization that would
eventually produce the humanistic studies represented in the pendentive paintings
(Fig. 58). Orpheus, traditionally identified as the first lawgiver, is referred to as the
"poetic legislator" in a review of the paintings.[21] The order and calm brought by
Orpheus are reflected in the blue-green sweep of mountains enclosing a stable, if
rather conventional, pyramidal composition.

At the opposite end of the library, Attila tramples civilization, which collapses in anarchy before his marauding host (Plate 7). The somber emotional tone of this scene reverberates in the clash of red and blue-green, in the diagonal thrust of limbs, and in the broad handling of Attila's charger, which occupies center stage beneath a dark cloud. A winged putto flees before the invader with a lyre and scroll, representing music and literature,[22] attributes that also refer to Orpheus, who holds a scroll. Beside this putto, near a crowned and fallen allegory of Italy, the art of eloquence is represented by a tearful woman fleeing with a caduceus and laurel leaves.[23]

Hopmans has dated the conception of the Orpheus and Attila hemicycles as subsequent to the publication of two articles in the *Revue des deux mondes,* January 1 and 15, 1843, passages of which Delacroix copied on sheets bearing studies for the library hemicycles. The first passage refers to James Barry's painting *Orpheus Instructing a Savage People in Theology and the Arts of Social Life* (1777–84) in the Royal Society of Arts building, London. The second compares Napoleon's destruction of Moscow to the ravages of Attila.[24] Although this discovery demonstrates that the hemicycle subjects were determined surprisingly late, Orpheus the civilizing legislator was nonetheless, like Attila and the barbarian invasion, a familiar point of reference in Delacroix's France. The familiarity of these motifs, moreover, made them all the more appropriate for use in a state commission.

According to classical tradition, Orpheus was the initiator of law and civilization. The treatment of this theme by Horace in the *Ars Poetica* was imitated by Boileau in his *Poetic Art* (1674), that canonical monument of French classicism.[25] Boileau emphasized the civilizing force of the first laws associated with Orpheus:

> Before reason, borne by speech,
> Had instructed humankind and brought it laws,
> People knew only base instinct.
> Dispersed in the woods, they ran off to feed.
> Force usurped right and equity;
> Murder went unpunished.
> But finally the harmonious skill of discourse
> Tempered the rudeness of these savage customs;
> Assembled the people scattered in the forests;
> Enclosed cities with walls and ramparts;

Frightened insolence with the threat of punishment;
And placed feeble innocence under the law's protection.
This order, they say, sprang from the first verses.
From those have arisen the rumors heard by all,
That tigers were tamed by the tones of Orpheus's voice
As it resounded among the mountains of Thrace.[26]

More recently, the Lyonnais mystic Pierre-Simon Ballanche had treated the theme at length in his philosophical novel *Orphée* (1829).[27] Delacroix's placement of the slaughter of a deer and the cultivation of the soil at either side of the central group of Orpheus and his rustic pupils recalls a lesson of this odd but ambitious book that so delighted Delacroix's friend George Sand.[28] Orpheus, revealing "the foundations of the laws on which human institutions rest," teaches that "the first way to civilize men is to teach them to sow wheat." People will remain in a savage state, Ballanche maintains, as long as they continue to live from day to day, hunting animals and eating roots and wild fruit.[29]

Delacroix was not the first to associate Orpheus with the national legislature. The reverse of the identification medals by Nicolas-Marie Gatteaux, distributed under the Directory to the Council of Five Hundred and the Council of Ancients, bears an emblematic panoply that includes an Orphic lyre (Fig. 66; see obverse, Fig. 8). With ingenious economy, Gatteaux concealed the strings of the instrument behind the rods of a fasces topped by a Phrygian cap and flanked by boughs of laurel and oak. The arms of the instrument serve as the ends of two cornucopias. This design was repeated in medals for the legislature in successive years; examples are in the collection of the Palais-Bourbon library.

Attila and his barbarian hordes were as familiar as Orpheus to literate citizens under the July Monarchy. Since the beginning of the nineteenth century, the barbarian invasion had been a common point of reference for French authors. The motif was often employed—sometimes pejoratively, sometimes not—in the treatment of such large historical themes as the condition of France since the Revolution and the progress of democracy.[30] A distinguished example occurs in Lamartine's poem "Les Révolutions," written in early December 1831 under the influence of the insurrection in Lyon and published in 1832:

Levez-vous, Gaule et Germanie,
L'heure de la vengeance est là!

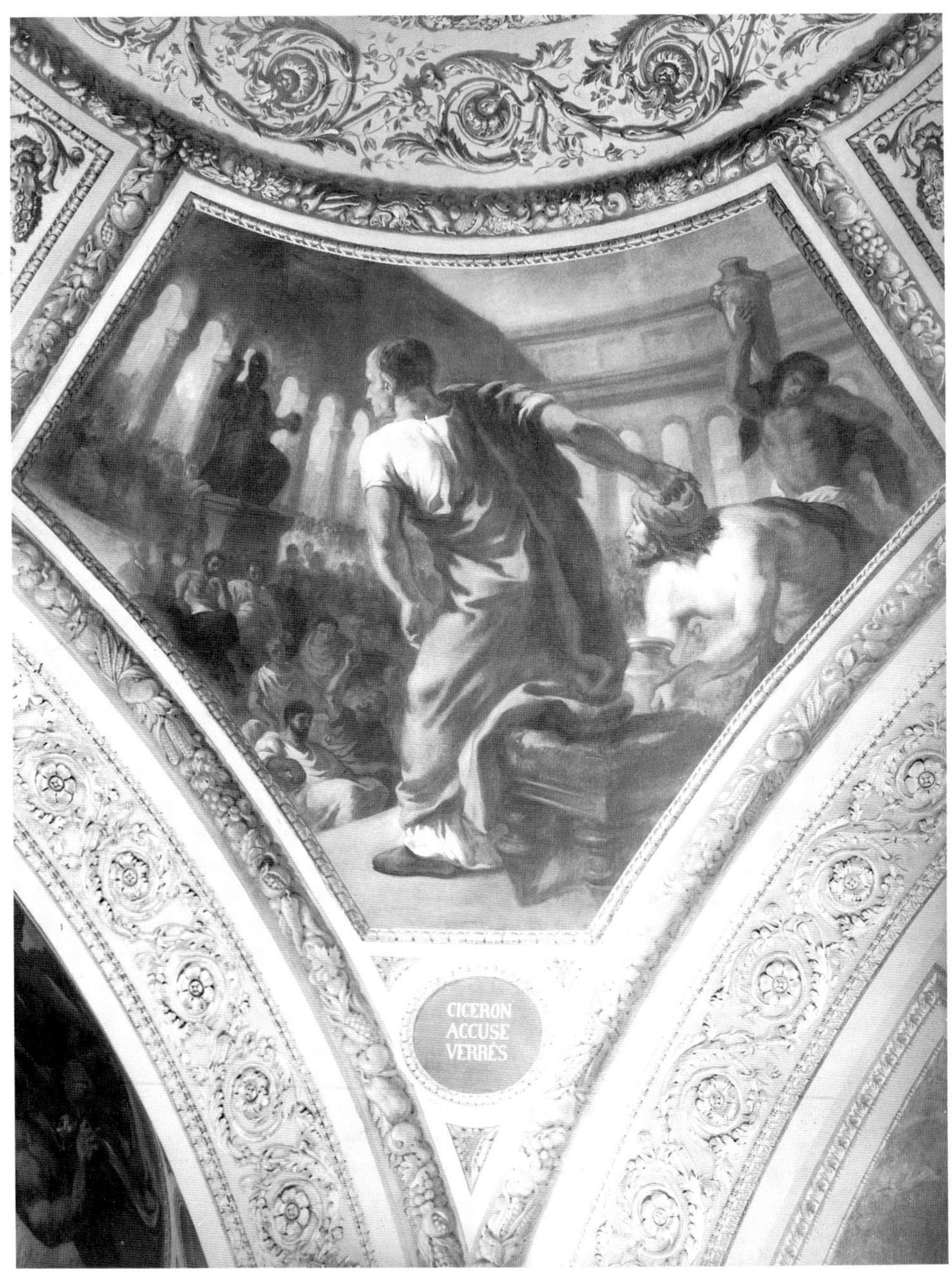

FIG. 65.   E. Delacroix, *Cicero Accuses Verres*. Palais-Bourbon, Paris.

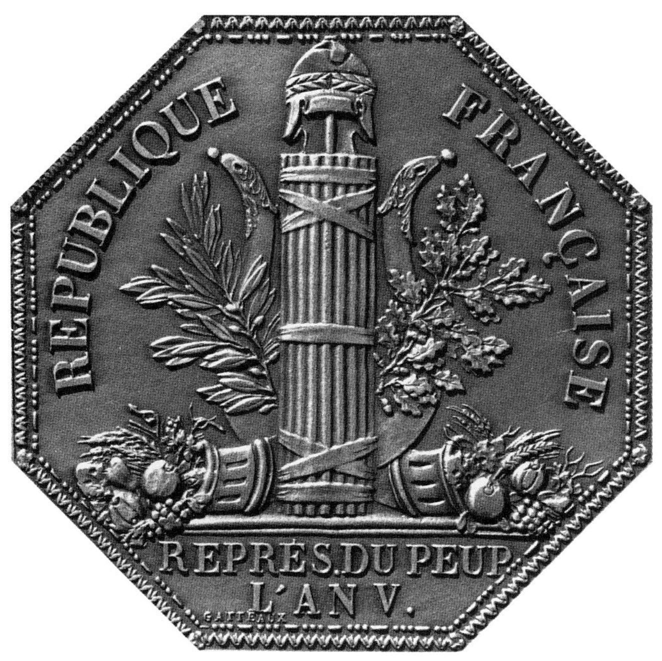

FIG. 66.   N.-M. Gatteaux, membership medal for Council of Ancients
(reverse), 1797. Musée de la Monnaie,
Paris.

Des ruines, c'est le génie
Qui prend les rênes d'Attila!
Lois, forum, dieux, faisceaux, tout croule;
Dans l'ornière de sang tout roule,
Tout s'éteint, tout fume. Il fait nuit,
Il fait nuit, pour que l'ombre encore
Fasse mieux éclater l'aurore
Du jour* où son doigt vous conduit![31]

Rise, Gaul and Germany,
The hour of vengeance has come!
The spirit of ruin
Drives Attila on!
Laws, forum, gods, fasces, all crumble;

*Christianity [Lamartine's note].

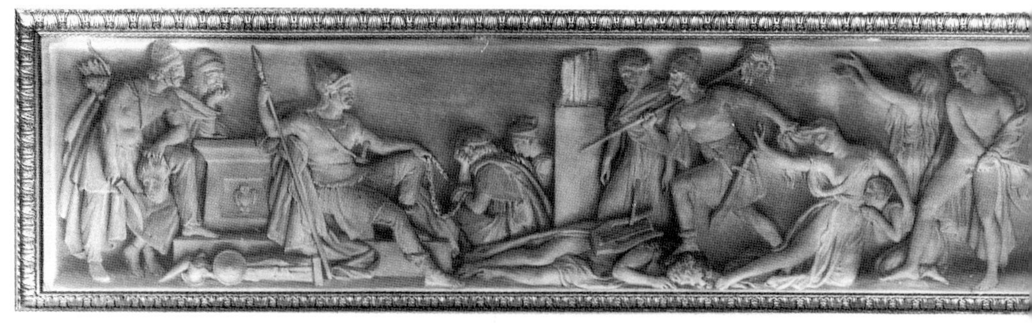

All tumble onto the bloody, rutted earth,
All are snuffed out, all smoke. Night has fallen,
Night has fallen so that against the darkness
The [Christian] dawn into which you are led
Will shine all the more brightly!

Although it is unlikely that Delacroix identified with Lamartine's Christian piety (later he said some unkind things about the poet),[32] the *vanitas* theme in this poem resembles that of Delacroix's pessimistic *Journal*.

Three images of barbarian invasion offer further examples of the theme. In the year following the commissioning of Delacroix's Council of State *Justinian*, Auguste Vinchon and Nicolas Gosse painted illusionistic reliefs in grisaille for the Louvre's Musée Charles X, including an *Orpheus Singing* as well as *The Barbarians Destroying the Monuments of Greece* (Salon of 1827).[33] In the latter, a slain Greek lies with a lyre pinned to his back by the shaft of a weapon (Fig. 67). Delacroix could have known, in reproduction, a grandiose *Battle of the Huns* by the Munich court painter Wilhelm von Kaulbach (1805–1874) in which barbarism and Christianity are locked in airborne combat (Fig. 68).[34] Although Delacroix would not have been impressed by the dry linearity and turgid melodrama of this

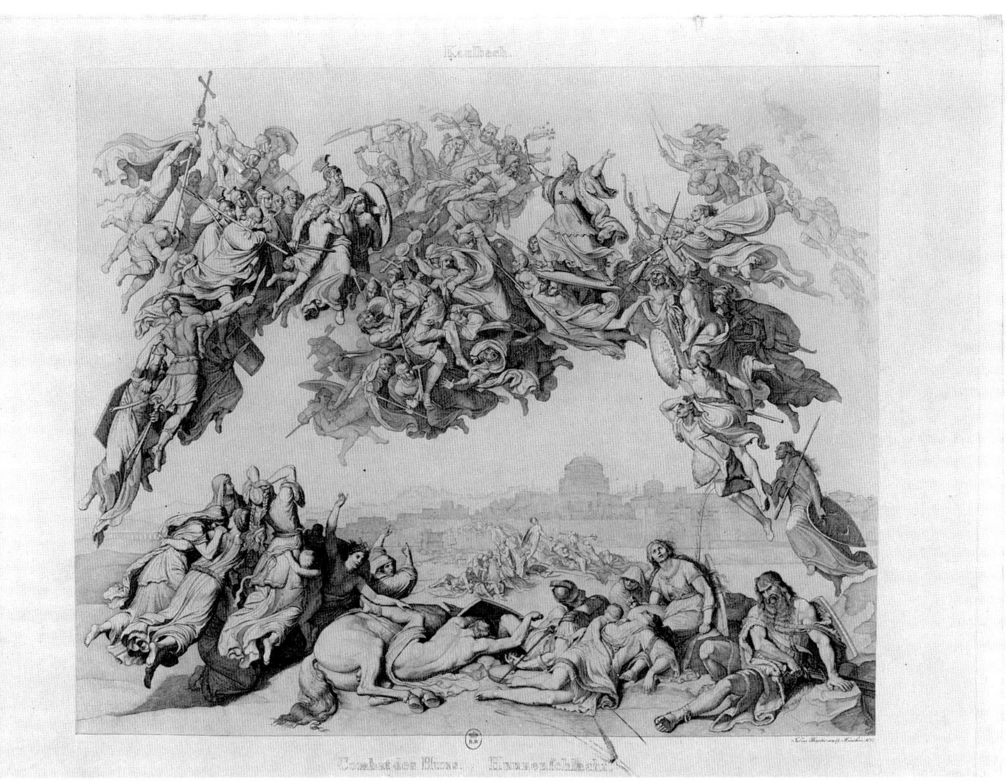

FIG. 68.   J. Thaeter after W. von
Kaulbach, *Battle of the Huns,* 1837.
Bibliothèque Nationale, Paris.

German image, both he and Kaulbach address the theme allegorically. The motif
of barbarian invasion also appeared in the popular satirical press. The October 13,
1831, issue of *La Caricature* included Denis-Auguste-Marie Raffet's pessimistic
"Barbarism and Cholera Morbus Enter Europe," which denounced the impotence
of France and the other European powers in the face of Russia's tyranny over
rebellious Poland (Fig. 69). The caricaturist links political oppression with the
looming specter of a cholera epidemic.[35]

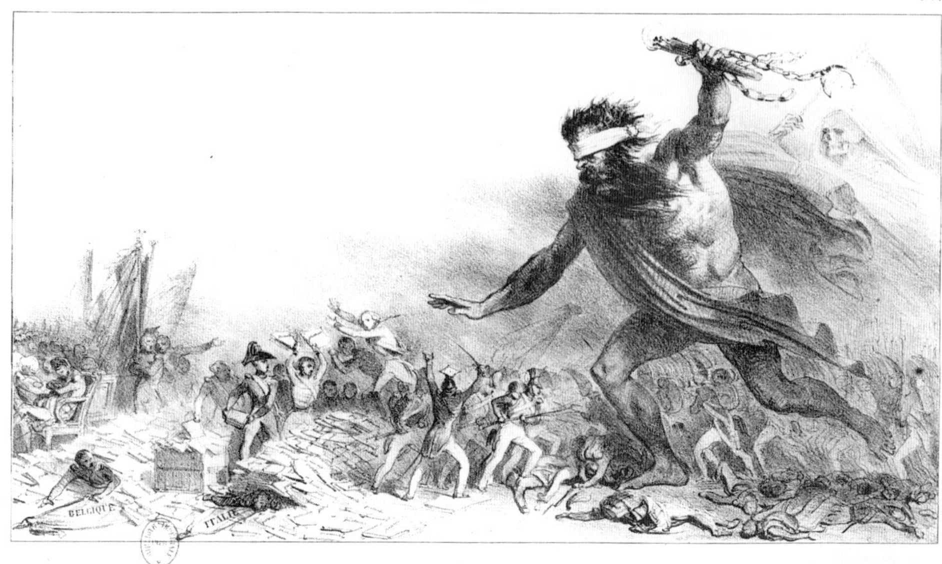

FIG. 69.   D.-A.-M. Raffet, "Barbarism and Cholera Morbus Enter Europe." *La Caricature,* October 13, 1831.

Whereas these images suggest that in the *Attila* hemicycle Delacroix employed a familiar motif, a more concrete analogy can be drawn between his representation of Italy, defenseless and bare-breasted, under the hoofs of the Hun's steed and that of a mother trampled in the foreground of *The Destruction of Jerusalem* (Fig. 70) by François-Joseph Heim (1787–1865).[36] In this vast Restoration *machine,* Heim portrayed an invasion as terrible as that of Attila, "the scourge of God," and, like it, providentially ordained. The destruction of Jerusalem by Titus was traditionally viewed as divine punishment of the Jews for their rejection of Christ.[37]

Delacroix was not the first to pair an Orphic legislator with Attila. In *Attila et le troubadour,* a play staged once in 1824, the invader is subdued by the patriotic French troubadour Roger, who accompanies himself on his lyre as he sings of his vocation: "He is the legislator of burgeoning nations. . . . He cultivates those he

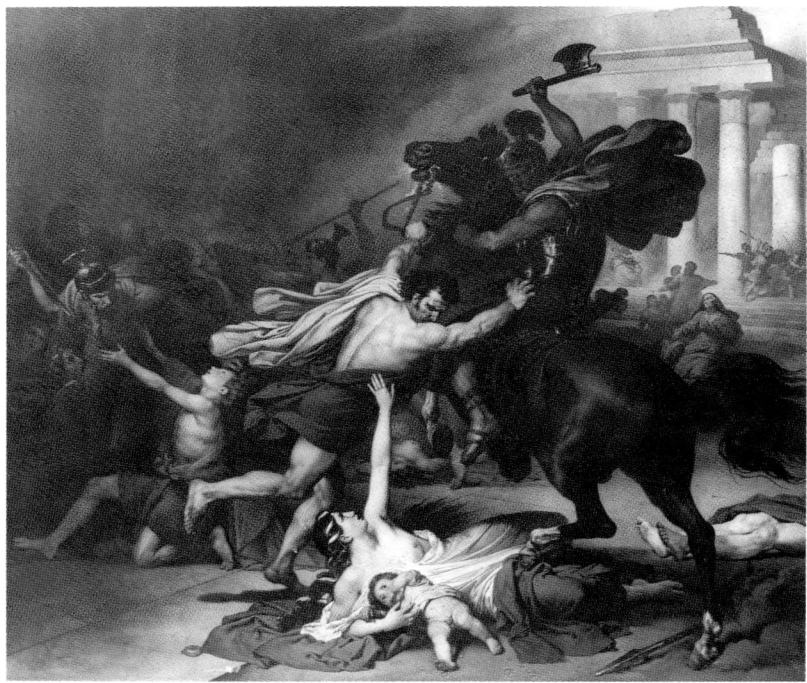

FIG. 70.   F.-J. Heim, *The Destruction of Jerusalem,* Salon of 1824. Louvre, Paris.

assembles. His art masters hearts and minds. His voice brings harvests and cities, commerce and laws to the sterile plains. And in his poor sanctuary, he is richer, more tranquil, and greater than Attila."[38]

Even if Orpheus, Attila, and the barbarian invasion were familiar motifs, Delacroix's choice of them for the Palais-Bourbon library was as bold as the style in which he painted *Attila.* Like the *Orpheus* and *Attila* paintings, Triqueti's monumental *Protecting Law* and *Avenging Law* reliefs—whose position in the nearby Salle Louis-Philippe parallels that of the library hemicycles—represent the dependence of civilization upon law. Whereas Triqueti gives this theme conventional, if elegant, allegorical form, Delacroix's hemicycles are imbued with a mythic amplitude that sets them apart from most official allegory of the period. Delacroix, moreover, offers a pathos-ridden contrast between the calm dawn of civilization

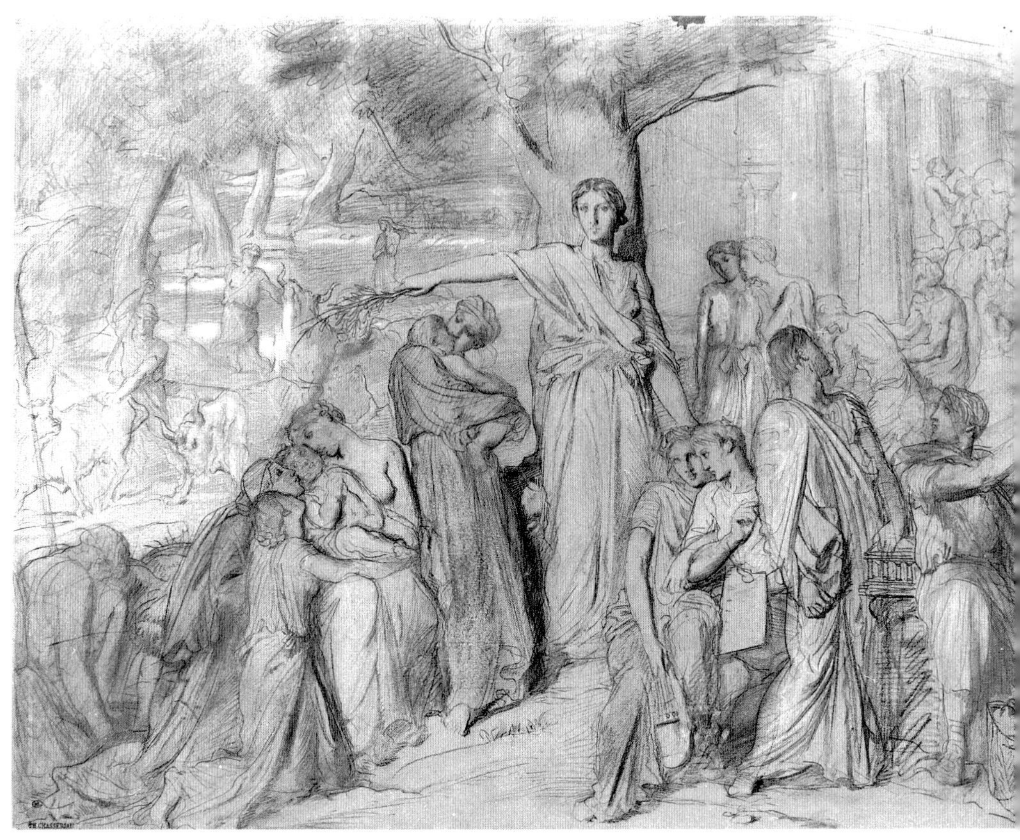

FIG. 71.   T. Chassériau, study for
Peace for Cour des Comptes, 1844–48.
Cabinet des Dessins, Louvre, Paris.

and its violent end, whereas Triqueti idealistically glorifies the law. In their setting, Triqueti's reliefs constitute an abstract allegorical component of a program
that celebrates French constitutional law (its principal ornament was Jacquot's
colossal statue *Louis-Philippe Swearing Loyalty to the Charter*). Delacroix's decoration of the library, in contrast, operates on the plane of legend rather than historical specificity.

Allegory in the library hemicycles shows none of the narrow didacticism found
elsewhere in the Palais-Bourbon; Delacroix's breadth of reference recalls the
epic polarity of Ingres's *Age of Gold* and *Age of Iron* murals at the Château of

Dampierre (begun in 1843 and left unfinished in 1850). The murals *War* and *Peace* (now mostly destroyed) that Delacroix's young admirer Théodore Chassériau painted in the ill-fated Palais d'Orsay for the Court of Accounts (1844–48) reveal a similar thematic breadth; I reproduce a study for *Peace* (Fig. 71).[39] In a general way, Delacroix's counterpoint of Orpheus and Attila reflects a fascination with universal history and providential design that was widespread under the July Monarchy. But Delacroix gives no hint of the dogmatic optimism of contemporary utopian theorists vis-à-vis human history and destiny. The skeptical artist had little patience with would-be saviors of humanity.[40]

The central cupola, both honoring and setting a high example for the Chamber of Deputies with references to the legendary orators and lawgivers of antiquity, stands equidistant from the hemicycle paintings representing civilization's birth and collapse. Delacroix alluded to the Chamber of Deputies in the library paintings in other ways as well.

All twenty pendentives refer to the disciplines represented in the library collection. This loosely defined program could have accommodated an almost limitless variety of subjects; such openness led to an ongoing revision of the themes projected for inclusion. Although any attempt to link the remaining sixteen pendentives to the legislative function of the library would misconstrue the irregular development of the cycle, some of the subjects seem to have been selected for their thematic relevance to the function of the Palais-Bourbon.

For example, *The Drachma of Tribute* (Fig. 72), an uncommon subject in the theology cupola that especially puzzled one commentator,[41] illustrates the fulfillment of Christ's prediction that money to pay a tax would be found in a fish (Matthew 17:24). It is one of the most complex compositions in the library. The astonishment of Peter and the other witnesses to the miracle is accented by great flourishes of windswept cloth that cut irregular silhouettes against the seaside sky. Like the decision to grant pride of place to the legislation-eloquence paintings, the choice of this story of how the payment of a tax received divine sanction was particularly appropriate to the institutional setting of the library. For tax legislation was not only one of the principal responsibilities of the Chamber of Deputies but also the sole domain in which the charter granted the deputies hegemony in the legislative process.[42]

Delacroix's concern to address the library's function could account for his curious idea of devoting a pendentive to the theme of education. As Hopmans has

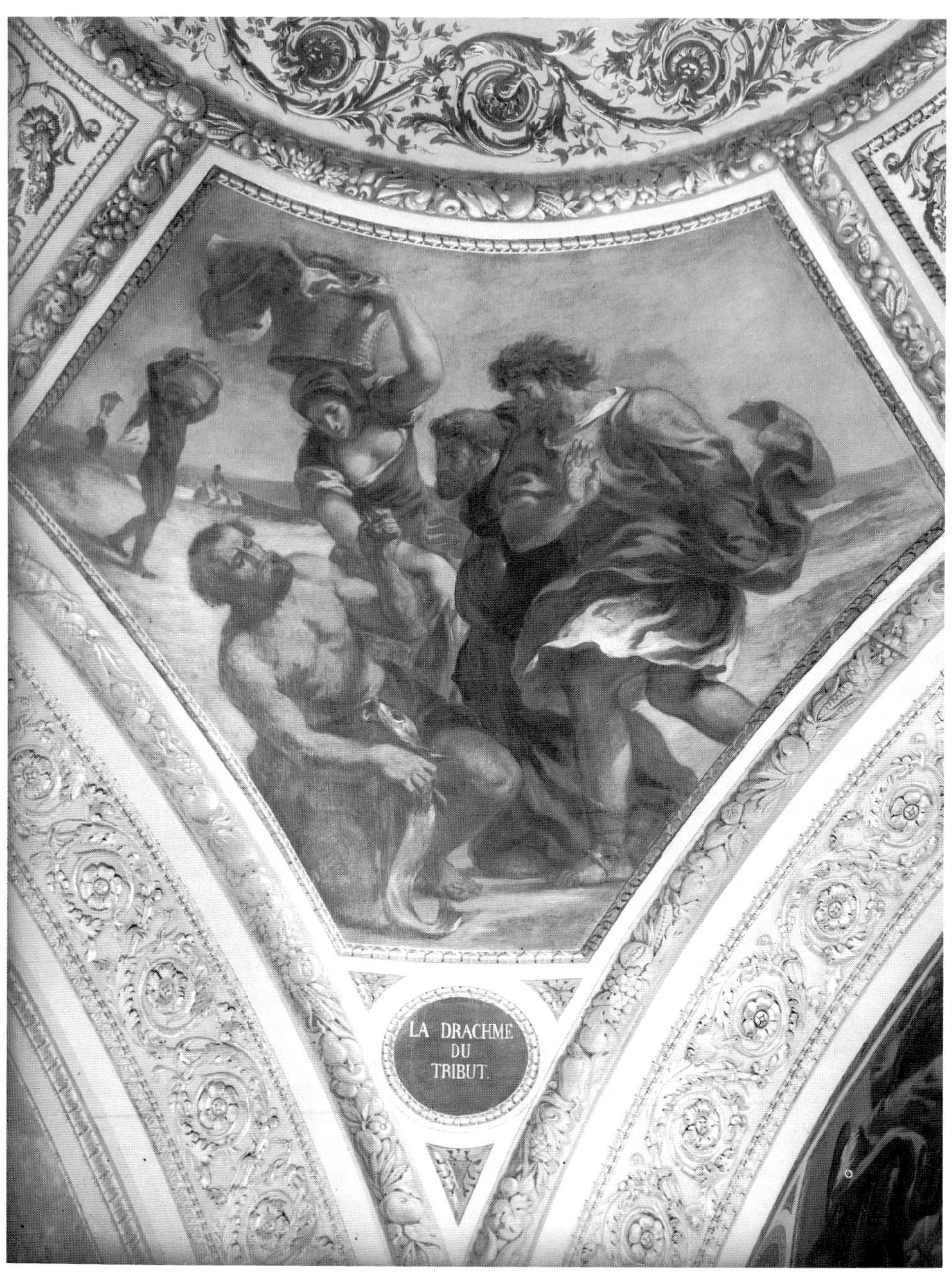

FIG. 72.   E. Delacroix, *The Drachma of Tribute*. Palais-Bourbon, Paris.

pointed out, he departed from Brunet's system of book classification and included *The Education of Achilles* in the poetry cupola, despite its apparent thematic inconsistency with the three companion pendentives.[43] *The Education of Achilles* provides a buoyant and muscular counterpart to the adjacent scene of Hesiod and his floating muse (cf. Figs. 61 and 73). This was clearly a sympathetic subject for the exalted imagination of the artist. But two considerations should be added to the "subject's special charm," which Hopmans sees as the principal reason for its inclusion. Clearly, *The Education of Achilles* refers to the function of the library. But its theme seems all the more appropriate in light of the notion, inherited from the Enlightenment, that the legislator was a moral tutor, responsible for educating the citizenry in virtue and civic patriotism.[44]

Before receiving the library commission, Delacroix had proposed an aggressively nationalistic program for the ceiling of the Salle des Pas Perdus (grand foyer) of the Palais-Bourbon, a surface eventually covered, to his disgust, by Horace Vernet.[45] Delacroix's unrealized project, illustrating historical examples of France's military and cultural hegemony, is echoed by two pendentives with broader historical reference and greater subtlety that offer models of patriotic conduct to the Chamber of Deputies. In the science cupola, the incorruptible Hippocrates refuses to treat the Persian enemy despite their offer of treasure. The adjacent *Death of Pliny the Elder* (Fig. 74) also offers an example of patriotic resolve. "Pliny studied nature to better admire Italy; he boasted of his country as the most beautiful"—thus sang the heroine of Madame de Staël's popular novel *Corinne, or Italy* (1807) at Cape Miseno, in an episode made all the more famous when François Gérard (1770–1837) painted it (Fig. 75).[46] "In pursuit of scientific knowledge . . . he left this very promontory to observe Vesuvius through the flames, and these consumed him."[47] With a rhetoric of *terribilità* that recalls Gérard's *Corinne*, Delacroix's Pliny dictates to his scribe as he sacrifices himself to science and the glory of Italy.[48] This inspired dictation is derived from that of the Council of State *Justinian*.

The theme of devotion to the homeland is echoed by three subjects that evoke the pain of exile, each a mournful counterpart to the patriotism of Hippocrates and Pliny: the Babylonian captivity, the expulsion of Adam and Eve, and Ovid in exile. The surprising inclusion of these subjects in the theology and poetry cupolas stems from an attraction to a theme that was an integral part of modern French history, from the flight of the aristocracy during the Revolution to the

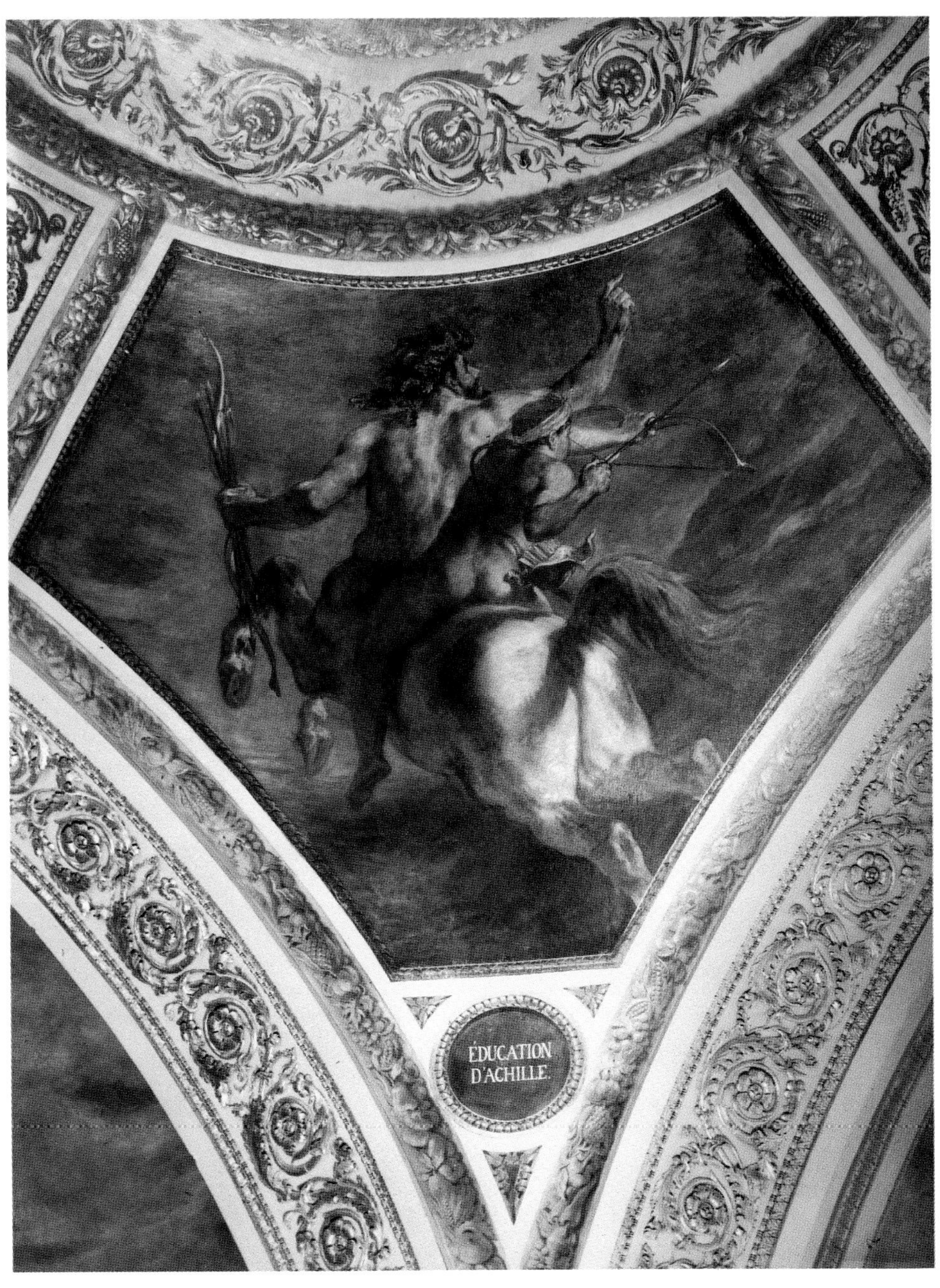

FIG. 73.   E. Delacroix, *The Education of Achilles*. Palais-Bourbon, Paris.

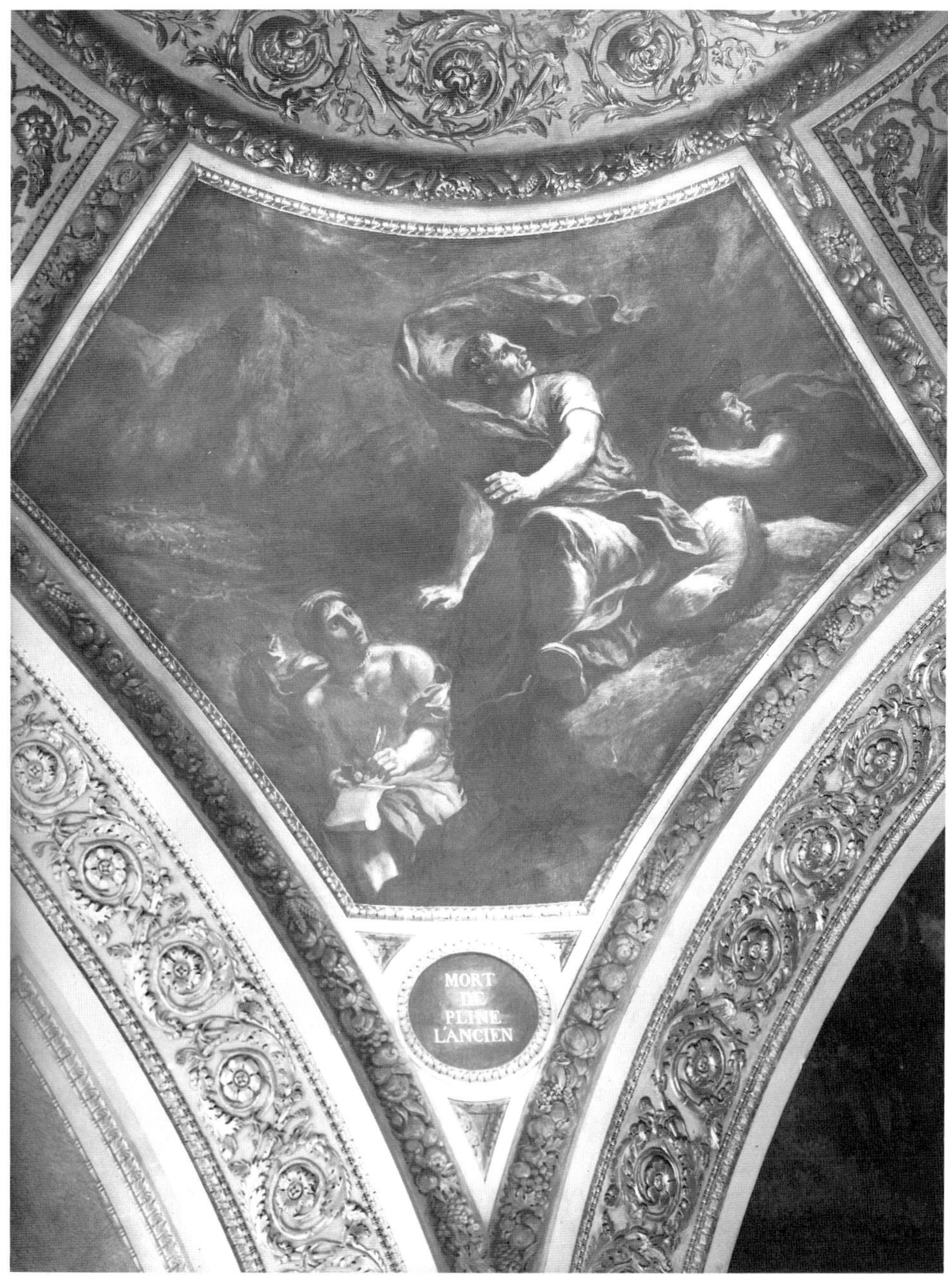

FIG. 74.   E. Delacroix, *The Death of Pliny the Elder*. Palais-Bourbon, Paris.

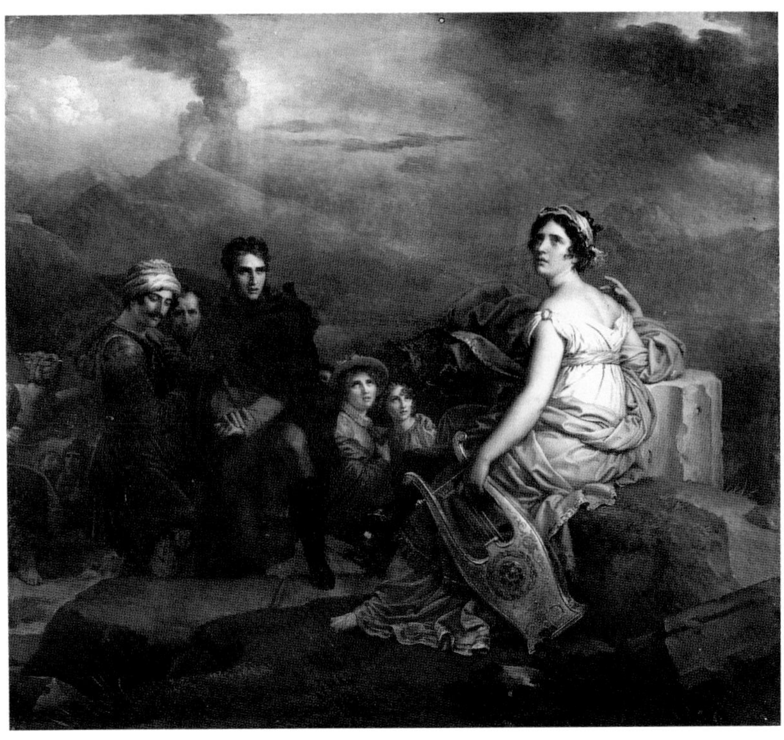

FIG. 75.　　F. Gérard, *Corinne at Cape Miseno,* 1822. Musée des Beaux-Arts, Lyon.

confinement of Napoleon on the island of Saint Helena. "Everywhere . . . the exile elicits a generous interest," according to the contemporary *Encyclopédie des gens du monde;* "one is moved by the sight of him, and one feels then how piteous is he who must drag out his existence on foreign soil, far from the tender mother who carried him in her womb and nourished him with her milk, far from a white-haired father who . . . fears to die without seeing his son!"[49] Such feelings were fanned by the plight of Poland following the failed insurrection of 1831, when such Poles as Delacroix's dear friend Chopin found sanctuary in Paris.[50]

In Delacroix's *Babylonian Captivity,* "a weeping family, seated at the edge of a river, sadly contemplates the waves while thinking of home."[51] The subject comes from Psalm 137 in which the Hebrews, driven from their homeland following the fall of Jerusalem, vow never to sing their national songs before their captors (Fig. 76). Long admired by French authors, this psalm was one of the most

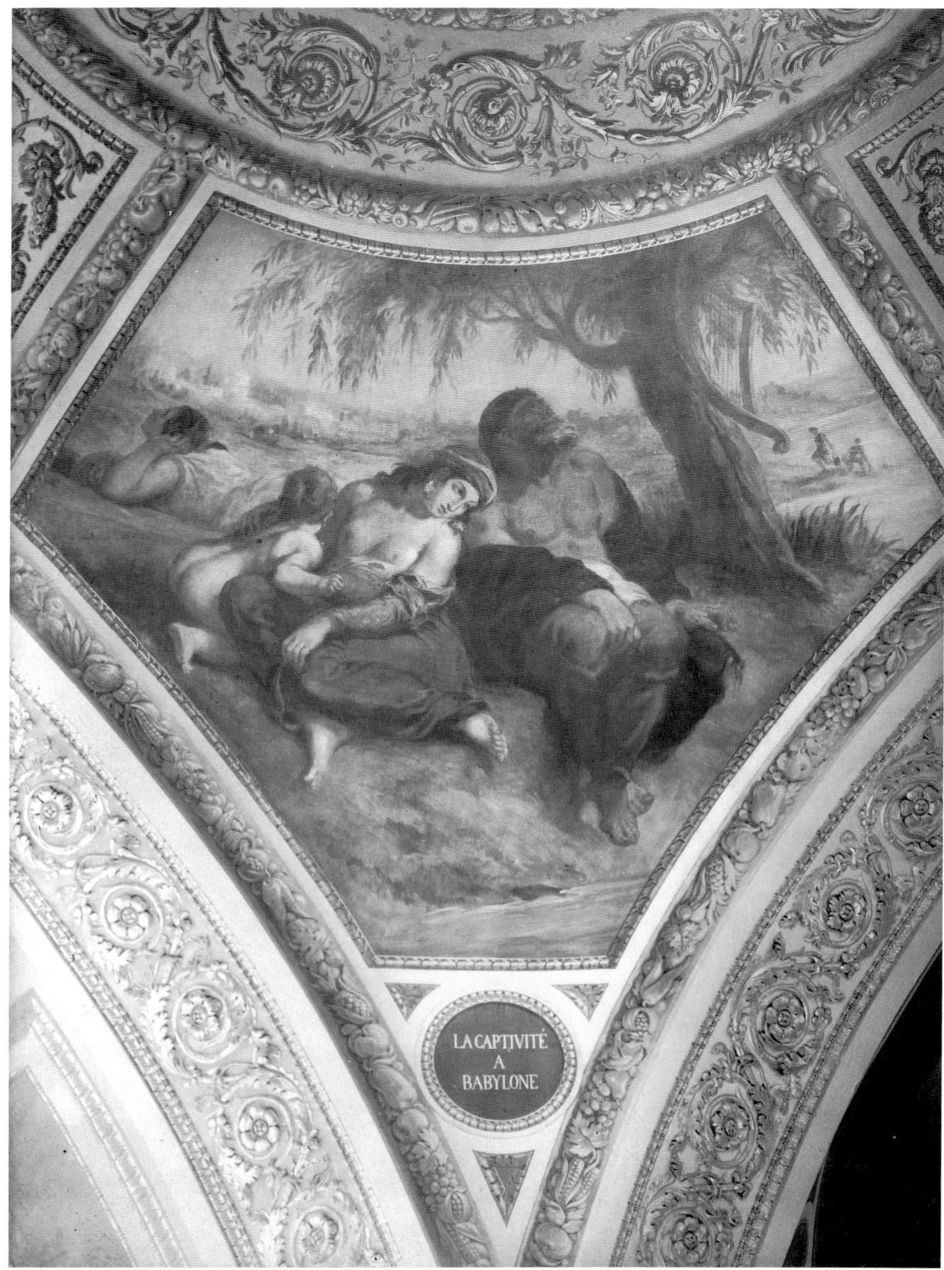

FIG. 76.   E. Delacroix, *The Babylonian Captivity.* Palais-Bourbon, Paris.

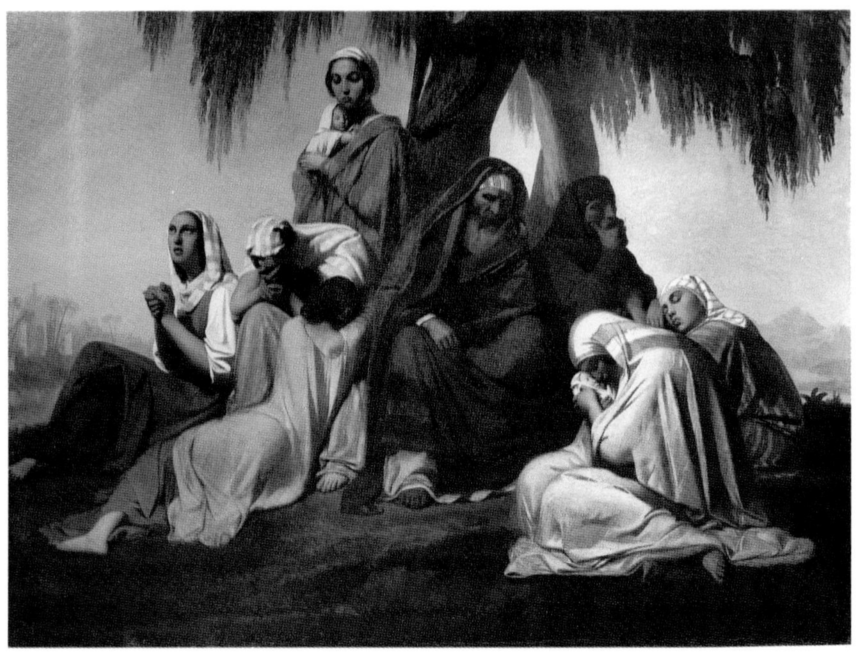

frequently translated and paraphrased passages of the Bible during the eighteenth century.[52] Racine imitated it in the chorus for *Esther;* Lord Byron paraphrased it in *A Selection of Hebrew Melodies* (1815; translated into French, 1821);[53] and the hero of Casimir Delavigne's "Jeune diacre, ou La Grèce chrétienne" (1822) invoked it. Delavigne's poem, written to elicit sympathy for the cause of Greek independence, provided Delacroix with the subject for a sketch.[54]

Before Delacroix painted it in the theology cupola of the library, the Babylonian captivity theme had appeared in Salon paintings (Figs. 77, 78) by Romain Cazes (1810–1881) and Angel Joyard (1809–?).[55] Louis de Planet (1814–1875), a close friend of Cazes's and one of Delacroix's principal assistants on the library commission, also treated the subject in a painting that may have inspired the library pendentive (Fig. 79).[56] With neither Planet's overblown gesticulation nor Cazes's and Joyard's ingratiating details of costume and setting, the Delacroix pendentive has a poignant breadth and economy that are even more pronounced in a related

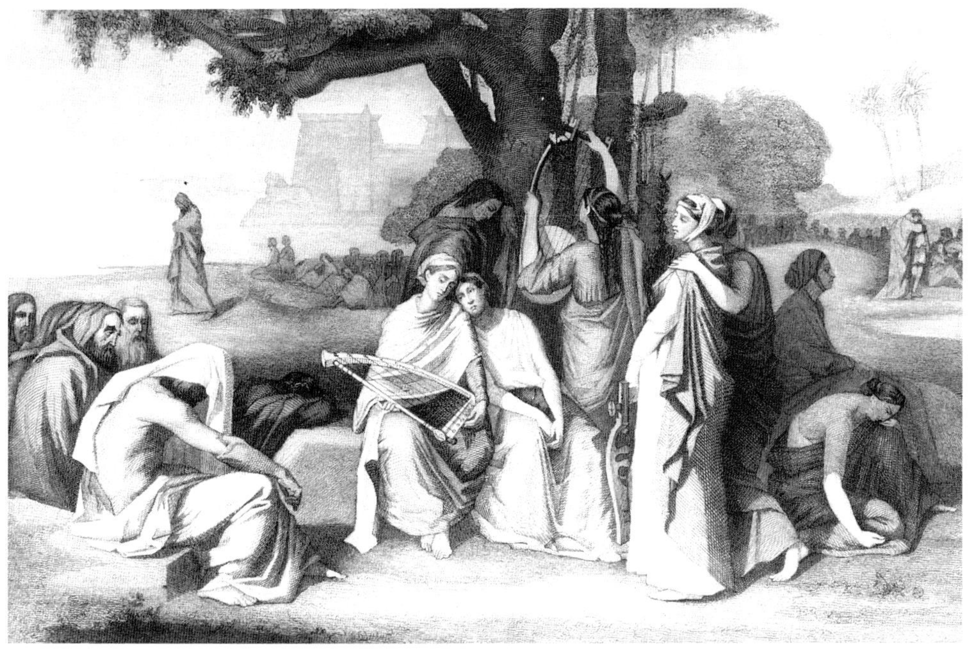

FIG. 78.   A. Joyard, "The Babylonian
Captivity." *L'Artiste,* 2d series, VIII, 1841.
Thomas J. Watson Library, Metropolitan
Museum of Art, New York.

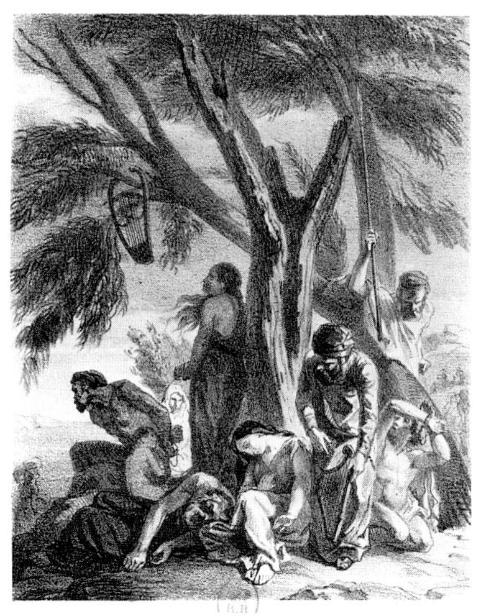

FIG. 79.   Mouilleron after L. de
Planet, "The Babylonian Captivity,"
1842–43, *Bulletin de l'ami des arts.*
Bibliothèque Nationale, Paris.

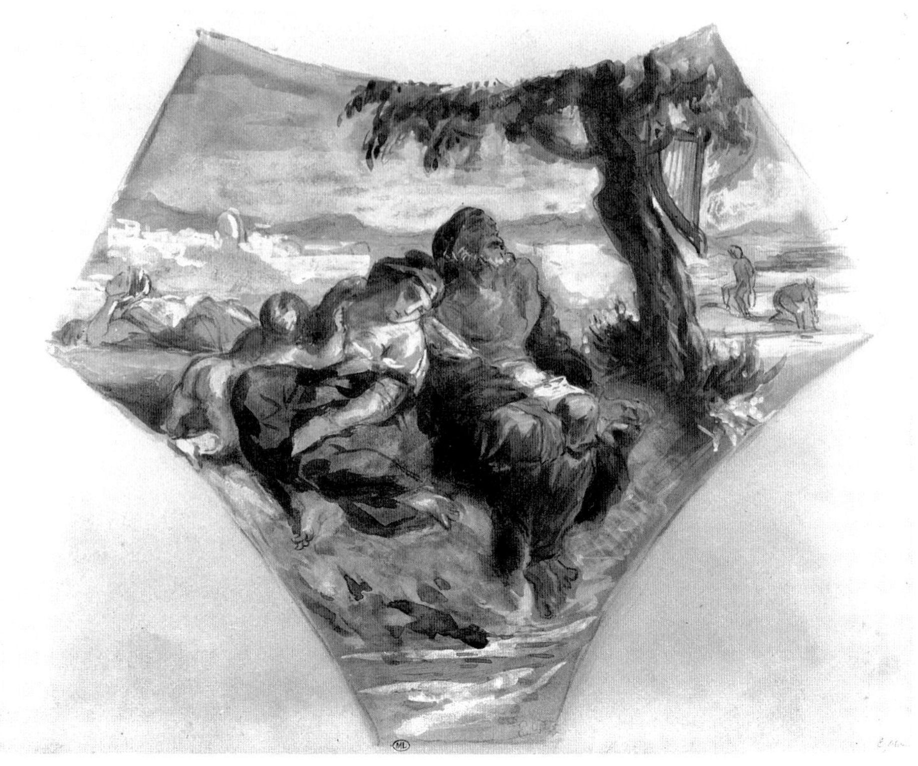

watercolor from the artist's hand (Fig. 80).[57] At the same time, the library pendentive, like other paintings on the theme, is charged with a torpor that recalls the sense of national bereavement in France under Louis-Philippe, one expressed in the fascination with Napoleon that Delacroix shared with so many of his fellow citizens.

Two years after receiving the commission for the Palais-Bourbon library, Delacroix was chosen by the government to decorate the library of France's other legislative body, the Chamber of Peers, in the Palais du Luxembourg. Delacroix's decoration here provides an instructive comparison with his more elaborate work at the Palais-Bourbon. His distinct treatment of each commission, moreover, indicates his concern to tailor his work to the institution.

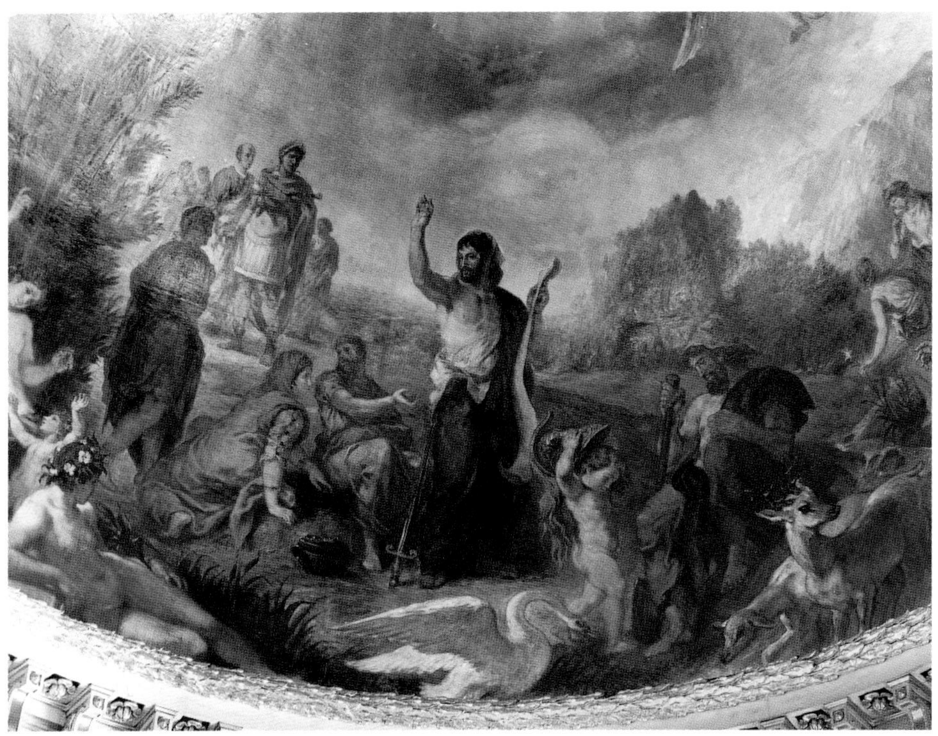

FIG. 81.   E. Delacroix, dome of the
Palais du Luxembourg library (detail),
1840–46. Palais du Luxembourg, Paris.

In the domical cupola at the center of the Luxembourg library Delacroix portrayed four groups of great philosophers, poets, legislators, and heroes, an assembly loosely based on the description of limbo in canto iv of Dante's *Inferno* (Fig. 81).[58] In the principal group Virgil introduces Dante to Homer, who is accompanied by the poets Ovid, Statius, and Horace. To one side of this group are such illustrious Greeks as Achilles, Socrates, Plato, and Demosthenes; to the other side are famous Romans, including Cato of Utica, Marcus Aurelius, Trajan, and Cicero. Opposite the Homer group, Orpheus sings before Sappho and Hesiod. "In brief," Delacroix wrote to the critic Gustave Planche, "one sees there [in the Luxembourg dome] as many great men as possible, walking and sitting at their pleasure."[59] This serene gathering, crowned by inscriptions from Dante borne aloft by an eagle and two winged putti, is complemented by the pendentive paintings *Eloquence, Poetry, Theology (Saint Jerome)*, and *Philosophy* and by the fan-shaped mural *Alexander Ordering That the Poems of Homer Be Placed in a Golden Casket* in a hemicycle below. The last work, whose subject was also featured in the poetry cupola of the Palais-Bourbon library, showed how a mighty ruler respected works of genius.[60]

Commentators on the two library commissions have failed to remark that the contrast between the luminous apotheosis Delacroix placed above the peers and the dynamic, often violent, imagery of the Palais-Bourbon library mirrors the distinction between the two legislative assemblies. Whereas the Chamber of Deputies was a controversial forum, an elective body answerable to approximately 250,000 adult French males with property taxes sufficient to qualify as voters, the Chamber of Peers, whose members were appointed by the king, was a deliberative, conservative assembly. Significantly, the artist discarded an early project for the Palais-Bourbon library with hemicycles depicting a coronation of Petrarch and Socrates and his pupils discussing the immortality of the soul.[61] This project apparently would have paid homage to the iconographic tradition established by Raphael's frescoes in the Stanza della Segnatura and continued by Ingres's *Apotheosis of Homer*. Close in spirit to the sedate work Delacroix painted in the dome of the Chamber of Peers' library, this proposal was superseded by the dynamic counterpoint of Orpheus and Attila.

Although it is not certain that Delacroix entered into a conscious dialogue with the visual and literary prototypes I discuss, my examples comprise only those he could have known. The evidence, moreover, suggests that the subjects Delacroix chose and the thematic relations I detect had currency in France under Louis-Philippe. Delacroix was concerned to choose subjects that would be familiar as well as appropriate.

The internal coherence of the Palais-Bourbon library paintings and their suitability to their setting, elements clear enough in retrospect, do not alter the bewilderment that even sympathetic contemporaries felt before the cycle. Delacroix, recognizing the program's potential for misinterpretation, provided his supporter Thoré with a description of the work for publication.[62] The opacity of the program merits further consideration.

At the outset Delacroix wrote his learned friend Frédéric Villot that what was needed was "a fertile idea, neither too real nor too allegorical, that has, finally, something for every taste."[63] Such concern to accommodate his audience, we have seen, guided the artist's choice of familiar subjects that at once glorified the humanistic studies represented in the library's collection and cited the inspiration, authority, and patriotism of ancient luminaries whom contemporaries could have considered "legislators" in their own right. For in this period the word *legislator* could mean "one who establishes the principles of an art, [or] of a science."[64] Delacroix's effort to link reality and allegory is also evident in his use of complex, expressive narratives in a context that conventionally called for something more static and emblematic. Such an approach had been successful in his earlier *Greece on the Ruins of Missolonghi* (1826) and *Liberty Leading the People* (1830), to which full-blooded corporeality gave a sense of immediacy and actuality. But in decorating, as the artist noted in his journal, "one is compelled to subordinate many parts" (July 1, 1847).[65] Delacroix was unable to do this in the Palais-Bourbon library, where diverse, emotionally charged narrative overpowers the program's larger themes.

Delacroix gave the ensemble a measure of unity by linking disparate motifs under large thematic categories. The *Hippocrates* and *Pliny* pendentives can be associated with the theme of patriotism; *The Babylonian Captivity, Adam and Eve,* and *Ovid in Exile* all pertain to exile; the theme of divine inspiration, represented by *Lycurgus, Numa, Hesiod,* and *Socrates,* is echoed in the *Pliny* pendentive. This decorative cycle thus shows the consistency of theme and expressive tenor that link diverse subjects Delacroix treated in his career. For example, he repeatedly used the storm-tossed boat motif—in the *Barque of Dante* (Salon of 1822), *The Shipwreck of Don Juan* (Salon of 1841), and the versions of *Christ on the Sea of Galilee* (1853–54).[66] But the storm-tossed boat paintings have a private, autobiographical meaning at odds with the public character of an official decorative cycle. Delacroix's subordination of subject to theme—his willingness to offer multiple variations of related subjects to satisfy the expressive needs of a larger obsessive theme—does not lend itself to the discursive clarity critics hoped to find in his paintings for the Palais-Bourbon library.

Although the Chamber of Deputies' library is untroubled by Delacroix's calm *Orpheus, Numa and Egeria,* and *Hesiod and the Muse,* the artist gave free rein there to the proclivity for the tragic evident since his *Barque of Dante, Massacre of Chios,* and *Death of Sardanapalus* had brought damnation, blood, and flame to the Salons of the Restoration. "My tragic inclinations always dominate me," he confessed, "and the Graces rarely smile on me."[67] The severed head of John the Baptist, the stoical suicide of Seneca, the bitterness of exile, and the murder of Archimedes as he sits engrossed in study (Fig. 82)—the last a chilling example of studious absorption for the library clientele—cast a pall over the didactic idealism of the ensemble.[68]

Of the twenty-two paintings in the library, the *Attila* hemicycle is the most impressive. It evokes the pessimism of the artist's journal. "The most extreme civilization," he wrote on a sheet enclosed in a notebook of 1847, "cannot banish from our cities the most atrocious crimes, which seem to belong to peoples blinded by barbarism."[69] "Sickness, death, poverty, the torments of the soul, all are eternal, and will torture humanity under every kind of government; the form, democratic or monarchical, has nothing to do with the case."[70]

Such pessimism was only confirmed by the vicissitudes of mid-century French politics. In the year following the collapse of the July Monarchy, the artist wrote in his journal:

> From knowledge which has been growing inescapable for a year, I believe one can affirm that all progress must necessarily carry with it not a still greater progress, but finally the negation of progress, a return to the point from which we set out. The history of the human race is there to prove it. . . . Is it not evident that progress, toward good or toward evil, has today brought society to the edge of an abyss into which it may very well fall, to make way for a state of complete barbarism?[71]

And the following year brought no relief:

> Man himself, when he gives way to the savage instinct which is the very basis of his nature, does he not conspire with the elements to destroy the works of beauty? Does not barbarism, like the Fury who watches Sisyphus rolling his stone to the top of the mountain, return almost periodically to overthrow and confound, to bring forth night after a too brilliant day? . . . Almost all the great men have had a life more thwarted, more miserable than that of other men.[72]

The tragic vision of the Palais-Bourbon library paintings competes with their ostensible function as embellishments of the legislative palace. This dichotomy

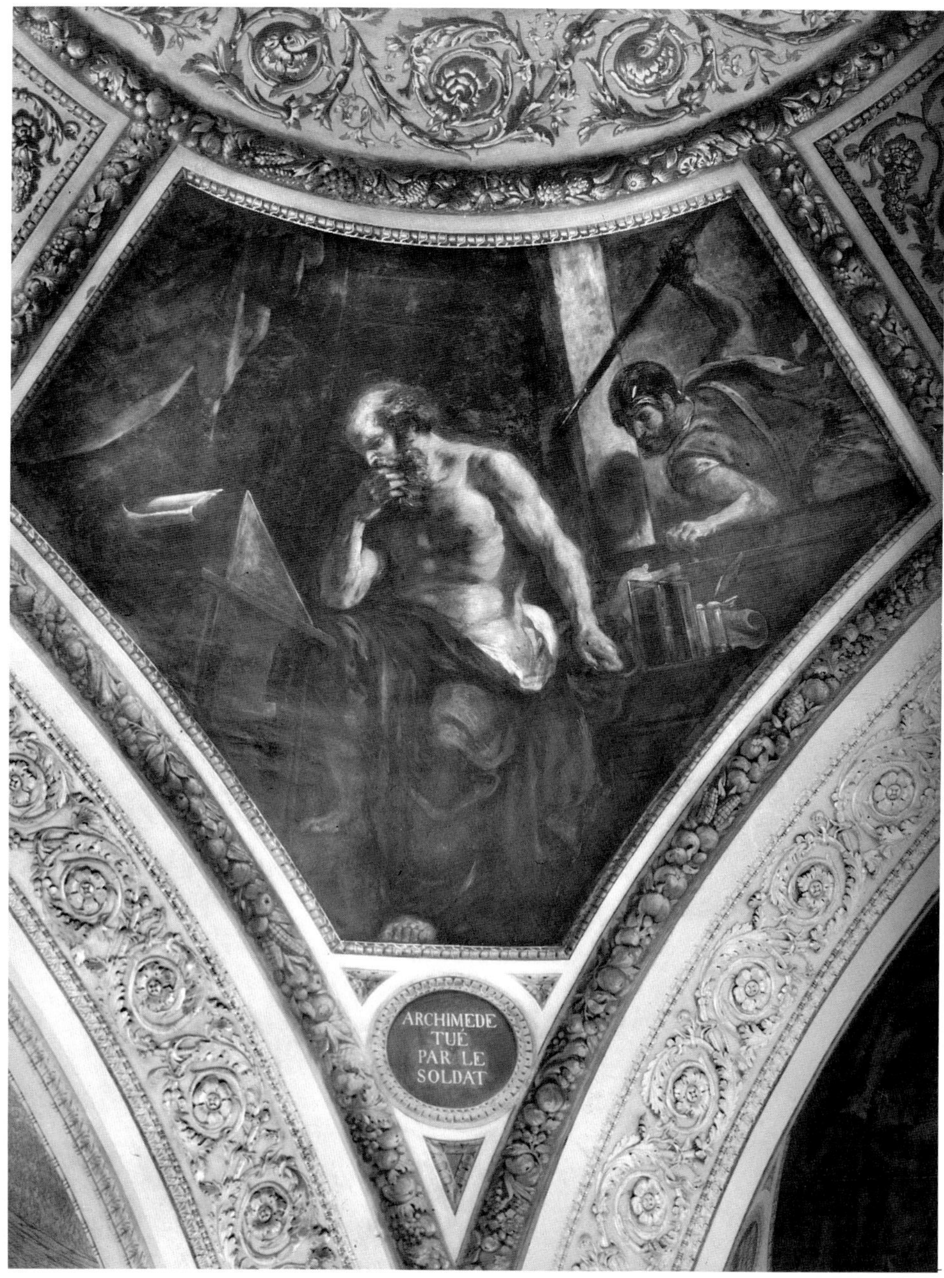

FIG. 82.　E. Delacroix, *Archimedes Killed by the Soldier.* Palais-Bourbon, Paris.

distinguishes the work from the earlier, less extensive, commission to decorate the Salon du Roi. It is likely that Delacroix's work there—it was his first major decorative commission—received official guidance and approval from Thiers, the sympathetic minister in charge of the project. Notwithstanding the stylistic innovation of these paintings, they conform to the functional requirement, to glorify the monarch who was the focus of attention when the Salon du Roi was in ceremonial use. In the library, where Delacroix had a more elaborate interior space at his disposal and was apparently free to determine his own program, he produced a decorative cycle that, if more evocative, bears a less apparent connection to the institution it adorns.

Together with his contemporary work for the Chamber of Peers, Delacroix's decoration of the Palais-Bourbon library represents one of the final triumphs of a tradition of heroic allegorical decoration largely moribund since the century of Tiepolo and Le Moyne. Unlike the works commissioned under the Restoration for the Council of State, for example, the paintings in the Palais-Bourbon library are integrated with their architectural setting even as they escape the narrow didacticism of most contemporary official art. But Delacroix's success in revitalizing this languishing heritage was tempered by the idiosyncrasy of the program. Although Delacroix confidently employed the lofty rhetoric of baroque allegory, with its goddesses, personifications, and muses, his cycle lacks the serene faith in divine Providence that informs the earlier tradition.

This problematic embrace of tradition recalls Delacroix's frustrated ambition to be accepted by the official art establishment, a goal he finally accomplished in 1857, six years before his death, with his admission to the Institut de France after seven failures in twenty years. And in the artist's erratic and ambitious search for noble subjects to glorify Western civilization there is an element of comic pathos that foreshadows the ridiculous foray into universal knowledge undertaken by Flaubert's Bouvard and Pécuchet.

Although Delacroix's decoration of the Palais-Bourbon and Luxembourg libraries has a sense of conviction rare among the many public decorative commissions of the July Monarchy, his exalted imagery is anachronistic. With the fall of the July Monarchy—the regime that had been so generous in awarding decorative commissions to Delacroix—the brilliant aura that had surrounded law and the legislator since 1789 was dimmed.

When, to Delacroix's dismay, the revolutionaries of February 1848 attempted to establish an egalitarian republic, the cult of law that had arisen in France's first legislative assemblies had been blunted by more than half a century of banal parliamentary government and nine constitutions. Lamartine's election to the Chamber of Deputies in 1833 might have seemed to vindicate the Romantic notion of the poet-legislator; the prosaic legislative work pursued in the Palais-Bourbon, however, justified the satiric question asked as Lamartine began his legislative career: "Giant, why does he come to struggle against dwarfs?"[73]

For such dwarfs Delacroix provided the exalted imagery of the libraries of the Bourbon and Luxembourg palaces. Alexis de Tocqueville—one of the most distinguished members of the Chamber of Deputies under Louis-Philippe—witnessed the legislature's decline in prestige that is so painfully evident in Daumier's *Legislative Belly*. Looking back on the regime that fell in February of 1848 he wrote:

> I do not know whether any parliament . . . has ever comprised more varied and brilliant talents than ours during the last years of the monarchy of July. I can affirm, however, that these great orators detested listening to each other, and, all the worse, the entire nation was bored hearing them. The nation inadvertently became accustomed to seeing in the struggles of the Chambers exercises of wit rather than serious discussions and, in all that divided the different political parties, . . . domestic quarrels between children . . . trying to cheat each other in the distribution of the family inheritance.[74]

The peers enjoyed no more prestige than the quarrelsome children of the Palais-Bourbon. Although the Chamber of Peers was described in article 20 of the 1830 charter as "an essential part of the legislative power," under Louis-Philippe the Luxembourg Palace was, in the words of one historian, "a house of rest" under whose roof could be found mostly "men fatigued by age."[75] Unencumbered by Delacroix's obligation to dignify the legislature, Heinrich Heine summed up the relation between the peers and deputies: "The few grey-headed old men who sit in the Luxembourg murmur more and more softly, or half lost in sleep nod their assent to the decisions of the younger Chamber."[76]

The peers' sleep was troubled during the period when their Chamber served as a high court of justice in the trial of 121 defendants arrested after insurrections

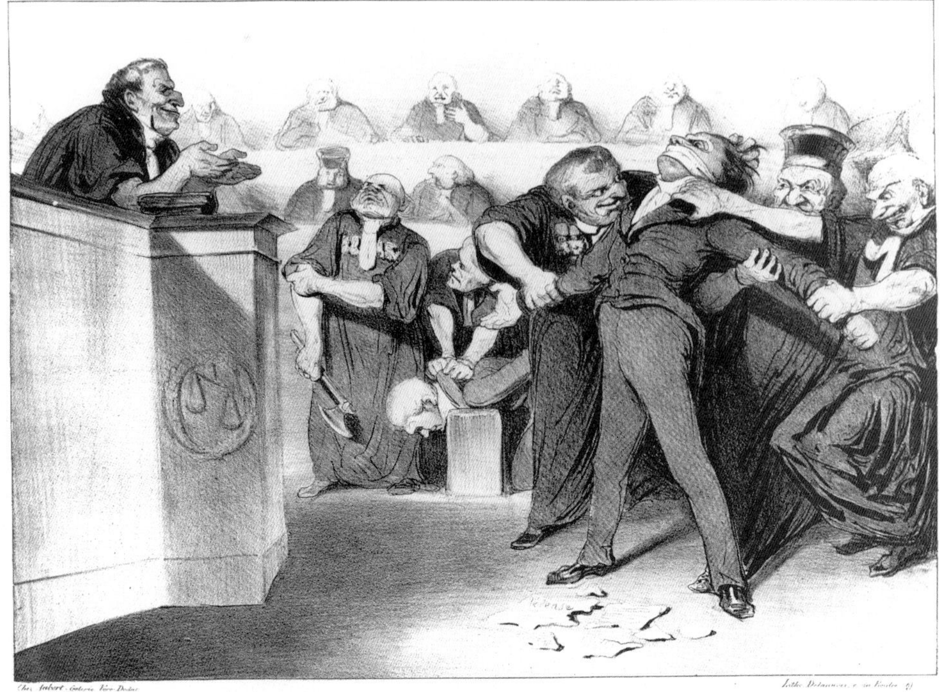

FIG. 83.   H. Daumier, "You Have the Floor, Explain Yourself, You Are Free!" *La Caricature,* May 14, 1835. Boston Public Library.

that began in Lyon in April 1834 and spread to Paris, site of the Rue Transnonain Massacre. In the May 14, 1835, issue of *La Caricature,* Daumier summarized the proceedings of what became known as the *procès monstre* (monster trial) in a manner that the censorship laws, enacted the following September, would have prohibited. His defense torn at his feet, a forcibly restrained defendant is told: "You have the floor, explain yourself, you are free!" Before a somnolent audience of peers, another hapless victim of injustice is prepared for execution (Fig. 83).[77] Like Daumier's *Legislative Belly,* this travesty of the peers exercising their most solemn duty keenly insulted a regime founded on legal integrity.

With the discrediting of the legislature, how could Delacroix's glorification of
the civilizing force of law, his representation of the lawgiver's divine inspiration,
and his invocation of the patriotism expected of the nation's representatives continue to speak to visitors to the Palais-Bourbon library? Delacroix himself, recalling a tiresome evening at the home of the former prime minister, revealed that he
regarded legislative affairs with the very indifference Tocqueville found so lamen-
tably widespread. "Dined at the house of M. Thiers," he recorded on January 26,
1847. "I don't know what to say to the people that I meet at his house, and they
don't know what to say to me. From time to time, noticing the deep boredom
produced in me by those conversations of politicians about the Chamber, etc.,
they talk painting with me."[78] Such impatience could only have compounded
Delacroix's difficulties in providing a lofty and cohesive ensemble for the Palais-
Bourbon library in the twilight of the cult of law.

The Romantic Moses

On June 9, 1841, Jean-François Millet wrote from Paris to the Municipal Council of Cherbourg that it would soon receive, as a gift, a work now known as the *Self-Portrait as Moses* (Plate 9).[1] The provincial authorities must have been taken aback by Millet's generosity, for relations between the twenty-seven-year-old artist and the city had not been altogether happy. Having come to Cherbourg in 1833 from the rural hamlet of Gruchy to pursue his art, Millet had received a scholarship from the city to study in Paris. But this support was terminated in 1839 when he dropped out of the Ecole des Beaux-Arts following an unsuccessful effort to win the Prix de Rome. More recently, Millet had protested the Municipal Council's bad faith in a portrait commission. The *Self-Portrait as Moses,* which has remained on the margins of Millet scholarship, deserves reconsideration, for it offers a poignant example of Mosaic imagery used in a discourse of legitimation and empowerment outside the realm of national politics.

The circumstances surrounding the creation of this work have been recounted by Millet's biographers, Etienne Moreau-Nélaton and Alfred Sensier. Early in 1841 the Municipal Council of Cherbourg had commissioned Millet to paint a posthumous portrait of Colonel Javain, a former mayor of the town. Millet was supplied with a poor miniature that dated from Javain's youth. He was to be paid three hundred francs for the portrait, intended for the assembly hall of the Municipal Council. The likeness presented to the council on March 30, 1841, however, was judged unsatisfactory (Fig. 84). The council's displeasure was aggravated by a rumor that Millet had modeled the portrait's hands on those of a boy who had been imprisoned.[2] Millet defended his painting, arguing that the portrait conformed to the commission as he and the subject's son and son-in-law understood it. The work was not "a family portrait whose principal quality was its completely bourgeois resemblance"; it was intended, rather, to represent for posterity a man "worthy to fulfill the mission with which he was charged during his life."[3]

In response to the artist's demand for payment, the Municipal Council reached a compromise: one hundred francs, a third of the commission, would be paid to Millet provided that the portrait remain in Cherbourg. Before Millet learned of this, he wrote to announce his donation to Cherbourg of the *Self-Portrait as Moses:*

> You will receive in a few days a painting that I beseech you to accept. I hope
> that this feeble result of my labors, so generously encouraged by you, justifies
> the expectation that determined your honorable choice. I have perhaps waited
> long to express my gratitude toward you; but you will understand, I am sure,
> that this delay was not caused by an ungrateful negligence. I have only waited
> until I felt capable of delineating some work worthy of you. In the painting
> that I submit to your good will, I have sought to represent Moses. I did not
> believe that I could offer a subject more appropriate to the magistrates of the
> city of Cherbourg than the image of this ancient and severe legislator of the
> Hebrews. I can only testify anew, Messieurs, to the gratitude of a schoolboy,
> whose first efforts have been aided by you, and to his keen desire to succeed in
> bringing you satisfaction.[4]

Making reference to Millet's terminated scholarship, this letter was written in a tone of mock humility that masks a spirit of defiance. Moreau-Nélaton has detected "a light touch of malice" in Millet's choice of subject,[5] and certainly the contrast between the "ancient and severe legislator of the Hebrews" and the provincial Municipal Council is comic. But this interpretation does not give sufficient weight to the aggressiveness of Millet's gesture.

The most audacious aspect of the work is the resemblance to the artist, evident in a comparison to *Self-Portrait,* a drawing of 1845–46 (cf. Plate 9 and Fig. 85). The arrogance of the assumed biblical identity is reinforced by Moses' assertiveness in facing the viewer as he points to the Ten Commandments. A portion of the frowning hawk-like countenance is illuminated against a mass of dark hair

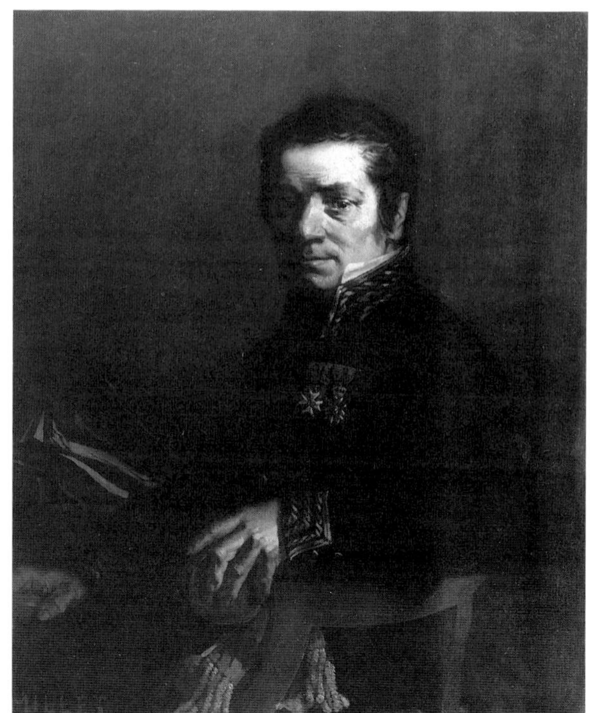

FIG. 84.   J.-F. Millet, *Portrait of
Colonel Javain,* 1841. Musée Thomas
Henry, Cherbourg.

and beard that set the nose into Semitic prominence. The horned silhouette is
enhanced by a zone of light in the sky, suggestive of divine inspiration.

The defiance underlying Millet's gift to Cherbourg is even clearer in light of
the idea that the artist and the poet were the true legislators of mankind,[6] a
notion, embraced by utopian theorists under the July Monarchy, that had become
a rhetorical commonplace in Paris by 1841. The Saint-Simonian Emile Barrault,
for example, said of the artist: "In his free flight, he soars above the earth, and
from the sky his inspired and often prophetic voice can be heard. . . . The artist
alone . . . by the power of the sympathy that makes him embrace God and society, is worthy to direct humanity."[7] This strain of utopian rhetoric was also pursued in references to Michelangelo's *Moses* as "the legislator-poet."[8] Millet's identification with Moses thus proclaims the artist's independence, dignity, and
authority.

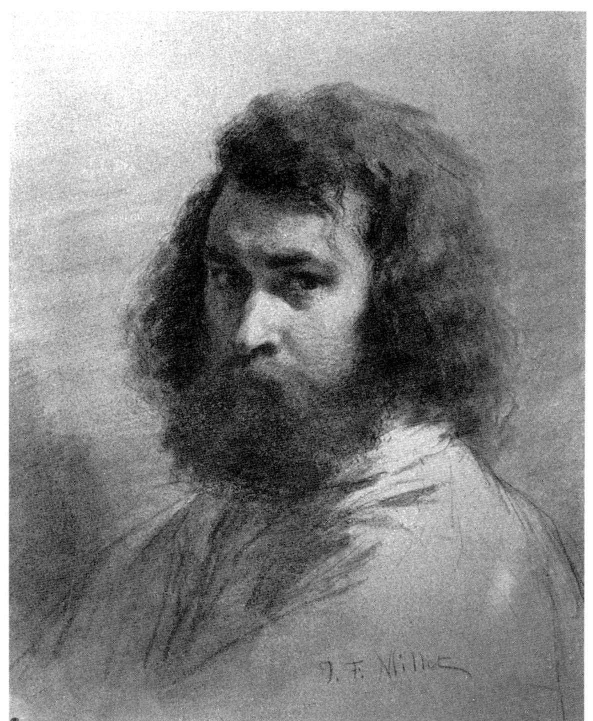

FIG. 85.   J.-F. Millet, *Self-Portrait,*
1845–46. Cabinet des Dessins, Louvre,
Paris.

The relevance of the *Self-Portrait as Moses* to Millet's dispute with the Municipal Council is also suggested by the gesture ("undecipherable" to one commentator) with which Millet's Moses points to the number of the Eighth
Commandment.[9] The Eighth Commandment prohibits bearing false witness, the
transgression Millet perceived as that of his patron. In treating Millet as an artisan
and in rejecting the Javain portrait, the Municipal Council was belying Millet's
calling as well as violating a contract. For Millet, the portrait would have borne
false witness if he had imitated a mediocre miniature.

A Moses comparable in severity to that of Millet's self-portrait was prominently
placed in Paris early in 1841, when Henri de Triqueti's monumental bronze doors
representing the Ten Commandments were moved from the founders' studio,
where they had been on display, and installed at the church of the Madeleine.
The forbidding Moses on the lintel resembles that of the *Self-Portrait as Moses*

(cf. Plate 9 and Fig. 50). Triqueti illustrated the Eighth Commandment with the judgment of Susanna and the punishment of the perjuring elders—a story relevant to Millet's dispute with the Municipal Council.

As a veiled gesture of independence, Millet's *Self-Portrait as Moses* prefigures Courbet's *Studio of the Painter* (1854–55); there Courbet asserted his artistic and moral authority after refusing Count de Nieuwerkerke's offer of government patronage.[10] The *Self-Portrait as Moses* reflects an aggressive self-aggrandizement that, some twelve years later, Delacroix found annoying. With aloof displeasure Delacroix described a meeting with Millet:

> During the morning, somebody brought Millet to me. He speaks of
> Michelangelo and the Bible, which, he says, is or almost is the only book that
> he reads. That explains the rather ambitious character (*tournure*) of his peas-
> ants. . . . He is certainly of the constellation or squadron of bearded artists who
> made the revolution of 1848, or who applauded it, apparently thinking that
> there would be equality of talents, as well as fortunes.[11]

Delacroix's disparagement of Millet as a bearded revolutionary who invested lowly subjects with inappropriate grandeur suggests the character of the young artist who painted the *Self-Portrait as Moses*. Millet portrayed himself with the full beard that, as Robert L. Herbert has observed, identified him with artists, writers, philosophers, and religious leaders rather than the bourgeoisie of Cherbourg.[12]

In combining earthy realism and lofty reference, the *Self-Portrait as Moses* pre-figures Millet's bold imputation of biblical and Michaelangelesque qualities to rural imagery, disliked by Delacroix and the mid-century Salon audience. At the same time, the very obscurity of the *Self-Portrait as Moses* suggests the problem of Millet's private appropriation of the theme of divine legislation.[13]

Millet's view of Moses as a source of legitimacy and authority is related to the ongoing tradition of Mosaic imagery in French official art. The *Self-Portrait as Moses* also continues a tradition of self-aggrandizement through biblical reference established by the young poets of the 1820s. Victor Hugo, like others in the circle of the short-lived Catholic and ultra-royalist literary magazine *La Muse française* (July 1823–June 1824), cherished a belief in the priestly and prophetic functions of the poet.[14] Accordingly, he turned to Scripture in evoking the poet's authority in "Le Poète" (1823; published 1824):

Les peuples prosternés en foule l'environnent;
Sina mystérieux, les foudres le couronnent,
    Et son front porte tout un Dieu![15]

Crowds bow down before him;
Inexplicable as Sinai, he is crowned with thunder,
    And his brow shines with divine radiance!

The prophet-poet, like Moses, stands amid the thunder of Sinai with a radiant brow (which one is tempted to associate with Hugo's own prominent forehead). Hugo employed similar imagery to honor his colleague Lamartine:

Chante, juge, bénis; ta bouche est inspirée!
Le Seigneur en passant t'a touché de sa main;
Et, pareil au rocher qu'avait frappé Moïse,
    Pour la foule au désert assise,
La poésie en flots s'échappe de ton sein![16]

Sing, judge, bless; your tongue is inspired!
The Lord, in passing, touched you with his hand;
And, like the torrent from rock that Moses struck
    For the multitude in the desert,
Poetry flows from your breast!

Hugo's scriptural reference reflects the literary prestige of the Bible early in the 1820s. But his use of Mosaic imagery is hardly religious. It resembles the secular transvaluation of Mosaic imagery by another young member of the circle around the *La Muse française,* Alfred de Vigny.[17]

Like Hugo's verse of the early 1820s, Vigny's "Moïse" (1822), though full of biblical reference, is entirely secular. Conflating the death of Moses (Deuteronomy 34) with the terrifying spectacle on Mount Sinai (Exodus 19–31 and Deuteronomy 5), Vigny gives Moses an overpowering individual presence at variance with the traditional conception of him as the obedient servant of God.[18] As Moses ascends Mount Nebo to meet his death—with six hundred thousand terrified Hebrews "bowed in the dust" below—he enumerates the divine powers he has received from God:

J'impose mes deux mains sur le front des nuages
Pour tarir dans leurs flancs la source des orages;
J'engloutis les cités sous les sables mouvants;
Je renverse les monts sous les ailes des vents;
Mon pied infatigable est plus fort que l'espace;
Le fleuve aux grandes eaux se range quand je passe,
Et la voix de la mer se tait devant ma voix.

I grasp the clouds with both hands
To dry up the source of storms in their flanks;
I bury cities under moving sands;
I topple mountains under the force of winds;
My tireless tread cannot be outdistanced;
The mighty river makes way when I pass,
And the voice of the sea falls silent at my voice.

This demigod, the envy of the angels, is filled with a melancholy alien to the biblical Moses. Like Job, Jeremiah, and Christ, Vigny's Moses laments the solitude that has been the cost of God's choosing him:

Sitôt que votre souffle a rempli le berger,
Les hommes se sont dit: Il nous est étranger;
Et leurs yeux se baissaient devant mes yeux de flamme,
Car ils venaient, hélas! d'y voir plus que mon âme.
J'ai vu l'amour s'éteindre et l'amitié tarir,
Les vierges se voilaient et craignaient de mourir.

As soon as your spirit passed into the shepherd,
Men said to themselves, He is a stranger to us,
And lowered their eyes before my flaming eyes
Because they had, alas, seen more there than my soul.
I have seen love extinguished and friendship dried up;
The virgins covered themselves in fear of death.

Weary of solitary grandeur, Moses asks God for the repose of death:

O Seigneur! j'ai vécu puissant et solitaire,
Laissez-moi m'endormir du sommeil de la terre.[19]

Oh Lord! I have lived in power and solitude;
Let me sleep the sleep of mortals.

Vigny's Moses is particularly unorthodox when he is compared with the Moses of Bossuet's *Discours sur l'histoire universelle* (1681), who dies content.[20] The grandiose narcissism of Vigny's Moses, moreover, was the very stuff of Romantic theater, as was the unrecognized young poet in Vigny's *Chatterton,* whose suicide in the face of bourgeois indifference created a sensation among Parisian audiences in 1835.

The critic Charles Magnin appreciated the tragic and secular elements of "Moïse," writing in the liberal paper *Le Globe* of Vigny's "sad and great idea, a modern idea that brings new life to an ancient myth whose primitive meaning had been weakened or lost." As Vigny severed his Moses from Scripture, he also transformed the solitude and frustration of his protagonist, by a Romantic alchemy, into attributes of empowerment and aggrandizement. Magnin wrote that Vigny evoked "that melancholy of omnipotence, that sadness of a superhuman superiority that isolates; that weighty disgust of genius, of command, of glory, of all those things that make of the poet, of the warrior, of the prophet a gigantic and solitary being, a pariah of grandeur."[21] Some sixteen years after writing "Moïse," Vigny offered a similar interpretation of the poem, which he then considered his best, for "its sadness." His Moses, he explained, "is not that of the Jews. This great name only serves as a mask for a man . . . more modern than antique: the man of genius, weary of his eternal widowhood and despairing to see his solitude all the more vast and more arid the more he grows."[22]

Vigny's "Moïse" and his gloss on the poem reflect the Romantic inclination both to elevate the "man of genius" by references to Moses (as in Millet's *Self-Portrait as Moses* and in the two poems by Hugo already discussed) and to reconstitute the biblical personage who is an instrument of Providence into a mighty individual will. From this perspective, Vigny's reinterpretation of the biblical Moses echoes the cult of the divine lawgiver that flourished under Napoleon.

The Romantic enhancement of Moses' stature as an individual is perceptible even amid the orthodoxy of the competition for the Prix de Rome. This contest, judged on the traditional academic criteria of composition, drawing of the nude, expression, and command of ancient history and literature, offered young artists the opportunity to study in Rome that Millet had been denied. Biblical subjects

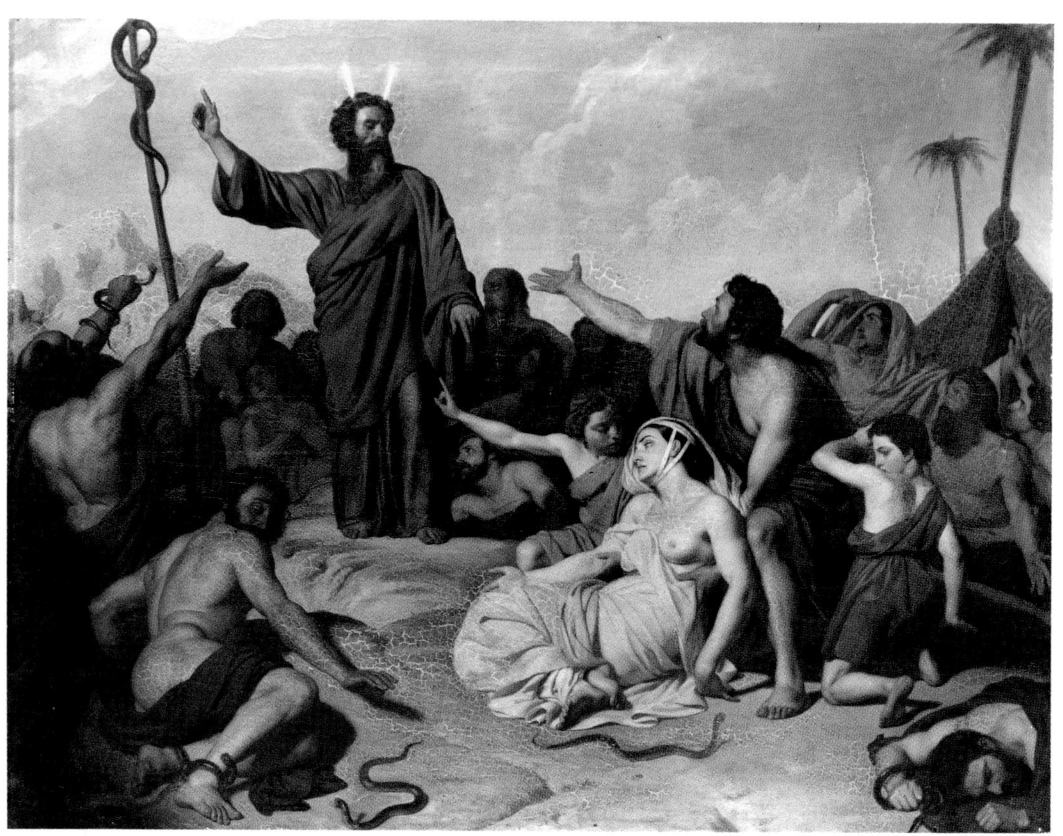

FIG. 86.   E. Roger, *Moses and the Brazen Serpent,* 1833. Ecole Nationale Supérieure des Beaux-Arts, Paris.

were not unusual in this competition, beginning with *Moses, Overcome with Indignation at the Sight of the Israelites Adoring the Golden Calf, Breaks the Tablets of the Law* (1663).[23] Poussin and Racine had established Old Testament narrative as part of the French classical tradition. In 1833 the Academy of Fine Arts offered Moses and the Brazen Serpent as the competition subject, a story (Numbers 21) of revolt, punishment, and reconciliation. God sent venomous snakes to attack the Hebrews in the desert after they began to grumble about Moses' leadership and the folly of having left the relative comfort and security of Egypt. Acting under divine inspiration, Moses raised a staff surmounted by a serpent of bronze

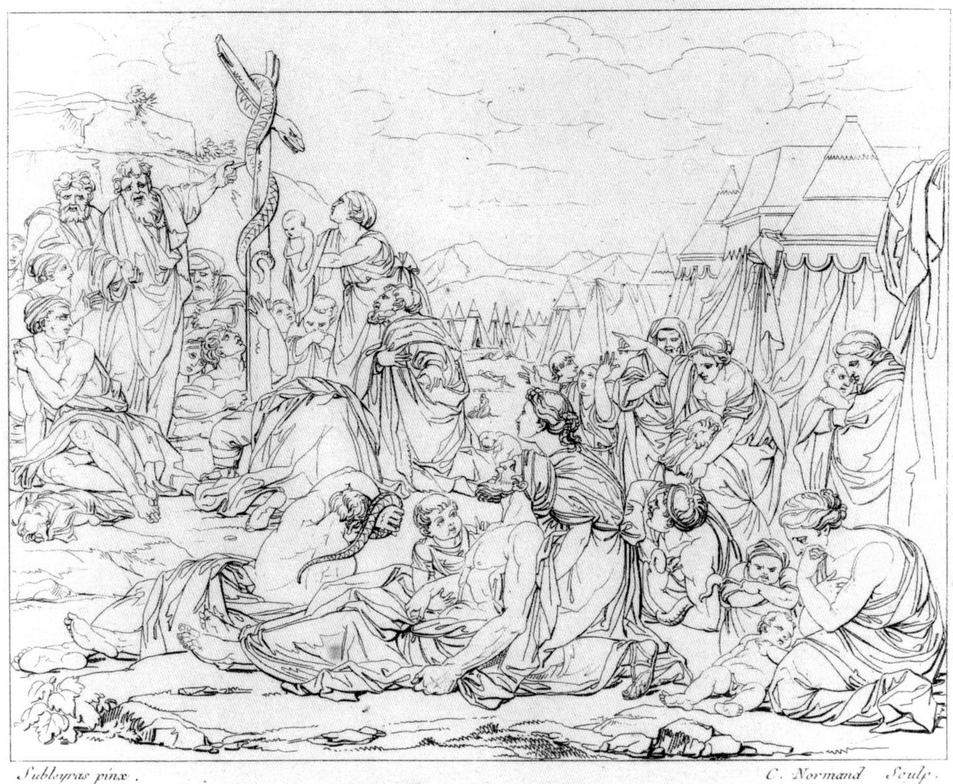

FIG. 87.   C. Normand after P. Subleyras, *The
Brazen Serpent* (1727), from C. P. Landon,
Annales du Musée, vol. 2, Paris, 1803, plate 32.

that had healing power for the Hebrews who would look on it. This episode, in
the Christian iconographic tradition, prefigured salvation through Christ.

The composition of the winning entry in 1833 (Fig. 86), by Eugène Roger
(1807–1840) was reminiscent of that of the winning entry of 1727, by Pierre-
Hubert Subleyras (1699–1749). Subleyras's painting, much admired in the early
nineteenth century, was reproduced in the 1802 and 1835 editions of Landon's
Annales du Musée, an illustrated compendium of old master and contemporary
paintings (Fig. 87).[24] Roger's modern sense of archaeological decorum—evident
in the bamboo staff, the palm trees, and the detailed headdress of the recumbent

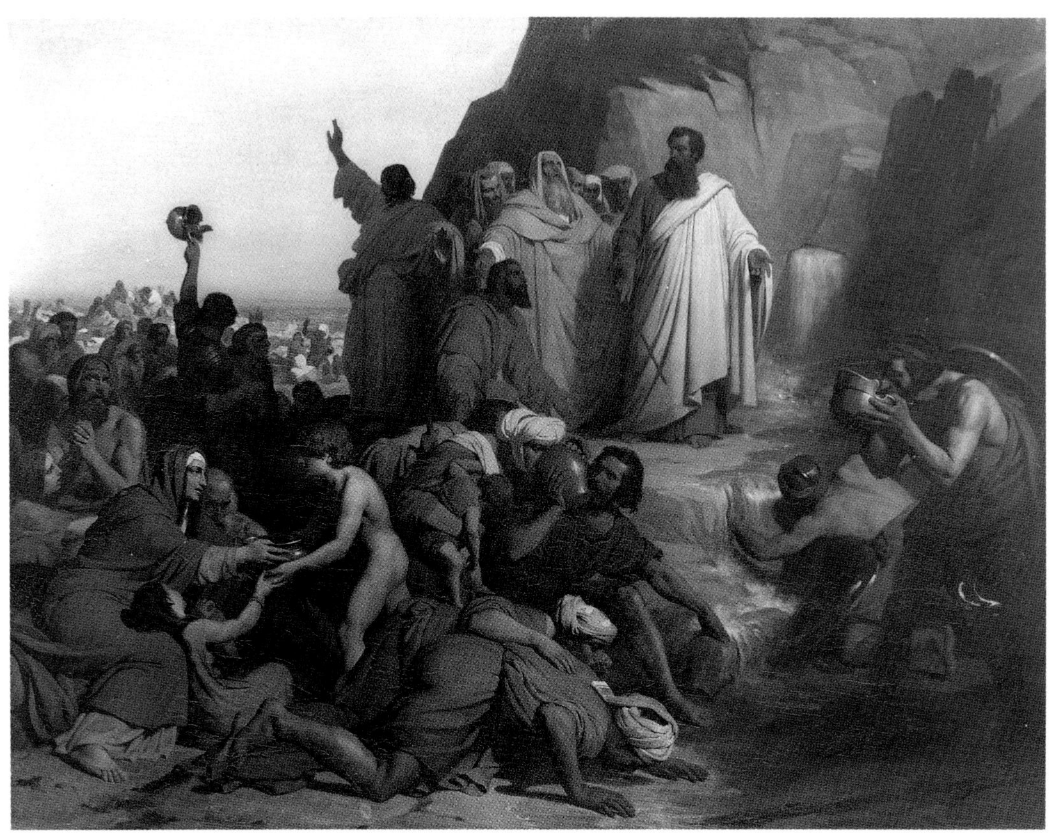

woman—however, departs from its classical prototype in giving prominence to Moses. Silhouetted against the sky, Roger's Moses combines the authoritative gestures of Plato and Aristotle in Raphael's *School of Athens*. He stands on raised ground, fully clad, above the seminude crowd at his feet.[25]

The Mosaic subject for the 1836 competition was the Striking of the Rock. A critic reviewing the entries in *L'Artiste* protested the Academy's choice of a theme so ambitious that most of the contestants have been "crushed by their subject"—a theme that called for no less than "the vast, profound, austere genius of Nicolas Poussin."[26] It was not surprising that the two winners, Dominique-Louis-Ferréol Papety (1815–1849) and Charles-Octave Blanchard (1814–1842) turned to Poussin

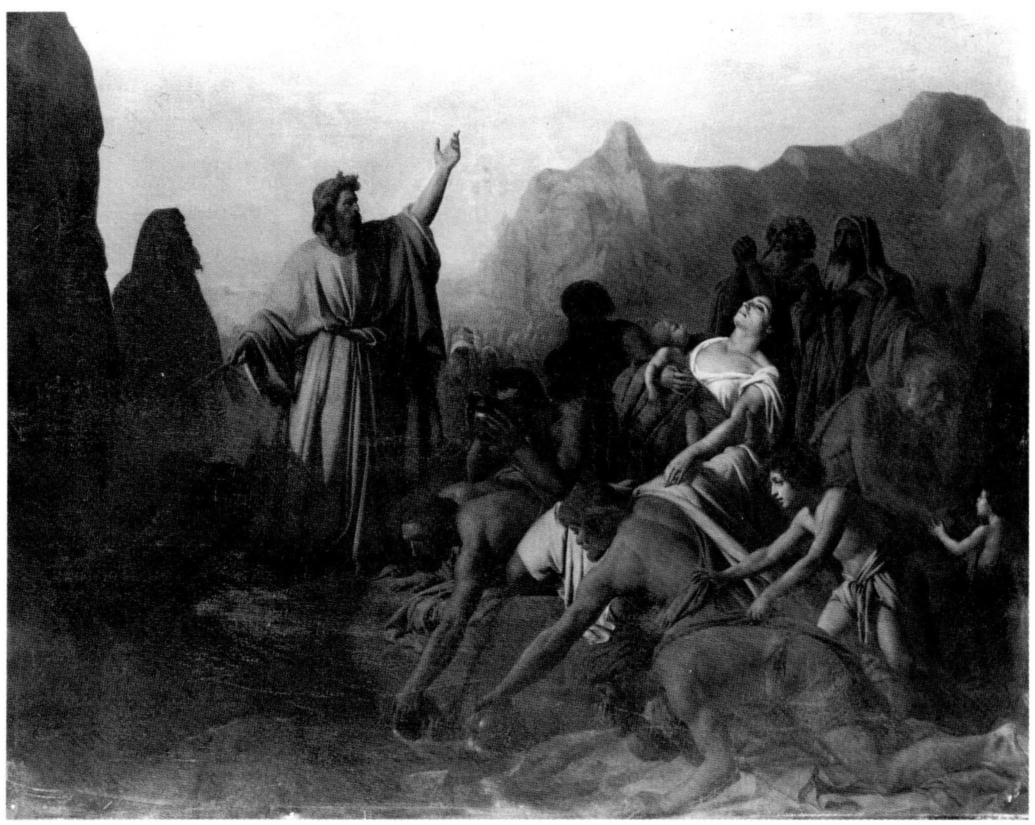

FIG. 89.   C.-O. Blanchard, *The Striking of the Rock,* 1836. Ecole Nationale Supérieure des Beaux-Arts, Paris.

(cf. Figs. 88–90). Papety, though he emulated the seventeenth-century master, emphasized Moses (whose prominent forehead and angular nose imitate those of Michelangelo's figure in San Pietro in Vincoli) in a characteristically nineteenth-century way.[27] The critic in *L'Artiste* wanted more: "The head of Moses has a handsome character, but it does not sufficiently dominate the crowd."[28] And Blanchard's painting, like those of Roger and Papety, melodramatically contrasts the untroubled authority of Moses with the heartfelt vulnerability of the crowds at his feet.

Chateaubriand's sole theater piece, *Moïse* (c. 1811–28)—a dramatic poem in the manner of Racine's *Athalie*—was an ambitious attempt to represent Moses in

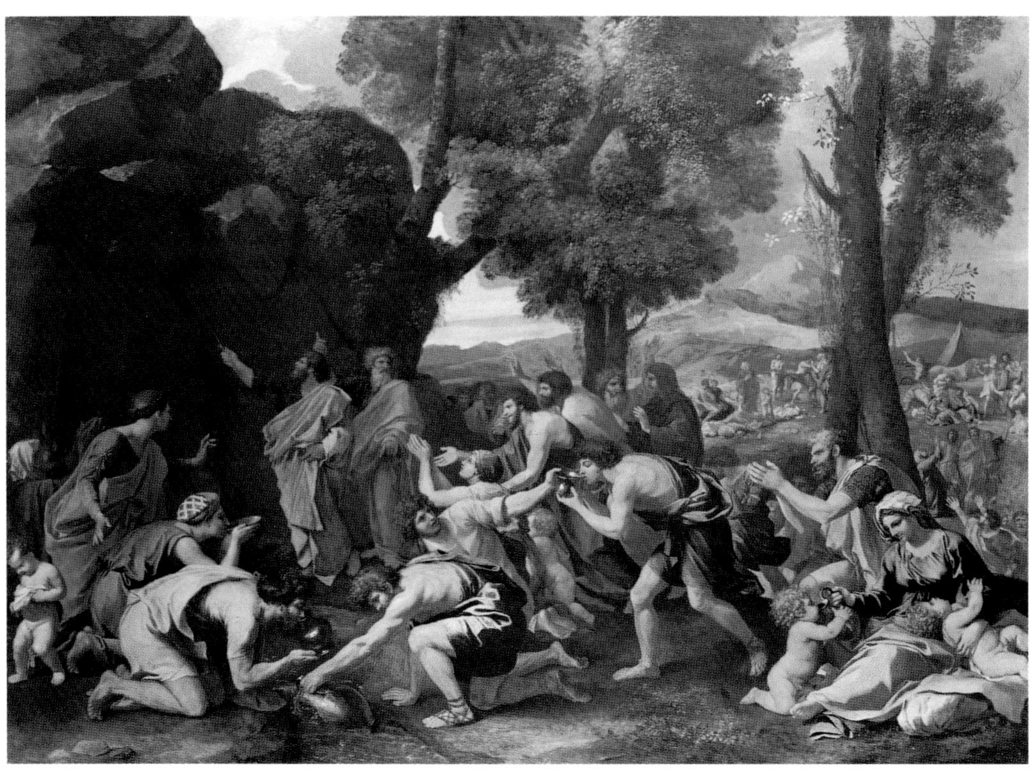

the language of French classicism.[29] Although in the *Génie du christianisme* Chateaubriand recommended the subject of Moses to poets, in the preface to *Moïse,* published in his *Complete Works,* he begged his readers' indulgence. Even Racine, he pointed out, was sometimes unequal to his scriptural source. And Chateaubriand had dared to conceive of a theater production featuring "that legislator with rays of fire on his brow, that prophet who delivered Israel, struck Egypt, opened the sea, wrote the history of Creation . . . and spoke to the Lord face-to-face." He predicted ("without vanity, for it is a question of material effect independent of the author's talent") that such details as "the descent of

Moses from Mount Sinai, by the light of the moon, bearing the tablets of the law [and] . . . the sets representing the Red Sea in the distance, Mount Sinai, [and] the desert with its palm trees" would bring variety and movement to classical tragedy.[30] Accepted by the Théâtre-Français in 1828, the work was staged October 2, 1834, at the Théâtre Municipal de Versailles under the title *Moïse au mont Sinaï, ou La Première Idolâtrie.* This spectacular flop saw five performances at Versailles and one at the Odéon in Paris.

Writing in *L'Artiste,* a professed admirer of Chateaubriand awaited the premiere with "astonishment and profound chagrin." For the "sublime child" had written *Moïse* as if it were to be played "in the presence of Mount Sinai, with the sound of thunder, by the glare of lightning." Chateaubriand had conceived the work without recognizing the limitations of "a theater of boards . . . a cardboard mountain, a sky of blue cloth . . . [and] players in flesh and blood."[31] The critic's apprehensions were borne out when, according to an anecdote attributed to Chateaubriand himself, such mirth greeted the production that Chateaubriand's butler congratulated him on the success of his comedy.[32] Sainte-Beuve aptly characterized this pompous creation: "Ô ennui! noble ennui!"[33]

Just as the Prix de Rome entries imply a revised conception of Moses, so too the range of responses to Michelangelo's representation of him (Fig. 91) suggests the protean vitality of the Romantic Moses. In the late eighteenth century the statue, whose awesome authority would so impress Freud, was not universally appreciated.[34] Repulsed by it, Francesco Milizia denounced it in terms approvingly paraphrased by Joseph de Maistre: "a satyr head with pig bristles . . . a frightful boor enveloped in the costume of a baker."[35] For the sculptor Etienne-Maurice Falconet (1716–1791), who likened the *Moses* to a convict, the figure Michelangelo had made fell far short of the magnificent original.[36] Seroux d'Agincourt, however, in his ground-breaking history of Italian art, published 1811–23 but written in the decade before the French Revolution, offered a very different opinion, which would be echoed in the nineteenth century: the *Moses* was Michelangelo's greatest work and perhaps the capital achievement of modern sculpture.[37]

The evocative force of Michelangelo's *Moses* for the Romantic period is suggested by the cloud of extraneous associations that interferes with the representation and description of the object. Two engravings (Figs. 92, 93) are telling examples. The first, included by Seroux d'Agincourt in his work on Italian art,

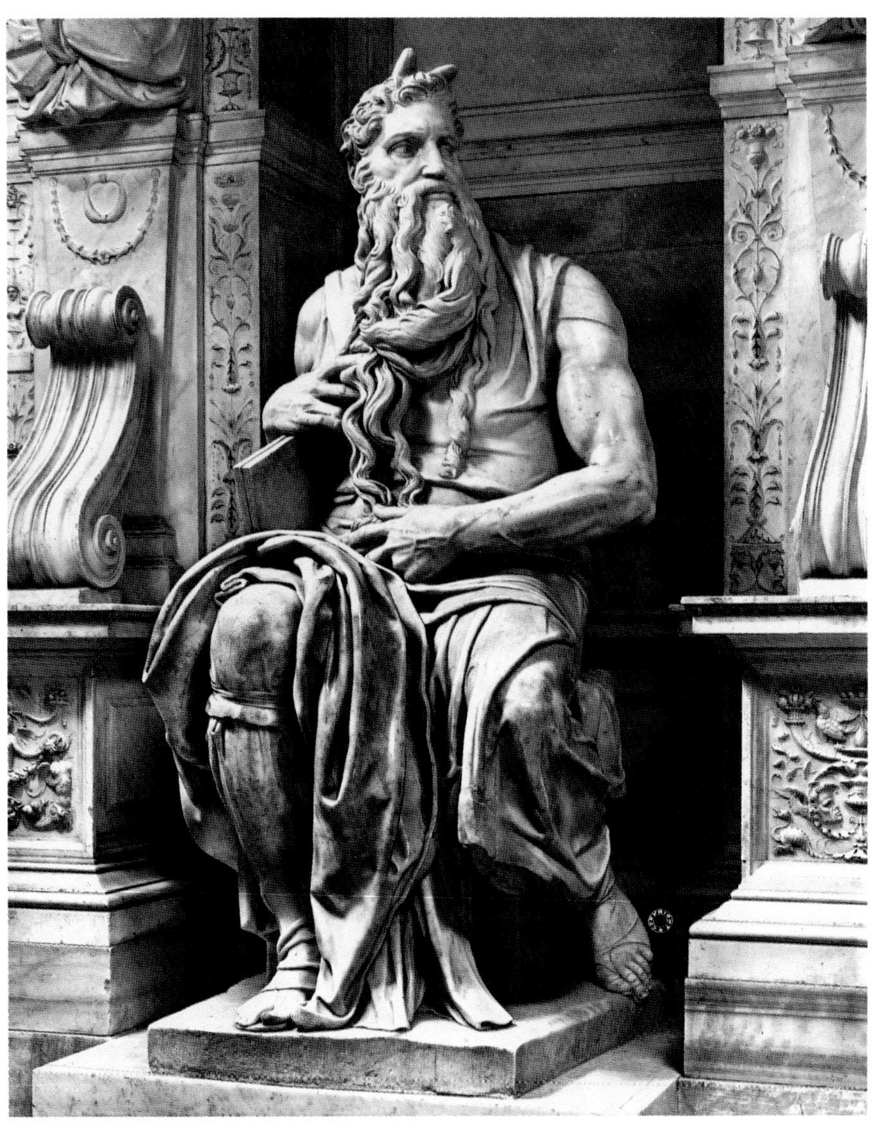

FIG. 91.   Michelangelo, *Moses,* c. 1515.
San Pietro in Vincoli, Rome.

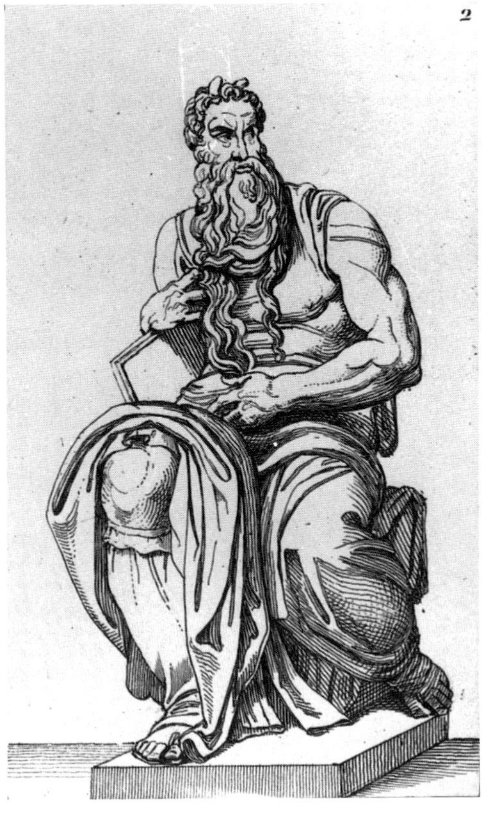
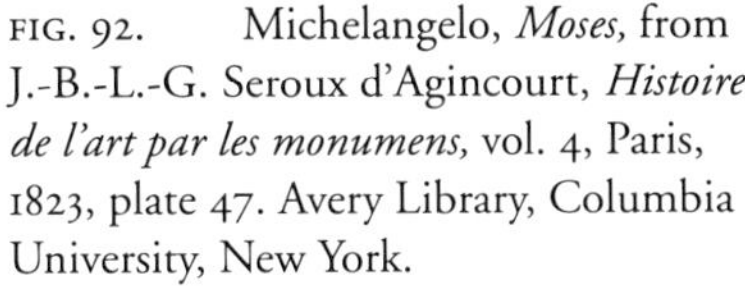
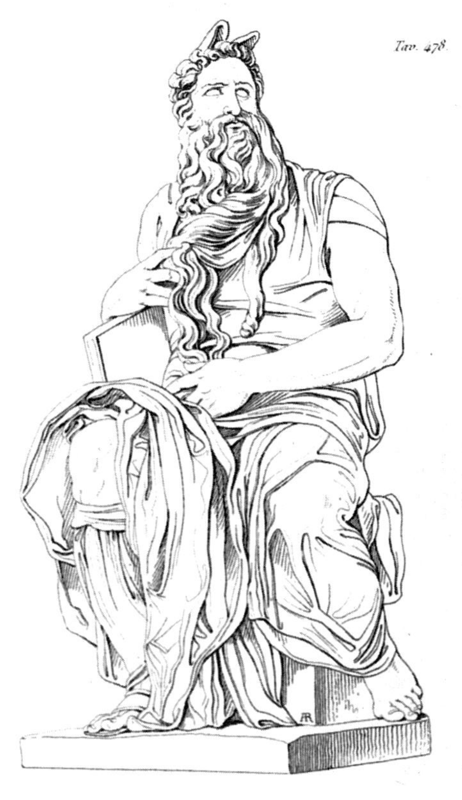

FIG. 92.   Michelangelo, *Moses,* from J.-B.-L.-G. Seroux d'Agincourt, *Histoire de l'art par les monumens,* vol. 4, Paris, 1823, plate 47. Avery Library, Columbia University, New York.

FIG. 93.   Michelangelo, *Moses,* from *Musée de peinture et de sculpture,* vol. 13, Paris, 1832, p. 924. Thomas J. Watson Library, Metropolitan Museum of Art, New York.

overemphasizes the curling musculature of the arms and lends a satyric expression to the face. Whereas Moses was Hellenized in this late eighteenth-century illustration, he was baptized in an engraving published in the *Musée de peinture et de sculpture.* Here the incision of pupils is omitted and the face given a slight backward tilt, suggesting a gaze upward with rolled eyeballs that is as reminiscent of ecstatic saints as it is foreign to the *Moses* of Michelangelo.

The *Moses* was canonized by a critic as well. Gustave Planche, in an 1834 article on Michelangelo, spoke of it as a figure of tearful and saintly majesty that produced "a mixture of sadness and veneration, a religious seizure, a shiver of pious ecstasy." In the expression of the *Moses* Planche perceived "a complete resignation, an absolute abnegation, a devotion without reserve"—in short, an Old Testament saint, who has shed generous and sympathetic tears: "Moses has wept, but wept on wounds he could not heal."[38]

Alexandre Dumas père, writing in *L'Artiste* in 1845, was impressed, on the contrary, by the animal energy and physicality of the *Moses;* he described the figure as a demigod seated in Olympian majesty with a "thick and secular beard spread in waves upon his vast chest like an overflowing torrent." Dumas compared the rays the sight of Jehovah had left on Moses' forehead to the horns of a goat:

> This emblem of savage energy and animal force adds I know not what of the strange and formidable to the physiognomy of the colossus; because, in truth, whether man or monster, reality or symbol, this being thinks, and the Hebrew people, as a poet [Vigny] said, would not have been entirely wrong to prostrate themselves before him.[39]

So overpowering is Michelangelo's *Moses* that Dumas declares it beyond the grasp of reason and taste:

> I pity the critics who have wanted to measure this giant according to their own dwarfish stature: so much grandeur crushes them. Here it is necessary to feel rather than reason. . . . It is a strange and colossal dream, translated into marble, during a night of insomnia and terror.[40]

Dumas's overblown evocation of the *Moses,* in which he pays homage to the Romantic cult of genius, is also pitched to a nostalgia for authority that had crowd-moving force in post-Napoleonic France—as when, for example, the emperor's remains were returned to Paris.

Like Vigny's "Moïse," Dumas's description of Michelangelo's *Moses* secularizes and magnifies the biblical lawgiver. While this treatment of the theme contrasts with Millet's and Hugo's self-aggrandizing identification with Moses, both tendencies echo the discourse of legitimacy and authority associated with the law in official art since the French Revolution. The diversity of sentiment that found expression through reference to Moses under the Restoration and July Monarchy suggests that the figure of the lawgiver remained evocative for artists and writers when the cult of the law was in decline.

Epilogue: Twilight of the Rights of Man

The preceding pages testify to the immediacy with which images of the round-headed tablets of the law and of Moses, Numa, and other divinely inspired law-givers spoke to a nation bereft of the religious and political certitudes of the Old Regime. We have seen how during the Revolution the law replaced monarch and religion as the site of authority and focus of veneration. And we have followed the destiny of the revolutionary cult of the law as it became personalized under Napoleon, monarchist under the Restoration, and defensive under Louis-Philippe.

Against this pattern of disruption and instability, some unexpected points of continuity have been set into relief. The different regimes that governed France between 1789 and 1848 used and reused a common vocabulary of legislative imagery, reflecting a pattern that is especially striking under the Bourbon Restoration, when the Napoleonic theme of the divinely inspired legislator was revived and both ends of the political spectrum identified with Moses. Similarly, the prestige of law and lawgiving during the Revolution and Empire was echoed under the Restoration and July Monarchy in the Romantic cult of Moses.

More surprising, the history of the cult of the law in French art indicates the role France's Catholic and monarchic heritage played in establishing its modern constitutional tradition. The tenacious association between modern French law and the laws of Moses, from the Revolution through the July Monarchy, is a secular variant of the tradition that Christian doctrine was rooted in Old Testament prototypes. The ongoing attempt to establish a divine sanction for the law—whether that of the revolutionary constitutions, the Code Napoléon, or the charters of Louis XVIII and Louis-Philippe—suggests the vitality of the Old Regime's linking of temporal authority and divine Providence. In this regard, it is telling that Bossuet was one of the earliest French writers to use the word *constitution* in its modern sense. And Rousseau's insistence that laws be grounded in a myth of divine origin is fully anticipated in Bossuet's classic defense of divine right absolutism, *Politique tirée des propres paroles de l'Ecriture sainte* (*Politics drawn from the very words of Holy Scripture*). Bossuet, citing the classical tradition of the divinely inspired legislator—according to which Minos of Crete, Lycurgus, and Numa had derived their laws from the gods—argued that laws associated with divinity are unbreakable: "That is why all peoples have wanted to give a divine origin to their laws; and those that did not have one have feigned one."[1]

With the collapse of the July Monarchy in 1848, the cult of the law was no longer vital in French politics. Accordingly, by mid-century French artists and their governmental patrons show little interest in representing the law and lawgiving. As we have seen, however, the cult of the law and the creation of a supportive body of legislative symbolism were troubled from the outset: the *Acts of the Apostles* mocked the National Constituent Assembly, and *La Caricature* contemptuously assaulted the July Monarchy. The sanctity and permanence of the numerous constitutions of the period, moreover, were repeatedly belied by the lurching instability of the political landscape. In the alternating exaltation and disappointment of French constitutional history between the revolutions of 1789 and 1848, the cult of the law was perilously fragile.

Specialists in French legal and institutional history have discussed the decline during the nineteenth and twentieth centuries of the exalted notion of law bequeathed to France by the Revolution.[2] A key element in this process of erosion was the new urgency of social issues that by the mid-nineteenth century placed into question the revolutionary legislative heritage with its individualistic cult of property and emphasis on the rights of man. With the increasing awareness of hunger and unemployment, universal suffrage and national workshops commanded attention rather than a constitutional tradition that guaranteed the security of property holders. Whereas the insurgents of 1830 had fought in defense of the law, in 1848 the law was eclipsed by social issues on which France's legislators had remained silent.

As the revolutionary infatuation with constitutional law declined, the prestige of the Code Napoléon deteriorated. The German attack on the conceptual foundation of the code that had helped consolidate the French empire was decisive. In the vanguard of this offensive was Friedrich Karl von Savigny (1779–1861), professor at the University of Berlin, who challenged the notion that a corpus of law could have universal validity. From the German perspective, the imported Code Napoléon was harmful and invasive. Savigny and his followers rejected the notion that laws could be made at will and according to reason, without regard for the spontaneous life of national customs; this historically oriented German current pervaded France during the 1820s.[3] Like the revolutionary Declarations of the Rights of Man, the Code Napoléon sanctified private property. Consequently, with the rise of social criticism at mid-century Napoleonic jurisprudence—anathema to Proudhon and Marx—was tarnished.[4]

The revolutionary legislative heritage came under especially fierce attack during the final quarter of the nineteenth century. But as early as 1851 Jules Barbey d'Aurevilly, in *Les Prophètes du passé,* denounced constitutional government as "absolutely contrary to the nature of man."[5] More ominous than this nostalgic tribute to Joseph de Maistre and his counter-revolutionary allies were the withering accusations of Hippolyte Taine's *Origines de la France contemporaine* (1875–93). Characterizing the articles of the Declaration of the Rights of Man and Citizen as "daggers aimed at human society,"[6] Taine indicted the Constituent Assembly as a grotesque and anarchic farce that destroyed the very customs, nurtured over the centuries, that offered the only hope for development. Such pessimism reflected the bitter conclusion of the Second Empire in national defeat. But as Zeev Sternhell has pointed out, the events of 1870 only strengthened Taine's earlier belief that the republican heritage was bankrupt.[7]

The discrediting of the law is inadvertently suggested by a large painting commissioned from Henri Lehmann for the Hall of Acts of the Ecole de Droit in 1872 and exhibited in the Salon the following year. In *La Droit prime la force* (Law surpasses force; Fig. 94),[8] Law, flanked by putti bearing the codes of civil and public (i.e., constitutional) law and the tablets of the Ten Commandments, stands in beatific triumph before the Paris skyline. At her feet, Force bends in submission in an architectural setting whose woeful state recalls both the bombardment of Paris during the siege and the vandalism of the Commune. Viewed against the dismal record of defeat, lost territory, and civil war that had scarred recent French

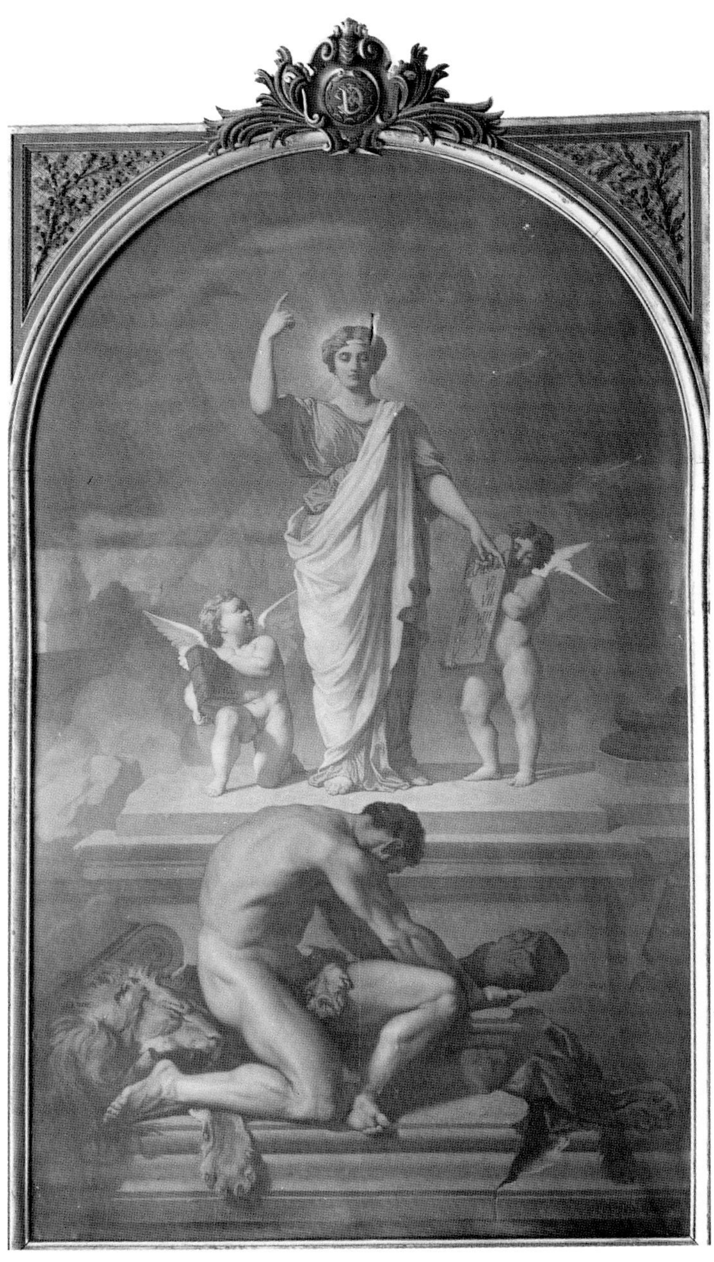

FIG. 94.   H. Lehmann, *Law Surpasses Force,* Salon of 1873. Musée d'Orsay, Paris (damaged).

history, this rhetorical triumph of Law over Force seems as willfully anachronistic as the middle-aged Ingriste's serene Ralphaelesque putti.

Taine's critique of both the Declaration of the Rights of Man and Citizen and the notion of universally valid law and his deterministic insistence on the imperatives of race and national tradition were sympathetically received by Maurice Barrès.[9] In *Les Déracinés* (The uprooted; 1897), the first of three volumes in Barrès's *Novel of National Energy*, the wisdom of Taine is contrasted with the destructive influence of the novel's opportunistic republican teacher, Bouteiller. Professing, in the author's words, a "cult of the law," Bouteiller poisons his pupils with a belief in abstract principles—an insidious pedagogy that uproots his students from their Lorraine ancestry and local customs and leads them to lives of cynicism and desperation in Paris. In keeping with the author's hostility to France's legislative heritage, one of Bouteiller's pupils learns from a newspaper editor named Portalis how to be an unscrupulous journalist. Barrès specifies that this unsavory character, whom the youngster admires as a combination of Machiavelli and Talleyrand, was the great-grandson of the venerable Napoleonic jurist.[10]

Barrès's hatred of the revolutionary legislative tradition found expression in a visceral anti-parliamentarianism that was a keynote of his activity as a political publicist. Elected in September 1889 to the very Chamber of Deputies that he abhorred, Barrès stood for a Boulangist program of constitutional revision that included the "suppression of the parliamentary regime that, under the Republic as under the monarchy, has only given proof of impotence and corruption."[11] Barrès's radicalism, like that of other late nineteenth-century French extremists, partook of elements dear to both the Right and the Left. Although he was hostile to the abstract and universal notion of law inherited from the revolutionary legislative assemblies, he embraced the tradition of popular insurrection represented by the *sans-culottes,* the insurgents of June 1848, and the Commune. And his tireless effort to destroy the bourgeois parliamentary order symbolized by "the dishonest babblers of the Palais-Bourbon"[12] can be seen as a fearsome sequel to the mockery of the legislators and ministers of the July Monarchy by Daumier and the staff of *La Caricature.* Since the Revolution, the law had been honored as the defining element of nationality. From the perspective of Barrès's Nationalism (with a capital *N*) the law was regarded with suspicion.

Barrès's hostility toward the revolutionary legislative heritage reveals another strain of hatred whose strength became evident in the Dreyfus Affair

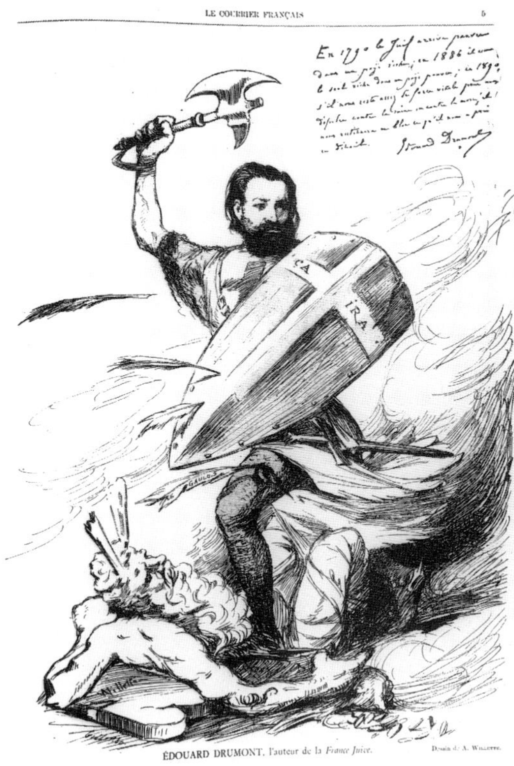

FIG. 95.   A. Willette, "Edouard Drumont, author of *La France Juive,*" *Le Courrier français,* May 16, 1886. Bibliothèque Nationale, Paris.

(1894–1906).[13] In 1889 Barrès and other supporters of the authoritarian General Boulanger failed to supplant the parliamentary order of the Third Republic. Afterward, influenced by the anti-Semitic publicist Edouard Drumont, Barrès championed a fusion of anti-parliamentarianism and anti-Semitism that came to define the radical Right's ideology in France.[14] In light of the traditional association between French law and the tablets of Moses, this development is bitterly ironic. Whereas references to Moses had previously brought luster to the law and the legislature, hatred of the Jews motivated Drumont, Barrès, and other enemies of the revolutionary legislative heritage.[15] A sympathetic caricature of Drumont drawn by the anti-Semite Adolphe Willette in 1886 provides a menacing sequel to the legislative imagery with which this study has been concerned (Fig. 95).[16] In the spirit of the radical Right, blending revolutionary militancy and reactionary nostalgia, Drumont is clothed as a Crusader, his shield emblazoned with the title of the revolutionary song "Ça Ira." Braving a barrage of pens launched by enemy journalists, France's leading anti-Semite tramples on Moses and his broken tablets.

INTRODUCTION

1. "La grande âme du Législateur est le vrai miracle qui doit prouver sa mission" (Rousseau, *Du Contrat social* [1762], ed. Ronald Grimsley, Oxford, 1972, p. 141).

2. Charles-Gilbert Romme, "Modèle des sentiments qui doivent animer les citoyens des campagnes," *Feuille Villageoise*, no. 43, July 21, 1791, p. 301. Quoted in Albert Mathiez, *Les Origines des Cultes révolutionnaires (1789–1792)*, Paris, 1904, p. 78.

3. The most thoroughly documented study of David's project is Philippe Bordes, *Le Serment du Jeu de Paume de Jacques-Louis David*, Paris, 1983. See also the review of Bordes by Thomas Crow, *Art Bulletin*, LXVIII, September 1986, pp. 499–501; and catalogue entries nos. 100–114 in Antoine Schnapper and Arlette Sérullaz, *Jacques-Louis David*, Paris, Musée du Louvre and Musée National du Château, Versailles, 1989, pp. 242–75.

4. *Description du serment et de la fête civique, célébrés au Bois de Boulogne par la Société du jeu de paume de Versailles, des 20 juin 1789 et 1790*, Paris, [1790], p. 2.

5. See Wolfgang Balzer, *Der junge Daumier und seine Kampfgefährten*, Dresden, 1965, pp. 58–60.

6. Alphonse de Lamartine, address of January 10, 1839, quoted in Mary Dorothy Rose Leys, *Between Two Empires: A History of French Politicians and People between 1814 and 1848*, London, 1955, p. 223.

7. My figure is based on the table of contents of Jacques Godechot, ed., *Les Constitutions de la France depuis 1789*, Paris, 1979, in which the three major modifications of the Constitution of Year VIII and Napoleon's Additional Act (1815) are treated as distinct constitutions.

8. See, for example, Bruno Foucart, *Le Renouveau de la peinture religieuse en France (1800–1860)*, Paris, 1987; and Michael Paul Driskel, *Representing Belief: Religion, Art, and Society in Nineteenth-Century France*, University Park, Pa., 1992.

9. This study developed from my dissertation, *"Le Peuple de Dieu:* Old Testament Motifs of Legislation, Prophecy, and Exile in French Art between the Empires," Institute of Fine Arts, New York University, 1986. For the treatment of Old Testament subjects by Romantic sculptors, see Ruth Butler, "Religious Sculpture in Post-Christian France," in the exhibition catalogue *The Romantics to Rodin,* ed. Peter Fusco and H. W. Janson, Los Angeles County Museum of Art, 1980, pp. 90–95.

10. See the exhibition catalogue *The Dreyfus Affair: Art, Truth, and Justice,* ed. Norman L. Kleeblatt, Berkeley and Los Angeles, 1987; Zeev Sternhell, *Maurice Barrès et le nationalisme française,* Brussels, 1985, and *La Droite révolutionnaire, 1885–1914,* Paris, 1978; and Michel Winock, *Nationalisme, antisémitisme et fascisme en France,* Paris, 1990.

CHAPTER 1

1. All constitutional citations in this book are from Jacques Godechot, ed., *Les Constitutions de la France depuis 1789,* Paris, 1979.

2. Charles Loyseau, *Traité des seigneuries,* 3d ed., Châteaudun, 1610, p. 26. For the legislative function of the French monarch, see Michel Antoine, "La Monarchie absolue," in *The French Revolution and the Creation of Modern Political Culture,* Oxford, 1987, 1:3–24; and Roland Mousnier, *The Institutions of France under the Absolute Monarchy, 1598–1789,* trans. Brian Pearce, Chicago, 1979, 1:665.

3. The Estates-General comprised representatives of the three divisions of the pre-revolutionary French population: the clergy, the aristocracy, and all other subjects of the crown. Its sessions were infrequent: the spring 1789 convocation of the Estates-General—which led to the formation of the National Assembly—was the first meeting of that body since 1614.

4. "At no point . . . was the legislative power of the monarchy viewed as a creative factor in legal development. At best, the rôle of the French monarchy was not to create law, but to formulate existing customs and to administer justice within the framework of tradition" (Réne David and Henry P. de Vries, *The French Legal System,* New York, 1958, p. 12).

5. Alexis de Tocqueville, *L'Ancien régime et la Révolution* [1856], ed. J.-P. Mayer, Paris, 1967, p. 140.

6. See Jean Carbonnier, "La Passion des lois au siècle des Lumières," in *Essais sur les lois,* Paris, 1979, pp. 203–23; and David Wisner, "Quelques représentations de législateurs antiques dans l'art de la période révolutionnaire," in *La Révolution française et l'antiquité,* ed. R. Chevallier, Tours, 1991, pp. 369–90.

7. *De la Législation,* in *Collection complète des oeuvres de l'abbé de Mably,* Paris, Year III [1794–95], p. 261.

8. *Encyclopédie, ou Dictionnaire raisonné,* Neuchâtel, 1765, s.v. "Législateur."

9. For the motif of the authoritative legislator-teacher in Rousseau's fiction and political writ-

ing, see Judith N. Shklar, *Men and Citizens,* Cambridge, Mass., 1969, pp. 128, 154–55, 160–61.

10. From an unpublished fragment "Produit net relativement à la société," in Emmanuel-Joseph Sieyès, *Ecrits politiques,* ed. Roberto Zapperi, Paris, 1985, p. 51.

11. Louis-Antoine Saint-Just, "Discours sur l'acte constitutionnel" (April 24, 1793), in *Chef d'oeuvres de l'eloquence parlementaire,* ed. Camille Lacroix, Paris, 1893, 2:160.

12. For the development of the modern notion of constitution, see Marina Valensise, "La Constitution française," in *The French Revolution and the Creation of Modern Political Culture,* 1:441–67. See also Paul Bastid, *L'Idée de constitution,* Paris, 1985.

13. For the text of the Tennis Court Oath, see François Furet and Denis Richet, *La Révolution française,* Paris, 1973, p. 77.

14. For the concept of constitution that evolved in the National Assembly, see François Furet and Mona Ozouf, eds., *A Criticial Dictionary of the French Revolution,* trans. Arthur Goldhammer, Cambridge, Mass., 1989, s.v. "Constitution," entry by Keith Michael Baker.

15. Emmanuel-Joseph Sieyès, *Qu'est-ce que le Tiers état?* ed. Roberto Zapperi, Geneva, 1970, p. 180; and Sieyès, "Préliminaire de la constitution: Reconnoissance et exposition raisonnée des droits de l'homme et du citoyen" (read to the Constitution Committee, July 20–21, 1789), in *Ecrits politiques,* p. 199.

16. This motif is discussed in R. Liebenwein-Krämer, "Säkularisierung und Sakralisierung," Ph.D. diss., Johann Wolfgang Goethe University, Frankfurt am Main, 1977, pp. 159–61.

17. Because it was the deputies' responsibility to have these insignia fabricated, they exist in variants. See the exhibition catalogue *Droits de l'homme & conquête des libertés,* Vizille, Musée de la Révolution française, 1986, no. 21, p. 23; and Sylvie de Turckheim-Pey, "Les Insignes révolutionnaires de la collection Claudius Côte," in *Autour des mentalités et des pratiques politiques sous la Révolution française,* Paris, 1987, pp. 137–49.

18. Constant Pierre, *Musique des fêtes et cérémonies de la Révolution française,* Paris, 1899, pp. 357–65. See Marie-Noëlle Polino, "Quatremère de Quincy et la Fête de la loi en l'honneur de Simoneau, maire d'Etampes (juin 1792), in *La Révolution française et l'antiquité,* ed. R. Chevallier, Tours, 1991, pp. 285–309.

19. *Convention nationale. Rapport sur le Code civil fait au nom du Comité de législation, le vendredi 9 août 1793 . . . par le citoyen Cambacérès, député du département de l'Hérault* [Paris, 1793], pp. 3, 11–12.

20. Jules Michelet, *Histoire de la Révolution française* [1847–53], ed. Gérard Walter, Paris, 1952, 1:418.

21. Maurice-Charles-Emmanuel Deslandres, *Histoire constitutionnelle,* Paris, 1932, 1:73.

22. See Albert Mathiez, *Les Origines des Cultes révolutionnaires (1789–1792),* Paris, 1904, pp. 33–34; 47–49.

23. Quoted in Mona Ozouf, *Festivals and the French Revolution,* trans. Alan Sheridan, Cambridge, Mass., 1988, p. 67.

24. The construction of this abortive monument was entrusted to Pierre-François Palloy (1775–1835), who made a business of selling Bastille memorabilia. See the exhibition catalogue *La Révolution française et l'Europe, 1789–1799,* no. 519, 2:405.

25. For a variant of this print without the artists' signatures see Bibliothèque Nationale, Département des estampes, *Un siècle d'histoire,* II, Paris, 1914, cat. no. 4236, p. 769.

26. Ozouf, *Festivals and the French Revolution,* pp. 83–84.

27. *Convention nationale. Procès-verbal des monuments, de la marche, et des discours de la Fête consacrée à l'inauguration de la Constitution . . . le 10 août 1793,* Paris, [1793], p. 7.

28. See Lynn Hunt, *Politics, Culture, and Class in the French Révolution,* Berkeley and Los Angeles, 1984, pp. 96–98.

29. *Convention nationale. Procès-verbal,* p. 10.

30. *Un siècle d'histoire,* III, Paris, 1921, cat. no. 4990, p. 223.

31. See Marcel Roux, *Bibliothèque Nationale, Département des estampes, Inventaire des fonds français, graveurs du dix-huitième siècle,* Paris, 1930, 1:149; and the color reproduction in Michel Vovelle, *La Révolution française: Images et récit,* Paris, 1986, 4:245.

32. According to Deslandres, "the memory of Moses clearly haunted the Convention" (*Histoire constitutionnelle,* 1:283). For the association of the Mountain with Mount Sinai, see also Liebenwein-Krämer, "Säkularisierung und Sakralisierung," pp. 160–61.

33. See Bibliothèque Nationale, *Un siècle d'histoire,* cat. no. 5012, 3:230–31.

34. This anonymous writer pushed biblical imagery to the edge of lunacy. He described monarchs as demons whose function has been to punish man for the idolatry in which he has been plunged by "the unpardonable neglect of the laws that Moses received from you, my God, on the mountain of Sinai; mountain whose [power of] regeneration has just saved the Republic" (Paris, Bibliothèque Nationale Lb[41] 1118).

35. *Archives parlementaires de 1787 à 1860,* 1st series, *1787–1799,* ed. J. Mavidal, E. Laurent, L. Lataste, Louis Claveau, Constant Pionnier, and André Ducom, Paris, 1903, 63:311, 64:32–33. See also J.-P. Babelon, *Archives Nationales, Musée de l'histoire de France,* vol. 4, *Salle de la Révolution française,* Paris, 1965, p. 84.

36. Gabriel Bouquier and Pierre-Louis Moline, *La Réunion du six août, ou l'Inauguration de la République française,* Paris, n.d., p. 37. For this play, performed fifty-two times after opening in March 1794, see Beatrice F. Hyslop, "The Parisian Theater during the Reign of Terror," *Journal of Modern History,* XVII, December 1945, pp. 344–45.

37. The work is dated 23 germinal Year II [April 12, 1794]. See *La Révolution française et l'Europe,* cat. no. 856, 3:654; and *Droits de l'homme & conquête des libertés,* cat. no. 35, pp. 33–34.

38. The quotation is from a directorial ordinance establishing a similar emblem for a seal to be placed on the official *Bulletin des lois* (*Messages, arrêtés et proclamations du Directoire exécutif,* no. 512, 2:121, 16 brumaire, Year V [November 7, 1796]). For Gatteaux's medal, see

[Michel Hennin], *Histoire numismatique de la Révolution française,* Paris, 1826, I, cat. no. 789; and Alain DiStefano, *Histoire des insignes et des costumes des sénateurs,* Paris, 1980, pp. 34–35.

39. For the development of anti-parliamentarianism in 1795, see Furet and Richet, *La Révolution française,* pp. 314, 320.

40. Ibid., pp. 489–92.

41. See Jacques Godechot, *The Counter-Revolution,* trans. Salvator Attanasio, Princeton, N.J., 1971; P. H. Beik, "The French Revolution Seen from the Right," *Transactions of the American Philosophical Society,* n.s. XLVI, part 1, 1956; and the incisive essay by George Steiner, "Aspects of Counter-Revolution," in *The Permanent Revolution: The French Revolution and Its Legacy, 1789–1989,* ed. G. Best, Chicago, 1989, pp. 129–53.

42. See Joan McDonald, *Rousseau and the French Revolution,* London, 1965, pp. 132–33.

43. Edmund Burke, *Reflections on the Revolution in France,* ed. Thomas H. D. Mahoney, Indianapolis, Ind., 1955, pp. 39, 79, 229.

44. See *Actes des apôtres,* VII, no. 210 [Dec. 1790 or Jan. 1791], pp. 3–5. The *Acts of the Apostles* published some of the earliest examples of royalist caricature, a genre that flourished between the opening of the Legislative Assembly, in autumn 1791, and the fall of the monarchy, August 10, 1792. See Claude Langlois, *La Caricature contre-révolutionnaire,* Paris, 1988, pp. 9–13.

45. "Stances sur l'ancien et le nouveau Sénat de France," *Actes des apôtres,* VIII, no. 214 [1791], p. 14.

46. Langlois, *La Caricature contre-révolutionnaire,* p. 65.

47. *Actes des apôtres,* II [1790], pp. 1–8 (preceding no. 31). In a similar vein of humor, an anonymous *Petit catéchisme national* defined *constitution* as "une émanation sortie avec grand bruit du corps constituant." See Frank Paul Bowman, "Les 'liturgies révolutionnaires': Pastiches ou parodies?" *Revue d'histoire littéraire de la France,* 1990, nos. 4–5, p. 601.

48. Bibliothèque Nationale, *Un siècle d'histoire,* cat. no. 4326, 2:794.

49. See Bibliothèque Nationale, *Un siècle d'histoire,* I, Paris, 1909, cat. no. 533, pp. 231–32; Langlois, *La Caricature contre-révolutionnaire,* pp. 194–95, 248, no. 119; and *La Révolution française et l'Europe,* cat. no. 770, 2:579.

50. The king's tormenter, astride a wigged centaur that resembles Robespierre, is identified below as "Robespierre mounted on [*à cheval sur,* i.e., 'a stickler for'] the constitution."

51. See catalogue entry no. 691 by David Bindman in *La Révolution française et l'Europe,* 2:515.

52. See Richard A. Lebrun, *Joseph de Maistre: An Intellectual Militant,* Kingston, Ontario, 1988; and Isaiah Berlin, "Joseph de Maistre and the Origins of Fascism," in *The Crooked Timber of Humanity,* New York, 1991, pp. 91–174.

53. Maistre, Comte Joseph de, *Considérations sur la France,* Lyon, 1847, p. 8.

54. See Maistre's *Essay on the Generative Principle of Constitutions* (1810), published in 1814.

55. Maistre, *Considérations sur la France,* pp. 67–68.

56. Ibid., pp. 92, 146.

57. See Henri Moulinié, "De Bonald," Ph.D. diss., University of Toulouse, 1915, which includes a useful summary of Bonald's thought, pp. 398–410.

58. Louis-Gabriel-Ambroise de Bonald, *Oeuvres complètes de M. de Bonald,* ed. Abbé Migne, Paris, 1859, 1:122 (emphasis in original).

59. See Godechot, *The Counter-Revolution,* p. 100. Bonald claimed that he sent a copy to Napoleon at the time of the return from Egypt. See Moulinié, "De Bonald," pp. 29–30.

60. Anne-Louise-Germaine Necker de Staël-Holstein, *Considérations sur les principaux événements de la Révolution française* (1818), in *French Literature and Thought since the Revolution,* ed. Ramon Guthrie and George E. Diller, New York, 1942, p. 33.

61. Bibliothèque Nationale, *Un siècle d'histoire,* IV, Paris, 1929, cat. no. 7414, p. 169.

62. Mary Dorothy George, *Catalogue of Political and Personal Satires,* London, 1942, vol. 7, no. 9426; and Bibliothèque Nationale, *Un siècle d'histoire,* cat. no. 7416, 4:170.

CHAPTER 2

1. Jacques Godechot, ed., *Les Constitutions de la France depuis 1789,* Paris, 1979, p. 146. Sieyès, like Bonaparte, had a copy of Bonald's banned counter-revolutionary treatise *Théorie du pouvoir.* Bonald sent Sieyès a copy, asking that he make the book known in France by any means, even a formal denunciation to the legislature. Although Bonald's request was apparently in vain, his choice of Sieyès is telling. See Charles-Augustin Sainte-Beuve, "M. de Bonald," in *Causeries de Lundi,* 4th ed., Paris, n.d., 4:430, n. 1.

2. Godechot, *Les Constitutions,* p. 162.

3. See Xavier Martin, "Politique et Droit privé après Thermidor," in *La Révolution et l'ordre juridique privé: Rationalité ou scandale?* ed. Michel Vovelle, Acts of the Colloquium of Orleans, September 11–13, 1986, Paris, 1988, 1:173–84.

4. Among these jurists were two experts on Roman and customary law: Jean Domat (1625–1696), the author of *Les Lois civiles dans leur ordre naturel* (1689–94) and Robert-Joseph Pothier of Orleans (1699–1772), the editor of the Pandects of Justinian (1748–52). For the origins of codification in France, see Réné David and Henry P. de Vries, *The French Legal System,* New York, 1958, pp. 9–16. For French legal sources, see André-Jean Arnaud, *Les Origines doctrinales du Code civil français,* Paris, 1969. For the Civil Code, see also Jean Carbonnier, "Le Code civil," in *Les Lieux de mémoire,* ed. P. Nora, vol. 2, *La Nation,* Paris, 1986, 2:293–315.

5. See catalogue entry no. 36 bis by Antoine Schnapper in *French Painting, 1774–1830: The Age of Revolution,* Detroit Institute of Arts, 1975, p. 373; and catalogue entries nos. 206–7 in Antoine Schnapper and Arlette Sérullaz, *Jacques-Louis David,* Paris, Musée du Louvre and Musée National du Château, Versailles, 1989, pp. 474–77.

6. See, for example, Fontanes's comments, January 14, 1805, at the inauguration of Antoine-Denis Chaudet's statue *The First Consul Presenting the Civil Code to the French People,* in Louis de Fontanes, *Collection complète des discours,* Paris, 1821, pp. 38–43.

7. Quoted in Anita Brookner, *Jacques-Louis David,* New York, 1987, p. 169.

8. See Lydie Schimséwitsch, "Portalis et son temps: L'Homme, le penseur, le législateur," Ph.D. diss., University of Paris, 1936.

9. Claire Constans, *Musée National du Château de Versailles: Catalogue de peintures,* Paris, 1980, no. 1848, p. 57. Gautherot's *Portalis* belonged to a series of ministerial portraits commissioned by Vivant Denon at the request of Napoleon and originally hung in the Galerie de Diane in the Tuileries Palace. See Charles-Otto Zieseniss, "Les Portraits des ministres et des grands officiers de la couronne," in *Les Arts à l'époque napoléonienne,* Archives de l'art français, n.s. XXIV, Paris, 1969, pp. 133–58.

10. P.-A. Fenet, *Recueil complet des travaux preparatoires du Code civil,* Paris, 1827, 15:611.

11. The Twelve Tables of Roman law and the laws of Justinian were also compilations of existing material, Portalis said in defense of the Civil Code ("Discours de presentation du Code civil," 3 frimaire Year X [November 23, 1801], in Jean-Etienne-Marie Portalis, *Discours, rapports et travaux inédits sur le Code civil,* ed. Vicomte Frédéric Portalis, Paris, 1844, pp. 95–96).

12. Quoted in Honoré Perouse, *Napoléon Ier et les lois civiles du Consulat et de l'Empire,* Paris, 1866, p. 37.

13. Quoted in Maurice-Charles-Emmanuel Deslandres, *Histoire constitutionnelle de la France de 1789 à 1870,* Paris, 1932, 1:541.

14. For Chaudet's statue, see Ferdinand Boyer, "Le Palais-Bourbon sous le Premier Empire," *Bulletin de la Société de l'Histoire de l'art français,* 1936, pp. 101–3; and Stanislas Lami, *Dictionnaire des sculpteurs de l'école française au dix-huitième siècle,* vol. 1, Paris, 1910, p. 187. The work, exhibited in the Salon of 1808 and the Decennial Exposition of 1810, was given by Louis XVIII to the king of Prussia. It disappeared from the orangery of Sans-Souci after the Russians captured Berlin in the Second World War.

15. The epithet is Fontanes's in a speech at the inauguration of the statue, 24 nivôse Year XIII (January 13, 1805), in *Collection complète des discours,* p. 38. For the engraving (c. 1820), see Jacques Lethève, Françoise Gardey, and Jean Adhémar, *Bibliothèque Nationale, Inventaire du fonds français après 1800,* Paris, 1963, 12:488. Chaudet's statue was reproduced on the medal struck to commemorate the Civil Code. See Aubin Louis Millin, *Medallic History of Napoleon,* London, 1819, cat. no. 82, pl. XXV.

16. See Louis Hautecoeur, *Histoire du Louvre,* Paris, [1928], p. 84; Count Frédéric de Clarac, *Musée de sculpture antique et moderne,* Paris, 1841, 1:444; Lami, *Dictionnaire des sculpteurs dix-huitième siècle,* vol. 2, Paris, 1911, p. 168; and Adlaïde-Marie-Anne Castellas Moitte, *Journal inédit de Madame Moitte,* ed. P. Cottin, 3d ed., Paris, 1932, pp. 25–29. The tablet held by History, inscribed "1806" over the traces of NAPOLEON LE GRAND, was effaced during the Restoration.

17. Napoleon's architect Fontaine noted on June 21, 1807, that the newly completed reliefs in the Cour Carré by Moitte, Philippe-Laurent Roland, and Chaudet had been well received (Pierre-François-Léonard Fontaine, *Journal, 1799–1853,* Paris, 1987, 1:162).

18. Four years later, with the birth of Napoleon's son, the King of Rome, reference to Numa again became an appropriate form of official flattery. See [Anne-Adrien-Firmin] Pillon-Duchemin, *Numa Pompilius au Palais des Tuileries: Hommage à l'occasion de la naissance de S.M. le Roi de Rome,* Paris, 1811. An image of Numa receiving a shield from heaven had adorned a triumphal arch erected for the coronation of Louis XVI. See Richard A. Jackson, *Vive le Roi! A History of the French Coronation from Charles V to Charles X,* Chapel Hill, N.C., 1984, p. 177.

19. See the description in C. P. Landon, *Annales du Musée,* vol. 2 of *Salon de 1812,* Paris, 1812, p. 91.

20. For the earlier design, see Michèle Beaulieu, "Esquisses de la décoration du Louvre au Département des sculptures," *Bulletin monumental,* CIV, 1946, pp. 251–53.

21. See Donald R. Kelley, *Historians and the Law in Postrevolutionary France,* Princeton, N.J., 1984, p. 47.

22. See Nathalie Volle, *Jean-Simon Barthélemy (1743–1811), peintre d'histoire,* Paris, 1979, cat. no. 106; and Pierre Lelièvre, "Vivant Denon," Ph.D. diss., University of Paris, 1942, p. 61.

23. Salon of 1808, *Explication des ouvrages,* Paris, 1808, no. 28.

24. See Volle, Barthélemy, pp. 20, 103.

25. See Georges Burdeau, "Essai sur l'évolution de la notion de loi en droit français," *Archives de Philosophie du droit,* nos. 1–2, 1939, pp. 24–27.

26. Quoted in R. R. Palmer, *The Age of the Democratic Revolution,* vol. 1, Princeton, N.J., 1959, p. 214.

27. Perouse, *Napoléon Ier,* p. 349.

28. *Considérations sur les principaux événements de la Révolution française* (1818), quoted in Louis Bergeron, *L'Episode napoléonien,* vol. 1, *Aspects intérieurs, 1799–1815,* Paris, 1972, p. 19.

29. The title of the code was to continue to change: Louis XVIII had it renamed Code civil (1816) and Napoleon III brought back Code Napoléon (1852); under the Third Republic it once again became the Code civil (1870).

30. "Corps législatif. Présidence de M. Fontanes. Suite de la séance du 3 septembre," *Gazette nationale, ou Le Moniteur universel,* no. 248, September 5, 1807.

31. See Jacques Lablée, "Vœu inscrit au registre ouvert sur la proposition du Consulat à vie," in *Couronne poétique de Napoléon-le-Grand,* ed. Jacques Lablée, Paris, 1807, p. 157.

32. Quoted in Georges Lefebvre, *Napoleon,* trans. Henry F. Stockhold, New York, 1969, p. 130.

33. Quoted in Bergeron, *L'Episode napoléonien,* 1:14.

34. See Lefebvre, *Napoleon*, pp. 147–49.

35. The fundamental study of this influential figure remains Aileen Wilson, *Fontanes (1757–1821)*, Paris, 1928.

36. See [Alexis Eymery, César de Proisy d'Eppe, Pierre-Jean Charrin, et al.], *Dictionnaire des Girouettes (1815), ou Nos contemporains peints d'après eux-mêmes*, Paris, 1815, pp. 157–69.

37. *Discours prononcé dans l'autre monde pour la réception de Napoléon Bonaparte le 5 mai 1821, par Louis Fontanes*, Paris, 1821.

38. Fontanes, *Collection complète des discours*, pp. 44–45.

39. See Irene Collins, *Napoleon and His Parliaments, 1800–1815*, London, 1979, p. 107.

40. The phrase is from a letter from Poyet to Champagny, minister of the interior, quoted in Marie-Louise Biver, *Le Paris de Napoléon*, Paris, 1963, p. 216.

41. For Napoleon's tirade against this work and French architecture in general, see Fontaine, *Journal, 1799–1853*, 1:278–79 (January 21, 1811).

42. On April 18, 1797, after conquering Italy, Napoleon presumed he had the authority to negotiate with Austria and signed the Preliminary Articles of Leoben. Though infuriated, the Directory acquiesced. Lethière's painting, exhibited in the Salon of 1806, is now in the Château de Versailles. For a discussion of this work, see Albert Boime, *Art in an Age of Bonapartism, 1800–1815*, vol. 2 of *A Social History of Modern Art*, Chicago, 1990, pp. 35–37. For a smaller version of the lost *Liberty and Death*, see *French Painting, 1774–1830*, cat. no. 150, pp. 580–81.

43. See Boyer, "Le Palais-Bourbon sous le Premier Empire," pp. 104–6.

44. See the catalogue entries by Jacques Foucart in *French Painting, 1774–1830*, no. 104, pp. 498–500; and D. Ternois in *Ingres*, Paris, Petit-Palais, 1967, no. 17, pp. 32–33; see also Robert Rosenblum, *Jean-Auguste-Dominique Ingres*, New York, 1967, reprint, New York, 1985, p. 68.

45. Susan L. Siegfried has argued that the association of Napoleon with Charlemagne had been discredited by the time the painting was exhibited and that the critics' fury was provoked by Ingres's representation of a political symbol agreeable to the Legislative Body but offensive to other political factions. See her "Politics of Criticism at the Salon of 1806," in Donald D. Howard, John L. Connolly, Jr., and Harold T. Parker, eds., *Proceedings of the Consortium on Revolutionary Europe, 1750–1850*, Athens, Ga., 1980, pp. 69–81. Regarding Ingres's *Napoleon*, see, in the same volume, John L. Connolly, Jr., "Napoleon and the Age of Gold," pp. 52–68.

46. See Boime, *Art in an Age of Bonapartism*, pp. 51–53.

47. See Louis Villefosse and Janine Bouissounouse, *The Scourge of the Eagle*, trans. and ed. Michael Ross, New York, 1972, p. 199.

48. Fontanes, *Collection complète des discours*, pp. 35–36 (December 26, 1804). Siegfried points out the accord between Ingres's image of Napoleon in the guise of a medieval ruler and

Fontanes's support of Napoleon's reinstatement of the French medieval tradition of Catholic monarchy. See "The Politics of Criticism," p. 72.

49. The Constituent Assembly had granted citizenship to French Jews. See Arthur Hertzberg, *The French Enlightenment and the Jews,* New York, 1968, chap. 10.

50. Robert Anchel, *Napoléon et les Juifs,* Paris, 1928, p. 188.

51. *Correspondance de Napoléon Ier, publiée par ordre de l'Empereur Napoléon III,* vol. 13, Paris, 1863, pp. 100–101.

52. See Renée Neher-Bernheim and Elisabeth Revel-Neher, "Une Iconographie juive de l'époque du grand Sanhédrin," in Bernhard Blumenkranz and Albert Soboul, eds., *Le Grand Sanhédrin de Napoléon,* Toulouse, 1979, pp. 135–39.

53. L. Bramsen, *Médaillier Napoléon le Grand . . . première partie, 1799–1809,* 1904–13, reprint, Hamburg, 1977, cat. no. 527, p. 86. According to Jean-Marie Darnis, archivist at the Musée de la Monnaie, Paris, the medal was designed by Denon, and Brenet intended the kneeling figure to be in imitation of Michelangelo's *Moses.* See Neher-Bernheim and Revel-Neher, "Une Iconographie juive," p. 142 nn. 16, 17. The face of the medal bears a profile of Napoleon originally used for a medal commemorating the Battle of Lutzen (1813). According to Bramsen, the Sanhedrin medal was first struck in 1815, in England. The medal's original dies, however, are in the collection of the Administration des Monnaies et Médailles. See *Administration des monnaies et médailles; Médailles françaises dont les coins sont conservés au Musée monétaire,* Paris, 1892, cat. no. 56, p. 361.

54. *Collection des procès-verbaux et décisions du Grand Sanhédrin, convoqué à Paris, . . . dans les mois de février et mars 1807,* ed. Diogène Tama, Paris, 1807, pp. 125, 130, reprinted in Blumenkranz and Soboul. For an annotated bibliography of works by Jews in praise of Napoleon, see E. Carmoly, "Napoléon et ses panégyristes hébreux," *Univers israélite,* no. 4, December 1849, pp. 162–70.

55. For the coercive aspect of Napoleonic policy toward the Jews, see Anchel, *Napoléon et les Juifs,* p. 577; and F. Delpech, "L'Histoire des Juifs en France de 1780 à 1840," in *Les Juifs et la Révolution française,* ed. Bernhard Blumenkranz and Albert Soboul, Toulouse, 1976, pp. 16–17.

56. See André Latreille, "Le Catéchisme impérial de 1806," Ph.D. diss., University of Paris, 1935.

57. *Catéchisme à l'usage de toutes les églises de l'empire français,* Paris, 1806, pp. 58–59. For Napoleon's draft, see Latreille, "Le Catéchisme impérial," pp. 55–56.

58. See Juliette Turlan, "Les Catéchismes politiques, ou De l'instruction à la propagande," in *Hommage à Robert Besnier,* Paris, 1980, p. 270.

59. See Frank Paul Bowman, *Le Christ romantique,* Geneva, 1973, pp. 46–61, and "Les 'Liturgies révolutionnaires,' pastiches ou parodies?" *Revue d'histoire littéraire de la France,* 1990, nos. 4–5, pp. 599–609.

60. *Catéchisme de la Constitution républicaine, Mis à la portée des jeunes citoyens français,* Paris, Year II [1793–94], p. 71.

61. Charles-Augustin Sainte-Beuve, *Chateaubriand et son groupe littéraire sous l'empire* [1861], ed. Maurice Allem, Paris, 1948, 1:225.

62. Under the Consulate the authoritative version of the Bible remained Louis-Isaac Lemaistre de Sacy's translation (1672–95). For the place of the Old Testament in nineteenth-century French Catholic practice, see Claude Savart, "Quelle Bible les Catholiques français lisaient-ils?" in Claude Savart and Jean-Noël Aletti, eds., *Le Monde contemporain et la Bible,* Paris, 1985, pp. 19–34, and, in the same volume, Elisabeth Germain, "Le Catéchisme et la prédication," pp. 49–59.

63. For French imitation and paraphrase of Scripture, see Paul Bénichou, *Le Sacre de l'écrivain, 1750–1830,* 2d ed., Paris, 1985, chap. 2; and Henri Tronchon, "La Fortune intellectuelle de Herder en France," Ph.D. diss., University of Paris, 1920, pp. 170–73.

64. The apocryphal Ossian poems, full of surreptitious biblical imitation, had an enhanced impact on French readers, who were unfamiliar with their source. See Paul Van Tieghem, *Ossian en France,* Paris, 1917, 1:215–16.

65. François-René de Chateaubriand, *Génie du christianisme,* ed. Pierre Reboul, Paris, 1966, 1:110–13.

66. The "Verses on the Hebrew People," by the royalist poet Jacques Delille, were similar in spirit to Chateaubriand's discussion of Mosaic law (*Mercure de France,* no. 37, 1 nivôse, Year X [December 21, 1801], pp. 9–10).

67. Quoted in Sainte-Beuve, *Chateaubriand et son groupe littéraire,* 1:226.

68. See Chateaubriand, "Sur la Législation primitive de M. le vicomte de Bonald (part 2)," in *Oeuvres complètes,* Paris, 1826, 21:174. Sainte-Beuve quotes Bonald's explanation of the difference between the critical fortunes of the *Génie* and *Législation primitive:* "I gave my drug straight and he gave his with sugar" (*Chateaubriand et son groupe littéraire,* 1:225 n. 2).

69. Louis-Gabriel-Ambroise de Bonald, *Oeuvres complètes de M. de Bonald,* ed. Abbé Migne, Paris, 1859, 1:1120. That the Ten Commandments were a common referent during the Consulate is further suggested by *Essai sur l'art de la législation, suivi d'un Plan abrégé de la rédaction d'un Code civil* (Carpentras, 1800) by Jean-de-Dieu d'Olivier, a judge in the court of appeals of Nîmes. Olivier claimed the Ten Commandments as the basis of all legislation: "This ancient charter of morality and social duties offers the elements of law in the briefest imaginable version" (p. 13). He urged that a French civil code be drafted without delay; the respect for property and paternal authority and the use of both Roman and customary law he recommended characterize the code promulgated in 1804.

70. Bonald, *Oeuvres complètes,* 1:1135, 1154–55, 1215.

71. Bossuet had served as preceptor to the dauphin (for whom he wrote the *Discours sur l'histoire universelle*); Bonald was offered the position of preceptor to Napoleon's son, the King of Rome, and to the son of Napoleon's brother Louis Bonaparte. Loyal to the exiled monarchy, Bonald refused the offer. Yielding, however, to the advice of his friend

Fontanes, he accepted an invitation to join the Council of the Imperial University (1810), which the former president of the Legislative Body headed as grand master.

72. A. M. Broadley, *Napoleon in Caricature, 1795–1821,* London, 1911, no. 13, 2:358.

73. This myth that bellicosity and despotism were intended to lay the foundation of a liberal and peaceful republic was later propagated by Louis-Napoleon Bonaparte, the future Napoleon III, in his book *Napoleonic Ideas* (1839).

74. Salon of 1833, *Explication des ouvrages,* Paris, 1833, no. 3130, *Napoléon; tableau allégorique.* For the painting by Mauzaisse, see Michael Marrinan, *Painting Politics for Louis-Philippe,* New Haven, Conn., 1988, p. 162. In the same volume, see pp. 202–3 for Hippolyte Flandrin's *Napoleon as Lawgiver* (Salon of 1847).

CHAPTER 3

1. For the political history of the period, see Guillaume de Bertier de Sauvigny, *The Bourbon Restoration,* trans. Lynn M. Case, Philadelphia, 1966.

2. Quoted from Archives Nationales AB XIX, 340, pp. 108 (bis)–109, in Pierre Simon, *L'Elaboration de la Charte constitutionnelle de 1814,* Paris, 1906, p. 111.

3. The passage continues: "Toute charte constitutive d'un état doit descendre du Ciel, pour être placée ensuite dans un sanctuaire impénétrable aux regards du vulgaire et même des sages, parce que les plus sages deviennent insensés, lorsqu'ils veulent sonder les vues de la Providence. . . . Il y a un autre prestige qui n'est pas moins puissant, c'est celui de l'antiquité. Tous les peuples en effet ont . . . été d'autant plus attachés à leurs institutions, qu'elles ont été plus enveloppées de ces augustes ténèbres, de ces illusions mystérieuses qui commandent le respect" (*Du Sentiment considéré dans ses rapports avec la littérature et les arts,* Lyon, 1801, pp. 142–43). Cf. also the opening passage from a counter-revolutionary work on Charlemagne's legislation: "Quand le temps qui règle et affermit les empires, a établi et cimenté un ordre de choses, l'homme sage le respecte et ne lève que d'une main religieuse le voile, que en cache l'origine" (Bonnaire de Pronville, *Pouvoir législatif sous Charlemagne,* Brunswick, 1800, p. 1).

4. According to Beugnot, "M. de Fontanes had few occasions to read preambles of laws, and it was not there that the orators generally went to seek models. The piece that he provided contained . . . lofty thoughts couched in eloquent forms; but these thoughts were too general, these forms had too much luster. It was a beautiful page, but not a preamble" (*Mémoires du comte Beugnot, 1779–1815,* ed. Robert Lacour-Gayet, Paris, 1959, p. 288). Like Fontanes, Beugnot (1761–1835) had a distinguished Napoleonic past. He served as Lucien Bonaparte's favorite advisor in the Ministry of the Interior, entered the Council of State in 1806, and was made count of the empire two years later.

5. *Catalogue générale illustré des éditions de la monnaie de Paris,* [Paris], 1978, 2:105.

6. For the pre-revolutionary origins of the Council of State and its revival (at the suggestion of Sieyès) under Napoleon, see Tony Sauvel, "Du Palais de la Cité au Palais-Royal," in *Le*

Conseil d'Etat: Livre jubilaire, publié pour commémorer son cent-cinquantième anniversaire, 4 nivôse an VIII, 24 December 1949, Paris, 1952, pp. 32–39.

7. Napoleon's Council of State sat in the Tuileries; prior to the relocation under Charles X, the committees were dispersed, with infrequent general assemblies in the Chancellerie, Place Vendôme. Under the July Monarchy, the Council of State was moved to the Hôtel Molé (1832) and then to the Palais d'Orsay (1840) where some of the paintings, including Delacroix's *Justinian,* were destroyed when the palace was burned during the Commune.

8. Count de Peyronnet, letter of April 10, 1824, to Marquis Jacques-Alexandre-Bernard Law de Lauriston, the minister in charge of the royal household, regarding the proposed move of the Council of State to the Louvre (Archives Nationales BB17ᴬ32, dossier 4).

9. See Ch. Léonardi, "Le Conseil d'état sous la restauration," Ph.D. diss., University of Paris, 1909, pp. 63–65; and Bernard Olivier-Martin, "Le Conseil d'état de la restauration," Ph.D. diss., University of Paris, 1941.

10. See François Guizot, *Mémoires pour servir à l'histoire de mon temps* [1858–68], ed. Michel Richard, Paris, 1971, pp. 94–95.

11. See Count Frédéric de Clarac, *Musée de sculpture antique et moderne,* Paris, 1841, 1:545–99; and Norman D. Ziff, *Paul Delaroche: A Study in Nineteenth-Century French History Painting,* New York, 1977, pp. 62–63.

12. From Delécluze, *Journal,* quoted in Ziff, *Paul Delaroche,* p. 63.

13. See the engraved reproductions in *Musée de peinture et de sculpture,* vol. 4, Paris, 1829. See also the list of Louvre paintings on deposit in other locations, compiled by Elisabeth Foucart-Walter, in Isabelle Compin and Anne Roquebert, *Catalogue sommaire illustré,* Paris, 1986, 5:194–375. A description of this program was sent by Forbin to the minister of justice and keeper of the seals, with a request for permission to erect scaffolding, October 6, 1826 (Archives Nationales BB17ᴬ49, dossier 1, item 12). In the same dossier is the response of the minister, October 10, 1826: "The choice of subjects appears very proper, and I gladly give them my approval."

14. Louvre inv. no. 2628. See Compin and Roquebert, *Catalogue sommaire illustré,* 3:65; and Salon of 1827, *Explication des ouvrages,* Paris, 1827, pp. 17–18.

15. Quoted from the description of the program sent by Forbin to the minister of justice. Archives Nationales BB17ᴬ49, dossier 1, item 12.

16. "Salon de 1827. Peintures du Conseil d'état," *Journal du Commerce,* January 11, 1828.

17. Ibid.

18. According to the critic of the *Journal du Commerce,* a portrait of Charles X by Paulin-Jean-Baptiste Guérin (called Paulin-Guérin) hung in the same room.

19. Louvre inv. no. 6551. Compin and Roquebert, *Catalogue sommaire illustré,* 4:76.

20. *Lycurgus and the Deputies of Sparta* (Jacques-Charles Bordier du Bignon); *Numa and the Nymph Egeria* (Charles-Nicolas-Rafael Lafond); and *Solon Drafting the Laws of Athens* (René-Théodore Berthon) were included in a group of four overdoor paintings of ancient

lawgivers commissioned for the Salon de la Pendule, Château de Versailles (c. 1819). See Archives Nationales o³1395; and Eudore Soulié, *Notice des peintures et sculptures composant le Musée Impérial de Versailles,* Versailles, 1855, part 2, p. 175. Roland Bossard, secretary of documentation at the Château de Versailles, informed me that the four paintings were destroyed during World War II while on deposit in the French embassy in Warsaw.

21. Archives Nationales BB17ᴬ49, dossier 1, item 12. In 1841 Mauzaisse painted a revised version of *Divine Wisdom Giving the Laws to the Kings and Legislators,* in which Napoleon is included next to the French monarchs (Musée Napoléon, Ile d'Aix, inv. no. MG 100).

22. Auguste Jal, *Esquisses, croquis, pochades, ou Tout ce qu'on voudra, sur le Salon de 1827,* Paris, 1828, pp. 454–56.

23. Mauzaisse's painting is related thematically to a Napoleonic ceiling painting in the Louvre's Hall of Greek Civilization, Charles Meynier's *Earth Receiving from the Emperors Hadrian and Justinian the Code of Roman Laws Dictated by Nature, Justice, and Wisdom* (commissioned 1801; signed and dated Year XI [1802–3]), Louvre inv. no. 20092. Compin and Roquebert, *Catalogue sommaire illustré,* 4:87.

24. The *Moses* and *Numa* were sent to the museum of Saint-Brieuc in 1872. Blondel's *Solon* and *Lycurgus* are in the museum of Amiens.

25. Since 1962 Drolling's painting has been concealed by a false ceiling (Compin and Roquebert, *Catalogue sommaire illustré,* 3:230).

26. See Lee Johnson, *The Paintings of Eugène Delacroix,* vol. 1, Oxford, 1981, pp. 110–12; and F. A. Trapp, "An Early Photograph of a Lost Delacroix," *Burlington Magazine,* CVI, June 1964, pp. 266–69.

27. See Claire Constans, *Musée National du Château de Versailles,* Paris, 1980, cat. no. 4023, p. 117.

28. For this painting, see Ziff, *Paul Delaroche,* pp. 62–66.

29. Donald R. Kelley, *Historians and the Law in Postrevolutionary France,* Princeton, N.J., 1984, p. 43, cites Delacroix's *Justinian* as an example of the continuation under the Restoration of Napoleonic legislative pretensions.

30. See the dedication of "La Poésie sacrée" from *Méditations poétiques* (1820) where Lamartine explained his admiration of Genoude: "Until now we only knew the sense of the books of Job, of Isaiah, of David; thanks to him, the expression, the color, the movement, the energy live today in our tongue" (*Oeuvres poétiques,* ed. Marius-François Guyard, Paris, 1963, p. 76). The Genoude Bible (1815–24) was based on the seventeenth-century translation by Lemaistre de Sacy. For the vogue for scriptural imitation among Restoration playwrights, see Anna Louise Catharina Kromsigt, "Le Théâtre biblique à la veille du romantisme (1789–1830)," Ph.D. diss., Univ. of Amsterdam, 1931.

31. From "Nabuchodnosor" (1821), in *Oeuvres de P. J. de Béranger,* Paris, 1876, 2:4–6.

32. See Maurice Z. Shroder, *Icarus: The Image of the Artist in French Romanticism,* Cambridge, Mass., 1961, p. 69.

33. Chateaubriand, *Mémoires d'outre-tombe* [1849–50], ed. Maurice Levaillant and Georges Moulinier, Paris, 1951, 1:905.

34. See Jean-Marie Darnis, *Les Monuments expiatoires du supplice de Louis XVI et de Marie-Antoinette sous l'Empire et la Restauration, 1812–1830,* Paris, 1981 (for Chateaubriand's support of the chapel, see p. 9). See also Louis Hautecoeur, *Histoire de l'architecture classique en France,* Paris, 1955, 6:12. Darnis (pp. 9–10) indicates that the chapel, privately financed by Louis XVIII and the Duchess of Angoulême, was a family monument and was not intended originally to carry the national expiatory significance it acquired by popular sentiment with the encouragement of Chateaubriand.

35. Louis-Pierre Fontaine (not to be confused with the architect) and Antoine Etex also worked on the pendentives and other parts of the interior decoration. See Darnis, *Les Monuments expiatoires,* p. 42.

36. According to Fontaine, the sculptural program was specified at the outset and was executed as planned. But the choice of inscriptions became a matter of some controversy as Cardinal de Croy, grand almoner of France and archbishop of Rouen, insisted on modifying those originally projected. The inscription for the pendentive with the tablets of the law, originally "Dat robur fert auxilium" (It gives strength), was among those altered by Croy. Fontaine's reference to the inscription as "Si vis ad vitam beatam ingredire serva mandata" (If you wish to enter a beatific life, you must serve) varies slightly from the inscription as executed. See P.-F.-L. Fontaine, *Journal, 1799–1853,* Paris, 1987, 2:700–701 (February 23, 1826).

37. Louis-Gabriel-Ambroise de Bonald, *Législation primitive,* in *Oeuvres complètes de M. de Bonald,* ed. Abbé Migne, Paris, 1859, 1:1111.

38. Lamartine's lover, Julie Charles, in her last letter to him, told him his ode had won Bonald's admiration. See Arsène Soreil, *Etude littéraire sur le vicomte de Bonald,* Brussels, 1942, p. 54.

39. Lamartine, *Oeuvres poétiques,* pp. 53–54.

40. François-René de Chateaubriand, *Génie du christianisme,* ed. Pierre Reboul, 1:447–48.

41. Lamartine, *Cours familier de littérature, un entretien par mois,* Paris, 1856, 2:273.

42. See Hubert Juin, *Victor Hugo,* vol. 1, *1802–1843,* Paris, 1980, pp. 465–75.

43. *Vie de Rossini* [1823], ed. H. Prunières, Paris, 1922, 2:66–67.

44. Quoted in Gabriel Salvador, *J. Salvador: Sa vie, ses oeuvres et ses critiques,* Paris, 1881, pp. 9–10. A similar argument for the liberal nature of Mosaic legislation had already been voiced by a lawyer, de La Serve, in *De la Royauté selon les lois divines révélées, les lois naturelles et la Charte constitutionnelle,* Paris, 1819, pp. 7, 11. Similarly, the republican academician Népomucène Lemercier (1771–1840), in the preface to his epic poem *Moyse* (1823), offered the tenacious loyalty of the Jewish people to Mosaic law as an edifying example: "J'ai pensé qu'il serait utile d'offrir le simulacre le plus frappant de la conservation constante d'une loi jurée, au peuple français, de qui le naturel n'est que trop incon-

stant à tout ce qu'il veut fonder" (*Moyse, Poëme en quatre chants,* Paris, 1823, p. vii). The young, independently wealthy Salvador came from Montpellier, where he was trained in medicine. His Jewish father, whose forebears fled Spain during the Inquisition, claimed descent from the Maccabees; his mother was Catholic.

45. E.L., review of *Histoire des institutions de Moïse et du peuple hébreu,* by Joseph Salvador, *Le Globe,* April 19, 1829, p. 243.

46. The most notable objection to Salvador's argument was that of the liberal lawyer Dupin, whose counter-argument—that Christ had been denied due process and subjected to cruel irregularities—was solidly in the liberal tradition of respect for the law. See André-Marie-Jean-Jacques Dupin, *Jésus devant Caïphe et Pilate, ou Réfutation du chapitre de M. Salvador intitulé: "Jugement et condamnation de Jésus,"* Paris, 1828.

47. Quoted in Salvador, *J. Salvador,* p. 46.

48. The readiness of contemporaries to associate Moses with politics was mocked by a satirist commenting on a reading of Chateaubriand's play *Moïse.* The audience included a hypocritical "deputy of the extreme left" who, before launching into a diatribe against the control of the Council of State by the monarch, awkwardly attempted to present Moses as a precursor of progressive constitutional government. See "Lecture de Moyse de M. de Chateaubriand, à l'abbaye aux Bois, le 21 juin 1829," in [F. de Montherot], *Mémoires poétiques,* Paris, 1833, pp. 24–25. For Chateaubriand's play, see Chapter 6.

CHAPTER 4

1. François-René de Chateaubriand, *Mémoires d'outre-tombe* [1849–50], ed. Maurice Levaillant and Georges Moulinier, Paris, 1951, 2:394–95.

2. This fatal article of the 1814 charter was inspired by Napoleon's authoritarian Constitution of Year VIII (art. 44). See Jacques Godechot, ed., *Les Constitutions de la France depuis 1789,* Paris, 1979, pp. 214, 245.

3. François Guizot, *Mémoires pour servir à l'histoire de mon temps* [1858–68], ed. Michel Richard, Paris, 1971, p. 241.

4. Guizot, *Mémoires,* p. 241.

5. The phrase is that of the Count Marthe-Camille Bachasson de Montalivet, a member of Louis-Philippe's cabinet who cited this emphasis on the law as the distinguishing mark of Périer's politics. See *Cte. de Montalivet: Fragments et souvenirs,* ed. Georges Picot, vol. 1, Paris, 1899, p. 382.

6. Périer went on to distinguish the July Revolution in Paris—justified by its defense of the law—from the anarchic uprising in Lyon: "Il faut enseigner aux hommes . . . que le fusil des trois journées de Paris était consacré par la loi qu'il vengeait, et que celui des deux jours de Lyon est flétri par la révolte contre les lois qu'il a violées! (Mouvement très-prononcé d'adhésion dans l'immense majorité de l'assemblée.) . . . Ces avertissemens, ces

leçons ont été malheureusement écrits sur les murs de Lyon, en caractères de sang; mais ce sang même n'aura pas été perdu pour la liberté, si tout le monde comprend la leçon qu'il a tracée! (Sensation prolongée)" (*Communication faite au nom du gouvernement à la Chambre des députés, sur les troubles de Lyon, par M. le président du Conseil, ministre de l'intérieur,* Paris, December 1831, pp. 10–11).

7. See Michael Marrinan, *Painting Politics for Louis-Philippe,* New Haven, Conn., 1988, p. 65. Similarly, in Abel de Pujol's *Charter of 1830* (1838–40), a grisaille ceiling painting in the Palais-Bourbon's Salle des Distributions (adjacent to the Salle Louis-Philippe), a group of legislators swears allegiance to Mosaic tablets inscribed "Charter of 1830."

8. For the Palais-Bourbon, see Jules de Joly, *Plans, coupes, élévations et détails de la restauration de la Chambre des députés,* Paris, 1840; Violaine Lanselle, "Le Palais-Bourbon et l'hôtel de Lassay," extract from *Monuments historiques,* no. 144, [1985]; Jules Rais, "Le Palais Bourbon et la Chambre des députés," *Revue universelle,* October 15, 1902, pp. 501–20; and G. Demoget, "Notice sur le Palais-Bourbon," *Société d'iconographie parisienne,* n.s., 1929, pp. 25–44.

9. The statues, commissioned in 1833, represent Jean-Sylvain Bailly, first president of the National Assembly, and Mirabeau (both works are by Jean-Louis-Nicolas Jaley); General Maximilien-Sébastien Foy, an outspoken member of the liberal opposition under the Restoration (by Louis Desprez); and Casimir Périer (by Francisque-Joseph Duret). The statue of Louis-Phillipe, 1833–38 (by Georges Jacquot), was removed after the revolution of 1848 and later replaced by the colossal bronze relief sculpture by Jules Dalou, *Estates-General, Session of June 23, 1789* (*Mirabeau Responding to Dreux-Brézé*), 1883. The room is now designated the Salle Casimir-Périer.

10. Commissioned August 31, 1833, with payment completed November 31, 1834. Archives Nationales F²¹488. The most informative study of the artist remains Michèle Beaulieu, "Un sculpteur français d'origine italienne: Henri de Triqueti (1804–1874)," in *A travers l'art italien du XVᵉ au XXᵉ siècle,* ed. H. Bédarida, Publications de la Société d'Etudes italiennes, no. 2, Paris, 1949, pp. 203–22. See also Stanislas Lami, *Dictionnaire des sculpteurs de l'école française au dix-neuvième siècle,* vol. 4, Paris, 1921, pp. 318–24; and the catalogue entry by Judith Applegate in Peter Fusco and H. W. Janson, eds., *The Romantics to Rodin,* Los Angeles County Museum of Art, 1980, pp. 359–60.

11. See Jean-Etienne-Marie Portalis, *Discours, rapports et travaux inédits sur le Code civil,* ed. Vicomte Frédéric Portalis, Paris, 1844, pp. 21–22, 33.

12. Triqueti's work for the Salle Louis-Philippe is thematically similar to Jean-Baptiste Roman's large relief sculpture in the adjacent assembly hall, *The Charter: Protector of the Arts, Sciences, Agriculture, and Commerce* (1830–33).

13. Alphonse de Lamartine, *Oeuvres poétiques,* ed. Marius-François Guyard, Paris, 1963, pp. 743–48.

14. See Henri Guillemin, "Le *Jocelyn* de Lamartine," Ph.D. diss., University of Paris, 1935, pp. 558–59.

15. For Lamartine's parliamentary career, see William Fortescue, *Alphonse de Lamartine,* London, 1983.

16. Lamartine associated agriculture with social order. Thus in a parliamentary address of March 13, 1834, he blamed social disorder on industrialization, claiming that France had been protected against such strife when it was strictly agricultural (*Discours prononcé par M. de Lamartine . . . sur les associations,* Paris, 1834, p. 18).

17. Alphonse de Lamartine, address of May 13, 1834, in *La France parlementaire (1834–1851),* vol. 1, Paris, 1864, pp. 80, 83. For the cult of property in legal thought under the July Monarchy, see Donald R. Kelley, *Historians and the Law in Postrevolutionary France,* Princeton, N.J., 1984, pp. 133–35.

18. See Lee Johnson, *The Paintings of Eugène Delacroix,* vol. 5, Oxford, 1989, pp. 3–31.

19. From the artist's description of the Salon du Roi paintings published in J.-J. Guiffrey, "Le Salon du Roi," *L'Art,* XIII, 1878, pp. 257–68.

20. Following the collapse of the July Monarchy, the moderate republican Francis Wey bitterly noted that "under Louis-Philippe, all justice emanated from the king. . . . How slow is the progress of societies! It was necessary to wait until 1848 to efface the last vestiges of the feudal regime" (*Manuel des droits et des devoirs; Dictionnaire democratique,* Paris, 1848, s.v. "Justice"). For Wey's politics see T. J. Clark, *Image of the People: Gustave Courbet and the 1848 Revolution,* Princeton, N.J., 1982, p. 53.

21. Louis de Ronchaud, "Etudes sur l'art: La Peinture monumentale en France," *La Revue indépendante,* 2d ser., XII, November 10, 1847, pp. 44–45.

22. Gustave Planche, "Eugène Delacroix: Le Salon du Roi" (1837) in *Portraits d'artistes,* Paris, 1853, 2:30.

23. Henri [Heinrich] Heine, *De la France,* Paris, 1833, p. 121.

24. Planche, "Eugène Delacroix," pp. 30–31.

25. This source is mentioned in Robert Neubinger Beetem, "Delacroix's Mural Paintings, 1833–1847," Ph.D. diss., University of California, Berkeley, 1964, p. 25; and in Sara Lichtenstein, *Delacroix and Raphael,* New York, 1979, p. 174.

26. A suggestive detail in the painting of Justice, set into the ceiling above the throne niche, is a scroll to the right of the figure that suggests blocky pseudo-Hebrew characters.

27. The bronze doors, 10.38 meters high (including lintel), were commissioned February 24, 1834. For a description, see *Inventaire général des richesses d'art de la France, Paris, Monuments religieux,* Paris, 1876, 1:212–14. The work is discussed in the exhibition catalogue *La Sculpture française au XIXe siècle,* ed. Anne Pingeot et al., Paris, Galeries nationales du Grand Palais, 1986, pp. 202–4; and in H. W. Janson, *Nineteenth-Century Sculpture,* New York, 1985, pp. 121–24.

28. See Jean-Marie Darnis, *Les Monuments expiatoires du supplice de Louis XVI et de Marie-Antoinette sous l'Empire et la Restauration, 1812–1830,* Paris, 1981, pp. 65–76.

29. See Marrinan, *Painting Politics for Louis-Philippe,* parts III and IV.

30. For Cortot's expiatory monument to Louis XVI, destroyed at the foundry during the July Revolution, see Darnis, *Les Monuments expiatoires,* pp. 115–19, 155–65.

31. For Ziégler's painting, see Michael Paul Driskel, "Eclecticism and Ideology in the July Monarchy: Jules-Claude Ziegler's Vision of Christianity at the Madeleine," *Arts Magazine,* May 1982, pp. 119–29.

32. According to Adolphe Granier de Cassagnac, *Histoire de l'église de la Madeleine,* Paris, 1838, p. 38, Triqueti was responsible for the subject. Administration of the Madeleine passed to the city of Paris in 1842; documentary material on the bronze doors may have been lost when the Hôtel de Ville was burned during the Commune.

33. In the Salon of 1836 Triqueti exhibited the model for a vase decorated with a series of biblical mothers (no. 1989). Thiers had the work cast for his large art collection. See Baron August-Théodore de Girardot, *Catalogue de l'oeuvre du baron Henri de Triqueti,* Orleans, 1874, p. 16; and Lami, *Dictionnaire . . . dix-neuvième siècle,* 4:320. For Thiers's enthusiasm for the Old Testament, see Adolphe Thiers, *Salon de mil huit cent vingt-deux,* Paris, 1822, p. 73.

34. Charles-François Lhomond, *Histoire abrégée de la religion avant la venue de Jésus-Christ* [c. 1791], Angers, 1818, p. 134.

35. See A.-Z., "Revue de la semaine . . . la porte de la Madeleine . . . ," *L'Artiste,* 2d series, I, 1839, p. 387. *Christ Pardoning the Magdalen at the Last Judgment,* by Philippe-Joseph-Henri Lemaire (1830–34), is in the pediment of the church, high above Triqueti's doors.

36. The other panels feature *God Admires Creation* (commandment to honor the Sabbath); *Cham Cursed by Noah* (commandment to honor parents); *The Banishment of Cain* (the crime of murder); *Acham Condemned by Joshua* (Joshua 7; the crime of theft); *Daniel, Susanna, and the Elders* (the crime of false witness); and *Abimelech and Sara* (Genesis 20; the crime of coveting a neighbor's wife).

37. See Michael Paul Driskel, "Singing 'The Marseillaise' in 1840: The Case of Charlet's Censored Prints," *Art Bulletin,* LXIX, December 1987, pp. 604–25.

38. Duke Victor de Broglie, quoted in Paul Thureau-Dangin, *Histoire de la Monarchie de Juillet,* Paris, 1888, 2:320–21.

39. The iconographic significance of this urban scheme is pointed out in Donald David Schneider, *The Works and Doctrine of Jacques Ignace Hittorff, 1792–1867: Structural Innovation and Formal Expression in French Architecture, 1810–1867,* New York, 1977. On the relationship between this urban scheme and the hieroglyphic inscriptions on the obelisk, see Todd Porterfield, "Art in the Service of French Imperialism in the Near East, 1798–1848," Ph.D. diss., Boston University, 1990, pp. 209–10.

40. H.-D. Lacordaire, *Sainte Marie-Madeleine,* Paris, 1860, p. 223, quoted in Paul Léon, "L'Eglise de la Madeleine (1764–1842)," *Revue des deux mondes,* June 1, 1954, p. 424.

41. The identification of the Madeleine doors with the regime was bolstered by the statues by Charles-François Leboeuf (called Nanteuil) of the king's patron saints, Saint Louis and Saint Philippe, in niches flanking the entrance to the church.

42. The commentary published with the cartoon gives the comparison of the greedy regime to the biblical Hebrews an anti-Semitic twist. "Ce sont les poches et les tirelires de juifs qui, comme ceux du désert, n'ont pas soif d'eau claire" (pp. 1837–38).

43. For Traviès's caricature, see the exhibition catalogue by Gerd Unverfehrt, Klaus Lankheit, and Jurgen Döring, *La Caricature: Bildsatire in Frankreich 1830–1835 aus der Sammlung von Kritter,* Münster, Westfälisches Landesmuseum für Kunst und Kulturgeschichte, 1980, no. 88.

44. The profile in the print reverses that on the coin. See Jean Mazard, *Histoire monétaire et numismatique contemporaine, 1790 -1963,* Paris, 1965, cat. no. 962, 1:247.

45. Jeanne L. Wasserman, in the exhibition catalogue *Daumier Sculpture: A Critical and Comparative Study,* Cambridge, Mass., Fogg Art Museum, Harvard University, 1969, p. 125, associates the name Père-Scie with Persil's jagged profile and with the sound of the guillotine. The word *scie* is also slang for a tiresome person or thing.

46. *La Politique de Lamartine,* ed. Louis de Ronchaud, Paris, 1878, 1:77.

47. Edme Miel, "Salon de 1834," *Le Constitutionnel,* April 14, 1834. For Préault and his bibliography, see David Mower, "Antoine Augustin Préault (1809–1879)," *Art Bulletin,* LXIII, June 1981, pp. 288–307; and the catalogue entries by Charles W. Millard in Fusco and Janson, *The Romantics to Rodin,* pp. 323–25. Millard is the author of the manuscript "The Life and Work of Auguste Préault." For *Tuerie* see also the exhibition catalogue *La Sculpture française,* no. 191; and Alison Elizabeth West, "From Pajou to Préault: The Development of Neoclassicism and the Sublime in French Sculpture, 1760–1830," Ph.D. diss., Institute of Fine Arts, New York University, 1985, pp. 515–18.

48. See Théophile Silvestre, *Histoire des artistes vivants, français et étrangers,* Paris, 1856, p. 294.

49. Salon of 1834, *Explication des ouvrages,* Paris, 1834, no. 2124.

50. Hugh Honour, *Romanticism,* New York, 1979, pp. 143, 388.

51. Mower, "Antoine Augustin Préault," p. 293. Similarly, Nancy Davenport ("Sources for Préault's *Tuerie, fragment episodique d'un grand bas-relief,*" *Source: Notes in the History of Art,* XI, fall 1991, pp. 22–30) unconvincingly identifies the figures in *Tuerie* with specific characters from three plays. Caravaggio's *Kiss of Judas* (c. 1600–1601, Museum of Eastern and Western Art, Odessa), identified in the same article as a source for *Tuerie,* has some resemblance to the sculpture; but that resemblance is hardly strong enough to justify Davenport's claim that the Caravaggio supersedes all previously suggested visual sources. The Triqueti Law reliefs in the Salle Louis-Philippe that I compare to *Tuerie* (*Art Bulletin,* LXX, September 1988, pp. 486–501) are erroneously referred to by Davenport (p. 28) as Triqueti's Ten Commandments reliefs on the Madeleine doors.

52. De Caso's example, *Childebert assistant à des jeux* (Salon of 1833; Musée d'Amiens) by Théophile Caudron, does not appear to have been a source for any particular figural or compositional elements of *Tuerie,* but it is remarkable in anticipating the frenetic violence and aggressively projecting relief of Préault's sculpture. See Jacques De Caso, *David d'Angers,* Paris, 1988, pp. 98–99.

53. See *Le Salon de 1834,* Paris, 1834, p. 164.

54. See Ernest Chesneau, "Auguste Préault," *L'Art,* XVII, 1879, pp. 6–8; and Jean Gigoux, *Causeries sur les artistes de mon temps,* Paris, 1885, pp. 172–75.

55. Quoted in Silvestre, *Histoire des artistes vivants,* p. 286.

56. Albert Boime, in *Hollow Icons: The Politics of Sculpture in Nineteenth-Century France,* Kent, Ohio, 1987, compares *Tuerie* to Daumier's famous lithograph *Rue Transnonain, April 15, 1834,* rightly associating *Tuerie* with "the prevailing climate of tension and potential violence" of 1834. Boime's characterization of *Tuerie* as "a topical political statement akin to Daumier's *Rue Transnonain*" (pp. 48–50), however, oversimplifies the richly problematic relationship between Préault's sculpture and its political context.

57. See Jean Lucas-Dubreton, *La grande peur de 1832 (le choléra et l'émeute),* Paris, 1932.

58. Silvestre, *Histoire des artistes vivants,* p. 282.

59. Although Préault benefited from state patronage during his career, this support did not begin until the latter half of the July Monarchy. See the record of Préault's Salon refusals in Mower, p. 307. For Triqueti's position, see Beaulieu, "Un Sculpteur français," pp. 208–9. During the Second Republic Triqueti appealed to the prefect of the Seine for an official commission for a marble Crucifixion group for the church of Sainte-Clotilde, recalling that "like every good citizen" he had served in the National Guard during the June Days insurrection of 1848 and had been wounded in the defense of order: "Forcé comme tous les bons citoyens de sortir en juin 1848 de ma paisible et laborieuse vie d'artiste, j'avais été atteint de plusieurs balles à l'attaque des premières barricades et . . . j'étais resté une année entière malade et éloigné de mes travaux sans que j'ai cherché à être indeminisé en aucune manière de mes pertes et de mes souffrances" (Archives de la Seine D4, AZ, 309; letter of March 9, 1851).

60. A reproduction by Nanteuil of Préault's *Parias,* rejected by the Salon jury of 1834, was published in *L'Artiste,* 1st series, VII, 1834, with the inscription "Célestin Nanteuil à son ami Préault 1834." For a reproduction of the print, see Mower, "Antoine Augustin Préault," p. 291 fig. 3. The previous year Nanteuil's illustration of a scene from Borel's "Dina, la belle juive," one of the stories in *Champavert, contes immoraux,* was reproduced in *L'Artiste,* 1st series, V, 1833. For Borel, see Paul Bénichou, *Le Sacre de l'écrivain, 1750–1830,* 2d ed., Paris, 1985, pp. 435–39; Mario Praz, *The Romantic Agony,* trans. Angus Davidson, 2d ed., Oxford, 1970, pp. 13–36; and Enid Starkie, *Petrus Borel the Lycanthrope: His Life and Times,* Norfolk, Conn., 1954.

61. Théophile Gautier, *Histoire du romantisme* [1874], Paris, 1927, p. 97.

62. This outburst is attributed to Préault in Luc Benoist, *La Sculpture romantique,* Paris, [1928], p. 62. The remark is given to Prince Ernest de Saxe-Cobourg in Adèle Hugo, *Victor Hugo raconté par un témoin de sa vie,* Paris, 1867, 2:283. The varying attribution of the remark as well as the probability that it was a "common enough slogan" is discussed in Malcolm Easton, *Artists and Writers in Paris: The Bohemian Idea, 1803–1867,* London, 1964, p. 61 n. 9. Easton associates Préault's hostility to middle-class taste with Borel's

hatred of middle-class morals and manners: "It is only a short step from Préault's 'Guillotine the baldpates!' . . . to Borel's 'In Paris there's a den of robbers and a den of murderers: the first is the Stock Exchange and the second the Law Courts.'" Borel is quoted from *Champavert, contes immoraux,* in *Oeuvres complètes de Pétrus Borel "le lycanthrope,"* ed. Aristide Marie, Paris, 1922, 3:35.

63. Pétrus Borel, "Des artistes penseurs et des artistes creux," *L'Artiste,* 1st series, V, 1833, p. 258. For Préault's *Two Poor Women* and *Beggary,* see Salon of 1833, *Explication des ouvrages,* Paris, 1833, nos. 2646, 2647. Borel ("Des artistes penseurs," p. 259) referred to *Beggary (La Mendicité)* as *La Misère.*

64. "Loi! vertu! honneur! vous êtes satisfaits; tenez, reprenez vôtre proie!... Monde barbare, tu l'as voulu, tiens, regarde, c'est ton oeuvre, à toi. Es-tu content de ta victime? [. . .] Bâtard! c'est bien effronté à vous, d'avoir voulu naître sans autorisation royale, sans bans! Eh! la loi? eh! l'honneur? [. . .] Loi barbare! préjugé féroce! honneur infâme! hommes! société! tenez! tenez votre proie!... Je vous la rends!!!..." (Borel, *Champavert,* pp. 382–83; suspension points in original). Denunciation of society and its laws in such exclamatory outbursts was popularized by Alexandre Dumas's melodramatic play *Antony,* which premiered in 1831. For the "Antonisme" vogue, see Louis Maigron, *Le Romantisme et les moeurs: Essai d'étude historique et sociale d'après des documents inédits,* Paris, 1910, pp. 356–89.

65. "Qu'ils viennent donc les imposteurs, que je les étrangle! les fourbes qui chantent l'amour, qui le *guirlandent* et le *mirlitonnent,* qui le font un enfant joufflu, joufflu de jouissances, qu'ils viennent donc, les imposteurs, que je les étrangle! Chanter l'amour!... pour moi, l'amour, c'est de la haine, des gémissemens, des cris, de la honte, du deuil, du fer, des larmes, du sang, des cadavres, des ossemens, des remords, je n'en ai pas connu d'autre!... Allons, roses pastoureaux, chantez donc l'amour, dérision! mascarade amère!" (Borel, *Champavert,* pp. 357–58; suspension points and emphasis in original).

66. G. L. [Gabriel Laviron], review of *Champavert, contes immoraux,* by Pétrus Borel, *L'Artiste,* 1st series, V, 1833, p. 67. Laviron, a socialist, participated in the storming of the Constitutional Assembly on May 15, 1848, by a pro-Polish leftist mob and died in the service of Garibaldi in 1849. See Benoist, *La Sculpture romantique,* p. 33; and René Jasinski, *Les Années romantiques de Th. Gautier,* Paris, 1929, p. 131. Beaulieu's contrasting of Triqueti, who, he said, perfectly represented bourgeois society, with Laviron, who was an enemy of that society, underscores Laviron's affinity with Préault and Borel ("Un Sculpteur français," p. 205).

67. "It is certain that after July [1830] the young Romantics were attracted to republican and revolutionary ideology. What is dubious is that a common and coherent impulse tying poetry and art to revolution existed in the midst of the *petit cénacle* [Borel's circle]" (Paul Bénichou, "Jeune-France et Bousingots," *Revue d'histoire littéraire de la France,* LXXI, May–June 1971, p. 455).

68. Philibert Audebrand, "Scènes de la vie d'artiste, Auguste Préault," *L'Art,* XXXI, 1882, pp. 261–62.

1. For the construction of the library (1831–35), see Jean Marchand, *La Bibliothèque de l'Assemblée nationale,* Bordeaux, 1979, pp. 137–45.

2. These were the holdings when Jules de Joly published his *Plans, coupes, élévations et détails de la restauration de la Chambre des députés,* Paris, 1840 (p. 12).

3. Théophile Thoré, "Les Peintures de la Bibliothèque de la Chambre des députés," *Le Constitutionnel,* January 31, 1848.

4. As Lee Johnson points out, these rubrics are not specifically defined by the artist (*The Paintings of Eugène Delacroix,* vol. 5, Oxford, 1989, p. 34 n. 4).

5. Villot maintained that he and Delacroix had decided on the programs of the Palais-Bourbon library and the Salon du Roi only after endless discussions and "laborious research." See Villot's letter of July 27, 1869, to Alfred Sensier, quoted in Raymond Escholier, *Delacroix: Peintre, graveur, écrivain,* vol. 3, Paris, 1929, p. 50. For the development of the program, see Anita Hopmans, "Delacroix's Decorations in the Palais Bourbon Library," *Simiolus,* XVII, no. 4, 1987, pp. 240–69. See also the descriptions of unexecuted projects for the library quoted in Maurice Sérullaz, *Les Peintures murales de Delacroix,* Paris, 1963, pp. 49–52; and in Pierre Angrand, "Genèse des travaux d'Eugène Delacroix à la Bibliothèque de la Chambre," in *A travers l'art français (du moyen âge au XXᵉ siècle),* Archives de l'art français, n.s. XXV, 1978, pp. 313–35; and the notations on studies for the library in Maurice Sérullaz et al., *Musée du Louvre, Cabinet des dessins. Inventaire générale des dessins,* Paris, 1984, 1:150–66.

6. Louis de Ronchaud, "Etude sur l'art: La Peinture monumentale en France," *La Revue indépendante,* 2d series, XII, November 10, 1847, pp. 48–49.

7. Louis Clément de Ris, "La Bibliothèque et le Salon de la Paix à la Chambre des députés," *L'Artiste,* 4th series, XI, January 9, 1848, pp. 154–56.

8. George L. Hersey, "Delacroix's Imagery in the Palais Bourbon Library," *Journal of the Warburg and Courtauld Institutes,* XXXI, 1968, pp. 383–403. Regarding the theoretical discussion of the cycle by Norman Bryson (*Tradition and Desire from David to Delacroix,* Cambridge, Eng., 1984, chap. 6), see the review by Lorenz Eitner in *Times Literary Supplement,* April 12, 1985, pp. 413–14.

9. Delacroix's reliance on Brunet's classification system is noted in Robert Neubinger Beetem, "Delacroix's Mural Paintings, 1833–1847," Ph.D. diss., University of California, Berkeley, 1964, p. 5.

10. Hopmans, "Delacroix's Decorations," pp. 266, 268–69. Beetem similarly maintains that "beyond the *Orpheus-Attila* polarity . . . the search for an iconographical meaning that ties all the subjects together is fruitless" ("Delacroix's Mural Paintings," p. 54).

11. The architect anticipated that in addition to the paintings in the hemicycles and cupolas the library decoration would include portraits of scholars. See the proposal signed by Joly and dated November 22, 1836, Archives Nationales F²¹752, item 179. A similar proposal,

neither signed nor dated, refers to these as "portraits of scholars, historians, and writers executed on gold ground" (Archives Nationales F²¹752, item 180). For the history of library decoration, with a brief discussion of the Palais-Bourbon library paintings (pp. 61–62), see André Masson, *The Pictorial Catalogue: Mural Decoration in Libraries,* trans. David Gerard, Oxford, 1981.

12. Hopmans, "Delacroix's Decorations," pp. 244, 263–64. Although in a project predating the commission Delacroix proposed to devote the central cupola of the library to the sciences, with subjects drawn from the lives of Galileo, Aristotle, Archimedes, and Newton, apparently he did not at this point consider this cupola the center of a symmetrical scheme (Archives Nationales F²¹752, cited in Sérullaz, *Les Peintures murales de Delacroix,* p. 51). Johnson incorrectly states that the central cupola in this early project was to be devoted to the arts. See *The Paintings of Eugène Delacroix,* 5:34.

13. This decision was made prior to July 1845, when Joly requested permission from the minister of public works to mount the completed paintings of the final three cupolas. See the "Chronology" in Johnson, *The Paintings of Eugène Delacroix,* 5:40. On p. 34 of the same work, Johnson indicates the appropriateness of the central placement of the cupola devoted to legislation and eloquence. See also Johnson, *Delacroix,* New York, 1963, p. 90.

14. Johnson, *The Paintings of Eugène Delacroix,* 5:33.

15. See Marchand, *La Bibliothèque,* pp. 123–24.

16. The example of the Council of State rooms had already been followed in the new Palais-Bourbon assembly hall (1828–32), whose ceiling was adorned with portraits of Numa, Solon, Charlemagne, and Justinian by Jean-Victor Adam and Nicolas Gosse.

17. Inv. no. RF 9935, Sérullaz et al., *Musée du Louvre,* I, cat. no. 263. Delacroix considered including a Justinian in the program, under the subhead Roman law, in a cupola devoted to jurisprudence. See Hopmans, "Delacroix's Decorations," p. 256.

18. Thoré, "Les Peintures de la Bibliothèque."

19. See Joly, *Plans,* p. x. On French eloquence, see Jean Starobinski, "La chaire, la tribune, le barreau," in *Les Lieux de mémoire,* ed. Pierre Nora, vol. 2, *La Nation,* Paris, 1986, 2:425–85.

20. The companion statues in the old assembly hall, *Brutus* and *Lycurgus,* both by François-Frédéric Lemot; *Solon,* by Claude Ramey; and *Cato of Utica,* by Claude Michallon (misidentified by Joly as *Epaminondas*), were moved to the Vestibule of the Four Columns. See Joly, *Plans,* p. 16. For the series of legislator statues commissioned under the Directory for the assembly hall of the Council of Five Hundred in the Palais-Bourbon, see Ferdinand Boyer, "Six statues de législateurs antiques pour le Palais-Bourbon sous le Directoire," *Bulletin de la Société de l'Histoire de l'art français,* 1958, pp. 91–94.

21. Clément de Ris, "La Bibliothèque," p. 155. Similarly, the critic Gustave Planche warmly referred to the protagonist of Vigny's "Moïse" as "the prophet-legislator, Orpheus of a nascent civilization" ("Poètes et romanciers modernes de la France, II: Alfred de Vigny," *Revue des deux mondes,* 1st series, VII, 1832, p. 305).

22. Johnson, *The Paintings of Eugène Delacroix,* 5:61.

23. See ibid. for the appropriateness of the theme of eloquence both here and in the central cupola.

24. Hopmans, "Delacroix's Decorations," pp. 244–50.

25. See *Horace's Satires and Epistles,* trans. Jacob Fuchs, New York, 1977, p. 93. Horace's *Ars Poetica* is presented as a source for the *Orpheus* hemicycle in Hersey, "Delacroix's Imagery," p. 391.

26. Boileau, *Le Lutrin et l'Art poetique,* ed. René d'Hermies, 10th ed., Paris, Larousse, n.d., p. 100:

> Avant que la raison, s'expliquant par la voix,
> Eût instruit les humains, eût enseigné des lois,
> Tous les hommes suivaient la grossière nature,
> Dispersés dans les bois couraient à la pâture:
> La force tenait lieu de droit et d'équité;
> Le meurtre s'exerçait avec impunité.
> Mais du discours enfin l'harmonieuse adresse
> De ces sauvages moeurs adoucit la rudesse,
> Rassembla les humains dans les forêts épars,
> Enferma les cités de murs et de remparts,
> De l'aspect du supplice effraya l'insolence,
> Et sous l'appui des lois mit la faible innocence,
> Cet ordre fut, dit-on, le fruit des premiers vers:
> De là sont nés ces bruits reçus dans l'univers,
> Qu'aux accents dont Orphée emplit les monts de Thrace,
> Les tigres amollis dépouillaient leur audace.

27. Ballanche's treatment of the Orpheus theme is noted in Hersey, "Delacroix's Imagery," p. 391. Another reflection of the classical motif of Orpheus the legislator can be found in the jurist Jean-de-Dieu d'Olivier's introduction to his essays on the moral effects of music. Olivier recounts that Orpheus came to him in a dream and brought the realization that one should not neglect the study of "l'esprit d'ORPHÉE LÉGISLATEUR" (*L'Esprit d'Orphée, ou De l'influence respective de la musique, de la morale et de la législation,* vol. 1, Paris, 1798, p. 16). For Orpheus, see Dorothy M. Kosinski, *Orpheus in Nineteenth-Century Symbolism,* Ann Arbor, Mich., 1989; and Brian Juden, *Traditions orphiques et tendances mystiques dans le Romanticisme français (1800–1855),* Paris, 1971.

28. See George Sand, *Les Sept Cordes de la lyre,* ed. René Bourgeois, Paris, 1973, p. 19, a script for a drama (published in the *Revue des deux mondes,* April 15 and May 1, 1839) in which an enchanted lyre prompts the scholar Albertus to meditate on the Chinese belief that the

gods revealed "to the first legislators the important mystery of a new cord added to the lyre, emblem of civilization for those hard-working, practical people" (p. 128).

29. *Orphée,* in *Oeuvres de M. Ballanche de l'Académie de Lyon,* Paris, 1833, 5:248–49.

30. See Paul Bénichou, *Le Temps des prophètes,* Paris, 1977, pp. 198, 477, 545, and *Le Sacre de l'écrivain, 1750–1830,* 2d ed., Paris, 1985, pp. 236–38.

31. Alphonse de Lamartine, *Oeuvres poétiques,* ed. Marius-François Guyard, Paris, 1963, p. 515.

32. See *The Journal of Eugène Delacroix,* trans. Walter Pach, New York, 1972, pp. 185 (February 26, 1849) and 382–83 (April 30, 1854).

33. Isabelle Compin and Anne Roquebert, *Catalogue sommaire illustré,* Paris, 1986, 3:284, inv. no. 8472. In the 1827 Salon catalogue, *The Barbarians* is referred to as *Decadence of the Arts in Greece.*

34. The engraving of *Battle of the Huns* (Fig. 68) was reproduced in an album accompanying Count Athanasius Raczynski, *Histoire de l'art modern en Allemagne,* Paris, 1836–41.

35. See Wolfgang Balzer, *Der junge Daumier und seine Kampfgefährten,* Dresden, 1965, p. 227.

36. Compin and Roquebert, *Catalogue sommaire illustré,* 3:305, inv. no. 5305 (3.92 x 4.6 meters).

37. See Jacques-Bénigne Bossuet, *Discours sur l'histoire universelle* [1681], ed. Jacques Truchet, Paris, 1966, pp. 258–66.

38. Benjamin [Benjamin Antier, pseud. for Benjamin Chevrillon (1787–1870)], *Attila et le troubadour, comédie-vaudeville en un acte,* Paris, 1824, pp. 31–32:

> Des nations naissaintes
> C'est le législateur.
> . . . .
> Des hommes qu'il rassemble
> Il adoucit les moeurs,
> Son art maîtrise ensemble
> Les esprits et les coeurs.
> Dans les plaines stériles
> Fleurissent à sa voix
> Les moissons et les villes,
> Le commerce et les loix.
> Et dans son pauvre asile
> Il est avec cela
> Plus riche, plus tranquille
> Et plus grand qu'Attila.

Antier, in his preface to the play, attributes the story to a Baron de Bilderberg and indicates that the work, published in its entirety, had been performed in a mutilated version, as demanded by the government censors. See Théodore Muret, *L'Histoire par le théâtre, 1789–1851*, Paris, 1865, 2:136–42. Muret refers to a rumor that the play was co-authored by the republican songwriter Pierre-Jean de Béranger.

39. See Carol Ockman, "The Restoration of the Château of Dampierre: Ingres, the Duc de Luynes, and an Unrealized Vision of History," Ph.D. diss., Yale University, 1982; and Marc Sandoz, *Théodore Chassériau, 1819–1856: Catalogue raisonné des peintures et estampes*, Paris, 1974, pp. 39–54. For mural painting under the July Monarchy, see Léon Rosenthal, *Du Romantisme au réalisme*, Paris, 1914, chap. 8.

40. Delacroix spoke disdainfully (*Journal*, trans. Pach, pp. 172–73 [September 5, 1847]) of one such theorist, who was greatly admired by George Sand:

> [Pierre] Leroux has most assuredly found the great word, if not the thing itself, to save humanity and to pull it out of the mire: "Man is born free," he says, following Rousseau. Never has a heavier piece of foolishness been uttered, no matter how great the philosopher who spoke it. . . . Is there in all creation a being who is more of a *slave* than man? . . . The passions that he finds within himself are the cruelest tyrants he has to fight, and one may add that to resist them is to resist his very nature.

41. See Lucien Rudrauf, *Eugène Delacroix et le problème du romantisme artistique*, Paris, 1942, p. 172.

42. According to article 15 of the charter, "The proposition of laws belongs to the king, to the Chamber of Peers and to the Chamber of Deputies. However, every tax law must first be passed by the Chamber of Deputies."

43. See Hopmans, "Delacroix's Decorations," p. 266 and n. 99.

44. See the *Encyclopédie*'s definition of *legislator*, quoted in Chapter 1. Delacroix also considered two subjects that referred to the austere practices associated with child rearing in Sparta, the *Spartan Girls Wrestling* and *The Spartan Children Whipped at the Altar of Diana*. For these subjects, see Angrand, "Genèse des travaux," p. 315.

45. See Delacroix, *Journal*, trans. Pach, p. 141 (February 4, 1847). For Vernet's ceiling, see Robert Neubinger Beetem, "Horace Vernet's Mural in the Palais Bourbon: Contemporary Imagery, Modern Technology, and Classical Allegory during the July Monarchy," *Art Bulletin*, LXVI, June 1984, pp. 254–69.

46. See Madeleine Vincent, *La Peinture des XIXe et XXe siècles*, vol. 7, *Catalogue du Musée de Lyon*, Lyon, 1956, pp. 13–17. See also Robert Rosenblum, *Transformations in Late Eighteenth Century Art*, 2d ed., Princeton, N.J., 1969, p. 118.

47. *Corinne, ou l'Italie*, in *Oeuvres de Mme de Staël*, Paris, 1864, p. 302.

48. Paul de Saint-Victor enthusiastically described Delacroix's *Pliny* as "the prophet of nature seated on his boiling tripod" ("Eugène Delacroix," *La Presse*, September 22, 1863). In its

tone of prophetic inspiration, the library pendentive is unlike two earlier versions of the subject (1827) located in the Musée Charles X in the Louvre: *The Death of Pliny* by Heim (inv. no. 5301) and *Pliny Observing Vesuvius* (inv. no. 8473), one of eight grisaille scenes of antique life by Vinchon and Gosse, in Compin and Roquebert, *Catalogue sommaire illustré,* 3:285, 305.

49. *Encyclopédie des gens du monde . . . par une société de savans, de littérateurs et d'artistes, français et étrangers,* vol. 10, Paris, 1838, s.v. "Exile."

50. See Lloyd S. Kramer, *Threshold of a New World: Intellectuals and the Exile Experience in Paris, 1830–1848,* Ithaca, N.Y., 1988.

51. Thoré, "Les Peintures de la Bibliothèque."

52. See Bénichou, *Le Sacre de l'écrivain, 1750–1830,* p. 85.

53. See Thomas L. Ashton, *Byron's Hebrew Melodies,* Austin, Tex., 1972; and Joseph Slater, "Byron's Hebrew Melodies," *Studies in Philology,* XLIX, January 1952, pp. 75–94.

54. See Nina M. Athanassoglou-Kallmyer, *French Images from the Greek War of Independence, 1821–1830: Art and Politics under the Restoration,* New Haven, Conn., 1989, pp. 15–19.

55. Millet, who exhibited a work on this subject in the Salon of 1848, later covered the canvas with the *Young Shepherdess Seated* (1869; Museum of Fine Arts, Boston). For the Babylonian captivity theme, see my doctoral dissertation, "*Le Peuple de Dieu:* Old Testament Motifs of Legislation, Prophecy, and Exile in French Art between the Empires," Institute of Fine Arts, New York University, 1986, pp. 126–42.

56. Planet's painting was exhibited at the Galerie des Beaux-Arts on the boulevard de Bonne-Nouvelle in 1843 and again in the Salon of 1849. This lost work reflects the influence of *The Massacre of Chios,* of which Planet made a copy, admired by Delacroix along with Planet's *Babylonian Captivity,* on a visit to his assistant's studio January 25, 1843; he had seen sketches for the latter work on an earlier visit, on December 2, 1842. See Hopmans, "Delacroix's Decorations," p. 264 n. 87; and Louis de Planet, "Souvenirs de travaux de peinture avec M. Eugène Delacroix," ed. A. Joubin, *Bulletin de la Société d'Histoire de l'art français,* 1928, pp. 421–28.

57. Inv. no. RF 4774, Sérullaz et al., Musée du Louvre, I, cat. no. 298. The watercolor may have been the model for the pendentive painting that, according to Johnson, was executed by Delacroix, himself. See *The Paintings of Eugène Delacroix,* 5:54, and cat. no. 557, p. 74. Cazes's painting follows the example of Horace Vernet, who used detailed Arab costume in his *Rebecca at the Fountain* (1833) and *Expulsion of Hagar* (1837). See the exhibition catalogue *Horace Vernet (1789–1863),* Rome, Académie de France à Rome, 1980, no. 68, pp. 93–94.

58. For the program of the Luxembourg library decoration, see Johnson, *The Paintings of Eugène Delacroix,* 5:87–92; and the artist's description published in *L'Artiste,* 4th series, VII, October 4, 1846, p. 221.

59. "Bref on y voit tous les grands hommes possibles se promenant et s'asseyant pour varier leur plaisir" (Delacroix, *Correspondance générale,* ed. André Joubin, 2:120 [August 9, 1842]).

60. Alexander, holding the casket with Homer's poems, is one of those paying homage to the poet in Ingres's *Apotheosis of Homer* (1827; Louvre).

61. See Sérullaz, *Les Peintures murales,* p. 50. The Luxembourg library dome was derived from a subject considered for the Palais-Bourbon library, the groves of academe. See Hopmans, "Delacroix's Decorations," pp. 260–62.

62. See Delacroix's letter to Thoré, January 5, 1848, in *Correspondance générale,* 2:338.

63. Ibid., 2:24 (September 13, 1838).

64. So maintains the 1835 edition of the *Dictionary of the French Academy,* which gives the following example: "Boileau is the legislator of French poetry" (Institut de France, *Dictionnaire de l'Académie française,* 6th ed., Paris, II, s.v. "Législateur").

65. Delacroix, *Journal,* trans. Pach, p. 171.

66. See Lorenz Eitner, "The Open Window and the Storm-Tossed Boat: An Essay in the Iconography of Romanticism," *Art Bulletin,* XXXVII, December 1955, p. 289.

67. Letter to Baron Charles Rivet, February 15, 1838, in Delacroix, *Correspondance générale,* 2:5.

68. The gloom and cruelty of the library paintings are emphasized in Mario Praz, *The Romantic Agony,* trans. Angus Davidson, 2d ed., Oxford, 1970, pp. 143–44.

69. Delacroix, *Journal,* trans. Pach, p. 179.

70. Ibid., p. 147 (February 20, 1847).

71. Ibid., pp. 196–97 (April 23, 1849).

72. Ibid., pp. 219–20 (May 1, 1850).

73. [F. de Montherot], "A Lamartine, Député; à Beyrouth, Syrie," January 1833, in *Mémoires poétiques,* Paris, 1833, p. 101.

74. Alexis de Tocqueville, *Souvenirs* [1850–51], ed. Luc Mounier et al., Paris, 1978, pp. 45–46.

75. Paul Bastid, *Les Institutions politiques de la monarchie parlementaire française (1814–1848),* Paris, 1954, p. 244.

76. Heinrich Heine, *Lutetia,* in *French Affairs: Letters from Paris,* vol. 2, *1840–1843,* New York, 1906, p. 109 (July 3, 1840).

77. Loys Delteil, *Le Peintre-Graveur illustré: Daumier,* vol. 20, Paris, 1925, cat. no. 116.

78. Delacroix, *Journal,* trans. Pach, p. 134. A less than respectful attitude toward the Chamber is also suggested when in a letter to George Sand, September 5, 1838, the artist comically compared his own renewed pleasure at returning to the sea with that of Louis-Philippe at seeing "his dear deputies" (*Correspondance générale,* 2:21).

1. See Etienne Moreau-Nélaton, *Millet raconté par lui-même,* Paris, 1921, 1:33–44; and Alfred Sensier, *La Vie et l'oeuvre de J.-F. Millet,* ed. Paul Mantz, Paris, 1881, pp. 72–74. See also Lucien Lepoittevin, *Jean-François Millet, portraitiste: Essai et catalogue,* Paris, 1971, I, no. 42; and the exhibition catalogues *Jean-François Millet 1814–1875,* Musée Thomas Henry, Cherbourg, 1971, no. 19; and Lucien Lepoittevin, *Cent cinquantième anniversaire de la naissance de Jean-François Millet 1814–1875,* Musée Thomas Henry, Cherbourg, 1964, no. 28.

2. See Sensier, *La Vie et l'oeuvre,* p. 73.

3. Letter from Paris, April 9, 1841, quoted in Moreau-Nélaton, *Millet raconté par lui-même,* 1:36.

4. Quoted in Moreau-Nélaton, 1:39. In a letter to the mayor of Cherbourg, July 19, 1841 (ibid.), Millet requested that the *Moses* be exhibited.

5. Ibid.

6. See Paul Bénichou, *Le Temps des prophètes,* Paris, 1977, and *Le Sacre de l'écrivain, 1750–1830,* 2d ed., Paris, 1985. The Romantics identified poetry with legislation. Shelley, for example, declared in "A Defense of Poetry" (1821) that "poets are the unacknowledged legislators of the world" (*The Selected Poetry and Prose of Shelley,* ed. Harold Bloom, New York, 1966, p. 448). Gert Schiff brought this reference to my attention.

7. Emile Barrault, *Aux artistes. Du passé et de l'avenir des beaux-arts,* Paris, 1830, p. 78.

8. Philippe Busoni, "Michel-Ange," *L'Artiste,* 1st series, VI, 1833, p. 294.

9. Lepoittevin attributes the comment to Moreau-Nélaton in *Millet, portraitiste,* I, cat. no. 42.

10. See Klaus Herding, *Courbet: To Venture Independence,* trans. John William Gabriel, New Haven, Conn., 1991, chap. 3.

11. *Journal de Eugène Delacroix,* ed. André Joubin and Jean-Louis Vaudoyer, Paris, 1932, 2:19–20 (April 16, 1853).

12. See Fig. 84 for the portrait Herbert had in mind. See also Herbert's catalogue *Jean-François Millet,* Hayward Gallery, London, 1976, no. 8, p. 42.

13. In the 1840s the Saint-Simonian high priest Père Barthélemy-Prosper Enfantin (1796–1864) urged the sect's official musician, Félicien David, to compose an oratorio on the subject of Moses. Reference to Moses was especially pertinent to Enfantin, for he viewed his role in the leadership of mankind as that of a new Moses, a self-image reinforced by his belief that the building of the Suez Canal in Egypt would help realize his utopia. David's *Moïse au Sinaï,* intended by Enfantin to spread the Saint-Simonian gospel, was received unenthusiastically when it premiered at the Paris Opera on March 24, 1846. See Dorothy Veinus Hagan, *Félicien David, 1810–1876: A Composer and a Cause,* Syracuse, N.Y., 1985, pp. 87–102. See also Jacques-Gabriel Prod'homme, "Correspondance inédite

de Félicien David et du Père Enfantin (1845)," *Mercure de France,* LXXXV, May 1, 1910, pp. 67–86.

14. See Bénichou, *Le Sacre de l'écrivain,* pp. 288–300. For this aspect of Hugo's thought see also Bénichou, *Les Mages romantiques,* Paris, 1988, pp. 273–530; and Maurice Z. Shroder, *Icarus: The Image of the Artist in French Romanticism,* Cambridge, Mass., 1961, chap. 2.

15. Victor Hugo, *Odes et ballades,* ed. Pierre Albouy, Paris, 1969, p. 202.

16. Hugo, *Odes et ballades,* p. 156.

17. Although Vigny was part of this ultra-royalist circle and served during the Restoration as an officer in the Bourbon army, his poetry lacks the militant counter-revolutionary piety of Hugo's early work.

18. See Fernande Bartfeld, *Vigny et la figure de Moïse,* Paris, 1968; and Bénichou, *Le Sacre de l'écrivain,* pp. 370–71. The poetic license of Vigny's "Moïse" was anticipated by the republican academician Népomucène Lemercier in his epic poem *Moyse,* the last of his hymns to four great representatives of poetry, war, science, and legislation that also included *Homère* and *Alexandre* (both 1800) and *Atlantiade* (dedicated to Newton; 1812). *Moyse* includes a meeting between Moses and Job—an innovation that allowed the author "to enrich my painting with the variety of colors offered by a combination of two of the most beautiful books of the Bible." See Lemercier, *Fragments d'un poème intitulé: Moïse, sur la délivrance des Israélites. Lus par M. Le Mercier à l'Académie française, le 24 août 1819,* Paris, 1819, p. 6.

19. Alfred de Vigny, *Oeuvres poétiques,* ed. J.-P. Saint-Gerand, Paris, 1978, pp. 65–66.

20. Jacques-Bénigne Bossuet, *Discours sur l'histoire universelle,* ed. Jacques Truchet, Paris, 1966, pp. 182–83.

21. Charles Magnin, "Poèmes, par M. le comte Alfred de Vigny. Seconde et troisième éditions," *Le Globe,* October 21, 1829, p. 667.

22. Alfred de Vigny, letters of December 21 and December 27, 1838, in "Lettres à une puritaine, I," ed. P. Godet, *Revue de Paris,* IV, August 15, 1897.

23. See A. Duvivier, "Liste des élèves . . . de l'Ecole des Beaux-Arts qui ont remporté les grands prix," *Archives de l'art français, Documents,* 1857–58, 5:273. See also Philippe Grunchec, *Le Grand Prix de Peinture: Les concours des Prix de Rome de 1797 à 1863,* Paris, 1983.

24. For the painting by Subleyras (Louvre inv. no. 7999, on deposit in the Musée des Beaux-Arts, Nîmes) and for other engravings of the work, see the exhibition catalogue Olivier Michel and Pierre Rosenberg, *Subleyras, 1699–1749,* Musée du Luxembourg, Paris, 1987, no. 4, pp. 147–49. Both Roger's *Brazen Serpent* and the engraving in Landon reverse the composition of Subleyras's painting.

25. Moses is similarly prominent in a version of the subject painted in 1819 for the city of Paris by C.-L.-F. Smith reproduced in C. P. Landon, *Annales du Musée,* vol. 1 of *Salon de 1819,* Paris, 1819, p. 7. Landon complained that with the gray sky and background of the

work Moses was not set into relief. The work has apparently been removed from the Church of Saint-Paul-Saint-Louis, to which it was sent by the Préfecture de la Seine (Archives de la Seine, 10624, 72, 1).

26. "Concours pour le Grand Prix de Peinture," *L'Artiste,* 1st series, XII, 1836, p. 97.

27. The version of this subject that I reproduce as Fig. 90 (now in the National Gallery of Scotland, Edinburgh) had been engraved. See Anthony Blunt, *The Paintings of Nicolas Poussin: A Critical Catalogue,* London, 1966, no. 22, p. 19. Blanchard's entry recalls another version of the subject by Poussin (Hermitage, Leningrad), reproduced in *Musée de peinture et de sculpture,* vol. 10, Paris, 1831, p. 683. According to the *Journal des artistes* another contestant, Jean-Baptiste-Auguste Leloir, also quoted from Michelangelo's *Moses.* See Grunchec, *Le Grand Prix de Peinture,* p. 395.

28. The same critic approved the way another contestant (Louis-François-Marie Roulin) had understood that "*Moses* must be detached from the crowd and dominate it" ("Concours," pp. 97–98).

29. See the edition of Chateaubriand's *Moïse* by Fernande Bassan (Paris, 1983); Charles Comte, "Chateaubriand poète," *Mémoires de la Société des sciences morales de Seine-et-Oise,* 1894, pp. 15–51; and Anna Louise Catharina Kromsigt, "Le Théâtre biblique à la veille du romantisme (1789–1830)," Ph.D. diss., University of Amsterdam, 1931, pp. 86–87.

30. *Moïse, tragédie en cinq actes en vers,* in *Oeuvres complètes de Chateaubriand,* Paris, Garnier [1929–38], 3:575–76.

31. "Le *Moïse* de M. de Chateaubriand," *L'Artiste,* 1st series, VII, 1834, pp. 281–82.

32. See Virginie Ancelot, *Les Salons de Paris,* 2d ed., Paris, 1858, pp. 195–96.

33. Charles-Augustin Sainte-Beuve, *Chateaubriand et son groupe littéraire sous l'empire* [1861], ed. Maurice Allem, Paris, 1948, 2:77.

34. See Freud's essay "The Moses of Michelangelo" (1914).

35. Joseph de Maistre, *Cinq paradoxes* (1795), in *Oeuvres complètes de Joseph de Maistre,* Lyon, 1893, 7:320. See also Francesco Milizia, *De l'Art de voir dans les beaux-arts* [1786], trans. from the Italian by Général Pommereul, Paris, Year VI [1797–98], pp. 2–3.

36. Falconet knew the work only through "models, drawings, and engravings." See "Observations sur la statue de Marc-Aurèle" (1770) in *Oeuvres d'Etienne Falconet statuaire,* Lausanne, 1781, 1:321, 324.

37. Jean-Baptiste-Louis-Georges Seroux d'Agincourt, *Histoire de l'art par les monumens, depuis sa décadence au IVe siècle jusqu'à son renouvellement au XVIe siècle,* vol. 3, Paris, 1823, p. 41. Regarding this work, see Francis Haskell, *Rediscoveries in Art,* Ithaca, N.Y., 1980, pp. 71–73. Quatremère de Quincy was similarly enthusiastic about the *Moses,* despite its lack of reference to the art of classical antiquity. See Antoine-Chrysostôme Quatremère de Quincy, *Dictionnaire historique de l'architecture,* Paris, 1832, 1:254. The international reach of this revised opinion is suggested by Washington Allston's choice of the *Moses* as the model for a grandiose image of prophetic inspiration, *Jeremiah Dictating His Prophecies to the Scribe*

Baruch (1820; Yale University Art Gallery). See the exhibition catalogue by William H. Gerdts and Theodore E. Stebbins, Jr., *"A Man of Genius": The Art of Washington Allston (1779–1843)*, Museum of Fine Arts, Boston, 1979, p. 119.

38. Gustave Planche, "Michel-Ange," in *Portraits d'artistes*, Paris, 1853, 1:76–77. See Pontus Grate, *Deux critiques d'art de l'époque romantique: Gustave Planche et Théophile Thoré*, Figura 12, Stockholm, 1959.

39. Dumas, "Michel-Ange," *L'Artiste*, 3d series, III, 1845, p. 388; previously published in *Michel-Ange, suivi de Titien Vecelli*, Brussels, 1844. Another comparison of Vigny's poem and Michelangelo's statue was made by Charles Magnin, who in the "bitter and somber prayer" of Vigny's Moses perceived "a breadth, an assurance, a facility with the colossal that recall and seem to explain the *Moses* of Michelangelo" ("Poèmes, par M. le comte Alfred de Vigny," p. 667).

40. Dumas, "Michel-Ange," pp. 387–88.

ILOGUE

1. "C'est pourquoi tous les peuples ont voulu donner à leurs lois une origine divine; et ceux qui ne l'ont pas eue ont feint de l'avoir" (Jacques-Bénigne Bossuet, *Extraits des oeuvres diverses*, ed. Gustave Lanson, Paris, 1899, p. 211). Begun in 1677, Bossuet's *Politique* was published posthumously in 1709. As Rousseau acknowledged in *The Social Contract*, Machiavelli observed (*Discourses*, bk. 1, chap. 11) that all great lawgivers have claimed divine authority.

2. The classic study of this phenomenon is G. Burdeau, "Essai sur l'évolution de la notion de loi en droit français," *Archives de Philosophie du droit*, 1939, nos. 1–2, pp. 7–55. See also Burdeau, "Une Survivance: La Notion de Constitution," in *L'Evolution du droit public: Etudes en l'honneur d'Achille Mestre*, Paris, 1956, pp. 53–62; Pierre Legendre, *Histoire de l'administration*, Paris, 1968, pp. 460–63; André Sauvageot, "Dévaluation de la loi," *Revue politique et parlementaire*, no. 555, April 10, 1946, pp. 29–38, and no. 556, May 10, 1946, pp. 112–23; André-Jean Arnaud, *Les Juristes face à la société du XIXᵉ siècle à nos jours*, Paris, 1975; and Jean Carbonnier, "La Passion des lois au siècle des Lumières," in *Essais sur les lois*, Paris, 1979, pp. 217–19.

3. See Donald R. Kelley, *Historians and the Law in Postrevolutionary France*, Princeton, N.J., 1984, chap. 6.

4. For this development, ibid., chaps. 11, 12.

5. Jules Barbey d'Aurevilly, *Les Prophètes du passé*, Paris and Brussels, 1880, p. 140. See also, Lamartine's denunciation of the abstract and a priori character of the Declaration of the Rights of Man and Citizen in his *Histoire des constituants*, Paris, 1855, 2:217.

6. Taine, *Les Origines de la France contemporaine*, 23d ed., vol. 4, Paris, 1900, p. 47.

7. Zeev Sternhell, *La Droit révolutionnaire, 1885–1914: Les Origines françaises du fascisme,* Paris, 1978, pp. 84–87.

8. Musée d'Orsay inv. no. 20738. See Marie-Madeleine Aubrun, *Henri Lehmann, 1814–1882: Catalogue raisonné de l'oeuvre,* Nantes, 1984, no. 1036, 1:244; Isabelle Compin and Anne Roquebert, *Catalogue sommaire illustré,* Paris, 1986, 4:46; and Jacques Foucart and Louis-Antoine Prat, "Quelques oeuvres inédites d'Henri Lehmann," *Revue du Louvre et des Musées de France,* 1983, no. 1, pp. 16–24.

9. See the lucid study by Zeev Sternhell, *Maurice Barrès et le nationalisme français,* Brussels, 1985.

10. Maurice Barrès, *Les Déracinés,* ed. Hubert Juin, Paris, 1986, pp. 32, 51.

11. Quoted in *Le Nationalisme français, 1871–1914,* ed. Raoul Girardet, Paris, 1966, p. 136.

12. Quoted in Sternhell, *Barrès,* p. 127 n. 41.

13. See Norman L. Kleeblatt, ed., *The Dreyfus Affair: Art, Truth, and Justice,* Berkeley and Los Angeles, 1987.

14. See Sternhell, *Barrès,* pp. 232–45.

15. In Drumont's scandalously popular pseudo-historical diatribe *La France juive* (Jewish France), the royalist caricature *The New Calvary* (see Fig. 12)—in which the crucified Louis XVI stands on the roundheaded tablets of the Rights of Man—was held up as evidence that "the immense majority of the nation" realized that the Revolution's crimes against the monarchy were the work of a secret Jewish conspiracy (*La France juive: Essai d'histoire contemporaine,* Paris, Blériot n.d., pp. 225–26).

16. See Phillip Dennis Cate, "The Paris Cry: Graphic Artists and the Dreyfus Affair," in Kleeblatt, *The Dreyfus Affair,* cat. no. 70, p. 66.

Anchel, Robert. *Napoléon et les Juifs.* Paris, 1928.

Angrand, Pierre, "Genèse des travaux d'Eugène Delacroix à la Bibliothèque de la Chambre." In *A travers l'art français (du moyen âge au XXe siècle): Hommage à René Jullian.* Archives de l'art français, n.s. 25 (1978): 313–35.

Arendt, Hannah. *The Origins of Totalitarianism.* San Diego, 1979.

Arnaud, André-Jean. *Les Juristes face à la société du XIXe siècle à nos jours.* Paris, 1975.

———. *Les Origines doctrinales du Code civil français.* Bibliothèque de philosophie du droit, no. 9. Paris, 1969.

Baecque, Antoine de, Wolfgang Schmale, and Michel Vovelle, eds. *L'An 1 des droits de l'homme.* Paris, 1988.

Baldensperger, Fernand. *Le Mouvement des idées dans l'émigration française (1789–1815).* 2 vols. Paris, 1924. Reprint. New York, 1968.

Balzer, Wolfgang. *Der junge Daumier und seine Kampfgefährten: Politische Karikatur in Frankreich, 1830 bis 1835.* Dresden, 1965.

Bartfeld, Fernande. *Vigny et la figure de Moïse.* Paris, 1968.

Bastid, Paul. *L'Idée de constitution.* Paris, 1985.

———. *Les Institutions politiques de la monarchie parlementaire française (1814–1848).* Paris, 1954.

Beaulieu, Michèle. "Un sculpteur français d'origine italienne: Henri de Triqueti (1804–1874)." In *A travers l'art italien du XVe au XXe siècle.* Edited by Henri Bédarida, 203–22. Publications de la Société d'Etudes italiennes, no. 2. Paris, 1949.

Beetem, Robert Neubinger. "Delacroix's Mural Paintings, 1833–1847." Ph.D. diss., University of California, Berkeley, 1964.

Bénichou, Paul. "Jeune-France et Bousingots: Essai de mise au point." *Revue d'histoire littéraire de la France* 71, (May–June 1971): 439–62.

———. *Le Sacre de l'écrivain, 1750–1830: Essai sur l'avènement d'un pouvoir spirituel laïque dans la France moderne.* 2d ed. Paris, 1985.

———. *Le Temps des prophètes: Doctrines de l'âge romantique.* Paris, 1977.

Benoist, Luc. *La Sculpture romantique.* Paris, [1928].

Bergeron, Louis. *L'Episode napoléonien.* Vol. 1, *Aspects intérieurs, 1799–1815.* Nouvelle histoire de la France contemporaine, no. 4. Paris, 1972.

Berlin, Isaiah. *The Crooked Timber of Humanity: Chapters in the History of Ideas.* New York, 1991.

Bertier de Sauvigny, Guillaume de. *The Bourbon Restoration.* Translated by Lynn M. Case. Philadelphia, 1966.

Bezucha, Robert J., Michael Paul Driskel, Patricia Condon, Gabriel P. Weisberg, and Petra ten-Doesschate Chu. *The Art of the July Monarchy: France 1830 to 1848.* Exh. cat. Columbia: Museum of Art and Archaeology, University of Missouri-Columbia, 1990.

Bibliothèque Nationale, Département des estampes. *Un Siècle d'histoire de France par l'estampe, 1770–1871: Collection de Vinck. Inventaire analytique.* Vol. 1, François-Louis Bruel. *L'Ancien régime.* Paris, 1909; Vol. 2, François-Louis Bruel. *La Constituante.* Paris, 1914; Vol. 3, Marcel Aubert and Marcel Roux. *La Législative et la Convention.* Paris, 1921; Vol. 4, Marcel Roux. *Napoléon et son temps.* Paris, 1929.

Biver, Marie-Louise. *Fêtes révolutionnaires à Paris.* Paris, 1979.

———. *Le Paris de Napoléon.* Paris, 1963.

Blumenkranz, Bernhard, and Albert Soboul, eds. *Le Grand Sanhédrin de Napoléon.* Toulouse, 1979.

Boime, Albert. *Art in an Age of Revolution, 1750–1800.* Vol. 1 of *A Social History of Modern Art.* Chicago, 1987.

———. *Art in an Age of Bonapartism, 1800–1815.* Vol. 2 of *A Social History of Modern Art.* Chicago, 1990.

———. *Hollow Icons: The Politics of Sculpture in Nineteenth-Century France.* Kent, Ohio, 1987.

Bonald, Viscount Louis-Gabriel-Ambroise de. *Oeuvres complètes de M. de Bonald.* Edited by l'abbé Migne. 3 vols. Paris, 1859–64.

Bordes, Philippe. *Le Serment du Jeu de Paume de Jacques-Louis David: Le Peintre, son milieu et son temps de 1789 à 1792.* Notes et documents des Musées de France, no. 8. Paris, 1983.

Bordes, Philippe, and Régis Michel, eds. *Aux armes & aux arts! Les Arts de la Révolution, 1789–1799.* Paris, 1988.

Borel, Pétrus. *Champavert, contes immoraux.* In *Oeuvres complètes de Pétrus Borel "le Lycanthrope"* [1833]. Edited by Aristide Marie. Vol. 3, Paris, 1922.

Bossuet, Jacques-Bénigne. *Discours sur l'histoire universelle* [1681]. Edited by Jacques Truchet. Paris, 1966.

Bowman, Frank Paul. *Le Christ romantique.* Histoire des idées et critique littéraire, no. 134. Geneva, 1973.

———. *French Romanticism: Intertextual and Interdisciplinary Readings.* Baltimore, 1990.

Boyer, Ferdinand. "Le Palais-Bourbon sous le Premier Empire." *Bulletin de la Société de l'Histoire de l'art français* (1936): 91–123.

Burdeau, Georges. "Essai sur l'évolution de la notion de loi en droit français." *Archives de philosophie du droit et de sociologie juridique,* nos. 1–2 (1939): 7–55.

Carbonnier, Jean. *Essais sur les lois.* Paris, 1979.

Caso, Jacques de. *David d'Angers: L'Avenir de la mémoire. Etude sur l'art signalétique à l'époque romantique.* Paris, 1988.

Chateaubriand, Vicomte François-René de. *Génie du christianisme* [1802]. Edited by Pierre Reboul. 2 vols. Paris, 1966.

Chateaubriand politique. Edited by Jean-Paul Clément. Paris, 1987.

Chesneau, Ernest. "Auguste Préault." *L'Art* 17 (1879): 3–15.

Chevallier, Jean-Jacques. *Histoire des institutions et des régimes politiques de 1789 à nos jours.* 6th ed. Paris, 1981.

Clarac, Count Frédéric de. *Musée de sculpture antique et moderne, ou Description historique et graphique du Louvre et de toutes ses parties.* 6 vols. Paris, 1841–53.

Clark, T. J. *The Absolute Bourgeois: Artists and Politics in France, 1848–1851.* London, 1973.

Le Code civil, 1804–1904: Livre du centenaire. 2 vols. Paris, 1904.

Code Napoléon. Edition originale et seule officielle. Paris, 1808.

Collins, Irene. *Napoleon and His Parliaments, 1800–1815.* London, 1979.

Compin, Isabelle, and Anne Roquebert. *Catalogue sommaire illustré des peintures du Musée du Louvre et du Musée d'Orsay.* Vols. 3–5, *Ecole française.* Paris, 1986.

Le Conseil d'Etat: Livre jubilaire, publié pour commémorer son cent cinquantième anniversaire, 4 nivôse an VIII, 24 Décembre 1949. Paris, 1952.

Le Conseil d'Etat: Son histoire à travers les documents d'époque 1799–1974. Paris, 1974.

Constans, Claire. *Musée National du Château de Versailles: Catalogue de peintures.* Paris, 1980.

Cotteret, Jean-Marie. *Le Pouvoir législatif en France.* Paris, 1962.

Crow, Thomas E. *Painters and Public Life in Eighteenth-Century Paris.* New Haven, Conn., 1985.

Cuno, James. "The Business and Politics of Caricature: Charles Philipon and La Maison Aubert." *Gazette des beaux-arts* 106 (October 1985): 95–112.

Cuno, James, Michel Melot, Lynn Hunt, Claude Langlois, Ronald Paulson, Albert Boime, and Klaus Herding. *French Caricature and the French Revolution, 1789–1799.* Exh. cat. Los Angeles: Grunwald Center for the Graphic Arts, Wight Art Gallery, University of California, 1988.

Darnis, Jean-Marie. *Les Monuments expiatoires du supplice de Louis XVI et de Marie-Antoinette sous l'Empire et la Restauration, 1812–1830.* Paris, 1981.

David, Réné. *Le Droit français.* Vol. 1, *Les Données fondamentales du droit français.* Paris, 1960.

David, Réné, and Henry P. de Vries. *The French Legal System: An Introduction to Civil Law Systems.* New York, 1958.

Davois, Gustave. *Bibliographie napoléonienne française jusqu'en 1908.* 3 vols. Paris, 1909–11.

Delacroix, Eugène. "La Bibliothèque du Luxembourg." *L'Artiste* 7, 4th ser. (October 4, 1846): 221.

———. *Correspondance générale d'Eugène Delacroix.* Edited by André Joubin. 5 vols. Paris, 1935–38.

———. *Journal de Eugène Delacroix.* Edited by André Joubin and Jean-Louis Vaudoyer. 3 vols. Paris, 1932.

———. *The Journal of Eugène Delacroix.* Translated by Walter Pach. New York, 1972.

Deslandres, Maurice-Charles-Emmanuel. *Histoire constitutionnelle de la France de 1789 à 1870.* 2 vols. Paris, 1932.

Dowd, David Lloyd. *Pageant-Master of the Republic: Jacques-Louis David and the French Revolution.* Lincoln, Nebraska, 1948.

Droits de l'Homme & Conquête des libertés. Exh. cat. Vizille: Musée de la Révolution française, 1986.

Duclos, Pierre. "La Notion de constitution dans l'oeuvre de l'Assemblée constituante de 1789." Ph.D. diss., University of Poitiers, 1932.

Dumas [père], Alexandre, "Michel-Ange," *L'Artiste* 3, 3d ser. (1845): 342–47, 357–61, 371–78, 387–90, 402–5.

Easton, Malcolm. *Artists and Writers in Paris: The Bohemian Idea, 1803–1867.* London, 1964.

Ellul, Jacques. *Histoire des institutions.* Vol. 5, *Le XIXe siècle.* 8th ed. Paris, 1982.

Escholier, Raymond. *Delacroix: Peintre, graveur, écrivain.* 3 vols. Paris, 1926–29.

Fontaine, Pierre-François-Léonard. *Journal, 1799–1853.* 2 vols. Paris, 1987.

Fontanes, Louis de. *Collection complète des discours de M. de Fontanes.* Paris, 1821.

———. *Oeuvres de M. de Fontanes.* 2 vols. Paris, 1839.

Fortescue, William. *Alphonse de Lamartine: A Political Biography.* London, 1983.

French Painting, 1774–1830: The Age of Revolution. Exh. cat. Detroit: Detroit Institute of Arts, 1975.

The French Revolution and the Creation of Modern Political Culture. Vol. 1, *The Political Culture of the Old Regime.* Edited by Keith Michael Baker. Oxford, 1987; Vol. 2, *The Political Culture of the French Revolution.* Edited by Colin Lucas. Oxford, 1988; Vol. 3, *The Transformation of Political Culture, 1789–1848.* Edited by François Furet and Mona Ozouf. Oxford, 1989.

Furet, François. *Penser la Révolution française.* Paris, 1983.

Furet, François, and Denis Richet. *La Révolution française.* Paris, 1973.

Furet, François, and Mona Ozouf, eds. *A Critical Dictionary of the French Revolution.* Translated by Arthur Goldhammer. Cambridge, Mass., 1989.

Fusco, Peter, and H. W. Janson, eds. *The Romantics to Rodin: French Nineteenth-Century Sculpture from North American Collections.* Exh. cat. Los Angeles: Los Angeles County Museum of Art, 1980.

Garrisson, F. *Histoire du droit et des institutions.* Vol. 1, *Le Pouvoir des temps féodaux à la Révolution.* Paris, 1977.

Gautier, Théophile. *Histoire du romantisme* [1874]. Paris, 1927.

———. *Les Jeunes-France, romans goguenards.* Paris, 1875.

Geffroy, Gustave. "Les Peintures d'Eugène Delacroix à la Bibliothèque de la Chambre des députés." *Revue de l'art ancien et moderne* 13 (1903): 65–78, 139–52.

George, Mary Dorothy. *Catalogue of Political and Personal Satires Preserved in the Department of Prints and Drawings in the British Museum.* Vol. 6, *1784–1792.* London, 1938; Vol. 7, *1793–1800.* London, 1942.

Gigoux, Jean. *Causeries sur les artistes de mon temps.* Paris, 1885.

Girardot, Baron August-Théodore de. *Catalogue de l'oeuvre du baron Henri de Triqueti, précédé d'une notice sur ce sculpteur.* Orleans, 1874.

Godechot, Jacques. *The Counter-Revolution: Doctrine and Action, 1789–1804.* Translated by Salvator Attanasio. Princeton, N.J., 1981.

———. *Les Institutions de la France sous la Révolution et l'Empire.* 3d ed. Paris, 1985.

———, ed. *Les Constitutions de la France depuis 1789.* Paris, 1979.

Grunchec, Philippe. *Le Grand Prix de Peinture: Les concours des Prix de Rome de 1797 à 1863.* Paris, 1983.

Guiffrey, J.-J. "Le Salon du Roi au Palais de le Chambre des Députés. Peintures decoratives d'Eugène Delacroix décrites par l'artiste." *L'Art* 13 (1878): 257–68.

Guizot, François. *Mémoires pour servir à l'histoire de mon temps* [1858–68]. Abridged and edited by Michel Richard. Paris, 1971.

Hautecoeur, Louis. *Histoire du Louvre. Le Chateau, le Palais, le Musée des origines à nos jours, 1200–1928.* Paris, [1928].

Heine, Henri [Heinrich]. *De la France.* Paris, 1833.

Herbert, Robert L. *David, Voltaire, Brutus, and the French Revolution: An Essay in Art and Politics*. New York, 1972.

———. *Jean François Millet*. Exh. cat. London: Hayward Gallery, 1976.

Herding, Klaus, and Rolf Reichardt. *Die Bildpublizistik der Französischen Revolution*. Frankfurt am Main, 1989.

Hersey, George L. "Delacroix's Imagery in the Palais Bourbon Library." *Journal of the Warburg and Courtauld Institutes* 31 (1968): 383–403.

Honour, Hugh. *Neo-classicism*. Harmondsworth, 1968.

———. *Romanticism*. London, 1979.

Hopmans, Anita. "Delacroix's Decorations in the Palais Bourbon Library: A Classic Example of an Unacademic Approach." *Simiolus* 17, no. 4 (1987): 240–69.

Howard, Donald D., John L. Connolly, Jr., and Harold T. Parker, eds. *Proceedings of the Consortium on Revolutionary Europe, 1750–1850. Florida State University, Tallahassee, Florida* 2. Athens, Ga., 1980.

Hugo, Victor. *Odes et ballades*. Edited by Pierre Albouy. Paris, 1969.

———. *Oeuvres poétiques*. Vol. 1, *Avant l'exil, 1802–1851*. Edited by Gaëtan Picon and Pierre Albouy. Paris, 1964.

Hunt, Lynn. *Politics, Culture, and Class in the French Revolution*. Berkeley and Los Angeles, 1984.

Jal, Auguste. *Esquisses, croquis, pochades, ou Tout ce qu'on voudra, sur le Salon de 1827*. Paris, 1828.

Janson, H. W., and Judith Herschman. *An Iconographic Index to Stanislas Lami's "Dictionnaire des sculpteurs de l'école française au dix-neuvième siècle."* New York, 1983.

Jardin, André, and André-Jean Tudesq. *La France des notables*. Nouvelle histoire de la France contemporaine, nos. 6, 7. Paris, 1973.

Johnson, Lee. *The Paintings of Eugène Delacroix: A Critical Catalogue*. 6 vols. Oxford, 1981–89.

Joly, Jules de. *Plans, coupes, élévations et détails de la restauration de la Chambre des députés, de sa nouvelle Salle des séances, de sa Bibliothèque et de toutes ses dépendances. . . .* Paris, 1840.

Jones, Colin. *The Longman Companion to the French Revolution*. London, 1988.

Kelley, Donald R. *Historians and the Law in Postrevolutionary France*. Princeton, N.J., 1984.

Kennedy, Emmet. *A Cultural History of the French Revolution*. New Haven, Conn., 1989.

Kriéger, Antoine. *La Madeleine*. Paris, 1937.

Krieger, Leonard. *Kings and Philosophers, 1689–1789*. New York, 1970.

Lamartine, Alphonse-Marie-Louis de. *La France parlementaire (1834–1851). Oeuvres oratoires et écrits politiques*. 6 vols. Paris, 1864–65.

————. *Oeuvres poétiques.* Edited by Marius-François Guyard. Paris, 1963.

Lamartine: Le Poète et l'homme. Exh. cat. Paris: Bibliothèque Nationale, 1969.

Lami, Stanislas. *Dictionnaire des sculpteurs de l'école française au dix-huitième siècle.* 2 vols. Paris, 1910–11.

————. *Dictionnaire des sculpteurs de l'école française au dix-neuvième siècle.* 4 vols. Paris, 1914–21.

Landon, C. P. *Annales du Musée et de l'école moderne des Beaux-Arts.* 2d ed. 44 vols. Paris, 1823–35.

Langlois, Claude. *La Caricature contre-révolutionnaire.* Paris, 1988.

Latreille, André. "Le Catéchisme impérial de 1806: Etudes et documents pour servir à l'histoire des rapports de Napoléon et du clergé concordataire." Ph.D. diss., University of Paris, 1935.

Lefebvre, Georges. *The Coming of the French Revolution.* Translated by R. R. Palmer. Princeton, N.J., 1947.

————. *The French Revolution.* Vol. 1, *From Its Origins to 1793.* Translated by Elizabeth Moss Evanson. London, 1962; Vol. 2, *From 1793 to 1799.* Translated by John Hall Stewart and James Friguglietti. London, 1964.

————. *Napoleon: From 18 Brumaire to Tilsit, 1799–1807.* Translated by Henry F. Stockhold. New York, 1969.

Legendre, Pierre. *Histoire de l'administration de 1750 à nos jours.* Paris, 1968.

Léon, Paul. "L'Eglise de la Madeleine (1764–1842)." *Revue des deux mondes* (June 1, 1954): 406–26.

Lepoittevin, Lucien. *Jean-François Millet, portraitiste: Essai et catalogue.* 2 vols. Paris, 1971.

Leroy, Maxime. *La Loi: Essai sur la théorie de l'autorité dans la démocratie.* Paris, 1908.

Lidderdale, D. W. S. *The Parliament of France.* New York, 1952.

Liebenwein-Krämer, Renate. "Säkularisierung und Sakralisierung: Studien zum Bedeutungswandel christlicher Bildformen in der Kunst des 19. Jahrhunderts." Ph.D. diss., Johann Wolfgang Goethe University, Frankfurt am Main, 1977.

Les Lieux de mémoire. Edited by Pierre Nora. Vol. 1, *La République.* Paris, 1984; Vol. 2, *La Nation* (3 vols.). Paris, 1984–86.

Lucas-Dubreton, Jean. *La Restauration et la Monarchie de Juillet.* Paris, 1926.

Maistre, Comte Joseph de. *Considerations sur la France* [1796]. Lyon, 1847.

Malafosse, Jehan de. *Histoire des institutions et des régimes politiques de la Révolution à la IVᵉ République.* Paris, 1975.

Marchand, Jean. *La Bibliothèque de l'Assemblée nationale.* Bordeaux, 1979.

Marmottan, Paul. *Elisa Bonaparte.* Paris, 1898.

Marrinan, Michael. *Painting Politics for Louis-Philippe: Art and Ideology in Orléanist France, 1830–1848.* New Haven, Conn., 1988.

Mathiez, Albert. *Les Origines des Cultes révolutionnaires (1789–1792)*. Paris, 1904.

Mazard, Jean. *Histoire monétaire et numismatique contemporaine, 1790–1963*. Vol. 1, *1790–1848*. Paris, 1965.

McClelland, J. S., ed. *The French Right (from de Maistre to Maurras)*. Roots of the Right: Readings in Fascist, Racist and Elitist Ideology. General ed., George Steiner. London, 1970.

Michel, Régis, and Marie-Catherine Sahut. *David: L'Art et le politique*. Paris, 1988.

Michelet, Jules. *Histoire de la Révolution française* [1847–53]. Edited by Gérard Walter. 2 vols. Paris, 1952.

[Montherot, F. de]. *Mémoires poétiques. Evénemens contemporains, voyages, facéties*. Paris, 1833.

Moreau-Nélaton, Etienne. *Millet raconté par lui-même*. 3 vols. Paris, 1921.

Moulinié, Henri. "De Bonald." Ph.D. diss., University of Toulouse, 1915.

Mousnier, Roland. *The Institutions of France under the Absolute Monarchy, 1598–1789*. Vol. 1, *Society and the State*. Translated by Brian Pearce. Chicago, 1979.

Mower, David. "Antoine Augustin Préault (1809–1879)." *Art Bulletin* 63 (June 1981): 288–307.

Muret, Théodore. *L'Histoire par le théâtre, 1789–1851*. 3 vols. Paris, 1865.

Musée de peinture et de sculpture, ou Recueil des principaux tableaux, statues et bas-reliefs des collections publiques et particulières de l'Europe. Dessiné et gravé à l'eau forte par Réveil, avec des notices descriptives, critiques et historiques par Duchesne aîné. 16 vols. Paris, 1829–34.

Ozouf, Mona. *Festivals and the French Revolution*. Translated by Alan Sheridan. Cambridge, Mass., 1988.

Palmer, R. R. *The Age of the Democratic Revolution: A Political History of Europe and America, 1760–1800*. 2 vols. Princeton, N.J., 1959–64.

Perouse, Honoré. *Napoléon Ier et les lois civiles du Consulat et de l'Empire*. Paris, 1866.

Planche, Gustave. *Etudes sur l'Ecole française (1831–1852), peinture et sculpture*. 2 vols. Paris, 1855.

———. *Portraits d'artistes: Peintres et sculpteurs*. 2 vols. Paris, 1853.

Ponteil, Félix. *Les Institutions de la France de 1814 à 1870*. Paris, 1966.

———. *Napoléon Ier et l'organisation autoritaire de la France*. 2d ed. Paris, 1965.

Portalis, Jean-Etienne-Marie. *Discours, rapports et travaux inédits sur le Code civil*. Edited by Vicomte Frédéric Portalis. Paris, 1844.

Praz, Mario. *The Romantic Agony*. Translated by Angus Davidson. 2d ed. Oxford, 1970.

Raffin, Léonce. *La Madeleine, son histoire et ses oeuvres d'art*. Paris, 1950.

La Révolution française et l'Europe, 1789–1799. Exh. cat. 3 vols. Paris: Galeries Nationales du Grand Palais, 1989.

Ribner, Jonathan P. "Henri de Triqueti, Auguste Préault, and the Glorification of Law under the July Monarchy." *Art Bulletin* 70 (September 1988): 486–501.

———. "*Le Peuple de Dieu:* Old Testament Motifs of Legislation, Prophecy, and Exile in French Art between the Empires." Ph.D. diss., Institute of Fine Arts, New York University, 1986.

The Romantics to Rodin: French Nineteenth-Century Sculpture from North American Collections. Exh. cat. Edited by Peter Fusco and H. W. Janson. Los Angeles: Los Angeles County Museum of Art, 1980.

Ronchaud, Louis de. "Etudes sur l'art: La peinture monumentale en France." *La Revue indépendante* 12, 2d ser. (November 10, 1847): 24–78.

Rosenblum, Robert. *Jean-Auguste-Dominique Ingres.* New York, 1967. Reprint, New York, 1985.

———. *Transformations in Late Eighteenth Century Art.* 2d ed. Princeton, N.J., 1969.

Rosenblum, Robert, and H. W. Janson. *Nineteenth-Century Art.* New York, 1984.

Rosenthal, Léon. *Du Romantisme au réalisme: Essai sur l'évolution de la peinture en France de 1830 à 1848.* Paris, 1914.

Rousseau, Jean-Jacques. *Du Contrat social* [1762]. Edited by Ronald Grimsley. Oxford, 1972.

Sainte-Beuve, Charles-Augustin. *Chateaubriand et son groupe littéraire sous l'empire. Cours professé à Liège en 1848–1849* [1861]. Edited by Maurice Allem. 2 vols. Paris, 1948.

Salvador, Gabriel. *J. Salvador: Sa vie, ses oeuvres et ses critiques.* Paris, 1881.

Salvador, Dr. Joseph. *Histoire des institutions de Moïse et du peuple hébreu.* 3 vols. Paris, 1828.

———. *Loi de Moïse, ou Système religieux et politique des Hébreux.* Paris, 1822.

Savart, Claude, and Jean-Noël Aletti, eds. *Le Monde contemporain et la Bible.* Paris, 1985.

Schama, Simon. *Citizens: A Chronicle of the French Revolution.* New York, 1989.

Schimséwitsch, Lydie. "Portalis et son temps: L'Homme, le penseur, le législateur." Ph.D. diss., University of Paris, 1936.

Schnapper, Antoine. *David.* Translated by Helga Harrison. New York, 1982.

Schnapper, Antoine, and Arlette Sérullaz. *Jacques-Louis David, 1748–1825.* Exh. cat. Paris: Musée du Louvre and Musée National du Château, Versailles, 1989.

La Sculpture française au XIXe siècle. Exh. cat. Edited by Anne Pingeot, Philippe Durey, Antoinette Le Normand-Romain, and Isabelle Leroy-Jay Lemaistre. Paris: Galeries Nationales du Grand Palais, 1986.

Sensier, Alfred. *La Vie et l'oeuvre de J.-F. Millet.* Edited by Paul Mantz. Paris, 1881.

Sérullaz, Maurice. *Mémorial de l'exposition Eugène Delacroix organisée au Musée du Louvre à l'occasion du centenaire de la mort de l'artiste.* Paris, 1963.

———. *Les Peintures murales de Delacroix.* Paris, 1963.

Sérullaz, Maurice, Arlette Sérullaz, Louis-Antoine Prat, and Claudine Ganeval. *Musée du Louvre, Cabinet des dessins. Inventaire général des dessins. Ecole française. Dessins d'Eugène Delacroix, 1798–1863.* 2 vols. Paris, 1984.

1789: L'Assemblée nationale. Exh. cat. Paris: Palais-Bourbon, 1989.

Shklar, Judith N. *Men and Citizens: A Study of Rousseau's Social Theory.* Cambridge, Mass., 1969.

Shroder, Maurice Z. *Icarus: The Image of the Artist in French Romanticism.* Cambridge, Mass., 1961.

Silvestre, Théophile. *Histoire des artistes vivants, français et étrangers.* Paris, 1856.

Simon, Pierre. *L'Elaboration de la Charte constitutionnelle de 1814.* Bibliothèque d'histoire moderne 2, fas. 2. Paris, 1906.

Soboul, Albert. "Sentiment religieux et Cultes populaires pendant la Révolution: Saintes patriotes et martyrs de la liberté." *Annales historiques de la Révolution française* 29 (July–September 1957): 193–213.

Starkie, Enid. *Petrus Borel the Lycanthrope: His Life and Times.* Norfolk, Conn., 1954.

Starobinski, Jean. *1789: Les Emblèmes de la raison.* Paris, 1979.

Stendhal [Henri Beyle]. *Vie de Rossini [1823], suivi des Notes d'un dilettante.* Edited by Henry Prunières. 2 vols. Paris, 1922.

Sternhell, Zeev. *La Droite révolutionnaire, 1885–1914: Les Origines françaises du fascisme.* Paris, 1978.

———. *Maurice Barrès et le nationalisme français.* Brussels, 1985.

Sutherland, D. M. G. *France 1789–1815: Revolution and Counterrevolution.* New York, 1986.

Sydenham, M. J. *The French Revolution.* New York, 1965.

Taine, Hippolyte. *Les Origines de la France contemporaine [1875–1893].* 23d ed. 12 vols. Paris, 1900–1901.

Thoré, Théophile. "Les Peintures de la Bibliothèque de la Chambre des députés." *Le Constitutionnel,* January 31, 1848.

Thureau-Dangin, Paul. *Histoire de la Monarchie de Juillet.* 2d ed. 7 vols. Paris, 1888–92.

Tocqueville, Alexis de. *L'Ancien régime et la Révolution* [1856]. Edited by J.-P. Mayer. Paris, 1967.

———. *Souvenirs* [1850–51]. Edited by Luc Monnier et al. Paris, 1978.

Tourneux, Maurice. *Salons et Expositions d'art à Paris (1801 -1870): Essai bibliographique.* Paris, 1919.

Toussaint, Hélène. *Les Portraits d'Ingres: Peintures des Musées nationaux.* Paris, 1985.

Tulard, Jean, ed. *Dictionnaire Napoléon.* Paris, 1987.

Unverfehrt, Gerd, Klaus Lankheit, and Jurgen Döring. *La Caricature: Bildsatire in Frank-*

reich 1830–1835 aus der Sammlung von Kritter. Exh. cat. Münster: Westfälisches Landesmuseum für Kunst und Kulturgeschichte, 1980.

Vigny, Alfred de. "Lettres à une puritaine, I." Edited by Philippe Godet. *Revue de Paris* 4 (August 15, 1897): 673–95.

———. *Oeuvres complètes.* Edited by F. Baldensperger. 2 vols. Paris, 1948–50.

Villefosse, Louis, and Janine Bouissounouse. *The Scourge of the Eagle.* Translated and edited by Michael Ross. New York, 1972.

Vovelle, Michel. *La Chute de la monarchie, 1787–1792.* Nouvelle histoire de la France contemporaine, no. 1. Paris, 1972.

———. *La Révolution française: Images et récit.* 5 vols. Paris, 1986.

———, ed. *L'Image de la Révolution française: Communications présentés lors du Congrès mondial pour le Bicentenaire de la Révolution, Sorbonne, Paris, 6–12 juillet 1989.* 4 vols. Paris, 1990.

Wechsler, Judith. *A Human Comedy: Physiognomy and Caricature in Nineteenth Century Paris.* Chicago, 1982.

Wilson, Aileen. *Fontanes (1757–1821): Essai biographique et littéraire.* Paris, 1928.

Winock, Michel. *Nationalisme, antisémitisme et fascisme en France.* Paris, 1990.

Wisner, David. "Quelques représentations de législateurs antiques dans l'art de la période révolutionnaire (1789–1799)." In *La Révolution française et l'antiquité.* Acts of the colloquium at Tours, December 2–3, 1988. Edited by R. Chevallier. Collection Caesarodunum, no. 25 bis, Tours, 1991, pp. 369–90.

Index

Delavigne, Casimir, 126
Delécluze, Etienne-Jean, 55
Demane-Demartrais, Michel-
    François, 41, *42*
Demosthenes: and Delacroix's
    *Demosthenes Harangues the
    Waves of the Sea,* 103, 105,
    108; and Delacroix's Palais
    du Luxembourg painting,
    129; and Dupasquier's
    Demosthenes, 105, *109*
Denon, Vivant, 32, 35, 41, *43,*
    169n9, 172n53
Depersonalization, of law, 8, 13
Les Déracinés (Barrès), 160
Deslandres, Maurice-Charles-
    Emmanuel, 9, 166n32
Desprez, Louis, 179n9
The Destruction of Jerusalem
    (Heim), 116, *117*
Detroit Institute of Arts, Age of
    Revolution exhibition at, 4
Dictionnaire des girouttes
    (Fontanes), 38
Directory, 18, 26, 35, 37, 105,
    111, 171n42
Discours sur l'histoire universelle
    (Bossuet), 145, 173n71
Divine right, 1, 2, 4, 9, 157;
    and Ballanche's *Du sentiment,*
    51; and Bonald's *Législation
    primitive,* 45–46; and Bour-
    bon Restoration, 50–51, 57;
    and Delacroix's *Emperor
    Justinian,* 59, 82; and Maistre's
    Considérations sur la France,
    25–26; and Mauzaisse's
    Divine Wisdom, 57; and
    Napoleonic government, 40,
    44
*Divine Wisdom Giving the Laws
    to the Kings and Legislators*
    (Mauzaisse), 57, 176nn21,23
Domat, Jean, 168n4
Douglas, Alexander, 30
The Drachma of Tribute
    (Delacroix), 119, *120*
Dreyfus Affair, 4–5, 160–61

Drolling, Michel-Martin,
    57–58, 59, 176n25
Drumont, Edouard, 161, *161,*
    196n15
Ducos, Pierre-Roger, 30
Dumas, Alexandre, 154,
    184n64
Dupasquier, Antoine-Léonard,
    105, *109*
Dupin, André-Marie-Jean-
    Jacques, 178n46
Duprès. *See* Brenet, Nicolas-
    Guy-Antoine
Duret, Francisque-Joseph,
    179n9
Du sentiment (Ballanche), 51

Ecole des Beaux-Arts, 77, 138
Edict of Nantes, 55
The Education of Achilles
    (Delacroix), 121, *122*
Egeria, 4, 35; and Delacroix's
    Numa and Egeria, 103, 105,
    131
Egyptian art, 10, 88
Egyptian mythology, 35
Eloquence, representations of,
    105, 110, 130
*The Emancipation of the Serfs by
    Louis VI* (Blondel), 104
*Emperor Justinian Drafting His
    Laws* (Delacroix), 58–59, 60,
    103, 105, 114, 121, 175n7,
    176n29
Encyclopédie, 7
Enfantin, Barthélemy-Prosper,
    192n13
Enlightenment, 7, 13, 64, 121
Estates-General, 6, 7, 164n3,
    179n9
Esther (Racine), 45, 126
Exit Libertè a la Francois!
    (Gillray), 28, *28*
Expiatory Chapel, 62–63, *62,*
    83
Expulsion of Hagar (Vernet),
    190n57
Eyck, Jan van, 38, 40

Falconet, Etienne-Maurice, 151,
    194n36
Family, representation of, 77–80
Fénélon, François de Salignac de
    La Mothe, 4
Festival of the Federation, 7, 13
Festival of Unity and Indivisi-
    bility, 10, 13, *13,* 16
Fields of May, 103–4
*The First Consul Offering the
    Civil Code* (Chaudet), 32, *33,*
    35, 38, 169n14
Flaubert, Gustave, 134
Fleury, Claude, 45
Fontaine, Pierre-François-
    Léonard, 62, 170n17,
    177n36
Fontanes, Louis de: and
    Bourbon Restoration, 46,
    51–52, 174n4; and Catholi-
    cism, 40, 44, 45; as Legis-
    lative Body president, 30,
    37–38, 40, 44
Forbin, Louis-Nicolas-Philippe-
    Auguste de, 54, 175n13
Foy, Maximilien-Sébastien,
    179n9
*France, in the Midst of the
    Legislator Kings* (Blondel), 55,
    56
La France juive (Drumont),
    196n15
The French Constitution (print),
    23, *23,* 75, 77
*The French People Crushing the
    Hydra of Federalism* (sculp-
    ture), 10
Freud, Sigmund, 151
Fructidor, anti-royalist coup of,
    31, 38

Galerie des Beaux-Arts, Paris,
    190n56
Galileo Galilei, 186n12
Gates of Paradise (Ghiberti), 85
Gatteaux, Nicolas-Marie, 18,
    19, 111, *113*
Gautherot, Claude, 31, *31,* 169n9

Photographic Credits

Author, Figs. 48, 50; Plate 7

Boston, by courtesy of the Boston Public Library, Print Department, Fig. 83

Boston, by courtesy of the Trustees of the Boston Public Library, Fig. 53

Cambridge, Mass., Harvard College Library, Figs. 9, 87

Cherbourg, Musée Thomas Henry, Fig. 84; Plate 9

Edinburgh, Duke of Sutherland Collection, on loan to the National Gallery of Scotland, Fig. 90

London, Conway Library, Courtauld Institute of Art, Figs. 43, 44, 49

Lyon, Musée des Beaux-Arts, Fig. 75

New Haven, Conn., Yale Center for British Art, Paul Mellon Collection, Fig. 14

New York, Alinari/Art Resource, Fig. 91

New York, Avery Architectural and Fine Arts Library, Columbia University in the City of New York, Fig. 92

New York, Thomas J. Watson Library, The Metropolitan Museum of Art, Figs. 78, 93

Paris, Archives Nationales, Fig. 6; Plate 3

Paris, © Arch. Phot/S.P.A.D.E.M., Figs. 7, 19, 29, 30, 32, 47, 51, 52, 58, 59, 61, 62, 63, 65, 67, 70, 72, 73, 74, 76, 82

Paris, Assemblée Nationale, Plate 8

Paris, Bibliothèque Nationale, Figs. 1, 2, 3, 4, 5, 10, 11, 12, 13, 15, 16, 18, 23, 25, 28, 35, 36, 37, 38, 40, 41, 42, 54, 55, 68, 69, 79, 95; Plate 2

Paris, Ecole Nationale Supérieure des Beaux-Arts, Figs. 45, 46

Paris, J. Feuillie/© C.N.M.H.S./S.P.A.D.E.M., Figs. 21, 57, 81

Paris, Giraudon, Figs. 86, 88, 89

Paris, Musée de la Monnaie, Figs. 8, 24, 27, 66

Paris, Photo Bulloz, Figs. 26, 34, 56, 64; Plate 6

Paris, © R.M.N., Figs. 17, 20, 22, 33, 39, 60, 71, 77, 80, 85, 94; Plates 1, 5

Saint-Brieuc, Musée d'Histoire, Fig. 31

Washington, National Gallery of Art, Samuel H. Kress Collection, Plate 4

Designer: Steve Renick
Compositor: G & S Typesetters, Inc.
Text: 10/13 Adobe Garamond
Display: Adobe Garamond
Printer: Malloy Lithographing, Inc.
Binder: John H. Dekker & Sons